W E I S E R ♀ C L A S S I C S

The Weiser Classics series offers essential works from renowned authors and spiritual teachers, foundational texts, as well as introductory guides on an array of topics written by contemporary authors. The series represents the full range of subjects and genres that have been part of Weiser's over sixty-year-long publishing program—from divination and magick to alchemy and occult philosophy. Each volume in the series will whenever possible include new material from its author or a contributor and other valuable additions and will be printed and produced using acid-free paper in a durable paperback binding

---

THE MEANING OF WITCHCRAFT

THE MEANING OF WITCHCRAFT

GERALD GARDNER

Foreword by PAM GROSSMAN

This edition first published in 2022 by Weiser Books, an imprint of
Red Wheel/Weiser, LLC
With offices at:
65 Parker Street, Suite 7
Newburyport, MA 01950
www.redwheelweiser.com

 Originally published in the U.K. in 1959 by Aquarian, London. Previously published in 2004 as *The Meaning of Witchcraft* by Weiser Books, ISBN: 978-1-57863-309-8.
This new Weiser Classics edition includes a new foreword by Pam Grossman.

ISBN: 978-1-57863-789-8
Library of Congress Cataloging-in-Publication Data available upon request.

Series Editors
Mike Conlon, Production Director, Red Wheel/Weiser Books
Judika Illes, Editor-at-Large, Weiser Books
Peter Turner, Associate Publisher, Weiser Books
Series Design
Kathryn Sky-Peck, Creative Director, Red Wheel/Weiser

Printed in the United States of America
IBI

10 9 8 7 6 5 4 3 2 1

Contents

Foreword

Today, identifying as a witch is rather in vogue, as evidenced by a proliferation of stylish occult shops, contemporary grimoires, and bewitching social media posts. But when *The Meaning of Witchcraft* was published in 1959, such developments would have been quite a shock to its author—although, one presumes, a delightful one. Back then, proclaiming oneself a witch was so transgressive that most witchcraft practitioners kept their mystical lives secret, lest they be ostracized or persecuted by those who wrongfully associated witches with diabolical doings. In England, the practice of witchcraft was illegal until 1951. But even with the law having been changed eight years earlier, this book's mission was a tall order, for it attempted to counteract centuries of negative PR against witches by putting witchcraft in a historical context—and a better light overall.

The history of witchcraft is a notoriously tricky thing to pin down, as one must first parse what is meant by terms like "magic" and "witch." One must consider that beliefs about witches are always an amalgam of the imaginary and the factual, because our conception of what a witch is has largely been conjured from a combination of myth, fear, and fantasy. Tropes of witches cavorting fiendishly under a full moon and throwing homicidal hexes were calcified in the Early Modern Period thanks in large part to Christian paranoia and a nascent printing revolution that rapidly spread word (and imagery) of this supposed supernatural threat.

The witch hunts of Western Europe and, subsequently, the New England colonies, were fatal to thousands of innocent people—primarily women. These victims lost their lives based on a false notion, for there is no proof that they were involved in any sort of satanic actions, nor would most of them have ever considered themselves to be witches in any regard, even secret ones. Up until the 19th century, the word "witch" was a negative epithet, and to self-identify as one would have been unthinkable.

This isn't to suggest that people across the world and throughout time haven't consistently engaged in magical activity. Metaphysical pursuits such as spell casting, divination, plant-based healing, communication with spirits and deities, and the celebration of sacred seasonal and lunar transitions have clearly been part of the human story for centuries. What has shifted in recent decades, however, is that the identity of "witch" has transmuted from an alleged occult villainess into an aspirational figure of divine feminine power. And though there are many reasons and people responsible for this evolution, one of the most prominent ones is, ironically perhaps, a man and the author of this book: Gerald Brosseau Gardner.

Gardner himself was many things: a sickly child born just outside Liverpool in 1884 to wealthy parents. A white, British ex-pat, who spent much of his life in colonial Southeast Asia working in the tea and rubber industries. A self-proclaimed "archaeologist and anthropologist," though one seemingly without any formal training or accreditation. An autodidact with a penchant for spirituality of all stripes, and a great appreciation for—and some might argue appropriation of—the rites and rituals of the indigenous peoples of the regions in which he lived. He describes his life as being "devoted to an interest in folklore, anthropology, psychic research, magic, and knocking about in some of the odd places of the world in general."

When he retired at age fifty-two, he and his wife Donna moved back to England, to Highcliffe near the New Forest. Here his esoteric studies (not to mention well-funded free time) eventually—and, it must be said, allegedly—led him to being initiated by a woman named "Old Dorothy Clutterbuck" into one of the last surviving English covens, via which he was supposedly taught the magical techniques and worship practices of a long line of British Pagan witches. He would eventually go on to start his own coven, and ultimately become what he is now most commonly known as: the Father of Wicca.

Not that Wicca was the term he used to describe the religion he helped usher forth. "The Craft of the Wicca," as he called it, was positioned as being a continuation of the practices of an ancient "witch cult," and many of his ideas were based upon a now-controversial theory put forth by Egyptology professor and eventual Folklore Society president, Dr. Margaret Murray. Murray herself would go on to write the introduction to Gardner's first non-fiction book, *Witchcraft Today,* stating that the beliefs and customs Gardner described therein were "a true survival and not a mere revival copied out of books."

Complicating matters is the fact that many of Gardner's coven's rituals were, in fact, later revealed to be just that, as he drew from "biblical verses, the Mathers edition of the Key of Solomon, the Goetia, a work on the cabbala, three different books by [Aleister] Crowley, the Waite-Smith tarot pack, and one or two unidentified grimoires," according to witchcraft scholar Ronald Hutton, as well as the writings of Charles Godfrey Leland and Murray's own books. These writings were further refined by Gardner's creative partners, including High Priestess and poet Doreen Valiente. Then again, this alchemization of influences can also be considered evidence of Gardner's true genius. For what he and his comrades ultimately did was to develop a brand-new religion, albeit one they framed as being based on something quite old.

It remains debatable whether or not Gardner's own witchcraft practice was drawn from an actual unbroken British Pagan lineage or was derived from his imaginings and those of his cohort's—or some combination thereof. What is incontrovertible, however, is the impact that Gardner had on the millions of 20th- and 21st-century witches who followed in his magical footsteps.

I count myself as one of these spiritual progeny, though these days I prefer the term Pagan to Wiccan, as it feels more elastic and more encompassing of my own Eastern European ancestry. "Witch" is a word I have chosen for myself, because it represents someone who reveres nature, who acknowledges—and, crucially, collaborates with—immaterial forces, and who views feminine power as sacred. Due to its complex history, it also suggests a stance of sympathy toward those who are marginalized and a rebellious attitude against a repressive, and often oppressive, patriarchal status quo. That this word has shapeshifted from a damning insult into a badge of honor is largely because of Gardner and his life's work.

The Meaning of Witchcraft was published when Gardner was seventy-five years old, five years before his death. His primary intentions with the book were twofold: first, to expand upon his notions of the historical precedent for the witchcraft that had become so dear to him and that he had begun exploring in Witchcraft Today; second, to thoroughly refute the common belief that witchcraft was in any way associated with

Satan or with evil in general. As he put it, "If this book serves no purpose than to debunk this poisonous rubbish, it will have done a good job."

On the first point, his understanding of history is drawn from the (inconsistently cited) sources to which he had access, and it must be said that some of his ideas were his own conjecture or have since been proven false. Many historians now believe that it was approximately 100,000 people who lost their lives during the witch hunts, for example, and not the nine million that Gardner and the writers he quotes claimed. As for the false rumors that witches are in league with the devil? Horror films and conservative propaganda are still with us, though I'm happy to report that Gardner's positive PR campaign has been otherwise effective, as today modern witchcraft is considered one of the fastest-growing spiritual systems.

For me, however, this book serves a greater purpose. For amongst these pages, he puts forth what he and his cohort of midcentury witches valued and embodied. In the book, he describes a communal practice that is both religious and magical, and which lauds women and the Goddess on par with—if not superior to—men and the (Horned) God. This alone was radical for 1959 and even by today's standards sixty-three years later. That the covens he details are always led by a High Priestess who chooses her High Priest is nothing short of a micro-matriarchy. As he cheerfully retorts at one point in his book, "I'd like to see anyone reprimand a witch High Priestess." Not happening!

Gardner was also a trailblazer in what we might today classify as "sex-positivity." He felt that the Christian concept of sex being a shameful activity only meant for the purpose of procreation was deplorable, and he thought that the body's capacity for pleasure and connection with another was a gift to be celebrated. He was a staunch proponent of naturism—what we in America call nudism—and his coven's rituals were highly sensual (and, one hopes, consensual) rites that positioned the body as a vessel of divinity and holy energy.

Still, as with many older texts, The Meaning of Witchcraft is riddled with language and ideas that by current measures are problematic if not outright offensive. Feminists like me will bristle at his insistence that a coven's human representative of the Goddess be "young and lovely . . . motherly and kind . . . Man's Ideal." His feminine-centric coven structure also draws from gender-essentialist notions, and his insistence that the six couples of his thirteen-person coven be made up of strictly male-female pairings belies an extremely limited view of the numinous. There is no room for homosexuality in Gardner's model, and his understanding of gender is extremely binary.

Though he does say that the High Priestess "can represent the God if necessary," he goes on to write that "no man can ever represent the Goddess." Presumably this is due his own valuation of feminine magic as being supreme, but one may certainly read deeper implications into this. On another note, while Gardner seems to have much respect for cultures outside his own, some terminology he uses is dated at best, racist at worst. And his occasional railings against "The Welfare State" and government handouts is difficult to swallow from a man who had access to great wealth and social privilege.

These shortcomings of Gardner's are not to be excused or dismissed. Any spiritual path may only be strengthened by examining past missteps so that better, more relevant, and more radiant iterations can be developed moving forward. However, I believe his work did far more good than harm, for it helped open a door for far more diverse identities and expressions of modern witchcraft to pour through. That today, people of all genders, sexualities, ages, and backgrounds feel safe enough—or at least emboldened enough—to call themselves witches is because Gardner and his coven mates made the world a bit more welcoming to those who subvert restrictive societal norms.

At his core, Gardner was a free thinker, a taboo buster, and devotee to self-actualization and collaborative empowerment. He was antifascist and anti-elitist, and he emphasized that while other forms of occultism were for an exclusive subset of learned men, "the witch belonged essentially to the people."

The people to which he was referring may have been part of a romanticized history. But I'm far more interested in Gardner's legacy. There are still those who misunderstand or willfully misrepresent modern witchcraft today. But there are also more witches. Those of us who use the word "witch" with all of the pride and fortification that it offers us do so thanks to Gardner's lucid, liberating vision. And that is meaningful indeed.

—Pam Grossman, author of
Waking the Witch: Reflections on Women, Magic, and Power
New York, Summer Solstice 2022

Chapter I

The Witch Cult in Britain

My Directorship of the Museum of Magic and Witchcraft at Castletown, Isle of Man, brings me a great deal of correspondence from all parts of the world; some interesting, some abusive (a very little, just enough to enliven matters), some fantastic, and some funny in all senses of the word.

However, my more serious correspondents want to know the origin of witchcraft. Where, they ask, did it come from? What is behind this thing that obsessed the minds of men for centuries? Is it an underground cult of devil-worship? A dark thread running through history? An irruption of the supernatural into normal life? Or is it an enormous delusion? What is the meaning of it all?

This is a matter which of late years has exercised the ingenuity of a number of writers. These may be roughly divided into three schools. Firstly, those who take the severely rationalist view that witchcraft was a kind of mass hysteria, arising from psychological causes. Secondly, those who maintain that witchcraft is real, and that it is the worship and service of Satan, in whom its devotees appear to be great believers. This is the attitude taken by that very prolific writer, the late Montague Summers, and his many imitators. Thirdly, that school, headed by anthropologists like Dr. Margaret Murray, which has tried to look at the subject without either superstitious terrors and theological argument on the one hand, or materialistic incredulity on the other. This school of thought maintains that witchcraft is simply the remains of the old pagan religion of Western Europe, dating back to the Stone Age, and that the reason for the Church's persecution of it was that it was a dangerous rival. I personally belong to this third school, because its findings accord with my own experience, and because it is the only theory which seems to me to make sense when viewed in the light of the facts of history.

Perhaps I had better state briefly what that experience is. I am at present the Director of the only museum in the world, so far as I know, which is exclusively concerned with magic and witchcraft. I was a Civil Servant in the Far East (Malaya) until my retirement, and I made a large collection of magical instruments, charms, etc., which formed the nucleus of the present collection here. I am also an archaeologist and an anthropologist, and through these studies I became interested in the part played in the life of mankind by magical beliefs, and by what people did as a result of these beliefs.

When I was out East, before I had any contact with witchcraft in Britain, I investigated much native magic without finding anything which could not be explained by telepathy, hypnotism, suggestion or coincidence, and frankly I considered magic as an instance of the curious things that people will believe. In those days I was very much interested in Dr. Margaret Murray's theory that witchcraft was the remains of an ancient religion; but as all authorities seemed agreed that while there was evidence that some people may have been witches, there was not the slightest evidence that witches had ever been organised into covens; and as Charles Godfrey Leland, who had known many witches in Italy and elsewhere, and wrote a lot about them, never mentioned any coven or any organisation, I dismissed witchcraft as something which had possibly happened once, but even if it had existed it had been "burnt out" three hundred years ago.

The earlier books I read on the subject all seemed to agree to a certain extent. They said that witches existed everywhere, and were both male and female. They were intensely wicked people. They worshipped the Devil, often in the form of a heathen god (but then, all heathen gods were the Devil). They had a big organisation, regular religious ceremonies on fixed dates, a priesthood with priests, priestesses and officers, and an organised form of religion; though their deity might be called "a god" and "the Devil" almost in the same sentence. This was explained by saying that all non-Christian gods were really the Devil in disguise.

However, in the late 17th and the 18th centuries public opinion seemed to change. In spite of the strong views of John Wesley and other clergymen, people did not believe in witches any more, to the extent that when two clergymen induced a jury to convict Jane Wenham of talking to the Devil in the form of a cat, and she was sentenced to death for this in 1712, the judges protested and she was released. In 1736 the penal laws against witchcraft were repealed; and I did not think that anyone, with the exception of the Rev. Montague Summers, dared hint that there might be anything in witchcraft today without being laughed at. Charles Godfrey Leland had been regarded as a romancer who had written up a few Italian fortune-tellers, and while Dr. Margaret Murray was known as a good anthropologist, it was thought that she was writing about things that happened three or four hundred years ago, when people were superstitious, and believed silly things.

However, after Dr. Murray's books appeared, some other people were bold enough to admit that there were some witches left, but said that they were only village fortune-tellers, impostors who knew nothing about the subject, and there never had been any organisation, and anyone who thought otherwise was just being imaginative. I was of these opinions in 1939, when, here in Britain, I met some people who compelled me to alter them. They were interested in curious things, reincarnation for one, and they were also interested in the fact that an ancestress of mine, Grizel Gairdner, had been burned as a witch. They kept saying that they had met me before. We went through everywhere we had been, and I could not ever have met them before in this life; but they claimed to have known me in previous lives. Although I believe in reincarnation, as many people do who have lived in the East, I do not remember my past lives clearly; I only wish I did. However, these people told me enough to make me think. Then some of these new (or old) friends said, "You belonged to us in the past. You are of the blood. Come back to where you belong."

I realised that I had stumbled on something interesting; but I was half-initiated before the word "Wica" which they used hit me like a thunderbolt, and I knew where I was, and that the Old Religion still existed. And so I found myself in the Circle, and there took the usual oath of secrecy, which bound me not to reveal certain things.

In this way I made the discovery that the witch cult, that people thought to have been persecuted out of existence, still lived. I found, too, what it was that made so many of our ancestors dare imprisonment, torture and death rather than give up the worship of the Old Gods and the love of the old ways. I discovered the inner meaning of that saying in one of Fiona MacLeod's books: *"The Old Gods are not dead. They think we are."*

I am a member of the Society for Psychical Research, and on the Committee of the Folklore Society; so I wanted to tell of my discovery.

But I was met with a determined refusal. "The Age of Persecution is not over," they told me; "give anyone half a chance and the fires will blaze up again." When I said to one of them, "Why do you keep all these things so secret still? There's no persecution nowadays!" I was told, "Oh, isn't there? If people knew what I was, every time a child in the village was ill, or somebody's chickens died, I should get the blame for it. Witchcraft doesn't pay for broken windows."

I can remember as a boy reading in the papers of a woman being burned alive in Southern Ireland as a witch; but I could not believe that there could be any persecution nowadays in England. So, against their better judgment, they agreed to let me write a little about the cult in the form of fiction, an historical novel where a witch says a little of what they believe and of how they were persecuted. This was published in 1949 under the title of *High Magic's Aid.*

In 1951 a very important event occurred. The Government of the day passed the Fraudulent Mediums Act, which repealed and replaced the last remaining Witchcraft Act, under which spiritualists used to be prosecuted in modern times. This Act is, I believe, unique in legally recognising the existence of genuine mediumship and psychic powers.

I thought that at last common sense and religious freedom had prevailed; but even so, the passage of this Act was highly obnoxious to certain religious bodies which had been preaching against Spiritualism for years and trying to outlaw it as "the work of Satan," together with any other societies to which they objected, including Freemasonry and, of course, witchcraft.

About a year previously, this Museum had been opened, and I had flattered myself that showing what witchcraft really is, an ancient religion, would arouse no hostility in any quarter. I was to find out in due course how wrong I was!

Any attempt to show witchcraft in anything even remotely resembling a favourable light, or to challenge the old representation of it as something uniformly evil and devilish, or even to present it as a legitimate object of study, can still arouse the most surprising reactions. The virtues of humanism, which Charles Saltman defined as "sensitivity, intelligence and erudition, together with integrity, curiosity and tolerance," have still quite a long way to go in their struggle against the mentality which produced the *Malleus Malejicarum.*

In 1952 Pennethorne Hughes wrote a book, *Witchcraft,* which gave a very good historical account of witchcraft, but stated that while in mediaeval times witches had a fully worked-out ritual of their own which they performed, modern witches were simply perverts who celebrated "Black Masses," which he described as being blasphemous imitations of the Christian Mass. This made some of my friends very angry, and I managed to persuade them that it might do good to write a factual book about witchcraft, and so I wrote *Witchcraft Today.** In writing this latter book, I soon found myself between Scylla and Charybdis. If I said too much, I ran the risk of offending people whom I had come to regard highly as friends. If I said too little, the publishers would not be interested. In this situation I did the best I could. In particular, I denied that witches celebrated the Black Mass, or that they killed animals—or even unbaptised babies—as blood sacrifices.

One of the first questions I had asked witches as soon as I had got "inside" was, "What about the Black Mass?" They all said, "We don't know how to perform it, and if we did, what would be the point of doing so?" They also said, "You know what happens at our meetings. There is the little religious ceremony, the greeting of the Old Gods; then any business which has to be talked over, or perhaps someone wants to do a rite for some purpose; next there is a little feast and a dance; then you have to hurry for the last bus home! There is no time or place for any nonsense of 'Black Masses,' and anyhow why should we want to do one?"

I think this is just common sense. To a Roman Catholic who believes in Transubstantiation, that is, that the bread and wine of the Mass are literally changed into the flesh and blood of Christ, a ceremonial insult to the Host would be the most awful blasphemy; *but witches do not believe this, so it would simply be absurd to them to try to insult a piece of bread.*

I am not the first to have pointed this out; Eliphas Levi, the celebrated French occultist, who was also a devote Catholic, stated in his book, *Dogme et Rituel de la Haute Magie,* that the first condition of success in the practice of black magic was to be prepared to profane the cultus in which we *believed.*

Some may hold that anyone who does not believe in Transubstantiation is lacking in the True Faith and doomed to Hell. I am told that certain Nonconformist ministers preaching against Transubstantiation obtained

* Rider, 1954.

consecrated Hosts and held them up to mockery in the pulpit; *but I have never heard that this made them witches.*

What about the Christian people who carry such consecrated Hosts about in lockets as personal charms? Are they being reverent or not? *And are they witches?* (We have some of these charms in this Museum.) I know very well that some people would be shocked at this practice, but this does not alter the fact that it is done.

The point which those writers who persistently link the witch cult with the Black Mass fail to appreciate is that they can *either* maintain that witches are pagans, *or* that they celebrate Black Masses; but that in the name of logic and common sense they cannot have it both ways.

Unlike a number of sensational writers, I do not wish to convey the impression that there are witches at work in every corner of the land. On the contrary, there are very few real witches left, and those keep themselves very much to themselves. They are generally the descendants of witch families, and have inherited a tradition which has been preserved for generations. This is, indeed, the traditional way in which witchcraft was spread and preserved; the children of witch families were taught by their parents, and initiated at an early age. In fact, this is very probably the origin of all those frightful stories of the witches bringing babies to the Sabbat to eat them; what really happened was that witch parents dared not omit to have their babies baptised, for fear of instantly arousing suspicion, so they used to bring the babies to the Sabbat first, and present them in dedication to the Old Gods. Then, they felt, it wouldn't matter if a ceremony of Christian baptism was later gone through "for show." ("When I bow my head in the house of Rimmon, the Lord pardon Thy servant in this thing.") However, as the persecution of the Old Religion grew more fierce, it became dangerous to admit children. Innocent children prattled among themselves about where their parents went and what they did, and one unlucky word overheard by the wrong person might have meant death to the whole family. There are terrible records of children being hanged or burned with their parents, merely because they were of the witch blood. Margaret Ine Quane, for instance, who was burned as a witch here in Castletown in 1617, had her young son burned with her, simply because he was her son. Hence the custom of initiating the children was less and less observed, and this, coupled with the wholesale extermination policy carried on at the Church's instigation, soon greatly reduced the numbers of the cult.

However, there is one factor in the continuity of the tradition which the opponents of the cult had not reckoned with. The witches are firm believers in reincarnation, and they say that "Once a witch, always a witch." They believe that people who have been initiated into the cult, and have really accepted the Old Religion and the Old Gods in their hearts, will return to it or have an urge towards it in life after life, even though they may have no conscious knowledge of their previous associations with it. There may be something in this; because I know personally of three people in one coven who discovered that, subsequent to their coming into the cult in this life, their ancestors had had links with it, and I have already mentioned the witches who "recommended" me.

Of course, witch rites today are somewhat different from what they used to be many centuries ago. Then the great meetings, called Sabbats, used to be attended by large numbers of the population, who arrived provided with the wherewithal to cook a meal for themselves (hence the "hellish Sabbat fires" we have heard so much about), and prepared to spend a night on the heath in merrymaking, once the more serious rites were over. In fact, most traditional country merrymakings have some connection with the Old Religion; the Puritan Stubbes, in his *Anatomie of Abuses,* fiercely denounces the people who stayed out all night in the woods "Maying" on the old Sabbat date of May Eve; and Christina Hole, in her *English Folklore,* notes how the Northamptonshire "guisers"—folk-dancers dressed in fantastic costumes—are called "witch-men" to this day. Such instances might be greatly multiplied.

The English climate, of course, did not always permit these gatherings to be held on the heath; and I think that in this event they probably took place in someone's barn, or in the hall of a great house whose owner was friendly to the cult. In the Basque country of Pays de Labourd in 1609 the official investigator from the Parlement of Bordeaux, Pierre de Lancre, was horrified to find that the Sabbat was sometimes held in the local church, apparently with the priest's consent. He was particularly scandalised to find how many Basque priests sympathised with the Old Religion.*

We are often told horrid tales of witch meetings in churchyards, and of witches who, in the words of Robert Burns, "in kirkyards renew their leagues owre howkit dead." But in the old times the churchyard was the regular place for village merrymakings. In those days a churchyard was

* De Lancre, *Tableau de L'Inconstance des Mauvais, Paris, 1612.*

not, as it is today, a place of grave-stones, but simply a green sward. From M. C. Anderson's *Looking for History in British Churches*[*] we may see that dancing in the churchyard was quite feasible in the old days as the author says that it was not the practice to erect gravestones to those who were buried there. "The great folks were buried beneath sculptured tombs within the church. . . . The little people remained anonymous in death before the 17th century."

Eileen Power, in her book, *Mediaeval People*[**] says, speaking of the peasants:

> They used to spend their holidays in dancing and singing and buffoonery, as country folk have always done until our own more gloomier, more self-conscious age. They were very merry and not at all refined, and the place they always chose for their dances was the churchyard; and unluckily the songs they sang as they danced in a ring were old pagan songs of their forefathers, left over from old Mayday festivities, which they could not forget, or ribald love-songs which the Church disliked. Over and over again we find the Church councils complaining that the peasants (and sometimes the priests, too) were singing 'wicked songs with a chorus of dancing women', or holding 'ballads and dancings and evil and wanton songs and such-like lures of the devil'; over and over again the bishops forbade these songs and dances; but in vain. In every country in Europe, right through the Middle Ages to the time of the Reformation, and after it, country folk continued to sing and dance in the churchyard.

She continues:

> Another later story still is told about a priest in Worcestershire, who was kept awake all night by the people dancing in his churchyard, and singing a song with the refrain 'Sweetheart have pity', so that he could not get it out of his head, and the next morning at Mass, instead of saying 'Dominus vobiscum', he said, 'Sweetheart have pity', and there was a dreadful scandal which got into a chronicle.[***]

However, I have never heard of a present-day witch meeting being held in a churchyard; I think those sensation-mongers who have described

* John Murray, 1951.

** Penguin Books, 1951.

*** The chronicle in question was that of Giraldus Cambrensis, *Gemma Ecclesiastica, pt. I, c. XLII.*

present-day witches as forgathering in graveyards are guessing, and their guess is a few centuries out.

Actually, witch meetings today may take place anywhere that is convenient, and only people who have been initiated into the cult are allowed to be present. The actual proceedings would probably greatly disappoint those who have been nurtured on tales of blood sacrifices, drunken orgies, obscene rites, etc., etc. Witches do not use blood sacrifices; and only the type of mind which considers all recognition of the Elder Gods and their symbols to be "diabolical" would call their rites "obscene." There are, on the other hand, people who consider many of the Church's beliefs and practices to be an insult to Divinity; a woman once told me, for instance, that she thought the Church of England's Marriage Service so disgusting that she could never bring herself to submit to it. Much depends upon one's point of view in these matters.

The taking of wine during the rites is part of the ceremony; it consists usually of two glasses at the most, and is not intended to be a "mockery" of anything, still less a "Black Mass." In fact, witches say that their rite of the "Cakes and Wine" (a ritual meal in which cakes and wine are consecrated and partaken of) is much older than the Christian ceremony, and that in fact it is the Christians who have copied the rites of older religions. In view of the fact that such ritual meals are known to have been part of the Mysteries of the goddess Cybele in ancient times, and that a similar ritual meal is partaken of, according to Arthur Avalon in *Shakti and Shakta,* by the Tantriks of India, who are also worshippers of a great Mother-Goddess, there seem to be some grounds for this statement.

In the old days, they tell me, ale or mead might be used instead of wine, any drink in fact that had "a kick" in it, because this represented "life." I wonder if this is why Shakespeare used the expression "cakes and ale" as a synonym for fun which was frowned on by the pious?

It is a tradition that fire in some form, generally a candle, must be present on the altar, which is placed in the middle of the circle, and candles are also placed about the circle itself. This circle is drawn with the idea of "containing" the "power" which is raised within it, of bringing it to a focus, so to speak, so that some end may be accomplished by raising it. This focusing of force is called "The Cone of Power."

Incense is also used, and I have read in Spiritualist literature that "power" is thought by some mediums to be given off by naked flames, by a bowl of water, and by incense. All these are present on the witches' altar. I once took a photograph of a witches' meeting-place while a rite was being performed there; this included none of the people present, deliberately, but merely the altar, etc., and part of the circle. When the photograph was developed it showed "extras" in the form of ribbon-like formations, some of which appeared to proceed from the candles. I assured myself that there was nothing in the composition of the candles which could account for this phenomenon, nor was there anything wrong with my camera. A copy of this photograph is on display in the Museum.

The great reservoir of "power," according to the witches, is the human body. Spiritualists generally share this belief. Upon the practical means used to raise and direct this "power" I do not propose to touch; but that it is not a mere flight of fancy to believe in its existence is proved by some of the researches of modern science. The radiesthesia journal, *The Pendulum,* for March, 1956, carried an article called "Living Tissue Rays," by Thomas Colson, from the *Electronic Medical Digest.* This told how Professor Otto Rahn of Cornell University had described to a meeting of the American Association for the Advancement of Science, at Syracuse, New York, how yeast cells can be killed by a person looking intently at them for a few minutes. The yeast cells were placed on a glass plate and held close to the person's eyes. The Professor explained this by saying that certain rays were emitted from the human eye which were capable of producing this result. For several years, he said, scientists had been reporting discoveries that living things produce ultraviolet rays. In the human body they had been found coming from working muscles, and in the blood.

> The finger-tip rays of several persons at Cornell killed yeast readily. The tip of the nose was discovered to be a fine ultra-violet 'tube'. Then came the eye. Human rays are not always harmful. From some persons they are beneficial to tiny plants. There seems to be no difference in the kind, but the volume differs. When large, it is lethal to yeast. The same person emits it at different rates. He may be 'killing' at one time and 'benign' at another. The right hand appears to radiate more than the left, even in left-handers. . . .
>
> These body rays seem to be given off most strongly by the parts of the body which are replaced most rapidly, such as the palms of the hands and the soles of the feet. . . . The tops of the fingers are very strong emitters of this energy. . . . The back gives off the least energy and the abdomen and

> chest slightly more. The sex organs in both sexes and breasts in women emit these rays quite strongly.
>
> The first scientific proof that there is a personal electric field, a sort of electrical aura, within and in the air around a living body, was announced to the Third International Cancer Congress. The report was made by Dr. Harold S. Burr, of Yale University. . . . Human eyes are powerful electric batteries. This discovery, showing that each eyeball is an independent battery, was announced to the National Academy of Sciences in 1938 by Dr. Walter H. Miles, Yale University pathologist. . . . The fact that eyes produce electricity has been known to science since 1860, when it was discovered in frogs, but the source of this electric power, its variations and especially its high power in human beings, is little known.

The above extract gives the reason for the witches' traditional ritual nudity. To their Christian opponents this was mere shamelessness; but students of comparative religion know that, apart from the practical magical reason given above, nudity in religious ceremonies is a very old and world-wide practice. This is, in fact, yet another indication of the witch cult's derivation from remotest antiquity.

It may seem strange that the beliefs of the witch and the discoveries of the man of science should ever find a realm in which they could meet and touch; yet this is not the first time such a thing has happened. The doctor who introduced the use of digitalis into medical practice bought the secret from a Shropshire witch, after taking an interest in her herbal cures.

The witches' belief that "the power" resides within themselves, and that their rites serve to bring it out, is the great difference between them and the practitioners of "ceremonial magic," black or white. The latter proceed by the invocation or evocation of spirits, sometimes of demons, whom they seek to compel to serve them. This is not the witches' way, though they believe that helpful spirits, human or otherwise, come of their own accord to assist in their rites, and that those present who have developed "the Sight" (i.e. clairvoyance) may see such spirits.

A popular belief about witchcraft, which is nevertheless erroneous, is the idea that a witches' coven must consist of thirteen people. Actually, it may consist of more or less than thirteen people; but thirteen is considered to be the ideal number. This may be because it is the best number of people to work in the witches' traditional nine-foot circle; six couples and a leader. Or it may be because witchcraft is a moon cult, and there are thirteen moons in a year and thirteen weeks in every quarter, each quarter of the year having its Sabbat. The four great Sabbats are Candlemass, May Eve, Lammas, and Halloween; the equinoxes and solstices are celebrated also, thus making the Eight Ritual Occasions, as the witches call them. On the great Sabbats all the covens that could forgather together would do so; but apart from these great Sabbats, minor meetings called Esbats are held. The word "Esbat" may come from the old French "s'esbattre," meaning "to frolic, to enjoy oneself." Traditionally, the Esbat is the meeting of the local coven for local matters, or simply for fun, and it is, or should be, held at or near the full moon.

As might be expected from a moon cult, the leading part in the ceremonies is played by the High Priestess, or Maiden. She has the position of authority, and may choose any man of sufficient rank in the cult to be her High Priest. In France the Maiden was sometimes called *La Reine du Sabbat;* in Scotland she seems to have been called the Queen of Elphame (i.e. Faery), and one old witch-trial has it that "she makes any man King whom she pleases."

Apart from the theory that the "fairies" were actually the primitive People of the Heaths, the smaller, darker aboriginal folk displaced by the Early Iron Age invaders, which I treated of in *Witchcraft Today,* there is another connection between them and the witches. In the popular mind, after the advent of Christianity the old Celtic Paradise to which the souls of pagans went when they died became the "Realm of Faerie," and the God and Goddess who were the rulers of the After-World became the deities of the witches, who held to the Old Religion, and also were considered as the King and Queen of Faery. Hence the High Priestess of a witch coven, who is considered as the Goddess's living representative, would naturally be called "the Queen of Elphame."

The original "Fairyland" was the pagan paradise, and the "fairies" of early romances, are very different from the dainty miniature creatures of later tales and children's stories, made up when their original significance had been forgotten. This is made abundantly clear by the descriptions given in the anonymous old English poem, "Sir Orfeo," of which the earliest MS. we have dates from the early fourteenth century. It is reminiscent of the Greek story of Orpheus and Eurydice, but with a happy ending instead of a tragic one, and contains a fine description of "The proude courte of Paradis," which was entered apparently through a hollow hill or rocky cave, and of its rulers, "The king o' fairy with his rout," and his queen, the White

Goddess; "As white as milke were her weeks" and so brightly shining that Orfeo could scarcely behold them.

A. E. Waite, in his introduction to *Elfin Music, an Anthology of English Fairy Poetry*[*] says: "The Elizabethan age commonly identified the fairies of Gothic superstition with the classic nymphs who attended Diana, while the elfin queen was Diana herself, and was called by one of the names of that goddess, that is, Titania, which is found in the Metamorphoses of Ovid as a title of the uranian queen." He states further that ". . . the original fairy of Frankish poetry and fiction was simply a female initiated into the mysteries and marvels of magic."

A third ingredient in the tales of "fairies" is, of course, actual non-human nature spirits which some people claim to be able to see, and it is fascinating for the student of folklore to disentangle these different strands that weave through old stories and beliefs.

The High Priest of a witch coven is, as we have seen, chosen by the Priestess. He is the person whom the Inquisitors and witch-hunters of old times used to call "the Devil," as being either an actual supernatural devil or else his human representative. Witches are constantly being accused of "worshipping the Devil." Now, when we use that word "Devil," what picture automatically forms itself in most people's minds? Is it not that of a strange-looking being who seems to be partly human and partly animal, having great horns on his head, and a body covered with hair, although his face is human? Have you ever stopped to wonder why this picture should automatically come into your mind in this way? *There is not one single text in the Bible which describes "the Devil" or "Satan" in this manner.* The only place in which you will find such a personage described is, curiously enough, among the gods of the ancient peoples. Here you will find quite a number of Horned Gods, and sometimes Horned Goddesses too, who were not, however, beings of evil, but deities beneficent to man. The reason why people picture "the Devil" in this way is because from the very earliest times the Church has taught that the Old God who possessed these attributes was the enemy of the Christian God, and hence must be Satan; and people have got so used to this concept that they have never stopped to question it.

It is evident from early pictures and descriptions (the earliest being the famous cave paintings found at Ariege in the Caverne des Trois Freres,

---

* Walter Scott, 1888.

done by men of the Stone Age), that the High Priest who was the god's representative sometimes wore a ritual disguise, consisting of a head-dress bearing the horns of a stag or a bull, and a kind of robe of animal skins; sometimes, too, a mask which concealed his features. This custom seems to have been more particularly followed at the big Sabbats, when many people gathered outside the circle who were not actual initiates of the witches' mysteries, but came "for luck" (i.e. for the blessing of the Old Gods) or simply to enjoy themselves. It made the proceedings more impressive, and at the same time safer, if the god's representative was masked and disguised, so that he could not be recognised. The horned figure, seen dimly by moonlight or by the light of torches, would have seemed to the outsiders to be a supernatural being, and the initiates would not have undeceived them. When only initiates were present, there was less need for the ritual disguise, so the custom of wearing it has tended to fade out.

It will be seen that witchcraft is a system involving both magic and religion. This in itself is an indication of great age, because in primitive times magic and religion were closely interrelated. The priest was also the magician, and the magician had perforce to be a priest. Indeed, when one comes to consider it, many religious rites today are directed towards ends which might be called magical. What is the essential difference, for instance, between prayers for rain, or for a good harvest, and the old fertility rites which were directed to the same end? And why must a King or a Queen undergo the ritual of Coronation? With regard to the Church's prayers and a fertility rite, the difference would seem to lie in the latter working on the principle that "God helps those who help themselves," whereas the former is content with petition. The question of the necessity of Coronation ritual raises the whole idea of the Divine King or Queen which has engaged the attention of anthropologists for many years. The idea that there is any connection between religion and magic may be indignantly repudiated by some orthodox believers; nevertheless, both spring from the same root.

As I explained in my previous book, there are certain secrets of the witch cult that I cannot by reason of my pledged word reveal; but many people write to me saying, "You said in your book, *Witchcraft Today* that all the ancient Mysteries were basically the same; so as we all know what these ancient Mysteries were, we know exactly what the witches' secrets are. So why don't you write another book telling everything?"

Now, while the ancient authors who were initiated into a number of the Mysteries agree that they were all the same basically, and there is a certain amount of agreement among modern authors about what their secrets were, I doubt very much if any of them realises the reason behind them, "what made them work," in fact; and what makes things work is the witches' secret. I think that this was probably the practical secret of the ancient Mysteries also.

However, I am not going to be drawn in this way to break my word; a statement which will, I hope, result in a saving of notepaper and stamps on the part of some of my more aggressive correspondents. Certain of the present-day enquiries of psychical research, archaeology, anthropology, and psychology are beginning to converge in a manner that is gradually revealing facts about ancient beliefs and their effect upon human evolution which have not been realised before. It is my hope that this book will be a useful contribution to these lines of enquiry, and perhaps assist in their convergence.

Upon the 1st March, 1956, Major Lloyd-George, then Home Secretary, as a result of a question asked in the House of Commons, said that black magic was an offence in common law. When pressed by M.P.s to define black magic, he said, "It is the opposite to white magic (at which there was laughter and ironical cheers) which is performed without the aid of the devil, so I assume the other is done with his aid."

If this be accepted as a definition, then authentic witchcraft is certainly not black magic, because witches do not even believe in the devil, let alone invoke him. The Old Horned God of the witches is *not* the Satan of Christianity, and no amount of theological argument will make him so. He is, in fact, the oldest deity known to man, and is depicted in the oldest representation of a divinity which has yet been found, namely the Stone Age painting in the innermost recess of the Caverne des Trois Freres at Ariege. He is the old phallic god of fertility who has come forth from the morning of the world, and who was already of immeasurable antiquity before Egypt and Babylon, let alone before the Christian era. Nor did he perish at the cry that Great Pan was dead. Secretly through the centuries, hidden deeper and deeper as time went on, his worship and that of the naked Moon Goddess, his bride, the Lady of Mystery and Magic and the forbidden joys, continued sometimes among the great ones of the land, sometimes in humble cottages, or on lonely heaths and in the depths of darkling woods, on summer nights when the moon rode high. It does so still.

From time to time the public have been treated to various highly coloured and highly unconvincing "revelations" in the popular Press and elsewhere upon the subject of "Black Magic," "Satanism," and similar matters, and occasionally these have been linked with witchcraft. Let me state right away that I personally maintain an attitude of thorough-going scepticism towards these things, and that even if they do exist I do not consider them to have any relation to the survival of the witch cult. Alleged "confessions," especially where witchcraft is mentioned, bear ample internal evidence of their own meretriciousness, in that they are obviously modelled upon sensational thrillers and reveal no knowledge whatever of genuine witch practices.

The real thing is deeper hidden than this. People, especially country people, are reluctant to talk about it; but no one, I think, can study folklore in this country for long without becoming convinced of the amazing vitality and tenacity of old beliefs.

Where the town-dweller usually goes astray in his conclusions about the witch cult is that he has been fed mentally upon the alleged "revelations" mentioned above, or upon works that associate witchcraft with some fantastic belief vaguely known as "Satanism," with the implication that it is, or was, a cult of evil and nothing else. I submit that this is an unreasonable view, and has been promulgated by persons who possess no qualifications beyond a bent for sensationalism or an outlook blinded by religious bigotry. The countryman and countrywoman preserve a belief through the centuries because they think it is some use to them, or because they derive some satisfaction from it. Of course, the benefit they derive from the belief may not always seem to us to be highly ethical. Nevertheless, no one but a maniac would deliberately cultivate evil for its own sake.

The foundation of magical beliefs, of which witchcraft is a form, is that unseen Powers exist, and that by performing the right sort of ritual these Powers can be contacted and either forced or persuaded to assist one in some way. People believed this in the Stone Age, and they believe it, consciously or not, today. It is now well-known that most superstition is in fact broken-down ritual.

The unseen Powers that have interested man most in his early history have been the powers of fertility and of contact with the spirit world; of

Life and Death. These are the elementary powers that became the divinities of the witches, and their worship is as old as civilisation itself. The meaning of witchcraft is to be found, not in strange religious theories about God and Satan, but in the deepest levels of the human mind, the collective unconscious, and in the earliest developments of human society. It is the deepness of the roots that has preserved the tree.

Chapter II

Witches' Memories and Beliefs

Many people have written to me saying they enjoyed my book, *Witchcraft Today,* and asking me to write more about the cult. The difficulty is, as I explained in the former book, that witchcraft has become one of the secret religions, wherein people can express their greatest longings and aspirations without being mocked at; those archetypal reverences which, arising from deep levels of the unconscious, so strangely stir the soul. These things I think are a true form of religion because they are natural; though constant bludgeoning and conditioning of the mind may blunt perception, and cause people to shut their intuitions away in the inmost recesses of their being.

With this Old Religion comes the knowledge of a type of magic, difficult at all times to learn, and more so in these days, when everything is against you in this respect; but which exists all the same as a closely guarded secret. Magic is in itself neither black nor white, bad nor good; it is how it is used, the intent or the knowledge behind it, that matters.

Other people write asking me to expound more fully my ideas of the origins of witchcraft, and the only true answer I can give is, "I don't know"; but I have been doing a lot of research on the subject, and this book is largely the result. It is just what I *think,* not what I *know,* because I do not see how anyone will ever find the first beginnings. They are probably something like this: very primitive men, still rather like their animal kindred, lived happily and thoughtlessly until they were menaced by the slow coming of an Ice Age. The trees grew thinner and thinner, and they had to search harder to get food. Their shambling gait may have resembled that of apes, sometimes perhaps even dropping to all fours; but when snow came they found that by walking upright they kept their hands warmer, and could see further. This upright position affected their brains, which grew keener. Their speech improved, and with it their ideas. The cold killed off much of the fruit they lived on, and made them congregate in caves, going out in bodies to hunt game, taking more and more to a meat diet. With the discovery of fire-making, ritual may have started. You did this and this, and up sprang the magical flame, a spirit at your command. Or it may have started with the custom of dancing to celebrate a successful hunt.

It became lucky to do certain rites to induce good hunting and gain power over the game. Then slowly certain people took to doing the rites, and something like a priesthood was formed; that is, they found who were the most magically powerful people and used them. The dance was the chief method performed, mimicking the stalking and slaying of game. Later it took the form of a fertility dance, when they became cattle breeders and not so dependent on hunting. Then came animism, and perhaps the worship of natural phenomena, moon, stars and sun.

Magic has been classed as a trick closely guarded by the primitive magician. Perhaps so; it is the trick of doing something so that something else will occur. The airmen who drop a bomb could not make the bomb itself; they make intelligent use of a certain force which they do not wholly understand; and that is what magic is. If they misuse that force, and detonate the bomb in their plane, they may destroy themselves. This also occurs in magic; you must know how to keep the effects away from yourself.

The witches' own traditions simply tell them that they existed from all time; but that they came to where they are now from the Summer Land in the distant past. When you ask them where the Summer Land is they do not know; but it seems to have been a place of warmth and happiness, the Earthly Paradise of which all races of mankind have some tradition, and which so many adventurers have risked their lives seeking. (It may be noted in this connection that in Welsh legend, "Gwlad yr Hav," "the Land of Summer," is the Celtic Other World, and also the place where the ancestors of the Cymir came from.)

Witches also say that they came because man wanted magical rites for hunting; the proper rites to procure increase in flocks and herds, to assure good fishing, and to make women fruitful; then, later, rites for good farming, etc., and whatever the clan needed, including help in time of war, to cure the sick, and to hold and regulate the greater and lesser festivals, to conduct the worship of the Goddess and the Horned God. They considered it good that men should dance and be happy, and that this worship and initiation was necessary for obtaining a favourable place in the After-World, and a reincarnation into your own tribe again, among those whom you loved and who loved you, and that you would remember, know, and love them again. They think that in the good old days all this was obvious to the whole tribe. Witches were supported by the community, and they gave their services freely to all who asked their help. (A primitive National Health Service?) It is partly because of this that there is a strong witch tradition that they may never take money for practising their art; that is, they may not work for hire.

As they worked for the good of the tribe, they were inclined to favour a strong chief or king, someone who would see that the laws were observed, that everyone had their fair share, and that everyone did their work properly. For this reason, too, they were inclined to dislike politics; anything that made the tribe fight among themselves they considered bad.

They think that they were not Druids, but representatives of an older faith; that the Druids were a good and strong male priesthood who worshipped the sun in the daytime, and were inclined to mix in politics, while the witches worshipped the moon by night. It is almost as if the Druids were the bishops, etc., who attended the House of Lords and made the laws, and had a magical religion, while the witches were the parish priests, who kept out of politics, and possessed a form of religion and magic of their own.

It must be understood clearly that witchcraft is a religion. Its patron god is the Horned God of hunting, death and magic, who, rather like Osiris of Egypt, rules over the After-World, his own Paradise, situated in a hollow hill, or at least in a place which is only approached through a cave, where he welcomes the dead and assigns them their places; where they are prepared, according to their merits and wisdom, for rebirth into a new body on this earth, for which they will be made ready by the love and power of the Goddess, the Great Mother, who is also the Eternal Virgin and the Primordial Enchantress, who gives rebirth and transmutation, and love on this earth, and in whose honour and by means of ritual the necessary power is raised to enable this to be done. They think that the God and the Goddess assist them in making their magic, as they assist the God and the Goddess in their turn by raising power for them by their dances and by other methods. In fact, they seem to consider the gods as being more like powerful friends than deities to be worshipped.

To them the concept of an All-Powerful God, one who could simply say, "Let there be peace. Let there be no sickness or misery," and all wars, sickness and misery would cease, and who for his own reasons will not say that word, and keeps men in fear and misery and want, is not fit to receive worship. They quite realise that there must be some great "Prime Mover," some Supreme Deity; but they think that if It gives them no means of knowing It, it is because It does not want to be known; also, possibly, at our present stage of evolution we are incapable of understanding It. So It has appointed what might be called various Under-Gods, who manifest as the tribal gods of different peoples; as the Elohim of the Jews, for instance, who made them in Their own image ("Elohim" being a plural noun), "male and female made They them"; Isis, Osiris and Horus of the Egyptians; the "portmanteau-word" of certain initiates, "Maben," which is MA, AB, BEN, or "Mother, Father and Son"; and the Horned God and the Goddess of the witches. They can see no reason why each people should not worship their national gods, or why anyone should strive to prevent them from doing so. This has always caused them to take a poor view of missionary enterprise, whether by the orthodox Church or by totalitarians such as the Communists. They think that many of the troubles in this world are caused by those various organisations which are formed "to make people do and believe what they don't want to, and to prevent them from doing and believing what they do want to."

It is usually said that to be made a witch one must abjure Christianity; this is not true; but they would naturally not receive into their ranks anyone who was a very narrow Christian. They do not think that the real Jesus was literally the Son of God, but are quite prepared to accept that he was one of the Enlightened Ones, or Holy Men. That is the reason why witches do not think they were hypocrites "in time of persecution" for going to church and honouring Christ, especially as so many of the old Sun-hero myths have been incorporated into Christianity; while others might bow to the Madonna, who is closely akin to their goddess of heaven. In former times attendance at church was compulsory by law, and absence both punishable and dangerous, in that it aroused suspicion; but of this more anon.

It must be understood that witches were, for the last two thousand years at least, the village priestesses, wise men and women, etc. They performed the rites which brought prosperity to the community; different from, but not opposed to, the official religion, which was at first Druidism. Then the Druids in Britain contacted the first Christian missionaries, who may have been led by Joseph of Arimathea. They had long had a god called

Hesus, and a tradition of a Divine Child, so it was not difficult for them to accept primitive Christian teaching. This tended to separate them further from the witch cult, but there is no evidence of any antagonism between them.

Then first the Roman, and later the Saxon invasions came. The kings, nobles, and the Christianised Druids suffered badly, and many fled to Ireland and Scotland, as did many good craftsmen, jewellers, etc. (and much of the wonderful Irish art was the work of these British craftsmen); but, contrary to what is often thought, the main population remained in their villages. The Saxons, at first heathen, were converted to Christianity by missionaries from Rome, and some laws against witchcraft were made.

After the Norman Conquest the Saxons became a race of serfs under Norman masters. Later the two races tended to amalgamate and intermarry, becoming English instead of British and Saxon. As there is no trace of Saxon customs in the cult, it does not seem that such Saxon witches as there were ever came into it; but when the Normans arrived they had a tradition of something like witchcraft. Whether this came from Norway or from Gaul I am not sure, but it certainly existed. At any rate, the British had always thought of the Saxons as oppressors who had robbed them of all the best in their country, and the witches disliked them because they made laws against witchcraft, so both were wryly amused to see the Saxons being bullied in their turn.

The Saxons were hard-working, thick-headed, stolid people, who stayed where they were and paid heavy taxes, while those "Britons" who were left were inclined to be vagabondish, gipsy-wandering, hunting and fighting types of people, who would take service easily with the Normans. They made good mercenary soldiers, who lived hard and liked fighting.

Christianity sat lightly upon the Normans. They were originally what in the East are called "rice-Christians." Their fathers had received lands from the French king to keep other pirates away, on the condition of accepting baptism. Not so many years ago in China, Feng Hu Sang, the Christian general, used to baptise his troops by playing hoses on them as they marched past, and as Charlemagne used to drive pagan tribes through rivers at swords point, having a bishop blessing it higher up. Such mass-conversions are apt not to be very sincere. But Christianity was at that time something to which, although you might not believe it or even clearly understand it, you had to conform if your ruler was a Christian convert, and to give up your pagan gods and declare them to be devils. You could do that easily, by word of mouth at any rate; but the customs and beliefs of centuries are not altered so readily or so quickly as this.

William the Conqueror had wisely proclaimed that he was the ruler of the Church, and he appointed his own Bishops; but as the Church at Rome became more powerful it insisted on appointing non-English Bishops to all offices of profit. This and other matters caused some of the Normans to take notice of the older faith. For if it was so difficult and expensive to get into the Christian Heaven and to dodge the Christian Hell, the witches' Paradise was simple and pleasant; but you had to keep your belief in it dark. This, to the younger men at least, was easy and romantic. You simply went out hunting with a few faithful retainers, and lost yourself in the woods for a while. Doubtless all the Castle knew where you had really been, but they didn't tell the Stoke (the Saxon village), or the priest; unless, as was often the case in the early days he had been there himself taking part in the rites.

There were several wars which troubled the countryside in places, but otherwise things remained much the same until about the time of Edward I, who expelled the Jews. Until then the Jews had been a race apart, who were merchants, money-lenders, tax collectors and doctors, living chiefly in the towns, marrying usually among themselves, hated but tolerated by the Church, their numbers kept down by occasional massacres. When King Edward banished them from England large numbers from the big towns left the country; though numbers went to ground, into the outland districts beyond the law; that is, into the British settlements, the witch districts. These probably had some connections there already. At least, it is a witch tradition that during the Jewish massacres they had always given them shelter when they could, and it is from these Jews that the witches got to know of the Qabalah, and obtained many of their ideas of the Jewish mystical and magical traditions, upon which most mediaeval magic was founded.

Neither the witches nor myself wish to argue as to the rights or wrongs of what the Jewish Qabalists taught. All I can say is that there is a witch tradition that this teaching among others was given and believed, namely that the ancient religion of Israel was the worship of the Elohim, the Supernal Father and the Supernal Mother, Who had made man in Their image, male and female (Genesis, Chap. I, v. 26–28); this mystery was symbolised by the sacred Twin Pillars, Jachin and Boar, of Solomon's Temple; but after Solomon's time wicked priests arose who perverted the true faith, and instead of the Gods of Love, preached a solitary God of hate and vengeance. To gain power and wealth, these priests had committed many pious forgeries of Holy Writ, and So led men from the truth.

In this connection, I may quote from the Introduction to S. L. MacGregor Mathers' book, *The Kabbalah Unveiled*. Speaking of the symbolism of the Sephiroth, the Ten Emanations of Deity, he says:

> Among these Sephiroth, jointly and severally, we find the development of the persons and attributes of God. Of these some are male and some female. Now, for some reason or other best known to themselves, the translators of the Bible have carefully crowded out of existence and smothered up every reference to the fact that the Deity is both masculine and feminine. They have translated a feminine plural by a masculine singular in the case of the word Elohim. They have, however, left an inadvertent admission of their knowledge that it was plural in Gen. I. v. 26, "And Elohim said: Let Us make man." Again (v. 27), how could Adam be made in the image of the Elohim, male and female, unless the Elohim were male and female also. The word Elohim is a plural formed from the feminine singular ALH, Eloh, by adding IM to the word. But inasmuch as IM is usually the termination of the masculine plural, and is here added to a feminine noun, it gives to the word Elohim the sense of a female potency united to a masculine idea, and thereby capable of producing an offspring. Now, we hear much of the Father and the Son, but we hear nothing of the Mother in the ordinary religions of the day. But in the Qabalah we find that the Ancient of Days conforms Himself simultaneously into the Father and the Mother, and thus begets the Son. Now, this Mother is Elohim. Again, we are usually told that the Holy Spirit is masculine. But the word RVCh, Ruach, Spirit, is feminine, as appears from the following passage of the Sepher Yetzirah: 'AChTh RVCh ALHIM ChIIM, Achath (feminine, not Achad, masculine) Ruach Elohim Chiim: One is She the Spirit of the Elohim of Life.

As I have previously mentioned, the witches were quite well affected towards the early Celtic Christians and the Culdees, the Druids who had become Christians, but were not so well affected towards the Saxons who had invaded them or towards their type of Christianity, which derived from Rome and denounced witch rites with puritanical fervour. It is noticeable that soon after the Qabalists began to mingle with them the Church began to persecute them. What seems to have happened is that the Jews in hiding disliked roughing it in the British type of village, and slowly came back into the towns; but they dared not be known as Jews. They had to pretend to be good Christians, and they could not be moneylenders any more. The Church, the Templars, and the Lombard goldsmiths had taken that lucrative job over; but they could be doctors and "wise men" generally, and many of them became the type we think of as "wizards," practitioners of ceremonial magic, sellers of cures and charms, and practised as astrologers, and there were many people who wanted their services.

Astrology was always respectable; many Churchmen practised it, and the law never bothered them. The fundamental idea of astrology is enshrined in the famous precept of Hermes Trismegistus, from the Smaragdine Tablet, "That which is below is like that which is above, and that which is above is like that which is below, for the performance of the miracles of the one substance." Everything was considered to have its astrological signature or rulership, and to know the astrological signatures of herbs and of the parts of the human body was an important branch of mediaeval medicine. The great authority for early astrologers was Claudius Ptolemy (2nd century A.D.). Cyril Fagan, in his *Zodiacs Old and New,* says, "Ptolemy's 'Great Construction' and 'Four Books' were translated into Arabic and with the Moorish invasion were introduced into western Europe during the Dark Ages. This was probably western Europe's first introduction to classical astrology. From the Arabic the books were rendered into Latin by the doctors of the church."

Witches are inclined to smile at learned magicians, saying that they never could do much without a witch to help them; but they do acknowledge that in the terrible "burning times" many witches were sheltered and protected by magicians and astrologers, and perhaps this is all the more reason why they pay attention to the teaching of the Qabalists. Astrological ideas form an integral part of the Hebrew Qabalah.

Under the Saxon kings there were laws against magic and witchcraft; but the punishment was usually only by a fine or by doing penance in church, and there is no record of it being actually inflicted. The first trial recorded for witchcraft in England was in the tenth year of the reign of King John, when the wife of Odo the merchant accused one Gideon of bewitching her. Gideon was tried by the ordeal of red-hot iron, and acquitted. As the ordeal by red-hot iron was a serious thing, either Gideon was favoured by the priests who conducted the ordeal, and who were said to have methods of protecting their favourites from the fire, or else he was able to work quite good magic, possibly of the self-hypnotic type, for recent experiments at the University of Texas have been producing remarkable results in the use of hypnotism for the treatment and cure of burns.

Witchcraft continued to be an ecclesiastical crime only in England for many years, and was largely mixed up with charges of denying the existence of demoniacal agency; for the Church said that denying a personal devil was equivalent to a confession of atheism and a denial of the Holy Scriptures themselves. In this way a great number of witches were doubtless convicted. They were accused of following or consorting with "the fairies," or Herne the Hunter, or Robin Hood, the Devil. To say he was not the Devil was heresy; and many people were brought to execution on that account. That is, it was put to them, "Do you believe Herne, or Robin, or the Queen of Elphame, as the case might be, is the Devil?" If they said "No," it was heresy. If they said "Yes," they were convicted of diabolism. At first they probably all denied that he or she was the Devil; but then the obvious question came, "If they are not the Devil, you must know them as a man or a woman. Who are they? Let them be arrested and tortured." Probably many confessed to dealings with the Devil, so as not to get someone else, a human leader of a coven, into trouble.

The mention of so popular a figure of legend as Robin Hood in this context may seem strange. However, he is one of the forms of the old god of the woods who presided over the May games. His name "Hood" probably means "Robin of the Woods," as his equivalent in France was called "Robin des Bois."*

Most of the general public had at least a shrewd idea of where to go if one wanted to get medicines that worked, or a bit of advice in time of trouble, and the country folk knew quite well that dances and rites were held at regular intervals to bring good crops, etc., and were aware who organised and took part in them; and so occasional "purges" were carried out by the church authorities. Some will doubtless say that even if the witches did not know they were doing wrong, they knew it as soon as the Church proclaimed witchcraft to be heretical and sinful; but to the witches it did not seem just that they should be condemned for doing what had been done for centuries and thought no ill of; what, they asked, was wrong with the old customs, anyway? And was not the Church always forbidding anything nice?

---

* See Chap. IV of *The Hero, by Lord Raglan.*

If in England, as on the Continent, the persecution had been everywhere at the same time, it might have seemed different; but there would be a wild flare-up of persecution in the domains of one lord, because he or his wife had suddenly "got religion," or because a new Bishop had come to the district. (I say "new Bishop" because it was possible that the old Bishop had been a regular attendant at the Sabbat, as the Bishop of Coventry was accused of being in 1303. The Pope accused him *Quod diabolo homagium fecerat, et eum fuerit osculatus in tergo.* (*Chartier* iii. p. 45.) So the persecution would flare up in one district, and some witches would be caught, while others escaped, across a river perhaps, or into another lord's lands.

Sir Matthew Hale (1609–1676), in his *History of the Pleas of the Crown,* says, "Witchcraft, *Sortilegium,* was by the ancient laws of England of ecclesiastical cognizance, and upon conviction thereof, without abjuration, punishable with death by writ *de haeretico comburendo.*"

What, incidentally, is this crime of heresy, that the early Church adjudged to be so terrible that it warranted burning alive the perpetrator of it? According to Cobham Brewer (*Dictionary of Phrase and Fable*), "Heretic means 'one who chooses', and 'heresy' means simply 'a choice'. A heretic is one who chooses his own creed, and does not adopt the creed authorised by the national church. (Greek *hairesis,* choice.)" It is a curious sidelight upon the evolution of human society that that which was a capital crime in the Middle Ages should have become one of the most cherished and fundamental rights of modern democracy.

In England the whole power of the State was not at first behind these persecutions. It was a matter for individual Bishops and nobles. It took longer, but was none the less thorough, because everyone knew who followed the Old Religion. They were marked down and "liquidated." Although Bishops occasionally burned witches as heretics, the general way of extermination in England was by hanging. Torture was not legal, but was used at times and conditions of imprisonment in those days were often torture.

Propaganda played an important part. It was unfortunate that the god of the witches wore a helmet with horns, because when the Church began to proclaim the doctrine of the devil as God's adversary they made him in the image of the Greek and Roman god Pan. There were many statues of Pan surviving, half-man, half-goat, with horns upon his head. The Church said very plausibly that the pagans would not have made such statues if they had no model to work from; they had had models for the other statues they made, men, women and animals, so there must be real creatures like this, and they must be devils, and have a Supreme Lord of Evil as their chief.

Public opinion can only be made to accept hangings, burnings and torturings, as righteous if it is turned against those who are to be the victims; and one of the surest ways in which this can happen is for people to become so thoroughly frightened that they lose their heads and their sense of proportion. Hence the ascribing to witches and other heretics of every crime, possible and impossible, that the human mind can conceive, until they are represented as being cohorts of Satan on earth. Human society, impelled by these ideas, became a tragic battleground; and perhaps the most pitiful aspect of this civil war of humanity was that it was sometimes waged by men of good-will and good faith, yet men so darkly misled that they honestly thought the pyre and the gallows a triumph for Christ and His Cross. That is surely one of the saddest things of all.

I have said that there were no severe civil laws against witchcraft in early England, and when Gideon was tried he was acquitted by the ordeal of red-hot iron; but this simply means there were no records, or at least none have survived, of trials in the Bishop's Courts, with the curious exception of that by a clerk of the Bishop of Ossory, Richard Ledrede, in Ireland, who it seems noted down some of the Bishop's songs (some of them rather curious for a Bishop: "Haro, je suis trahi, par fol amour de fausse amie" runs one of them), and included some notes on the case of Dame Alice Kyteler of Kilkenny, in 1324. She had been married four times, her first husband being the brother of Roger Outlaw, who was Head of the Order of the Knights of St. John in Ireland, and Lord Chancellor of Ireland. It was to enrich his nephew, her son, that she was said to have wrought spells with the aid of a "Devil," Robin Filius Artis, or Artisson, who is described as "Aethiopis," and with him she did "dirty work at the crossroads." Allowing for exaggeration, there seems not much doubt that she did attempt to bring her son luck, especially as one of the charms she is said to have used that of "sweeping dust inwards," is still used in the Isle of Man. Robin is also said to have appeared at times as "a black shaggy dog," like the spectral Moddey Dhoo, which is still said to roam about in Man. (May one wonder, not too seriously, if our Manx Moddey Dhoo is the originator of the "shaggy dog story"?)

None of these matters were crimes by the civil law; but the Bishop quoted Bulls against sorcery promulgated by Pope John XXII. The Bishop was actually imprisoned for making a false case; but the jailer was afraid of the Bishop, and complaints were made that his jail was "more like a ball of feasting" (where the Bishop doubtless sang his songs). While in jail he excommunicated his opponents, and placed the whole diocese under interdict, which brought the Archbishop of Dublin out against him for imposing an interdict without due enquiry. He left his easy jail in a grand procession, and attacked Lady Alice and her son again. The Archbishop of Dublin and the King's Justiciar summoned him to Dublin; but he refused to go, and set up a court of his own at Kilkenny, where he summoned Lord Arnold de la Poore, the King's Seneschal, who refused to attend. But the Archbishop of Dublin took his side over the question of his "joyous imprisonment," and had a number of people arrested, though not Dame Alice and her son. But eventually William Outlaw, the son, was taken and tried at Kilkenny before the Chancellor, the Lord Treasurer and others, when a verdict was arranged that he should hear three Masses a day for a year, maintaining a certain number of the poor, and pay for repairs to the Cathedral choir.

Dame Alice went to England where she was safe. The Bishop then attacked Roger Outlaw for disloyalty, who appealed to the King's Council. They deputed a number of high ecclesiastics to enquire into the case, who unanimously found him to be "loyal and upright, zealous in the faith, and ready to die for it." Meanwhile, the Bishop seized a number of lesser fry who were said to have belonged to Dame Alice's coven, flogged, tortured and burned alive Petronilla de Meath and others, and got away with it. If his clerk bad not written down the songs the Bishop made, it is unlikely that this curious witch trial would ever have been recorded. It is interesting that the people concerned were all great nobles, from England as well as Ireland, and all of them were on the side of the witches with the exception of the Bishop, who had the half-hearted support of the Archbishop.

If all this could go on without any record except the notes of a clerk writing down songs (and this was an outstanding case which lasted for years, involving many of the great ones of the realm), then it is evident that Bishops could and did do whatever they liked in their own dioceses, without any record being kept, at any rate none which survived the dissolution of the monasteries.

The witches have vague stories of the "burning time," which seems to have started about 1300, with persecutions springing up and dying down till about the time of Henry VIII; but the persecution was kept up by a spate of propaganda, until it was firmly fixed in the public mind that witches had commerce with the devil, that they raised storms at sea, caused abortions, and in fact were the authors of practically every evil that afflicts the human race. Even a modern author, Pennethorne Hughes, declared recently in his book *Witchcraft:*

> Witches cast spells; they raised havoc; they poisoned; they aborted cattle and inhibited human beings; they served the Devil, parodied Christian practices, allied themselves with the King's enemies. They copulated with other witches in male or female form, whom they took to be incubi or succubi; they committed abuses with domestic animals. More, they did these things consciously, in the belief that they served a diabolic master and challenged Heaven. Their motives were confused, their impulses were bemused, and their proceedings were more and more remote from any common original practice. Yet they did them, and the reasons for what they did lie in the earliest religions and beliefs. Beside these witches, thousands of technically innocent people died as the result of mass hysteria and pious fear.

William Temple, the then Archbishop of Canterbury, wrote in 1935, "Shelve the responsibility for human evil on Satan if you will; personally, I believe he exists, and that a large share of the responsibility belongs to him and to subordinate evil spirits."

With people nowadays believing things like this, it is easy to understand how when Henry VIII repealed any laws there were against witchcraft, the witches thought that at last the world was becoming a little saner, the fierce reformers, fresh from Geneva where Calvin was busy burning witches (and whoever it was who made a wax image of Queen Elizabeth I and stuck pins in it in Lincoln's Inn Fields), induced that queen to pass a law against magic and witchcraft again though the only penalty was the pillory. Her Catholic cousin, Mary Queen of Scots, made the Scottish law of burning for all witches and those who consulted them. Her son, James VI of Scotland, afterwards James I of England, burned witches with zest, and brought in the death penalty in England; but he could not get the English to allow burning. Torture, too, was legal in Scotland, but not in England.

The Puritans in England took up the persecutions and hangings with vigour. Matthew Hopkins, the notorious "Witch-finder General," and others who imitated him, made large amounts of money out of it. For instance, it is on record that he received £28 øs. 3d. from Stowmarket, where the people, bamboozled into thinking that he possessed a commission from Parliament, actually levied a rate to pay this charlatan and his retinue. This represents, at present-day values, a considerable sum. Another of his money-making schemes is shown by Matthew Hopkins' "talisman against witchcraft" that we have here in this museum. Hopkins sold these talismans as a preservative against witchcraft, asking a handsome price. If any refused to buy, they ran the risk of being denounced as "favouring witchcraft."

By ingenious methods he devised means of torturing prisoners and yet remaining technically within the law. However, people were ceasing to be as credulous as they formerly were; and a number of gentlemen, notably the Vicar of Great Staughton, John Gaule, protested against his activities. Hopkins seems to have come, in fact, to a rather mysterious end. He started his witch-finding career in 1644; and by 1648 he was dead. His partner, John Stearne, stated that Hopkins died of a consumption; but there is a tradition, noted in Samuel Butler's contemporary poem, "Hudibras," that some who were indignant at his cruelties got together and forcibly subjected him to one of his own tests, namely by swimming him in a pond with his hands and feet fastened together crosswise (the right hand to the left foot and vice versa); the idea being that if the person sank, he was innocent, but if he floated he was a witch, and consequently hanged. One story goes that Hopkins floated, so proving himself a witch, and got a severe chill from which he soon died. Certain it is that his career was somehow cut short. Not, however, before he had created a minor reign of terror in East Anglia, and had been the instrument of very many deaths.

Not before 1735 were the penal laws against witchcraft repealed; and not until 1951 was the last Witchcraft Act swept from the Statute Book. With all this history of persecution, can anyone wonder that members of the witch cult are not particularly fond of the orthodox Church, or that they distrust a faith which can take the teachings of its Master, who never persecuted anyone, and turn them into a frenzy of torture and horror? How many perished in the witch-mania throughout Western Europe, in the whole of its long course, will probably never be known; they are estimated to number nine million.

Even though all laws on the subject have now been repealed, this repeal has been received in some quarters with regret; and there are still attempts to whip up persecution by getting sensational scare-stories printed, endorsed by churchmen who issue solemn warnings about "black magic" and "devil-worship." Can anyone be surprised that adherents of this ancient cult prefer generally not to be known? Yet people are annoyed when I refuse to give them the names and addresses of persons whom I know to be witches, or to take them to where they can watch a witch meeting unobserved!

What does a witch get out of witchcraft? For one thing, she has the satisfaction of knowing that she is serving an ancient creed which she believes to be true. Nowadays, many people have only the simple pleasure of being themselves and following those things in which they are interested, among friends who understand them. To some there is the fun of belonging to a sort of secret society. This is a harmless type of amusement, realised by many organisations, such as that of Freemasonry. But in witchcraft there may be more. If you have any power, you are among people who will teach you how to use it. As one witch said to a reporter, "What do I get out of it? I get a life that holds infinite possibilities, and is entirely satisfying to me on all planes of consciousness. I have power to move in other dimensions and realms of being. I have communication with entities of different life forms, and by the development of new and magic gifts within myself I have certain powers of extra-sensory perception. I have knowledge, and the ability to bring about anything I really want in my own life. I experience forms of pleasures whose very existence is unknown to the majority of people. I have conquered fear. I have learned of the ordered pattern behind apparently unrelated things."

Another woman, a convert to witchcraft, told me, "When I was a little girl I used to be terrified of the dark and of being alone, because I often had the sensation of unseen presences around me. We were never encouraged to try to understand the spirit world. 'Spirits' were either banned altogether as a subject of conversation, or regarded with terror as evil. Since I have studied these things, however, I have lost this fear. Now I understand that just because an entity is not incarnate in flesh it is not necessarily evil, but that spirits are just like human beings in this respect; some are desirable companions and some are not. I know now how to deal with the 'undesirables', so I no longer dread them. This is one of the things that witchcraft has done for me."

Here is what two witches have said about their beliefs. When one is studying any belief or religion, an honest scholar asks the people concerned what they believe, or he reads what they themselves say about their beliefs. Anyone who wrote about the Roman Catholic religion, using only the works of the early Protestant reformers, or who wrote about the same Protestant reformers using only what Roman Catholic writers have said about the Protestants, would not be considered a serious critic; anyone searching for facts about contemporary life in England who only read the Communist newspapers of this and other countries would be apt to form distorted views. Yet it is a curious fact that until Dr. Margaret Murray investigated witchcraft about thirty years ago in her two monumental works, *The Witch Cult in Western Europe* and *The God of the Witches,* no writers ever seem to have thought, "The Church says that witches call up the devil, and fly through the air on broomsticks, and gives as proof the fact that people have been tortured until they confessed this, and that they caused storms and did all other sorts of evil. Now, I (whoever the writer may have been) do not believe in the devil, and I don't believe that anyone can fly on a broomstick; yet I am prepared to believe all the rest of what they were made to say under torture, and never try any further to discover what is the truth of the matter." Is this a logical or scholarly point of view to take?

At the time these authors were writing it would have been easy to investigate. Since then two wars, and changing social conditions, have disrupted the whole countryside. Only fragments of the old traditions remain. Here are some verses a member of the cult wrote a while ago:

O Moon that rid'st the night to wake,
Before the dawn is pale,
The hamadryad in the brake,
The satyr in the vale,
Caught in thy net of shadows
What dreams hast thou to show?
Who treads the silent meadows
To worship thee below?
The patter of the rain is hushed,

The wind's wild dance is done,
Cloud-mountains ruby-red were flushed
About the setting sun;
And now beneath thine argent beam
The wildwood standeth still,
Some spirit of an ancient dream
Breathes from the silent hill.
Witch-Goddess Moon, thy spell invokes
The Ancient Ones of night.
Once more the old stone altar smokes,
The fire is glimmering bright.
Scattered and few thy children be,
Yet gather we unknown
To dance the old round merrily
About the time-worn stone.
We ask no Heaven, we fear no Hell,
Nor mourn our outcast lot,
Treading the mazes of a spell
By priests and men forgot.

Chapter III

The Stone Age Origins of Witchcraft

I have endeavoured to tell as much as I can of what witches know and believe about themselves and their history. Now I am going to discuss the probable origins of the cult, and to do this I shall try to show the various influences which may have been brought to bear upon it in Britain. I hope this may encourage others to investigate along similar lines in this and other countries.

When you begin to examine the origin of witchcraft, it is like excavating one of those prehistoric caves in France which are still occupied. A few inches down you find a copper coin of Napoleon; a few inches further you find those of various French kings, then mediaeval pottery; a little lower Gallo-Roman remains and those of the Bronze Age, then beautifully polished stone axes of the New Stone Age; then rougher and more primitive work of the Old Stone Age; and these all serve to form the floor of this dwelling, as the people who made them were the ancestors of the people who live there today. So while I believe that we find the origin of witchcraft in the primitive hunting magic of the Old Stone Age people, one must try to see what different types of people have influenced it through the ages.

Everyone has heard of the cave paintings of France and Spain, but not so well known is the carving on a bone found in the Pin Hole Cave in Yorkshire, under six inches of stalagmite, showing a dancing man wearing an animal mask. Incidentally, the Pin Hole Cave is so called because it contained a deep hole into which the country people used to drop pins to gain their wishes; another instance of the way in which a magical tradition can linger about a place throughout the centuries.

In various caves in France and Spain, often half a mile or more from the entrance, in prehistoric times circles have been made by putting stones together, fires have been lighted inside, and pictures of animals painted on flat stones are carefully placed face-downwards inside them. Here it is obvious that magical rites have been performed inside the circles to affect the animals depicted upon the stones, which have then been placed face-downwards to prevent the power raised being dissipated. In other places clay figures of animals were found, which had been pierced with spears. When they were first discovered, archaeologists were puzzled as to their meaning; but the local peasants said, "It's just hunting-magic. We do that every year when we want to kill wolves. They're clever; you must gain power over them first, or they will get away." The researches of the Abbe Breuil and others show that the majority, if not all, of these old cave paintings were used for magic, and that originally the image or painting was done especially for the operation desired. The intense concentration necessary was obtained by painting the picture. At a later date, apparently, they had discovered other methods of inducing the concentration necessary, and they often used the same picture over again, only retouching it a little here and there.

Being an anthropologist, I am concerned with what people believe and what they do because of these beliefs. When I first began to write about witchcraft I realised that it seemed to be a Stone Age cult which began by practising hunting magic, and had found that the magic which would affect animals could be used to affect human beings, and to attempt to cause events to occur. I realised that the practice of magic had become a cult, which later grew into a religion, and that obviously at some later time foreign or exotic ideas had been introduced into the original simple folk-magic: but I thought that these ideas had only come in at a comparatively late date, via the Greek and Roman Mysteries. That is still the simplest explanation; yet in real life one finds that seemingly simple ideas are apt to prove complicated on examination. For instance, many people say, "There was no real religion in the world until Moses led the Children of Israel out of Egypt and set them worshipping the One True God in the Promised Land, and even then they were only Jews till Christ came on earth. All other religions weren't real religions; they were just idolatry." But on investigation you find that there were very many well developed religions before the time of Moses, and that many of the ideas of Christ had been expressed by Buddha nearly five hundred years before.

As an anthropologist, I am accustomed to talk to people and try to find out what they believe on certain points, at the same time attempting to avoid the trap of reading into their answers my own preconceived opinions. There are many people better equipped than I am for this work of investigating the witch cult; but as far as I know no one is doing it, and it should be done quickly before any more of the old knowledge is lost. I have this advantage, that having been initiated into a British witch coven I am in a position to talk to people who are initiated witches, and ask them what they believe, and they can trust me not to write down things which they do not wish to be known; because witches have a firmly rooted belief in their own powers, and the danger of these being misused if uninitiated people learn their methods. Also, they reverence their gods, and do not wish their names to be known, or bandied about and mocked. In fact, they of all people keep the commandment, "Thou shalt not take the name of thy God in vain." In investigating the witch cult I can only speak of British witches, because they are the only ones I know well enough and who trust me enough to tell me real things about themselves. Also, I think the same causes which have affected British witches would have affected those of most other European countries.

At first I thought it was just a matter of knowing what witches did and believed, and then seeing what race or tribe did and believed the same. But when I began to look closer, I found that so many people did and believed much, or all, that the witches did. Some could be only coincidences; but there were too many of them, and I knew that "Coincidence killed the Professor"; so I kept on until I began to think I saw a certain pattern shaping. People did things and believed things because they were the natural things to do and believe, and that meant that these things were probably true.

As elephant herds are led by an evil-tempered female, so early tribes of hunters were led by a matriarch; that is, the strongest and strongest-minded woman ruled the tribe, and the men. The matriarch and her daughters sat at home and governed the tribe because it was her magic which made the tribe. She made the babies. There are primitive tribes which have retained similar concepts to this day. Earl Russell, commenting on Malinowski's work, *The Sexual Life of Savages in North-West Melanesia,* points out that there is no word for "father" in the Trobriand language because no such concept exists. Charles Seltman, in his book, *Women in Antiquity* (Pan Books, 1956), says of this: "Missionaries could not get along without such an idea and name, and they were forced to teach the Islanders the facts of procreation, which these happy people dismissed laughingly as plain nonsense." Then perhaps some vigorous hunter, who liked experimenting, discovered that the matriarch's story that she made babies with the aid of a gooseberry bush, or her own magic, or whatever she told them, was not quite true. He saw that there were too many coincidences, and that these coincidences produced babies, and it struck him that he was the coincidence, and that the tribe could depend on him. The younger women were charmed at this discovery, and he began to throw his weight about and to think what a fine fellow he was. However, it was still a long time before the rule of the old matriarch gave way to patriarchy; that the understanding of the facts of procreation brought into prominence the male, phallic deity as "Opener of the Door of Life." The Great Mother acquired a partner; but he was not yet her lord.

Between the idea of the young woman he loved and the old woman he feared, man found a goddess to worship, who loved him and protected him, and at times punished him. Those modern psychologists who belong to the school of C. G. Jung tell us that buried deep in what they call the collective unconscious of humanity are certain primordial concepts which Jung calls "archetypes." He defines these as "inherited predispositions to reaction," and as "perhaps comparable to the axial system of a crystal, which predetermines, as it were, the crystalline formation in the saturated solution, without itself possessing a material existence." We might call them "primordial images." Jung defines two of the most potent of these archetypes which dwell in the mysterious depths of the unconscious mind of man as "The Great Mother" and "The Old Wise Man," and judging from the description of them given in his works they are undoubtedly identical with the goddess and god of the witch cult. Dr. Jolan Jacobi, in *The Psychology of C. G. Jung*, says, "They are well known from the world of the primitives and from mythology in their good and evil, light and dark aspects, being represented as magician, prophet, mage, pilot of the dead, leader, or as goddess of fertility, sybil, priestess, Sophia, etc. From both figures emanates a mighty fascination. . . ." These are precisely the deities of the witches, and this fact may be a clue to the mystery of the cult's amazing endurance.

I mentioned before that the peasants in France and Spain knew what the clay figures of animals which had been thrust through with spears meant, because they in the twentieth century still hunted wolves that way. That is, this inherited magical custom or knowledge had descended from father to son for ten or twelve thousand years. Nominally, all sorts of people had occupied the land in turn, each with their different languages; but in fact all these invasions simply meant that some new people came in and possibly seized the best pieces of land and some of the women. The original inhabitants were elbowed out into the less fertile parts; but in a few generations the original stock, excepting perhaps some of the "bosses" or nobility, was much the same. Rudyard Kipling puts it neatly in his verses about a piece of land throughout the ages, with its different lords and owners, and the family of Hobdens who lived on it continuously and worked it according to their notions, ending with:

> . . . for now I understand,
> Whoever pays the taxes, Mus' Hobden owns the land.

Even so the case is in England and elsewhere today; the oldest families are the hereditary "witches" or "wise folk," although unfortunately they had not preserved records of their family trees.

Exactly when the cult became a religion I cannot say; but there is a celebrated prehistoric painting in a cave in France (La Caverne des Trois Freres, Ariege), usually called "The Magician," which obviously depicts a man in a mask and an animal's skin, with horns on his head. Evidently he is playing the ritual part of an animal. In the Stone Age, when man possessed as yet no metal weapons, he had to rely on knives, spears, axes and arrows made from flint or stone. It is no easy proposition to kill a great stag or buffalo with such weapons as these; so the Stone Age hunters adopted the strategy of luring a herd of game into some favourable position where they either could not escape and were shot with arrows, or where they fell over a cliff or into a pit, and were there caught and despatched. It has been suggested by anthropologists that in order to get the herd where the hunters wanted them one of their number, probably the chief because he would have to be brave and resourceful, used to dress up in the horns and skin of an animal in order to act as a decoy. Some primitive tribesmen hunt in this manner today. When I was in Borneo fifty years ago, the Government had taken all the people's guns away, so they used to go out hunting deer with a pair of horns set up on a pole. One man with these crept up to the right place, the rest of the party being on the other side of the herd. One of these would yell to startle the animals, then the man with the horns would put up the pole and run. The herd of deer, seeing horns moving, ran towards it, and were led into a swamp, the man with the horns having previously laid some logs ready for himself to run on and escape. In the swamp the deer were easily speared. The country there was brushwood five or six feet high, so it was not necessary to wear skins as well as the horns, but in Europe it would be more open country, and hence a more complete disguise would be necessary.

It is very probable that the man who took the chief part in the hunt also took the chief part in the magical ceremonies, and became the priest of the tribe; because in those days religion and magic were closely related. The purpose of contacting the gods was to keep contact with the forces of life, and these were identical with the forces of magic and fertility. It was the custom, too, of early man, indeed up to comparatively late times, for the priest to identify himself, and to be identified, with the god he served. Hence the horned hunter became the horned magician-priest, and eventually the Horned God.

However, the Horned God had another function besides being the provider of food. He was also the dealer of death. It was after his magical dance that the great stag was brought low. One day, the hunter knew, he too must leave this world by the gate of death. I do not think that primitive people were as afraid of death as many people are today. Living closer to nature, their psychic powers were more active, and they were used to the idea of communicating with their dead relatives and friends. They looked upon it as quite a natural thing. Hence the witches, among whom this ancient creed is still preserved in a fragmentary form, do not regard the Horned God in his form as Lord of the Gates of Death as a terrifying being, nor have they any conception of a burning "Hell" such as some Christians envisage. Their idea of the After-Life is rather that of a place of rest and refreshment, where people await their turn to be born again on this earth. This, of course, is the concept of reincarnation, which is widely held among primitive people of all kinds. To them, the most logical place for the souls of new-born babies to have come from is the Land of the Dead, where there are plenty of souls awaiting another body. Hence the Lord of the Gates of Death is also the phallic deity of fertility, the Opener of the Door of Life. This is the reason why the witches' god was incorporated into the Roman pantheon as Janus, the two-faced god who was Guardian of the Gates. He and his consort Diana are two of the oldest deities of Western Europe, and Diana is named in the Canon Episcopi of the early tenth century as being the goddess of the witches.

There is a famous cave painting at Cogul showing a number of women dancing round a naked man, who wears garters, though there were no stockings in those days. Presumably he represented the god, and this was some magical ceremony to give him power. One of these women seems to be holding what looks like a witch's Athame (magic knife); but unfortunately at some later date some-one painted a horned beast over her. Of course, this may be a coincidence; but the "garter" is part of the witches' insignia, and the whole picture resembles a witch gathering in other particulars.

Women seldom came into the pictures on the walls of the caves; but the Stone Age people made small statuettes of very fat naked women with their sexual attributes very much emphasised, obviously representing a fertility inducer or goddess. It is possible that they admired fat women; fatness is the sign of beauty in parts of Africa today. At any rate, they spent much time and skill in carving these figures out of ivory with stone tools, and we may presume that this was because they venerated this goddess and asked blessings from her, at a period when from hunters they had become cattle herders and wished for plentiful offspring, both animal and human. It is quite possible that the first priestess was the magician's (or god-representative's) wife. On the other hand matriarchy seems to have been very prevalent in early days, and it is probable that, as with witches today, the god-representative, or high priest, was the choice, and often the husband, of the goddess-representative, or high priestess. While Man went out to hunt or herd the cattle, Woman, the Witch, stayed by the camp fire and made medicines and spells. She had time to practise what we might call the natural powers of extra-sensory perception; which to primitive people, however, were all "magic." For remember, when I speak of magic I mean the magic which really exists, not what many people think of when magic is mentioned, such as waving a wand and something miraculous happening, or saying a rhyme and making signs and being forthwith rewarded by the appearance of a pantomime demon. A rhythmic form of words (a charm) is used sometimes by witches, to help to direct the power once it is raised; but the "magician" has to raise that power and know how to direct it in the first place.

What this amounts to is that certain people were born with natural psychic powers. They discovered that certain rites and processes increased these powers, and that if they directed them properly they could use them to benefit the community. So the community demanded that they should perform these rites, the more so when they discovered that they could join in the rites themselves, helping to raise power by wild dancing and in other ways. This meant that the witches had to learn to use their brains, because there are things you can do by magic, and there are things which are impossible: the witch doctor in Africa today becomes unpopular if he cannot invent a good excuse for not doing something that is impossible, and this may be sharply pointed out to him with a spear. So I presume that the ancient witches had also to explain certain things away, and that there were tricks of the trade as well as genuine manifestations.

In Britain, prior to 3000 B.C., there were only scattered tribes of Old Stone Age hunters. They were akin to those in France and Spain, and probably had the same beliefs. We usually think of them as cave dwellers because we generally find their remains in caves, where they have naturally been better preserved; but the majority of them lived much as the Red Indians did in America a few hundred years ago, in wigwams made of skins or clods of earth, moving about in search of game; and, like the Red Indian, the Zulus, the Picts, and the Highlanders and Irish of three hundred years ago, they were often almost naked, wearing only a skin as a blanket to keep off the wind, as the Irishman wore his big cloak and the Highlander his plaid for the same purpose. Being unafraid of nakedness, they were strong and healthy, for sun and fresh air are the best medicines known; but I will speak more of this anon. We can only guess what their religious views were; though, as I have said, I believe they had their horned hunting god and their naked goddess of generation. They buried objects with their dead, so it seems that they believed in a future life, or a next world, and we can reasonably assume that they connected this in some way with their gods. Their chief form of worship was probably the dance, a group dance performed with fanatic fervour in a circle, for by the circles they made in the depths of the caves they evidently had the concept that a circle magically constructed conserves power. They probably had crude drums, and there is a cave painting in France of a man dressed in a bull's hide with horns, dancing and twanging the string of a small bow. It is probable that by a number of people twanging bow-strings they could produce a harp-like effect. It was probably a symbolic dance performed with wild abandon till they reached a state of ecstasy. To primitive people a dance is a prayer, by which they attain at-onement with the gods.

Much capital has been made of the idea that the Ancient Britons were "naked savages." These early Britons lived much as the modern nudists live.

They were clean and healthy, in fact they were certainly much cleaner and healthier than, for instance, the inhabitants of rat-infested, plague-ridden mediaeval cities, where the streets were heaped with household garbage, and where the people regarded taking a bath as being a dangerous operation: or, for that matter, than the dwellers in our slum districts today. They were free from the diseases of nervous origin which plague us nowadays, and, as modern civilised women find, if you go "nudist" they seldom have any trouble or pain in bearing children. For many years doctors in foreign lands were puzzled as to why native women could bear children without any trouble, and go to work the next day. They know the answer nowadays: because the native woman who adopts "civilization" and wears clothes has quite as much trouble and pain in bearing children as European women have, though modern science can alleviate much of the trouble caused by "civilisation."

From 3000 B.C. there was a constant immigration of New Stone Age people into Britain, who, while they first appeared as hunters, scouting parties in fact, soon possessed domestic animals and settled down as farmers and cattle raisers. These people are said to have come from North Africa. At first they came overland by way of France and Spain; later they came by sea, and by about 2500 B.C. appear to have had good boats, capable of long sea voyages. They made magalithic burial mounds of the long barrow type, and appear to have had a cult of the dead akin to that of Osiris of Egypt; that is, a god of the dead, with his witch wife who mourned him and caused him to be reborn by her magic; while the dying god ruled the After-World and could get favourable conditions for you when you went there.

It appears that some early peoples, the Egyptians and Assyrians, believed in the unhappy After-World, where the wandering soul might suffer from hunger, thirst and darkness, though not from physical pain. They could be aided by the gods, who could rescue them from these conditions; but this aid was difficult for the common people to obtain, being reserved for the kings and mighty men who could be buried in appropriate tombs with the proper ceremonies, and who in their life-time had gone through the rites which taught them the way to rebirth; otherwise, who had gone through an initiation ceremony which mimicked being killed and revived again—death and resurrection. They, knowing the way to the Land of the Gods, could lead favoured followers there.

The people who built the magalithic long barrows may have believed that everyone who helped to build one of these great tombs would in time share in the buried leader's immortality under favoured circumstances, as it is thought was believed at one time in Egypt. At a later date it was the custom in that country to paint pictures of a noble and all his household on the sides of his tomb, and all who were thus depicted would share his paradise, though continuing to work for him as servants. This belief led to the curious custom of occasionally bribing the tomb builders so that at the last minute, after the funeral ceremonies were completed, and just as they were closing the tomb for good, they would scratch out the face of an unpopular person, usually an overseer, to deprive him of his share in the good After-World. They believed that in some mysterious way salvation depended on either the preservation of your body or of an image of it; so a great man would have a number of images of himself buried along with him, so that if the body was destroyed his life would continue by means of these magical images. While the Ancient Britons seem to have entertained the belief of the tomb of the king or hero being necessary to salvation, they do not appear to have held the Egyptian ideas about the images, or else they made them in forms which have not survived. It is likely, however, that this was a later Egyptian conception, possibly invented by priests and image-makers to get more money. Or perhaps the Neolithic immigrants adopted the native beliefs that at-onement with the gods by dances and other means was all that was really necessary, though being of the band or family of a king or hero helped greatly. The modern witches believe that at death the "Mighty Ones," the Old Ones of the cult, come for faithful followers and take them to a favoured place among other initiates who have gone before.

By now, I think, this body of primitive belief and practice had become a real religion. Whether they had only two gods, the old hunting god and the new god of death and resurrection, one cannot say; but there is a natural tendency to amalgamate gods, to regard two different gods as being really different manifestations of the same deity, and it appears to me that at some time the Great Hunter and the god of Death and What Lies Beyond became one and the same. Also, the Great Mother became amalgamated with the witch-wife who brought her slain husband to life again, the personification of feminine allure and excitement, "The World's Desire."

About 2000 B.C. the broad-headed "Beaker People" (so called because of a particular shape of pottery they made) began to come in from Spain, also by way of France and the Rhine. They had bronze weapons and built round barrows. These are the people who are supposed to have built Stonehenge and Avebury.

There is little doubt that ships from Crete came to this country regularly, and that they or the Mycenaeans brought the blue faience beads manufactured in Egypt circa 1400 B.C., large numbers of which have been found in graves in Wessex. The researches of the late Michael Ventris, and excavations at Pylos, show that there was a great civilisation on the mainland as well as in Crete from at least 2000 B.C. onwards, until the Mycenaean invasions. The power of Crete was broken by the Greeks of Mycenae, who sacked the great Cretan city of Cnossus about 1400 B.C., and the ships of Mycenae and of Troy took over and kept up this trade with Britain until about 1200 B.C., when they were conquered by the Dorians, who were not seamen. The sea power thus lost was slowly acquired by the Phoenicians and their colony Carthage, on the coast of North Africa opposite Sicily. They conquered most of Spain and stopped all passage of other nations through the Straits of Gibraltar. It is probable that they did have some communication with Britain; but by this time iron had ousted bronze, so there was no vital need for tin, which was Britain's great export at that time, from the mines of the West Country, and which was indispensable for making bronze weapons.

These are all more or less recognised historical facts, each of which has some bearing on the making of the faith of Ancient Britain, and consequently upon that fragmentary survival of it represented by witchcraft. It is well known that ideas of all kinds tend to follow the trade routes; and by this means, and by means of the various immigrations of settlers, different religious ideas arrived here.

Chapter IV

Some Religious Ideas of Early Britain

As I mentioned briefly in the previous chapter, the broad-headed "Beaker People" began coming to this country from Spain by way of France and the Rhine, by about 2000 B.C. They brought with them bronze weapons, and their arrival is generally considered as the commencement of the Bronze Age in Britain. Unlike the Neolithic peoples, who, as we have seen, built big communal tombs, the long barrows, these bronze-using immigrants buried their dead individually in round barrows. They laid the bodies in their graves in a curious manner, "crouching with the knees so close to the chin that the corpses must have been trussed into position," as say Jacquetta and Christopher Hawkes in their Prehistoric Britain. A body lying on its side in this position, under the rounded hillock of earth, may have been intended to mimic an unborn child lying in the womb of its mother. In other words, they laid their dead in the womb of Mother Earth, to be born again when the time should come, and this custom may well be a mute witness to a belief in reincarnation. With the body would be laid a few precious possessions, such as weapons and ornaments, and one of their characteristic beaker-shaped drinking vessels. We know that the Ancient Egyptians laid valuable possessions with their dead, and we are aware why; they thought that the dead person would be able to use these things, or a kind of spirit-simulacrum of them, in the next world; so the Beaker People may have held the same idea.

These are the people who are thought to have built Stonehenge, commenced circa 1800 B.C., and finished in its latest state circa 1200 B.C. They seem to have built Avebury circa 2000 B.C.; that is, the avenue and the inner circles.

The avenue at Avebury consists of stones in pairs, which have been roughly dressed on the sides which face one another. One stone is always long and thin, and the other short and almond-shaped, obviously the male and female principles. Perhaps I can best explain this by quoting what Gerald Yorke has said in an essay about the religion of the Tantrics of India: "It seeks the spiritual through the senses while denying validity to them. It is a religion of light, life and love, in which the sting is taken out of death by the rosary of skulls round the neck of the naked goddess Kali, and in which sex is regarded as sacred, and is freely portrayed in temple sculpture. Music, dancing and drama have not been secularised as in the West. . . . In the Macrocosm, that is, the Universe of the Hindu, the Sun signifies the creative aspect of God . . . the Moon is the receptive principle. In the Microcosm, that is, man and woman, these two planets are replaced by the lingam and yoni, which are worshipped in temples dedicated to them." The words "lingam" and "yoni" mean the male and female genital organs respectively.

While I think there was no direct connection between India and Britain, I believe there is a natural form of religion which was universal in the hearts of men, and it was universal because it is founded on certain facts.

Nowadays, every Church of England clergyman has to study Paley's "Evidences" to get his degree, and Paley's chief argument as to the existence of God is this: "Supposing you found a watch; looking at it one would realise that this was no natural object, so its existence involves a designer and a creator, who might be human; but if in this watch was a full set of machinery which enabled this watch to manufacture many other watches, each equipped with all machinery to construct many others, this would involve the existence of a God, to design and create such an article." This is the polite way of putting this analogy with human reproduction; but the primitive man was no prude. To him the phallus and its feminine counterpart were the only reasonable representation of the Divine creative energy. It was thus in Palestine in ancient times, and it seems that there was the same objection to shaping the stones which they set up as there was in Ancient Britain. They searched for stones naturally so formed. "Lifting up tools" on the stones took away their sacred character. The Bible tells of the "Asserim," the sacred twin pillars which were erected in the groves, and which seem to have been of this symbolic nature.

To the ancient world, as nowadays in Paley's "Evidences," the powers of generation were attributed to the bounty of God, and no one in those days would have dared to think that that which was the living symbol and evidence of God was "improper."

Some Jews may have come to Britain in the ships of Crete or Mycenae, or Phoenicia. I do not think there was any settlement, as some have postulated; but my view is that they came as merchants, and they saw here exactly what they saw at home, that which they called "High Places" or "Groves."

The Bronze Age people who built Stonehenge would appear to have worshipped the same principles. At any rate, according to the witch beliefs the inner "horseshoe" of stones at Stonehenge represents the womb, and what should be watched for at sunrise at the Summer Solstice, the longest day, is the shadow of the Hele Stone which enters this "womb" as the sun rises and fecundates it for the coming year. It is the local custom to watch for this, though it is generally said that it is to see the sun rise over the Hele Stone, which is obviously phallus-shaped.

There was a local legend, once thought to be a fairy tale, that the inner "Blue" stones had been transported from Ireland. Nowadays it is known that this fairy tale is nearly true; they were actually brought from South Wales. It is generally thought that they were brought round by sea, and then up the River Stour and across to their present site. Other people think they were brought across country direct from Wales. Whichever way it was done it was a colossal task, and there must have been a very strong driving force, either religious or political, to cause the people to undertake it. The gigantic sarsens of the outer circle, erected circa 1200 B.C., were brought about 25 miles, and their erection is another problem. There is one curious thing to be noted in connection with them; in ancient Crete they had noticed that if you erected a pillar which was dead straight it seemed to get smaller at the top, because it was further away from your eye, so they made their pillars wider at the top, to make them look straighter. The builders of the outer ring at Stonehenge employed this device, which strongly suggests that the man who designed it had seen Cretan buildings, and it has been suggested that Egyptian masons may have been imported as there are resemblances to temples built by Khofra of the Fourth Dynasty in Egypt, where the lintels meet halfway on the pillar tops and these lintels are fitted to engage the dowels, of which there are two on each pillar. This suggests a prototype in wood, and we know that at an earlier date the Stone Age people made wood circles; Woodhenge, for instance, is quite close. As nothing but the post holes remain it is impossible to say if Woodhenge had lintels on the tops of the pillars, and it has been suggested that it was roofed over, and was only a very large hut. A further reason for thinking that Stonehenge was built by foreign masons is that the surface of the pillars was dressed, then rubbed down with rubbing stones, an Egyptian technique; these rubbing stones were later used to pack the base of the pillars. It is on these pillars that carvings of early type bronze axes, and of daggers of Mycenaean type, have been found (in 1953).

However, Stonehenge is unlike Greek or Egyptian temples in being round, so whether it was built by foreign or British masons it is clear that it was built to British ideas, for British gods. It is possible that there was some alteration in religion bringing a change in the old Biblical idea that unhewn stone was sacred, and tooling it desecrated it. We have no real proof that this was the belief in Britain, and I am inclined to think that the early Stone Age people built largely with undressed stone, though they could dress stones a little. Then someone built a small circle of dressed stones in Wales; this became known as "lucky" or "powerful," and for this reason the great chief or high priest ordered it to be transported to Stonehenge, which was already a sacred place (the old post circle and the bank and ditch). Whether this was due to conquest of South Wales, or simply by order of the king, or high priest or priestess of the oracle, it is impossible to say; but it was done, and then this wonderful new temple was embellished by further works.

It is said that in the Fourth Dynasty in Egypt the king had one hundred large ships of cedar. This would seem to be about the time when the foreign stone circle was built in Wales. Perhaps at that time Egypt had no rivals at sea, and it is not impossible that some of these Egyptian ships came here exploring, seeking for gold, copper, tin, etc.; gold from Ireland and Wales, copper and tin, pearls and amber from Britain. As there was a constant migration up the coasts of Spain at the time, they would doubtless have fairly full information as to where to go, and as soon as they were past Finisterre the usual south-west wind would take them to Brittany, where there were great settlements of megalith builders who were in communication with the west of Britain. The Egyptian priests boasted to Solon (circa 600 B.C.) about the ancient glory of Egypt, and how their ships two thousand years before made voyages of discovery outside the Pillars of Hercules, i.e. the Straits of Gibraltar. (Egypt had lost her sea power by Solon's time.) Now, these dates seem to fit. There is nothing impossible in it; anyone could make the voyages in quite small boats if they went by easy stages and only travelled in good weather, that is if they were not pressed for time. What seems impossible is what we know was done, namely transporting the "foreign stones" from Wales.

All these wonderful works cannot have been done by "ignorant savages"; their leaders must have been very intelligent men who received some education and have had great wealth, if indeed they did import Egyptian masons. There are things which suggest Egyptian influence; that is, copying what was done in Egypt. Silbury Hill at Avebury was built on a plateau cut away from a slope; it covers an area of five acres. Khofra's Pyramid (Fourth Dynasty) is on a similar plateau; it also covers five acres, and the slope of the pyramid is the same as at Silbury Hill. It suggests that someone had seen the Egyptian work and tried to copy it in earth; but because of particular religious ideas had made it circular. Now, while I quite agree that a circle is the easiest way to build a mound, all other nations seem to have found it easier to build their stone buildings quadrangular; but Stonehenge is circular, even the lintels being rounded inside and out. This must have been for a good reason, and I can only think that they had found by experience that in some mysterious way a circle retains and conserves any power generated inside it, in the same way that a witches' circle functions. Also, there is a very ancient belief that a circle will keep out evil influences. I think there were priest-kings, magicians, who worshipped their gods and worked their magic in this and at least some of the many stone circles in Britain.

I have previously mentioned the fact of the sun rising over the Hele Stone on the morning of the Summer Solstice. The 1955 edition of the Ministry of Works Official Guidebook to Stonehenge points out that every sunrise during the year must have a sunset point directly opposite, and the opposite point of the sunrise on the longest day will be the sunset on the shortest day, the Winter Solstice. At Stonehenge on this latter date, an observer standing in the centre will see the sun set just to the left of the tallest stone, behind the altar, that is, the remaining upright of the great central trilithon, of which the other stone and the lintel have fallen.

It is calculated, therefore, that if the now fallen central stone of the Bluestone horseshoe was of the same height as its neighbours, the setting sun on the day of the Winter Solstice would have appeared exactly over it, and framed by the stones of the great trilithon.

The Hon. John Abercromby, in his book on Bronze Age Pottery, written in 1912, has called attention to this fact, and pointed out that in no religion or temple does one enter by a door, walk some way into a building, and then turn round to the entrance to face the chief point of worship. Now, the entrance to Stonehenge is at the north-east; hence if the most holy thing there is the point of the sun's rising, one has to turn one's back upon the altar at the south-west in order to view it. He therefore suggests that the great occasion here was the Winter Solstice, when the setting sun, on the day on which it symbolically "died," appeared framed in the great trilithon, over the altar. The writer of the Official Guide. R. S. Newall, F.S.A., suggests that the trilithon represents the door of the Netherworld, into which the sun passes at the Winter Solstice.

This, I think, is an important observation; but the trilithon has another significance beside that of a door into the Land of the Dead. In his very remarkable book, *The Great Mother: An Exploration of the Archetype,* Erich Neuman, a pupil of C. G. Jung, shows a number of representations in ancient art of the door, or gateway, or trilithon, as a symbol of the Great Mother, the Goddess from whom the sun-god is reborn. Hence the appearance of the red disk of the setting sun, glowing between the mighty stones of the great trilithon through the gathering winter dusk, would symbolise to those ancient people not only death but the promise of rebirth, alike perhaps for man as for the sun, from the womb of the Great Mother.

I have described in my previous book, *Witchcraft Today,* how present-day witches secretly conduct a rite at the Winter Solstice which represents exactly the same idea. The priestess, or female leader of the coven, stands behind a cauldron in which a fire is ignited, while the rest dance round her sunwise, with burning torches. They call it the Dance of the Wheel, or Yule, and its purpose is "to cause the sun to be reborn." The cauldron here represents the same idea as the "gate"; the Great Mother. The fire in it is the Sun-child in her womb.

Another ancient monument I must mention, as typifying the "male-and-female" imagery of early religion, is the Men-an-Tol, meaning "Stone with the Hole," near Penzance in Cornwall. Although it has been moved from its original site it consists of two upright stones, and between them a huge stone in the centre of which a hole has been carefully carved out large enough for a human being to crawl through it. The sexual significance of this group of stones is obvious; and the careful carving of the central stone must have entailed much labour, with the tools then available. The stones are still revered by Cornish people, and it is an old custom for people to take their children to the holed stone of the Men-an-Tol and cause them to pass through it "for luck," or to cure them of childhood ailments, notably rickets.

A persistent legend, often referred to in early English literature, is that when Troy fell a number of its princes with their followers took refuge in Western Europe; and in particular Brutus, the great-grandson of Aeneas, settled in Britain and founded a city that is now London. Hence an old poetic name for London is Trinovantum, New Troy. The poet Humphrey Gifford (circa 1580) addressed the young men of Britain as "Ye buds of Brutus' Land," when urging them to resist the Spanish Armada. When Troy was thought, in later years, to be a purely legendary locality, this old story was ridiculed; but modern archaeological research has given it a new lease of life.

When Cnossos was sacked circa 1400 B.C. Mycenaean power extended over Asia Minor and the Aegean, including Troy, and even after Mycenae was destroyed by the Dorians, Troy seems to have kept up trade with Britain until Troy itself was destroyed, circa 1100 B.C. When the home town of a great shipping nation is destroyed there is apt to be a huge crowd of fugitives, and then, as nowadays, closely settled states did not welcome them, so there is nothing impossible in the legend that a number of these came to Britain, and not being welcome in the closely settled West Country passed up the English Channel and up a wide river to the first high land suitable for defence, and there founded a city where London now stands.

They worshipped the Great Goddess Danae, or Danu, and it is suggested that another band of these refugees went to Ireland, where they were known as the Tuatha De Danaan, "the Children of the Goddess Dana." Nennius, the 9th century chronicler, wrote that Britain's earliest name was Albion, by which it was known to Pliny, from Albina (the White Goddess), the eldest of the Danaids. The Latins worshipped the White Goddess as Cardea; she was the mistress of Janus, the Keeper of the Door of Hades. She had great power at Alba (the White City), first colonised by emigrants from the Peloponnese at the time of the great dispersal. Janus was really the Oak God Dianus, Keeper of the Door. His wife was Jana, or Diana (Dione), goddess of the woods and the moon, and of witchcraft. Albina, the Barley Goddess, who gave her name to Britain, is the White

Lady of death and inspiration, also called Cerridwen, from "cerdd" in Irish and Welsh meaning "gain," and also "the inspired arts, especially poetry," and "wen," "white." She is also Keeper of the Door of Hades. She was identified with Isis, Paphian Venus who arose from the sea, Diana, Prosperpina, and Hecate, and we have seen her already as the lady in shining white raiment who presided over the Land of the Dead in the early 14th century poem "Sir Orfeo."

If we accept the witch legend that Stonehenge is the temple of their great goddess, symbolic of her womb, which the Druids called the Cauldron of Cerridwen and the Cauldron of Inspiration, combined with the great stone phallus, the Hele Stone, we may presume that the ancient worship was everywhere the same, that of the creative powers, as shown by the avenue at Avebury, the Cornish Men-an-Tol, the Asserim of the Old Testament, the Twin Pillars of Solomon's Temple, and the Jehovah and Ashtaroth whom he and the early Israelites worshipped, and who are still adored by the Qabalists as the Supernal Father and the Supernal Mother. While among the Jews the male god seems to have been chief, or at least equal to the goddess, in the early times it appears that, whether as a survival of the matriarchal system or from other causes, the goddess was the ruling partner. Thus at the Temple of Artemis the moon goddess, who was sometimes called Thetis at Iolcus, a great port in Thessaly, there were fifty priestesses. Every seven years one was chosen by lot to be Queen. She took a man to be her Oak King, representing the god; but he was sacrificed at the end of seven years, when a new queen was chosen. This has a resemblance to the witch custom; the High Priestess is the "Divine Power," and she chooses any man she pleases as High Priest. He is usually her own husband; but with them the High Priest is not sacrificed, at least not nowadays, and they have no legend of this ever having been the case. Personally, I very much doubt whether anyone would ever take on the job of being king for a year, or even seven years, knowing he would be sacrificed at the end of his term; though he might do so if there was a good chance of being able to arrange for a substitute.

Robert Graves, who has written extensively upon this subject, considers that in Biblical times David derived his title of King of the Jews from marrying the High Priestess of the Goddess Michal at Hebron. (This, incidentally, may explain the opposition of Samuel, the follower of Jehovah, to the people's demand for a king; and the fact that Saul was consecrated as the first king of Israel at Gilgal, a name meaning "circle," where there were twelve great stones, ostensibly placed there to commemorate the passing of the Jordan. It was probably a stone circle.) It seems that the husband of the High Priestess of the country's goddess automatically became king, or at least could only be recognised as being king through his wife; and if he died or were killed whoever married the widow would have a good claim to kingship. There are hints of these ideas in the legends of King Arthur, where it will be seen that Arthur acquires his famous "Round Table" by marriage with Guinevere, and there are various attempts to abduct Guinevere by rebel knights who wanted to usurp the kingdom, as if Guinevere and the kingdom went together.

It is said in a quotation from the lost Gospel to the Hebrews that when Christ was sent on earth the Lord called a mighty power called Michal, and this power was named Mary and she descended to earth with Christ in her womb, and he was born. Many mystical sects in the Middle Ages believed in a female Holy Ghost. In the Abbey Church at New Barnet, on the right side of the altar, is a large picture of Christ, and on the left is a large picture of the (feminine) Holy Ghost, shown as a woman in white, the White Goddess. The priests of this church told me some years ago that Christ was born of the Father, conceived by the Holy Ghost, and that only a woman could conceive. They had a number of proofs of this being a very ancient doctrine. This of course is the ancient trinity, the sacred "MA-AB-BEN," written as a "portmanteau word," "MABEN," the Mother-Father-Son trinity of the ancients, or Isis-Osiris-Horus. While Christianity attempted to replace this for a while by the all-male Trinity, the Mediterranean peoples always longed for a goddess, and so the Church was forced to exalt the virgin Mary, somewhat at the expense of the worship of the Father and the Holy Ghost. This Mother and Son worship is not so different from the cult of the witches, although it may be heresy to say so.

Accepting that in most people there seems to be an urge to have a god and a goddess, I think we may consider that this was the case four thousand years ago, and all the evidence of archaeology points to it. We presume that from about 2000 B.C. to about 1200 B.C. there was constant communication between the Eastern Mediterranean and Britain, probably by small trading boats which brought various goods valuable to the British; cargoes of beads, and workmen who knew the secret of casting bronze. They received in return tin, gold, pearls and amber. All would welcome these traders, and perhaps would learn religious ideas from them; but these might be only points of ritual, because the basic religious ideas were the same, though the gods and goddesses might have different names.

In the British Chronicle, Geoffrey of Monmouth tells of the founding of London by Brutus, great-grandson of Aeneas of Troy, in the year 1103 B.C. This was believed implicitly by all Londoners until Polydore Virgil was employed by the King of France and the Roman Church to discredit all records showing that the Tudors were descended from Arthur and the ancient kings, and all suggestions that there was any civilisation in Britain until the Romans conquered the country; and he succeeded so well that we are only just beginning to re-discover the truth about Ancient British civilisation. But at the time when Henry VIII was quarrelling with the Pope everything possible in the way of "propaganda-warfare" was done by the anti-British party, and this was part of it. From the standpoint of the present day, the political purpose of discrediting the old British traditions is plain. A Church of England which derived its authority from Henry VIII was in a weak position; but a Church deriving its authority from Joseph of Arimathea was a very different matter; almost equally dangerous was the tradition of an ancient civilisation independent of Rome altogether.

Geoffrey gave the lists of the ancient British kings and their reigns since Brutus, so the story was ably put about that as writing was unknown in Britain until the Romans came it was impossible that these names and records could have been preserved, so they must be false. Nowadays we know that such arguments are not valid. The Maoris of New Zealand have long pedigrees, learned by heart, which extend backwards for one thousand, five hundred years. Further, Caesar states of the Druids (*De Bello Gallico*, vi.):

> Report says that in the schools of the Druids they learn by heart a great number of verses, and therefore some persons remain twenty years under training. They do not think it proper to commit these utterances to writing, although in almost all other matters and in their public and private accounts they make use of Greek characters. I believe that they have adopted the practice for two reasons—that they do not wish the rule to become common property nor those who learn the rule to rely on writing, and so neglect the cultivation of the memory.

Later, however, the Ogham form of writing was evolved, seemingly in Ireland, and between the 2nd and 7th centuries A.D. it spread to Wales,

Cornwall, Devon, Hampshire, and the Isle of Man. This script appears to be indigenous to the British Isles, and knowledge of it was preserved in the Irish folk-memory down to the early 19th century.

In Polydore Virgil's day it was generally believed that there was no writing before the rise of Rome, or at least he spread that view. It was thought that the Phoenicians were the first navigators to visit Britain; they had no idea that the ships of Mycenae and Crete came here regularly. Troy itself was dismissed as a myth, until Schliemann, following his dream, went and dug up Troy, and found to his surprise that there were not one but six Troys, in one of which he found a piece of Irish gold work similar to those found by Sir Flinders Petrie at Gaza, thus proving trade connections between these cities and the British Isles. Also, no one knew then of the large amounts of Egyptian beads brought to Britain by Cretan and Mycenaean ships, or that the Trojans were great trading and seafaring people, so that when Troy was destroyed there is nothing impossible or even unlikely in a number of refugees going where they could get good land for the taking.

Another old British tradition, incidentally, was that the Tower of London was built by Julius Caesar. This, too, was laughed at, until it was discovered that the Tower is built on Roman foundations; so the original Tower was a Roman fortress though later than Caesar.

Though there do not seem to be any traces of Cretan traders other than the Egyptian beads and bronze goods they brought, it is very possible that they brought part of their cult of the Mother Goddess with them. "No traces found" does not mean that there are none, only that they are not yet found or identified. The old maze designs cut on rocks may be Cretan, and the various hill mazes, though traditionally called "Troy Town," may have been from the Cretan idea of the Labyrinth. One at least of these mazes, the Miz-Maze at Leigh, in Dorset, was noted as the meeting-place of witches, and also as the place where in old times the people of the district used to meet to make holiday, probably to observe the old Sabbats. The Miz-Maze is now almost obliterated, but it existed as late as 1800 in the form of banks made to follow an intricate pattern.

In Jutland there are old mazes laid out in stone paths; it is said that in quite modern times they would put a girl in the centre, and young men would go along the paths to find her, and the one who got her became her lover. I never quite got the idea of this, because the walls were only a foot high, and one could see everything ahead. I think the lads of the village would quickly learn where to start in order to get there first; or, of course, the girl may have known, and told her favourite boy, "You start at that gate."

It is said that there cannot have been any early British writing or some would have survived. However, we must remember the burning of the great library of Bangor, and other libraries which were obnoxious to the Roman Church (not to mention the English climate). Twenty years ago it was the great point of the Higher Critics of the Bible that the Jews were utterly illiterate; so nothing could have been written before the Babylonian Captivity, because in all Palestine only four pre-Exile inscriptions had been found, three very rough calendar stones, and the fourth was the Siloam tunnel inscription which was written by a Phoenician. But I was with the Wellcome Expedition digging up the city of Lakish in 1936, and we found in a guard-house a large number of potsherds inscribed in ink with a reed pen. They were chiefly copies of the records of a trial, and one of them apologised for writing to so great a man on potsherds, saying that owing to the war the supply of papyrus was exhausted. That explained matters; the pre-Exile Jews could and did write on papyrus imported from Egypt. But while papyrus lasts in a bone-dry Egyptian tomb it rots quickly in a damp country like Palestine. We also realised that there had been many inscriptions on stones, but the Maccabees, being intolerant puritans had destroyed them all because they were mostly religious inscriptions dedicated to the gods, the Elohim, whose worship they were attempting to crush out.

Similar destruction both by nature and by the hand of man may have occurred in Britain. We know that as late as during the reign of Henry VIII complaints were made by the Church that there was a Druid Priest in Wales named Hu, who had a great Oak idol, also named Hu, and that many people worshipped this idol, bringing offerings of cattle to it. So the King had them both brought to London, and burned together at Smithfield. This idol named Hu, was obviously Hu Gadarn, and so much knowledge must have been lost by the death of that unfortunate Druid. We must also remember the systematic destruction of the manuscripts of the Mayas, and the burning of the wooden tablets covered with hieroglyphics on Easter Island by Christian Missionaries. What I am attempting to show is that there is clear evidence that there was communication between Britain and the Eastern Mediterranean at an early date, and that through this communication various religious ideas might have been introduced to this country. What puzzled me at first was the resemblance between the Sumarian Mother Goddess and the Witch Goddess (unfortunately I am not permitted to say what this is). I thought that this must be only coincidence. Then I came across the writings of Mr. Ross Nichols on "The Great Zodiac of Glastonbury," in which he says, "This Zodiac has Sumarian affinities. Some Archaelogical evidence exists of the colonisation of Britain by people of Sumarian affinities before 2700 B.C. and ships of King Sargon . . . are said to have come to Britain and the name Sumer may indeed be the 'Summer-land' of Somersetshire whence in the sixth Welsh Triad the Patriarch Hu Gadarn is said to have conducted the Cymry to Wales."

T. A. Waddell, in the *Phoenician Origin of the Scots and Britons* (p. 43, Appnd.), tells of a road tablet of the great emperor Sargan, circa 2750 B.C. recording his vast conquests, among which are "The Tin Land Country, lying beyond the Mediterranean," which would seem to be Britain.

It appears that at a very early date someone unknown shaped a number of hill islands in Somerset into curious forms; also they drained a large part of a semi-marsh to form this amazing large scale design, that is, they made a huge star-map on the earth. It seems likely that the people who did this huge work were star worshippers, deprived of the wonderful sight of the Host of Heaven which they saw each night in their homeland, and who, being in a tract of land where they were obliged to make great earthworks in order to get land above the surface of the water, constructed it in these curious signs. It seems a curious thing to do; but bringing the foreign stones from Wales to Stonehenge was likewise a curious thing to do. All I can say is, these people *did* curious things, and you can be sure they were not done for fun. They had some very good reason, and it is sometimes profitable to attempt to find their reason. These huge figures are said to be of Sumerian design. Can it be that in King Sargon's time their fleets did come here, which conquered part of the country and fortified a group of islands among the marshes from which base they would send out raiding parties, to get slaves? Or, more probably, it was just a trading centre, from which merchants would buy tin from the natives, much as we used to do in Singapore and Hongkong. All nations found it much easier to set up trading stations where your ships can be safe and where you trade what you have a surplus of, for what you require. The Sumarians and Assyrians were a fine fighting race, they had most things close at hand, but though they had great mines of copper in

Cyprus, they needed tin to make bronze. If they did come to Britain for it, it was a long journey, and many would probably settle down here with native wives. They were used to floods and building mounds, so in their new home they would begin raising mounds and cutting drains. Their Gods were the Hosts of Heaven, the stars, which in their native land seemed so close at night. They had mapped out these stars in the signs of the Zodiac; but here in this cold damp land the skies were so often clouded, and even when you could see them the stars seemed so distant. Then they noticed that some of these hills looked rather like a Zodiac. Then some priest or oracle may have said: "Make a Star Temple here so the power of the stars may be with you." There are mentions in old tales of the first mighty labour of the land of Britain, the building of "Caer Arianrhod," the Temple of Heaven. The second mighty labour of Britain was Stonehenge. No one knows where this Temple of Heaven is; may it not be this giant Zodiac which is about twelve miles across and the figures are so huge they can only be seen from the air, but that there were known to be figures there is proved by many old stories? The facts seem to be that someone, somehow, discovered that these hills roughly suggested a Zodiac, and they cut away and built up to make them more perfect. This implies a strong central government, or a strong religious motive, at some very early date. It is noteworthy that long afterwards the British were in the habit of making huge hill figures, white horses, etc. But there are gods also. The Giant of Cerne Abbas, for instance, and the curious figures lately discovered on the Gog Magog hills near Cambridge, including one figure of the Naked Goddess. It always has been a puzzle why these figures seem to have been constructed as if they were intended to be seen from above and the Glastonbury figures are practically invisible except from the air. This has made me wonder, is there no way, apart from Atlantean Airships (which some people believe in) and Flying Saucers, in which primitive people could have flown, or at least risen in the air? And I think there are at least two different ways which were well within their means. About sixty years ago, before aeroplanes came into existence, there were two ways in which a general in wartime could see from the air what the enemy was doing, namely kites and balloons. A small kite was sent up, which in turn took up a bigger kite; this took up another big enough to carry a man who could observe the enemy and send written messages down the kite-string. The whole affair folded up into a small cart, and was more portable than the military balloon, with its apparatus for making gas, etc. But the first balloons were fire balloons. A French paper manufacturer named Montgolfier noticed that smoke rose upwards with considerable force and it struck him if he confined smoke in a bag, the bag would be carried up along with the smoke. The story goes that he was staying in an inn, when he got this idea, and with the help of a waiter he lighted a fire in an unmentionable utensil which they took from underneath the bed and held paper bags over it. The paper bags rose to the ceiling and Montgolfier was nearly burned as a witch, but ballooning was born. In June 1783, he succeeded in sending a big balloon to a height of over one thousand five hundred feet, by means of an iron chafing-dish burning ten pounds of moist straw and wool to produce smoke. In November of that year he and a companion sailed across Paris and in 1784 the English Channel was crossed by Blanchard and Jeffries in a balloon. It was soon discovered that it was heat and not smoke which caused the balloons to rise. Napoleon had a Hot Air Balloon Corps, and obtained important military information in this way and part of his plans for the invasion of England (which the witches claim to have foiled) involved the transport of troops by a large fleet of balloons. Now, if Montgolfier conceived the idea of utilising the ascending force, it is quite possible that some Sumerian Priest, watching the clouds of smoke arising from a sacrifice, might have conceived it also and attempted it without any danger to himself, and it is quite feasible that the secret was known hundreds if not thousands of years before. If any Sumerian Priest did discover it, his King would surely be glad to patronise an experiment which looked like being useful in war. There are, in fact, many ancient stories of "Flying machines" of various kinds, from many countries—the well-known Eastern "Flying Carpet," for instance. There is a British legend of King Bladud of Bath, who invented a contrivance with which he "Attempted to fly to the upper region of the air"; but he fell down upon the temple of Apollo in the City of Trinoventum (London) and was dashed to death. In Ireland a Druid called Mog Ruith possessed, according to story, a magical machine called the Roth Fail. St. Columba writes of this as a vast ship which could navigate both land and sea. (Much as anyone of those days would describe a balloon if they saw it.) The legend goes that Mog Ruith and his daughter Tlachtga flew in this "ship" to Italy, where he met the famous magician Simon Magus. The Druid lent him the Roth Fail to demonstrate to the Roman Emperor that the Heathen Gods had more power than the Christian but the machine crashed at the trials and Simon Magus was seriously injured. Christian onlookers claimed that this was because they made the sign of the cross. The story goes that Tlachtga collected the broken bits of the machine, and flew them back to Ireland where, presumably, she too crashed, as the machine became two masses of rock which are shown to this day. One is in Dublin County, the other in Tipperary. Now, if some clever man of ancient times did in fact precede Montgolfier in the invention of fire balloons, it would explain all these stories (except turning into rock), and the mystery of the construction of these great Earth figures may be considerably enlightened.

In a flat country, such as Sumaria, it would be very useful to have a man up aloft in war time, or even at ordinary times, to look out for bandits and raiders. They had good looms and could make very fine cloth; they used much incense composed of resins, so would know how to make a fine strong varnish, to make the balloon airtight. If they used these at home, would they not have been likely to employ them on a colonising expedition, to spy out the land? And if they found the hills of this land were shaped in a way which suggested a sign from the gods, might not their priests accept it as such? I am not saying this was so. I am only suggesting what might account for the facts as we find them. *Viz*, The Great Zodiac as it is and the apparent Sumerian influence in Witchcraft, which I cannot account for otherwise. About the period, circa 2500 B.C., it is said Assyria was the great power in the Mediterranean. She had good ships, and an abundant population. Bronze was a great necessity and for this they needed tin. If her ships went outside the Mediterranean they would find great numbers of Lybians (Berbers) emigrating northwards, to the "Green Land" where there was such good grazing for cattle, and whence came gold, pearls, amber and tin. Is it not likely they would wish to discover what this land was like and procure what was more valuable to them than anything else, abundant tin. They already had Cyprus, whence all the copper came, but tin was very rare indeed. One ship-load of tin returning would lead to an expedition being sent with orders to seize some easily defended base where their ships could shelter in winter whence they could go to the mines. Agreed it might have been nearer for them to seize a base in Cornwall, but possibly all sheltered places suitable were already occupied. The distance from home was so great, that two or three days more sailing would not matter. An unoccupied natural defensive position was their aim. A few raids would provide all the slaves they required. Possibly the mines were in the possession of warlike tribes whom it was not worth while attempting to conquer. The Black stone was useless to the stone age natives, and they would trade lots of it for beads and other goods which cost little. As far as we know, these Stone Age people were not warlike, most of their axes, etc., were tools, and metal armed and armoured people were much in the same position as European settlers with guns were among native tribes two hundred years ago. When Assyria lost her power, communications would probably be kept up with Britain by the people of Crete, Greeks and Trojans, then Phoenicians. In those days there was a sort of free trade, and it is possible that Egyptian ships may have made the voyage in early times. There are very curious rock carvings in Norway and Sweden which have always been supposed to record the visits of strange ships at very early dates, circa 2000 B.C. Some of these ships are very Egyptian in appearance. See Pages 117 and 143 *The Viking Age,* by Paul du Chaillu. Some carvings seem to show raids by ship people who lead captive women away. A number of these ships are shown with a sun over them, much resembling the Egyptian "Solar Bark." All this seems to point to the fact that during the Stone Age in Britain, a number of Mediterranean people did come by sea to Britain and further, and that this intercourse continued until the rise of Carthage which dominated Spain and cut off all trade with the outer sea by her competitors. Also this was in the iron age and so tin was not urgently needed.

If I am right, I would suggest that by the time Assyrian ships ceased to come to Britain there would have grown up a strong and compact settlement of descendants of Assyrian Fathers and native mothers in Somerset and it is not impossible that this name came from "Sumaria."

The Aristocracy and Priesthood would have the theory of a kingdom where the Priest Kings and High Priestess were obeyed. Possibly their empire expanded, and the seat of government would be changed to Avebury and Stonehenge.

Possibly religious changes came in and they made no more Zodiacs, but the tradition remained of making gigantic animals. The serpent-like avenue at Carnac in Brittany is quite as big as any of the Zodiac figures. And from this in time would come the custom of cutting the Hill Figures, which are not found in any other country. It should be remembered that while the outer circle at Stonehenge, circa 1200 B.C. was oriented to the Sun, the inner circle, circa 1800 B.C., was oriented to the stars and so would seem to have been built by a star worshipping people; who would presumably, have come from some country where the stars are brilliant and the skies clear. And, I can only imagine that some absolute monarch of the Assyrian type could have given the order: "There's a nice stone circle in Wales, bring it here." Now, the reader will ask, "Whatever has all this to do with witchcraft?" The answer is, I am trying to find out the history and origins of the tradition called "witchcraft," and as it appears to have come from prehistoric times I must look at prehistoric times and see what they were really like. Once I thought they resembled the popular conception of people who lived in caves, dressed in skins, and who spent their time hunting and being hunted by wild beasts and their leisure in braining each other with stone axes and hauling fair maidens into their caves by the hair, until Caesar and his Roman legions landed and British history commenced. I find instead that early Britons were apparently fairly peaceful people who were farmers and cattle-breeders, and who, while not erecting good brick County-Council-approved suburban villas to live in, nevertheless did construct the most amazing works, presumably for religious reasons. They understood the calendar, and knew when to expect the Summer and Winter Solstices. They seem to have believed in reincarnation. They worshipped a Great Mother goddess. They communicated fairly freely with the rest of the world. The Bronze Age Britons had garments of linen and woollen stuff, and ornaments of Yorkshire jet, Irish gold work, and blue beads brought by traders from Egypt. Beautiful drinking cups of gold and amber have been recovered from their graves. Even in Neolithic times, their flint and stone axes, arrowheads, etc., show delicate craftsmanship; and in later times the art of enamel work on metal was invented in Britain. Yet we can still find people, even archaeologists, enquiring doubtfully if there was any civilisation in Britain before the Romans came!

The answer is, of course, that, as Professor Joad used to say, it all depends what you mean by civilisation. We are rather inclined to set up two vague headings, "Civilisation" and "Barbarism," and to think people "civilised" who somewhat resemble ourselves. What those whom we label "savages" would honestly think of our own society is a subject upon which we rarely reflect, and which it is perhaps more tactful not to pursue.

Even when the Stone Age Britons could not make metal instruments themselves, they were in constant communication with people who used metal, though these might not have been always willing to supply them with such, even as European governments frown on supplying guns to primitive races. Such metal-using people appear to have constructed great works at Avebury and Stonehenge and other places, notably Glastonbury. A remarkable structure which may be seen at Glastonbury is the so-called Chalice Well, which rises near the foot of the two famous hills, Chalice Hill and the Tor. It consists of a spring, giving a copious volume of water, which is enclosed by massive masonry. According to the guide issued to visitors by the present owners of the Well, "The masonry of the Well has been the cause of much discussion and is believed to be of pre-Roman origin. Possibly it is connected with the Druids, since experts consider it to have been associated with the ancient rituals of sunlight and water. Certain it is that the massive stonework is orientated, as has been proved by measurements on Midsummer Day. Archaeologists who have examined the stones report that they are placed together in wedge formation as is the case in the Pyramids, and that they are 'ripple' marked by stone implements, as at Stonehenge. Sir Flinders Petrie was of the opinion that the Well might have been rock-hewn by Egyptian colonists in about the year 2000 B.C. The waters are chalybeate and radioactive, having a never-failing flow of two thousand, five hundred gallons per day, even during the severest drought. The Well is square, measuring 8½ feet deep from water level." A friend who recently visited Glastonbury tells me it is locally believed that the massive stones of the Well are made of the same Prescelly "blue" stone as the famous "foreign" stones at Stonehenge. Whether this is true or not I cannot say (and the extraordinary thing is that people seem to be so little interested in trying to find out!) but the existence of this ancient sacred Well proves that Glastonbury is a pre-Christian sacred place.

No one would have bothered to build a structure like this merely to conserve an ordinary water supply. Further, as might have been expected, where we find the Sacred Well, we also find the Sacred Tree. The Glastonbury Thorn, which traditionally stood on the opposite Wearyall Hill, may well be a Christianised version of a much older sanctity. It is notable that almost everywhere where a sacred well, or fount, or pool, is found, there is either a sacred tree nearby or else a local legend of one. This is yet another version of the primordial male-female, mother-father religious image. The well symbolises the womb, the deep container of life; and the green, living, up-springing tree, the phallus.

Later, the Sacred Well became a sacred cauldron, the Cauldron of Ceridwen. of which the Christian version was the Holy Grail, and the pagan one the cauldron of the witches.

A persistent connection will be noted between the Great Mother and water, or the sea. Venus arises from the sea. The moon goddess is associated with the sea, perhaps because of the tides. Shells are symbols of the Great Mother. Binah, the Supernal Mother of the Qabalists, is called the Great Sea. We know today that in actual fact the waters of the warm Palaeozoic seas were the womb of evolving life for the first living things upon earth.

The complementary element, fire, was also sacred and magical, and masculine where water was feminine. The altar fire, or the altar candle, is the universal symbol of a sacred place. Such reverence is natural; two things distinguished primitive man from the animals, the ability to make fire and the ability to construct cutting tools, and we probably need look no further for the explanation of the many cults of fire-worship and consecrated weapons. To this day, the witches preserve these traditions: the flame upon the altar, and the ritual knife with which the magic circle is drawn. Both may well have their origin in the very dawn of human civilisation. (Psychologically, of course, the weapon has also a phallic significance.)

The people of Bronze Age Britain may have used incense in their religious rites. A type of pottery vessel has been found, dating from that period, which archaeologists call an "incense-cup," as they are unable to ascribe any other use to it. Such vessels are small, and pierced with holes in the lower part, possibly to allow a good draught to keep alight the glowing charcoal upon which grains of incense are burned. We know that the religious rites of ancient times used incense extensively, and if ancient Britain could import Egyptian beads, as we know it did, there is no reason why it should not have imported Egyptian incense also.

I have previously noted the use by witches of incense in their rites. This is not necessarily a foreign importation, or an imitation of church practices, as will be seen from the foregoing.

To sum up, it seems that at a very early date in the Stone Age certain secrets were discovered whereby what we call magic could be practised. That is, its practitioners worked to obtain thereby certain benefits for themselves and their friends. This was perhaps a lot of superstition together with some practical facts. As it was first used to obtain good hunting it became part of the religion attached to the hunting god. Later, when it was also used to obtain fertility, a fertility goddess came into the cult. Concepts of the life after death, with which primitive people were much concerned, also played their part. The god of the cult became the ruler of the After-World, and understanding of his mysteries was thought to help his followers to adjust themselves to the conditions they found when they quitted this life and their souls arrived "on the Other Side." This faith was much the same throughout the ancient world, though of course with many local variations determined by national character.

There was no antagonism between old-world religions; no one claimed that his god was the only true one and all the others were false. On the contrary, travellers respected the indigenous gods of the countries they came to, recognising them as different theophanies of the same Cosmic Powers. Sectarianism and religious persecution were practically unknown. Hence religious ideas were freely exchanged, especially along the trade routes; and there is no real reason why almost any religious concept of the Bronze Age civilisations of Europe and the Mediterranean should have been unknown to Ancient Britain.

CHAPTER V

Druidism and the Aryan Celts

I am often asked, "Where do the Druids come in?" "Were the witches of the Druid belief?" I can only say, "If we only knew for certain exactly what the Druids believed, I could tell you; but there are very few thing we do know about these mysterious people." We are told by ancient writers that the Druids reverenced the sun, and we know that they were the priests of the Celtic people of the Hallstadt Iron Age culture who invaded Britain in the 5th century B.C. and occupied the south-eastern parts. Later, about 250 B.C., Belgic people of the La Tène Iron Age culture invaded Britain and occupied the south, driving the others northwards and westwards. These were Brythons, with some Teutonic blood, and are the "Britons" Caesar wrote about. La Tène was the Druidic centre of Gaul. About 50 B.C., just after Caesar's unsuccessful invasion, there was another Belgic invasion, and these captured all the country from Salisbury Plain to Surrey. Although a number of people got pushed about in these invasions, the defenders usually took refuge in their hill forts, which were almost impregnable to the aggressors' means of attack; but they were forced to surrender from hunger and thirst, as they had no water supply. The forts were only designed to be defended against short raids. This means it is unlikely that many of the defenders were killed, though they may have been reduced to a state of serfdom. The coming of successive waves of warlike invaders, especially when the latter began to be armed with iron weapons, turned the comparatively peaceful picture of Bronze Age Britain into one of strife and war, with each tribe set against its neighbours. The great number of the hill forts mentioned above which were built in this period bears witness to this state of affairs. The one unifying force was the Druid priesthood, with the Archdruid at its head whom even the petty kings had to obey.

There are many popular misconceptions about the Druids. For instance, it was at first thought, when British archaeology was in its infancy, that the Druids built Stonehenge. Today, archaeologists date the earliest part of Stonehenge at about 1800 B.C. and, as we have seen, the Druids did not come to Britain until the Early Iron Age invasions mentioned above. However, Jacquetta and Christopher Hawkes, in their book, Prehistoric Britain, have this to say about the Druids and Stonehenge:

> What, then, of the Druids, those mysterious priests of the Celtic Iron Age with whose bearded and long-robed figures many of us have loved to people the great circles of Stonehenge? The fountain-head for such picturesque ideas was in the imagination of Stukeley (Druids had an inevitable appeal to a Romantic), and for this reason it was long the pleasurable duty of the scientific mind to scorn and deny them. Yet the discovery of undoubted Iron Age pottery on the site, and also . . . of Iron Age stone holes, has shaken such scepticism. It is now possible and permissible to believe that there must have been a last phase when Stonehenge was administered by Celtic priests, though they had little share in its devising. It seems then, that Stukeley's hazards were really nearer the truth than he deserved.

The earliest mention of Druids is by a Greek, Sotion of Alexandria, about 200 B.C., and when Sotion wrote they already possessed a considerable reputation as philosophers. Most of what we know about Druidism comes from Julius Caesar and Pliny; though there is much traditional lore of the Welsh Bards enshrined in such books as Barddas, which was written down by Llewellyn Sion of Glamorgan, a Welsh bard and scholar, towards the end of the 16th century A.D. This manuscript has been edited and translated by J. A. Williams Ap Ithel for the Welsh Manuscripts Society; it purports to be the ancient Druidic teachings, but modern scholars doubt this. However, it certainly contains thought which is not Christian in origin, and it teaches reincarnation. Caesar's account in his De Bello Gallico is suspect, as its political motivation is obvious; and Pliny's is late, circa A.D. 77. Caesar relates the well-known gruesome story of how the Druids offered human sacrifices by filling great wicker-work images with living men, and setting fire to them; but this is an extremely impractical way of offering human sacrifices, as the first thing that would happen when such an image was set on fire would be that it would fall over and the inmates would break out. The Romans had a strong vested interest in atrocity stories against the Druids, as the latter were a unifying force among the tribes of Gaul and Britain, and it was the disunity of the British and Gaulish tribes which alone permitted the Roman conquest. However, I do not think the story of wicker-work images is pure invention. That they were used for human sacrifice seems unlikely; but wicker-work images have long been popular in carnival processions in England, France and elsewhere, often of huge size. These popular festivals mostly date back to pagan times, and the images may originally have been pagan gods. Wicker-work was about the most useful material available in olden times for a large portable image; stone or even wood was heavy and difficult to carry, if the statue were large; but a huge image of wicker-work, perhaps decked with flowers and green boughs, could make an impressive sight. I remember seeing in Salisbury Museum a fine wicker-work "town giant," who is still carried in popular processions.

Some students of Druidism indignantly deny the charge that the Druids offered human sacrifices. Alan Insole, in his book, *Immortal Britain*[*] says, "Our historians . . . ignore the fact that if a people were accustomed to celebrate their festivals in such a gruesome manner for generations, then on every sacred hill would have been found huge piles of burnt bones and skulls. But none has ever been found." A number of burials, cremated and otherwise, have been found at Stonehenge, but there is no evidence that they were sacrifices. The so-called "Slaughter Stone" is actually a fallen sarsen, and the peculiar indentations on its surface have been produced by weathering.

One interesting burial was found at Stonehenge which may bear out the witches' idea that the Blue-stone "horse-shoe" represents the womb. It was a "crouched burial," in which the body was laid in the earth in the crouched position of an unborn child, and it was found within the "horseshoe," just before the Altar Stone. This custom of "crouched burial," frequent among ancient peoples, may be a symbol of the belief I have mentioned previously, that the souls of the dead go to await rebirth in human form on this earth. It would here symbolise Life lying in the womb of the goddess, waiting to be reborn. The custom of burying shells with the dead may be another form of the same symbolism, as the shell is a female symbol (i.e. of the womb), and this, too, was a frequent custom among ancient peoples.

Julius Caesar's informants about Druidism were Gallic Druids, and they told him that their rule of life was discovered in Britain and transferred thence to Gaul. Irish writings say the same thing, and for that reason their students went from Ireland to Britain, as the Gauls did, to learn its secrets from the source, which sometimes involved a twenty years' course of study.

* Aquarian Press, 1952.

Caesar mentions their objections to writing down their secret teachings, and the cardinal doctrine which they taught, namely that souls do not perish at death, but pass from one body to another (we would call this idea reincarnation). This doctrine removed the fear of death, and hence was a great incentive to valour. We must remember that Romans in Caesar's time generally believed that a rather unpleasant Hades would be the lot of all, excepting a favoured few who could achieve demi-godship, so this belief would be curious to Caesar and the people for whom he was writing. He also says they had many discussions about the stars and their movements, the size of the Universe and the earth, the order of Nature, and the powers of the immortal gods, and that they handed down their lore to the young men.

Cicero (*De Divinatione*) says, "I knew a Druid myself, Divitaecus the Aeduan. He claimed to have a knowledge of Nature which the Greeks call 'Physiologia', and he used to make predictions, sometimes by means of augury and sometimes by conjecture." This Aeduan had been a friend of Caesar, and was a man of affairs and a politician and diplomat of established reputation throughout the whole of Gaul. There is a life-sized bronze statue of him in the Promenade des Mabres at Autun. According to tradition, a Druid called Abaris was a friend of Pythagoras, who, it will be remembered, was also a believer in reincarnation. Diodorus Siculus said of the Celts: "Among them the doctrine of Pythagoras prevails, according to which the souls of men are immortal, and after a fixed term recommence to live, taking upon themselves a new body."

G. Keeting in his *History of Ireland* mentions Irish Druids who divined by means of wrapping themselves in the skins of sacrificed bulls. Similar practices were known in Scotland and called "Tag-hairm." According to Pliny the Druids had a mysterious round stone, about the size of a small apple, which they called "the serpent's egg," and which they wore in a case hung round the neck. This may have been a show-stone, used like a crystal for scrying (a favourite device of witches). Some writers say that these "glane-stones," as they call them, were made of green glass, and a wonderful story was told of how they were engendered by a tangle of hissing serpents. This was probably a fable to scare the uninitiated. The Irish Druids seem to have been noted for their powers of prophecy. The word used in describing such prophecies is "Baile," meaning "speech of excitement." In Ireland, Druids were attached to the king's court, and were supposed to use their powers to help and protect him.

It has always been recognised that Witches had certain words such as Coven and Athame, which did not seem to belong to any known language, and the matter was complicated by the fact that people who were not necessarily witches were known to have used these words in the old days. I was in the Craft a long time before I realised that some of them were aware that there was an "Old Language" known to only a few; I don't think there is anyone who can really speak it well, but they do have a tremendous number of words, chiefly relating to things which affect the craft. Nowadays it has become only a sort of amusing slang, and some of what are said to be "Witch Words" are obviously "cant," as "Kicking the Wind"—their word for being hanged. Obviously dating from the days when Witches and others were publicly executed by being slowly strangled (before the "drop" was invented).

Some words they use, such as "Vavasour" (one who holds lands for another) are probably Norman-French. Other words are seemingly Celtic, but the main Corpus of the language is made up of words like "Halch," "Dwale," "Warrik," "Ganch," etc., which seem to belong to some older tongue. Unfortunately they will not permit me to give their meanings, or more of the old words.

It seems that in the original idea of kingship the king is the earthly representative of the god. This was the case in Egypt and Sumeria, and in Ancient Greece. In Egypt, from about 2750 B.C., the king was the sun-god Ra or Osiris, a deity in earthly form. In his veins ran the ichor of Ra, the gold of the gods and the goddesses. His business was to ensure the prosperity of the land and the people, to render the soil fertile, preserve the life-giving waters of the Nile, the fertility of women, etc. This was the case in Sumeria, also; but to preserve it the king had to enter into a form of sacred marriage with the goddess of fertility, by means of her priestess. Wherever the doctrine of the Divine King was observed, as in Britain, it was the king's job to see that the land was fruitful. If the crops failed, the king was held responsible; in some way he must have displeased the gods. Also, if the king were maltreated, the crops would fail. In Ireland, when the vassal clans revolted in the reign of Tuayhal Teachtmhor in the 1st century A.D., famine followed, and was blamed on to the revolt. If the king's wife were not virtuous, the earth would not yield. By his marriage the Divine King promoted the fertility of the country. At the festival of Lughnassad (Lammas) the Irish kings went through a ritual marriage with a priestess representing the land of Ireland, much as the priest of Nemi did when the representative of Diana as goddess of the earth annually married the King of the Wood (the hunting god?). Here we see the Druids, like the Sumerian priests, protecting the king and conducting a fertility cult, which apparently entailed a class of priestesses.

The Druids practised astrology and divination, and I think these are likely to have been the ancient customs of the country from at least the time when the Bronze Age invaders, the Proto-Celts, came here and built Stonehenge; and the priestly class of women who took the part of the goddess of the country in the sacred marriage were probably the witches, or wise women, initiated into the old mysteries. As we have already seen, the witches share the Druids' belief in reincarnation.

The prophecies of "Baile" are akin to witch practice, as is "Taghairm," though witches practise it without killing an animal. The objection of some writers that Boadicea acted without a Druid, so there could not have been Druids in her time (A.D. 61), I think rather proves the point. In the reign of the Emperor Claudius (A.D. 41–54) the Romans had suppressed the Druids in those territories of Britain and Gaul which were under Roman control, ostensibly on the grounds that the religion the Druids professed was barbarous and inhuman; but they may not have realised the strength of the witch cult, in which, while a man may not take the goddess's part, a high priestess may, by girding on a ritual sword, take the part of the god. It is notable that Boadicea performed her divination by means of observing the actions of a hare. Dio, in his *Roman History,* says, "When the British Queen Boadicea had finished speaking to her people, she employed a species of divination, letting a hare escape from the fold of her dress; and since it ran on what they considered the auspicious side, the whole multitude shouted with pleasure, and Boadicea, raising her hand towards heaven, said, 'I thank thee, Andraste . . . I supplicate and pray thee for victory.'" Andraste was a British goddess who is said to have given her name to that part of the country anciently called Anderida. Her name much resembles that of the very ancient Greek goddess Andrasteia, who was one of the three nurses of Zeus in the Dictean Cave, and whom the later Greeks identified with Nemesis. These three goddesses (the other two were called Lo and Amaltha) were the guardians of the Cornucopia, or Horn of Plenty, an attribute which is often pictured on Celtic statues of the Three Mothers (i.e. the triple moon goddess). If this identification is correct, Boadicea was invoking the moon goddess in her destructive aspect, that of the waning moon, symbolised as a terrible old woman, and praying for vengeance upon the Romans for her wrongs. (She had been cheated out of her kingdom, flogged like a criminal, and her daughters raped by Roman soldiers.) The hare has from time immemorial been sacred to the moon, and hence was a suitable animal for the follower of a moon-goddess to divine by. In later times hares may often be found traditionally associated with witches. From the fact that Boadicea released the hare from her dress, it may have been a tame one. Is this the earliest recorded instance of "a witch and her familiar"?

It would seem that Boadicea's prayer was answered. Her revolt gave the Roman power the biggest jolt it had had for years, and, although Boadicea herself seems to have lost her life in it, it led directly to the replacement of the tyrannical Suetonius Paulinus by officials who ruled mildly for the next ten years.

Early scholars believed that Druidism had its origin in the East. R. Borrow, in his *Asiatic Researches,* traced a great resemblance between the cults of the Druids and the Persian Magi (Pliny had formerly noticed the same thing), and General Charles Vallency believed that they were first Brahmins, then Chaldeans, then Magi. What I think myself is that there was an ancient cult possibly spreading from Sumeria and the Near East, and part of this required certain ceremonies in sacred groves of trees, "Paradises" as they were called, preferably on a hill, where at certain times a sacred marriage, in token or otherwise, took place in order to confer the Divine Kingship on the ruler, and on this the general prosperity of the land was thought to depend. In Britain this sacred grove was of oak, in Ireland of yew; in the East other trees were used. At a later date these sacred groves were constructed near every town, and from Christian or Jewish influence came to be called "Paradises." Originally they were probably a natural grove. There are a number of old place-names called "Paradise" to this day, notably one at Glastonbury. And there is one close to this museum, formerly used by the witches. The early Jews did the same thing, but having hills handy they usually planted their groves upon the "high places."

In the very early days, descent was traced, not through the father, but through the mother. It was the priestess who enroyalled the king by choosing him as her mate in the sacred marriage; and the heir to the throne was not the king's son, but the man who married the priestess-queen's daughter. Then, with the collapse of the older civilisations, like that of Minoan Crete, for instance, before the Aryan invasions of Europe, patriarchal ideas and descent through the male line were imposed upon society by the invaders. Male priesthoods grew up, and mythologies were altered to accord with the new ideas; though the old female powers were still feared and venerated among the common people, and had to a certain extent to be compromised with.

Is it not possible that the Proto-Celts, as they grew stronger in Britain, had introduced more and more of their own patriarchal ideas? In a damp cloudy country the sun god would be welcomed and revered, and the sun and the moon were identified with the twin sexual principles which were the real basis of ancient worship. Probably the sun was always venerated as the chief of the hosts of heaven; but we must remember that the Irish Celts seem to have given greater veneration to the moon, for the truly Irish reason that the sun only gave light in daytime, when you didn't need it, while the moon gave light at night, when you did. While I think some priesthood of the Proto-Celts (call them "Proto-Druids" if you like) had by 1200 B.C. converted the nation to a type of sun-worship, as the outer circle of Stonehenge circa 1200 B.C., is orientated to the sun, this possibly only meant that there was a male sect who mainly worshipped the sun-god and a female sect who worshipped the moon-goddess; both being really of the same religion, as we today have a monastery of monks who are dedicated, say, to St. Joseph, and a nunnery which venerates St. Anne, both being Christian. But I think that even at this date witches were the village wise women and priestesses, who chiefly worshipped in their own circle: though perhaps attending the main festivals and being assigned their own special place in the ceremonies, but not taking part in the education and politics of the nation. At least, while the Romans speak of orders of "Druidesses" (who may have been witches) they apparently did not attempt to disturb them, while they massacred the Druids because they incited the British to resistance, and took a hand in politics generally. The Druids were possibly evolved from a branch of the Old Religion which became the witch cult, and may have adopted many of its ideas; the use of the circle, for instance, to gain and conserve power. That they themselves realised there was some great power in the circle we can be sure, from their use of Stonehenge, etc.

Robert Graves and others have postulated the evolution of a male priesthood which gradually usurped the privileges of the ancient matriarchy, and took over the exercise of its powers. May the Druids have been such a priesthood, which, when it was destroyed in Britain by the Romans, left the priestesses of the older ways, who had been pushed into the background for that very reason, in possession of the field?

There *was* an alteration of religious ideas in Britain in the Middle Bronze Age, when more invaders came across the Channel and settled in the desirable Wessex lands around Stonehenge, forming the brilliant culture which has been called the Age of the Wessex Chieftains. It is evident that these people revered Stonehenge, from the large number of their richly-endowed barrow graves which have been found in its near vicinity; but instead of burying their dead like their predecessors, they cremated them and buried the ashes in a funerary urn, accompanied by rich ornaments, weapons and tools. Aerial photographs of the area around Stonehenge show many of their barrows, meticulously rounded, and, in the case of the so-called "disc" barrows, actually surrounded by a miniature bank and ditch, the idea being, perhaps, to enclose the grave with a protective magic circle.

By circa 900 B.C. archaeologists consider that, owing to the successive immigrations from the Continent, the language spoken in Britain must have been recognisably Celtic. These vigorous people, the Celts, who brought their culture and their Druid priesthood to Britain, were an offshoot of the great Aryan invasion of Europe, the Mediterranean, and India, which had such a tremendous impact upon the ancient world. These nomadic people spread from the general vicinity of what is now the Russian steppes, which in those days, circa 2000 B.C., were probably warmer and more fertile than they are now. Being nomadic, their society was more inclined to the patriarchal form than the settled matriarchal Bronze Age civilisations. They were at first wild barbarians, but they became apt pupils of the societies they invaded, and they themselves may be the discoverers of the process of iron smelting, which first arose in the Near East circa 1500 B.C. Another discovery of theirs was the taming and riding of horses. Gradually they overcame and transformed the older civilisations, and themselves became differentiated into the Greeks, the Latins, the Celts, the Persians, the Indians of Vedic times, etc. The language of the latter people, Sanskrit, is recognised as being the parent of most present-day European tongues, including Celtic.

However, in the old India of pre-Aryan times, as modern archaeologists have found by research at the old buried cities of Mohenjo-daro and Harappa, the people worshipped the very same horned god and mother goddess as they did in Europe. Many pottery figures of a goddess have been found at Mohenjo-daro, identical in appearance with those of the Great Mother in the ancient Near East. In both these old cities, too, just as in our own country, have been found upright conical stones, and large stone rings, symbolising the male and female principles respectively. Seal impressions from Mohenjo-daro show a male horned god, sometimes depicted with three faces, and with the very characteristic of the "Devil" of the witch sabbats; a flaming torch between the horns, which are sometimes those of a bull and sometimes those of a stag. He is naked except for ritual ornaments. In one seal impression he is sitting in a squatting posture, like those of yoga, and surrounded by various animals. He is evidently Lord of the Beasts. Perhaps the beasts are thought of as being under his protection. If so, then this Indian seal impression, dating from between 3000 and 2000 B.C., has its exact counterpart in the altar from ancient Celtic France, or Gaul as it was then called, found at Rheims, which depicts a horned god feeding a bull and a stag, and seated in a very similar cross-legged posture. The original may be seen in the Museum at St. Germain-en-Laye.

It is considered that the Great Mother of pre-Aryan India and her horned consort are the prototypes of the Lord Shiva, the Lord of the Beasts (*Pasupati*) and the Lord of Yoga, and his bride Shakti, the Great Mother whose rites among the Tantrics strongly resemble those of Western witch covens.

A number of representations of Gaulish gods have been found, and the Gauls also worshipped the Great Mother in triple form (the Virgin, the Bride, and the Hag). The district in France called the Marne is named after the Three Mothers, and a number of statues of them and of other goddesses have been found. As we know that the ancient Gauls worshipped gods and goddesses, and the ancient Irish did the same, and the priests of both were Druids, it seems to dispose of the contention of some writers upon Druidism that the Druids were monotheists, and in fact forerunners of the Christian message.

Certain writers on Druidism believe, however, that the Druids eagerly accepted the Christian faith when it appeared in Britain, and grafted Christianity on to their paganism. This I think was quite true of the type of early Christianity which came soon after Christ's death, but not of what Christianity had changed to by Augustin's time. It is not generally realised that Christianity came to Britain from two different sources; namely, what has been called "Celtic Christianity," traditionally brought to these shores by

Joseph of Arimathea, and the much later mission of Augustin Roman Catholics in A.D. 597. Whether or not it was Joseph of Arimathea himself who, as legend says, fled here with some companions after the Crucifixion and took refuge at the Druid centre of Glastonbury, it is certain that Christianity was established in Britain long before Augustin's time, and was of a different form from that which Augustin, the emissary of the Roman Church, preached; because in A.D. 607 the Archbishop of St. David's, with six Bishops and the Abbot of Bangor, met Augustin and flatly refused to acknowledge the supremacy of Rome. As a result, they were massacred at Bangor Abbey by the Saxons on the orders of the Roman Bishop, and Bangor Library, at that time one of the finest in the world, was burned; even as the Druids had been previously massacred by the Roman general Suetonius Paulinus, and their learning destroyed. These two events cannot but have made great gaps in our knowledge of the ancient traditions of our country.

Dr. O'Donovan, editing "The Annals of the Four Masters" says:

> Nothing is more clear than that St. Patrick engrafted Christianity on to the pagan superstition with so much skill that he won over the people to the Christian religion before they understood the difference between the two systems of belief.

Sir John Rhys says:

> Irish Druidism absorbed a certain amount of Christianity, and it would be a problem of considerable difficulty to fix on a point where it ceased to be Druidism and from which onwards it could be said to be Christianity in any restricted sense of the term.

They simply thought of certain saints and of Jesus himself as being great Druids. It is generally recognised that some Druids at least carried on their practices, but called themselves "Cele De," "Culdees," meaning Servants of God. They worshipped in the Church of St. Regulas at St. Andrews until the year A.D. 1124. At Ripon and York they functioned in the eighth century, also at Iona. In Ireland they held sway at Clones and Armagh, and in 1628 a deed was signed by Edward Burton, Prior of the Cathedral Church of Armagh, "on behalf of the Vicars choral and Culdees of the same." Archbishop Lanfranc was extremely horrified at finding they did not use the Roman style of worship, and would not recognise the Roman saints. The Roman Church was also shocked because they were not celibate, and their style of tonsure was said to have come from the Druids.

The witches and the Druids certainly share a number of beliefs: a belief in a future life and in reincarnation; in the efficacy of the magic circle; in forms of prophecy (or, as we would call it, clairvoyance); in the sacredness of Stonehenge and other stone circles, which in later times became the traditional meeting-places of witches; and in an acute dislike of committing their teachings to writing. But perhaps the most striking link between the Druids and the witches is that of the four great ritual occasions the witches call "Sabbats."

In Ireland, as has been said, there was a great annual festival on August 1st (Lammas), held at Tailltenn and presided over by Druids. It was said to be in honour of the sun-god Lugh. A similar festival was held in Gaul at Lugudunum (Lyons) in honour of Lugus, god of light and knowledge. The Tailltenn festival also honoured Lugh's foster-mother Tailltiu. It is closely associated with the cult of the dead, and Tailltiu being obviously the Great Mother. The energy expended in the games was thought of as giving new strength to the god to bring fertility to the land (Witches dance at Lammas today with the same object). The celebration of Lughnassad (Lammas) ensured plenty of corn, milk, etc., throughout Ireland. If the rites were poor the crops would be poor, and temporary marriages seem to have been a great feature of the rites. To this day "a Tailltenn marriage" is the word for the type of union "when you do not bother the priest with your private affairs." "Lughnassad" means "the marriage of Lugh," and he was supposed to take the land as his bride. The King of All Ireland was ceremonially married to the goddess, actually to a priestess representing her. This is exactly what was done in Sumeria, when each year the king, representing the god, married a priestess representing the goddess.

Samhain (November 1st), the winter festival of the Celts, was the beginning of their New Year, and on Samhain Eve (our Halloween) divinations to know the happenings of the coming year were made. In Ireland this was held at Tara, when all the Druids assembled to sacrifice to the gods. They sacrificed a black sheep, and offered libations to the spirits of those who had died during the year.

May 1st was Bealteinne (Beltane); two great fires were lighted by the Druids on each sacred hill, and the cattle were driven between them as a preservation against sickness. Later, in England, the May King and May Queen, "Robin Hood and Maid Marian," represented the old god and goddess of fertility. Their marriage and union were believed magically to assist the crops. The May Day revels were fiercely denounced by the Puritans, on account of the freedom of lovemaking which prevailed among those who took part in them.

Ross Nichols, in his little book, *Sassenach Stray*, says, speaking of old Gaelic traditions:

> The big sun, Beltane, reappears, replacing winter's wizened little sun on Mayday, when ceremonial fires of sympathetic magic were lit. On Hallowe'en the little sun substituted for the big sun; the underworld began to dominate the upper world and you could see into the future. At these changeovers supernatural beings became unstuck and flew about.

Now, the four great festivals the witch cult celebrates are Halloween, May Eve (the old "Walpurgis Night"), Lammas, and Candlemas, February 2nd. (It is noteworthy that, being a moon cult, they celebrate the night before the day of the festival.)

February 2nd is called by the Christian Church "The Purification of the Blessed Virgin Mary"; but it is actually derived from the rites of the Roman goddess Februa, who was worshipped with lighted torches. Oimelc, the festival of the moon goddess Bride among the ancient Celts and Gaels, was February 1st. Bride has in modern days been Christianised as "St. Bride" or "St. Briget"; but the Eve of St. Bride is still held as "uncanny" by the Gael, a belief which forms the theme of one of the weird stories of "Fiona Macleod," "By the Yellow Moonrock" (from *The Dominion of Dreams*). On Bride's Day serpents were supposed to awake from their winter sleep and come from their holes, and the Gaels have a charm against them which runs as follows:

> *Today is the day of Bride.*
> *The serpent shall come from its hole.*
> *I will not molest the serpent,*
> *And the serpent will not molest me.*

There is, however, another version of this charm which says:

> *On the day of Bride of the fair locks*
> *The noble queen will come from the hill;*
> *I will not molest the noble queen,*
> *Nor will the noble queen molest me.*

It is apparent that the serpent is in fact a form of the goddess, and we may recall in this connection the snake-goddess of Minoan Crete, and the "Lamias" of Greek legend whose weird beauty inspired one of Keats's poems.

It will be noticed that these four ancient festivals neatly divide the year into four parts, from which they are sometimes known as "the four Cross-Quarter Days." Their origin has been something of a puzzle. It has been suggested that they are connected with the seasons of fertility in animals.

I would like to advance a suggestion in this connection which I do not think has been made before. The four great Sabbats each take place when the sun is in one of the four fixed signs of the Zodiac; sometimes called the Kerubic Signs, because they are the Man, Eagle, Lion and Bull which, according to Kabalistic teaching, are the Kerubs or ruling symbols of the Four Elements. The Man is Aquarius, the fixed sign of Air; the Eagle is Scorpio, the fixed sign of water (or rather, the esoteric symbol thereof); the Lion is Leo, the fixed sign of Fire; and the Bull of Taurus, the fixed sign of Earth. In Christian times these were adopted as the symbols of the Four Evangelists, the Man for St. Matthews, the Eagle for St. John, the Lion for St. Mark, and the Bull for St. Luke.

In *Gods in the Making,* by T. Mawby Cole and Vera W. Reid, we find the following:

> These four fixed signs are perhaps the most universal of all religious symbols, for they are to be found in the human-faced beasts of the gods of Chaldea, in the four Assyrian sphinxes, in the Cherubim of the Kabbala. The same symbols are frequently mentioned by Ezekiel and are said to be sometimes depicted in the four arms of Siva in Hindu temples, while the whole four are assembled in the mysterious Sphinx of Egypt. . . . There can be no doubt that these symbols of the fixed signs so universally employed possess profound and pregnant esoteric significance. By their position in the Zodiac, midway between the cardinal points, they may be considered to mark the culmination peak of cosmic energy released by the Equinoxes and Solstices, or, again, to indicate vital, progressive stages in the unfoldment of consciousness.

The Sabbat of Candlemas takes place when the sun is in Aquarius; that of May Eve when the sun is in Taurus; that of Lammas when the sun is in Leo; and that of Halloween when the sun is in Scorpio.

Chapter VI

Witchcraft in Roman and Saxon Times

The position of the cult in Roman and Saxon times seems rather a puzzle. The great question is, were the witches and the Druids members of the same cult? The witches have no exact traditions on the subject. Personally, I think they were not; the witch cult was the religion of the soil, as it were, and the Druids were the more aristocratic religion, much as things were a thousand years later, when the witch cult was the religion of the peasants, but the Roman Church was the dominant power. The latter was not only a religion, but also the Civil Service, the educational system, the politicians, and the not so very "hidden hand" which ruled the kings. The Druids seem to have occupied a similar position.

The Roman Occupation lasted from A.D. 43 to A.D. 410. I doubt if the religion the Romans brought with them had much influence upon the witch cult. The official cult of the deified Emperors and Capitoline Jove was, I think, more of a national expression of feeling, like the figures of Britannia with trident and shield (though this is really a figure of the Great Mother Goddess), or "Uncle Sam" in striped trousers and a goatee beard or the pretty lady with short skirts, a very decolleté chemise, and the Cap of Liberty, labelled "La France." Men fought and died for them, but did they really believe in them as gods, though they believed in what they stood for? That is, they did not take them seriously (who could have taken the deified Emperors seriously?) but they conformed; as people, whatever their private feelings about royalty, stand when the National Anthem is played. But it is another matter when we think of the various Mystery Cults which the Romans brought with them, the cult of Serapis at York for instance, or the cult of Mithras, which had a number of temples in Britain and whose temple has recently been uncovered in London.

From what we know of this latter cult I doubt if it had any effect at all. It was an exclusive, puritanical, male cult of sun-worship, which appealed to stern, hard-living soldiers, and was very popular with the Roman Legionnaires. However, it is different when one comes to the Roman and Greek Mysteries. I have told at length in my previous book, *Witchcraft Today*, of the discoveries in the Villa of the Mysteries at Pompeii. All the Mysteries were similar; they had their sacred drama where the candidate reproduced certain events of the history of the god or goddess. This is the principle of the Holy Communion among Christians, the eating of the bread and drinking of the wine to identify themselves with the acts of Christ. When rituals of this type are performed impressively they become events in the candidate's life; they may actually change his character, making him a fit medium to obtain contact or communion with the god. They are definitely magical in intention; but this intention is to make the participants better men and more worthy of salvation in the future life. Orphism was perhaps the most important of the Mystery cults. It was an orgiastic, ecstatic religion, consisting mainly in the worship of Dionysus, and the initiate lived his myth over again to obtain at-onement with the god, and paringenesis, dying and being reborn again as the god had done. They usually had some sort of doctrine of original sin, or at least impurity, and the initiates were purged of this by certain mortifications of the flesh in the Mysteries (though this doctrine was not the same as the Christian Church's doctrine of original sin). The Mysteries were the great centres of Greek life, protected by the State, which paid the fees of the poor so that all citizens should be members, while people of bad character, no matter what their rank might be, were rigidly excluded. The secrets were thought necessary for the preservation of the State, and it was a penal offence to betray them. These Mysteries flourished uninterruptedly for over a thousand years, until the 4th century A.D., when the early Christians looted and destroyed the temples, and prevented the rites from being performed. (Deliberately desecrated temples have been found in Britain, too; such as the shrine of Conventina and the temple of Mithras at Carrawburgh.) The Temple of Eleusis itself was destroyed by the Goths, at the instigation of the monks who followed the host of Alaric.

The Roman Emperors Augustus, Claudius, Hadrian, Marcus Aurelius, Commodus, Septimus Severus, and probably Antoninus, were initiates of the Eleusinian Mysteries, though so far as is known, Hadrian was the only imperial initiate to receive all three degrees, and it was he who brought the celebration of these Mysteries to Rome. Dudley Wright, in *The Eleusinian Mysteries and Rites,* says:

> About the beginning of the fifth century Theodosius the Great prohibited and almost totally extinguished the pagan theology in the Roman Empire, and the Eleusinian Mysteries suffered in the general destruction. It is probable, however, that the Mysteries were celebrated secretly in spite of the severe edicts of Theodosius and that they were partly continued through the dark ages, though stripped of their splendour. It is certain that many rites of the pagan religion were performed under the dissembled name of convivial meetings, long after the publication of the Emperor's edicts, and Psellius informs us that the Mysteries of Ceres existed in Athens until the eighth century of the Christian era and were never totally suppressed.

In the Villa of the Mysteries at Pompeii have been found life-sized frescoes illustrating an initiation. I got some large-sized illustrations of these, which showed tiny details, and showed them to English witches, and they all said the same thing: "So they knew the secrets in those days."

Now, this could mean that the real witch secrets came to Britain by means of the Mysteries, that is to say, prior to, say, A.D. 100, and that the British witches were only village wise women; but I do not feel that this is the true explanation. I think it is usually agreed that the Greek Mysteries came originally from Egypt, and they may well have done so. There are certain things in the witch cult which might have originated in Egypt, too; but there are also ideas which may have been derived from Sumeria. My own impression is that all these things reached Britain in the early days, when there was communication and trade between Egypt, Crete and Syria direct. In those days religious ideas were freely exchanged and freely adopted; but it is possible that certain ideas and practices came to Britain via the Mysteries brought by the Romans. Bacchic and Orphic pavements have been found in Somerset; but there is little proof of Mysteries of a Dionysiac nature ever being celebrated in Britain.

The concept of witches as followers of the moon goddess, and enchantresses whom it was dangerous to meddle with, was already well known to the Roman world. Lucius Apuleius, who flourished in the 2nd century A.D., was a Roman provincial who wrote in Latin a wonderful and very popular romance, *The Golden Ass,* which has been described as the parent of modern romantic literature. It is essentially a romance of witchcraft. In it many of the concepts of the behaviour of mediaeval witches can be found. At the commencement of the tale, Lucius tells how he journeyed into Thessaly, a famous place for witchcraft, and how his travelling companions regaled him with most frightful and horrible stories of the powers of the Thessalian witches.

Before long Lucius was to have proof of these in his own person. The wife of his host in Thessaly was one Pamphiles, a famous witch. His cousin Byrrhena solemnly warned him, before the statue of the goddess Diana, not to meddle with Pamphiles or seek to spy upon her enchantments; but Lucius despised her warning, and determined to pry and "to bestow my money in learning of that art, and now wholly to become a witch."

Accordingly he made love to her wanton maid Fotia, and persuaded the girl to let him spy upon Pamphiles through the chink of a door, as she was working her magical rites. He saw the witch strip herself naked and anoint herself all over with some unguent, whereat she became changed into an owl and flew away. He begged Fotis to steal the magic unguent for him; but the girl stole the wrong box, and when he made use of it Lucius found himself changed, not into an owl, the bird of wisdom, but into an ass.

In this shape he passed through many hair-raising and ludicrous adventures, until, being by the sea-shore at the full moon, he solemnly prayed to the moon goddess to release him from the spell, expressing repentance for any offence he had committed against her. He was rewarded by a dream-vision of the goddess, in which she told him how to remove the spell, and in gratitude to her, after he had regained his human shape, he became a priest of Isis.

In the story, just as in mediaeval times, witches are said to be able to change themselves into various animals, to use magical ointments, to work enchantments upon persons by means of a piece of their hair, and to make spells by means of parts stolen from newly-buried corpses, fumigations of incense, and pentacles inscribed with magical characters. It should be remembered in this connection that for many centuries people had an extra-ordinary belief in the medicinal value of what would strike us as most grisly remedies; hence the use of such things does not necessarily indicate black magic. Mrs. C. Leyel, in her very interesting book, *The Magic of Herbs** tells us some of these. Perfectly respectable apothecaries sold mummy dust

* Jonathan Cape, 1932.

and human flesh; and a liquor prepared from criminals' skulls was prescribed for Charles II when he was suffering from a fit of apoplexy.

Lucius relates with relish a number of macabre stories of the powers of witches in his day. Yet they are not devotees of Satan, of whom Lucius had never heard. Their goddess is Hecate, and Hecate, in the vision which delivers Lucius from bondage, is declared to be identical with Isis, the gracious and lovely Queen of Heaven. That is, she is the same goddess in her dark and light aspects, as is natural to a goddess of the moon.

It is notable that Shakespeare in *Macbeth* makes his famous three witches invoke Hecate as the mistress of their charms. There is no "Satanism" there.

"Papus" (Dr. Gerrard Encausse), in his *Traite de Magie Pratique* (Paris, 1893), gives in an appendix of "Magic des Campagnes," or "country magic," amongst much other matter evidently taken from such sources as the Grand Albert and similar books, an extraordinary traditional spell which, if it is authentic (unfortunately he does not give its source), is an amazing illustration of the blending of old pagan practices with Christianity, an invocation of Hecate at the full moon mingled with the rites of the Church:

Evocation

> For nine entire days, when the moon is increasing in light, after her fifth day, burn incense in honour of the protecting powers of suffering souls; recite each time a Pater (i.e. Pater noster, the Lord's Prayer) solely for the repose of the said souls, and burn to this same intention a candle in honour of the spirits which protect suffering souls, for their acquiescence in the intention you have.
>
> From time to time, burn incense in honour of the spirits, to this end.
>
> For three nights following (avoid Friday) light a fire, and make three rounds, mentally forming a circle. Take some incense in your hand, and cast it in the fire, thinking of and imploring Hecate (goddess of enchantments); then retiring inside the circle and placing yourself in the middle, invoke the help of the stars by look and by thought, and say: "O Hecate, goddess in the heavens, goddess upon the earth, and Proserpine in hell; O mother of shadows, supreme queen of the host of the dead; send not against me thy legions, O Hecate, but rather cause them to serve me. O triple Hecate, great goddess who presides over enchantments, in this fire which is offered to thee the incense shall burn in thine honour. O Hecate, may thy divinity come unto me and thy power surround me, my

> Father in Heaven not being offended thereat! By Hecate, O spirit ruler of the air; by Hecate, suffering souls of the dead; by Hecate, O wandering souls of the region below; by Hecate, become my helpers, my servers, my guards."
>
> Then, leaving the circle, take the incense in your hand to offer it to the spirits, and formulate your demand.
>
> Afterwards, burn an offering of bread and wine for the benefit of suffering souls in general; and when this is done, say: "By Hecate, in the silence of the night I have called upon the legions of the air, the vast army of the Good Goddess; to some I have offered the incense which delights them, to others the bread for which they hunger. Now, while the stars shine in power, and the forces invoked move; like a sovereign in his mantle of purple, thy servant, O Hecate, will go to his bed in peace."

A veneer of Christianity is given to this ritual by the use of the Lord's Prayer and the proviso in the invocation, "My Father in Heaven not being offended thereat"; but the witch goddess is conceived of as being the ruler over "suffering souls," i.e. souls in Purgatory, which is conceived of as a sort of intermediate region, from which souls can revisit the earth. The word which I have translated as "the Good Goddess" is "Obs" in the original; this sounds like a worn-down version of "Ops," the goddess of earth and of fertility, the bride of Saturn, but may be connected with Obi Worship in Africa. The goddess who was the guardian of the seed hidden in the earth was, in many ancient Mysteries, also the guardian of the dead, whose promise of immortality and rebirth was symbolised by the rebirth of the corn each year. It will be noted that if the spell is performed as stated, for nine days when the moon is increasing in light, after the fifth day, it will be operated at the full moon. This was the traditional time for the local Esbat, when the power of the moon-goddess was at its height.

In A.D. 324 the converted Emperor Constantine decreed that Christianity should be the official religion of the Roman Empire. The temples of the Roman gods were destroyed or converted into Christian churches. This change in religion caused many political upheavals, as the triumphant Christians began to attack the followers of the older religions. The old Roman society became disrupted and began to disintegrate.

As Hendrik Willem Van Loon says in his *Story of Mankind,* "The Christians still formed a very small minority of all the people (not more than five or six per cent), and in order to win, they were forced to refuse all compromise. The old gods must be destroyed." The Emperor Justinian closed the school of philosophy at Athens, which had been founded by Plato, and, Van Loon continues, "That was the end of the old Greek world, in which man had been allowed to think his own thoughts and dream his own dreams according to his desires."

The certainties of the Old World were being swept away. Waves of barbarians from the east, the Huns, the Goths, the Vandals, and their wild, brigand-like followers, battered at the Roman Empire. Constantine, the first Christian Emperor, removed his court from Rome and took refuge in Byzantium, which was named Constantinople in his honour. The Empire was divided by his two sons into eastern and western provinces, with Constantinople as capital of the east and Rome as capital of the west. The elder son ruled at Rome, the younger at Constantinople.

The western empire presently collapsed utterly into the hands of the barbarian invaders. In A.D. 410 the Emperor Honorius recalled the Roman Legions from Britain, telling the Britons that he could no longer spare Roman troops to garrison the country; the need at home was too desperate. He bade the Britons to defend themselves against the barbarian raiders, the Angles and Saxons, who for some time had been seeking to overrun the country.

As the Roman Empire crumbled into decay, the old "Pax Romana" gave place to local anarchy; brigands flourished everywhere. The Church tried hard to produce something to replace the old Roman tradition, and to a great extent succeeded. The ecclesiastical authorities became the leaders of the people. They were bigoted, and generally poorly educated; but they did serve to hold the various provinces together when their natural leaders were thus abolished, and the curious position arose of Bishops commanding armies, or rather the local militia. They at any rate prevented a total collapse of all authority in provinces where the Legions had been withdrawn. For by this time the army was chiefly composed of conscripts from other provinces. The Roman Wall in Britain was chiefly garrisoned by mercenaries from Germany and conscripts from Spain, and local wars prevented reinforcements being sent.

The Church Councils, too, were busy; their concern was to extirpate the old religion, and to gain complete control of the State. The Council of Ancyra, A.D. 314, for instance, when Vitalis, Bishop of Antioch, St. Leontius of Caesarea, and many other Bishops, denounced pacts with the devil. They also objected to vegetarianism; at least, their 14th canon orders that "clergy shall be deprived if they obstinately refuse to eat meat, or vegetables cooked with meat." The 18th canon excommunicates those who, having been appointed Bishops and been refused by the people of the diocese to which they have been appointed, wish to invade other dioceses (a sidelight on the way in which Bishops were liable to behave in those days). The 24th canon gives five years' penance to those who use soothsaying or witchcraft to cure diseases, or who follow the customs of the Gentiles (i.e. the pagans). The 15th canon enacts that church property unlawfully sold by priests during a vacancy in the Bishopric shall be reclaimed by the Church (apparently without any recompense to the innocent buyer, a clear case of the old Roman law *Caveat emptor,* "Let the buyer beware"). The Church here is clearly superseding the civil law. This was brought out more clearly at the Council of Angers, A.D. 453, with Leo, Archbishop of Boudges, presiding, the 1st canon of which is to the effect "That since Bishops had been granted the power of trying civil cases, the clergy should, in every case of difference among themselves, apply to them instead of to the civil authorities. That in case of a dispute between the clergy and the laity, they should require it to be judged by their Bishop; but if the other party should not agree to this they should not go before any secular judge without permission of their Diocesan." This is a very clear case of attempting to overthrow the ordinary law of the land. The same Council ordered all wandering monks to be excommunicated. Priests were forbidden to *assault* or *mutilate their flock!* The 4th canon deprives those of the clergy who would not abstain from intercourse with all "strange women" (witches?).

So, while the Popes and Kings and Emperors squabbled, while the cities set up as small independent states, while various invaders settled down in new provinces (as the Northmen did in France by becoming baptised and calling themselves "Normans," though still retaining much of their pagan belief and entering into alliances, to say the least, with the local witches), while the great mass of the people swore fealty to any overlord who would and could protect them, the Church gradually created a faith, and used the devil to scare people into obedience. And the Church was the only force which was consistent. It might rack-rent its serfs, but it protected them. The Bishop's militia was a formidable force; but this security was only built up at the price of losing humanity and toleration.

Slowly the laws against heresy and witchcraft grew fiercer. The priest who would only be "deprived" for associating with the witches by the

Council of Angers would have been burned alive five hundred years later, if his Bishop wished it. (Of course, many Bishops did not; some possibly belonged to the cult themselves, especially the Norman Bishops.) The penalty for using witchcraft to cure diseases by the decree of the Council of Ancyra was five years' penance; in 1576 Bessie Dunlop of Ayr was convicted and burnt alive for the same offence. No one alleged that she had harmed anyone; her specific offence was curing. By the Council of Ancyra, priests were forbidden to assault or mutilate their flock; but in 1596 another Scotswoman, Alison Balfour, was brought to a confession of witchcraft by the expedient of putting the pilnie-winks, an instrument of torture for crushing the fingers, not upon her, but upon her seven-year-old daughter, in her presence. We had not yet reached these refinements of civilisation in the Dark Ages; but progress was starting on its way, even in spite of such reactionary activities as those of the Holy Synod of Paderborn in 785, which decreed that "Whoever, being fooled by the devil, maintains, in accordance with pagan belief, that witches exist and causes them to be burned at the stake, shall be punished with death."

While school books talk of the Romans leaving Britain, actually there were very few to leave, apart from the Army. One or two officials and a few traders may have gone; but the "Romans" in Britain then were Britons who were Roman citizens. Some of them may have had a little Roman blood, though their families had been living in Britain for several generations. They were well educated after Roman standards, but they were Britons, and almost at once split up into the various tribes in the areas in which they were when the Romans came three hundred and fifty years before. Thus, Northumberland alone had to resist all the attacks of the Picts and Scots without help from the other tribes. Also, all along the east coast various districts had to defend themselves against great Saxon attacks without help from the others, and with no Roman fleet to attack the invaders' ships. As all know, the result was that the Saxons conquered and occupied the greater part of Britain.

One result of the splitting up into separate clan areas was the break-up of the Roman system of cultivation by huge farms attached to villas. These were promptly deserted by the slaves or serfs who cultivated them. The Romano-British owner, thus deserted, had to leave also. Some of these serfs in time took to cultivating small patches for themselves; the result of which was that the nation's food supply was about halved. While the small farmers could just feed themselves, they had nothing over, so it was impossible for the new states to support anything like an army in the field. To repel a local attack, a crowd of local militia could be assembled for a few days only, then they would melt away. These circumstances would have tended to increase the influence of the witch cult. The witches believed in fertility rites, and would use all their powers to make each small community grow corn, etc., in their little fields, as they had done in the pre-Roman times. Also, I think that here we have a clue as to why we do not hear anything of witches in the Roman times. The Roman villa was much like a vast communal farm in Russia today. It was scientific farming by experts, the work being carried out by forced or slave labour bound to the land. They had no need for witches' fertility rites, though these lingered on in the "native villages" in out of the way places. When all the slave labour deserted the Roman villas, their owners deserted them too. We know this because the Roman villas we dig up have not been sacked or burned; they have simply been denuded of anything easily portable and abandoned, and slowly become buried.

If these British states had been left alone they would doubtless in time have got themselves into as good a condition as they were before the Roman invasion; but the constant Saxon invasions, coupled with the Danish raids, brought about a state of chaos. Most of the merchants and tradesmen seem to have emigrated to Ireland, which was at the time extremely prosperous, and it was they who made much of the exquisite "Irish" metal work and other artistic productions for which she was famous for the next three hundred years. A great part of the rest of the British population in course of time seems to have emigrated to Brittany and Wales; yet there was no wholesale clearing-out or massacre of the Celtic population as some books infer. What actually happened was that the Saxons liked the rich bottom land along the rivers. This was densely forested, but with great labour they cleared it and settled there. In a few of the larger towns, notably London and Exeter, they shared with the British population, there being British and Saxon quarters, each with their own churches and government. The Saxon kings made the laws, and the British had to obey them, more or less (chiefly less), much as it was in Ireland fifty years ago.

Up to that time it is doubtful if the Wica had a distinctive name for themselves. They were the people, the priests and priestesses of the Old Goddess, who were recognised as of the people. The Saxons hated and feared anything to do with magic. They worshipped Odin (Woden) and Thor and the other Scandinavian gods, and were extremely "respectable" in a Germanic way. When they became Christians they were more so. That Odin used to have a Wild Hunt resembling that of Herne, and Valkyries who were in some ways like the witches of legend, only they rode horses through the air instead of goats or broomsticks, made things worse; they hated the memory of Odin and the Valkyries because they were pagan divinities. I have been asked, "Did the Saxons make changes in the witch cult?" And I say, "I don't think so." Caesar records that the customs of the "Germans" were entirely different from those of the Celts. They had no Druids, and spent most of their time in hunting and warlike pursuits, recognising as gods only those things which they could see and which obviously benefited them, such as sun, moon and fire; "the other gods they have never even heard of." They were not agriculturists, settled farming being actively discouraged by their chiefs. Milk, cheese and meat were their principal foods. Altogether, Caesar paints a picture of the Germans (i.e. Teutonic tribes) of his day as leading a savage, semi-nomadic existence, and being partial to plundering raids upon other tribes. Tacitus in A.D. 98 describes them very similarly. They were originally yet another branch of the patriarchal Aryan nomads, and a study of their religion reveals once again the process of the imposition of a patriarchal masculine pantheon upon aboriginal matriarchy. Their gods were the warlike Aesir, headed by Woden (or Odin) and Thor; but there are hints of other, older, more peaceful gods, called the Vanir, the chief of whom were Frey and Freya, names which simply mean "the lord" and "the lady." Frey was the god of peace and plenty, and Adam of Bremen tells us that he was depicted "*cum ingenti priapo.*" Carl Clemen in his *Religions of the World* illustrates a phallic statue of Frey; and he was sometimes called Fricco. Freya was also called Frigga; and the names of these two ancient deities are the obvious origin of a number of words of a sexual connotation which are not usually considered printable. It is evident that Frey was originally the mate of Freya; but in later times she was "married" to Woden, and Frey became her "brother." Like Ishtar, one of Freya's attributes was her wonderful necklace, and in this she resembles the witch-goddess also. She is, in fact, the aboriginal Great Mother, and Frey is her phallic consort. The father-god Woden and his fierce followers are the gods of the patriarchal Ayran invaders.

By the time the Angles and Saxons started to invade Britain, they had acquired more civilisation than when Caesar and Tacitus described them. Even so there was a great difference between them and the cultured, literate Romano-British, many of whom were Christians of the old Celtic Church. It is to this period that King Arthur and his chivalry must have belonged, if he had an historical existence.

The Saxons came in as heathen conquerors; they looted and killed and raped. Most of the Celtic population were dispersed in these long wars, and the remnants lived in inaccessible places. Only in the big towns did the races meet and mix, and even there they were hated conquerors, who had dispossessed the Celts from their ancestral lands and forced them to live in the out-lands. Also, they hated magic. This is no condition for any mingling of cult practices. Then the Saxons became Christian, the new kind of intolerant, Roman Christian, which made matters even worse. And then, just as the Saxons were settling down nicely, the Danish invasions commenced. To them the Saxons were renegades who had forsaken the old faith of Odin and Thor, and so deserved exterminating. But in time these Danes themselves were baptised and made Christians, and lived in an uneasy confederacy with the Saxons.

By this time the Celts in their out-of-the-way dwellings were regaining their prosperity, and the Danish-Saxon lawgivers began making laws against the aboriginal magic they feared. As they had no witches of their own they had no special name for them; however, they made one up from *wig,* an idol, and *laer,* learning, *wiglaer,* which they shortened into *wicca.* They also used the terms *scin-laeca, galdor-craeftig,* and *morthwyrtha. Scin-laeca* seems to have been a phantom double or astral body, or the one who could project it. *Galdor-craeftig* is one skilled in spells. *Morthwyrtha* is a worshipper of the dead. They also had a word *dry* for a magician. Their laws were clear on the subject: "If any *wicca* or *wiglaer* (male witch), or false swearer, or *morthwyrtha* . . . or any foul, contaminated, manifest *horc-wenan* (whore, quean, or strumpet), be anywhere in the land, man shall drive them out. . . ." "We teach that every priest shall extinguish all heathendom, and forbid *Wilweorthunga* (fountain worship) and *licwiglunga* (incantations or invocations of the dead), *hwata* (omens or soothsayings), and *galdra* (magic), and man-worship, and the abominations that men use in the various craft of the Wica, and *frithspottum* with elms and other trees, and with stones ("going to the stones"?), and with many phantoms."

Penalties were provided for destroying anyone by "wicca crafte," or for driving sickness on a man, or for causing death, or for using "wicca crafte" to gain another's love, or for giving him to eat and drink of magic, or for divining (*wiglian*) by the moon, or for worshipping the sun or moon, fire or floods, wells or stones, or trees, or for "loving wicca crafte." There was also another word, *unlybban wyrce,* which seems to mean unlawful magic, that is, the deadly kind, or what is called nowadays black magic. It is a curious fact that when the witches became English-speaking they adopted their Saxon name "Wica."

The allusion to "man-worship" is notable, as it may well refer to the appearance of the old Horned God in the form of his priest, the god's representative, dressed in his ritual costume of skin and horns. The *Liber Poenitentialis* of Theodore, composed in the 7th century, lays down, *"Si quis in Kalendas Januarii in cervulo aut vetula vadit, id est, in ferarum habitus se commutant, et vestiuntur pellibus pecudum, et assumunt capita bestiarum; qui vero taliter in ferinas species se transformant, III annos poeniteant; quia hoc daemoniacum est"*; "Whoever at the Kalands of January goes about in the form of a stag, that is, changes himself into the form of an animal, dressing in the skin of a horned beast, and putting on the head of a beast, for those who in such wise transform themselves into the appearance of a wild animal, penance for three years, because this is devilish." Yet, in spite of this and similar laws, the custom of the "Christmas Bull" or the "Wooser" was kept up in Dorset until the end of the 19th century; as witness the curious mask known as the "Dorset Ooser" illustrated in Margaret Murray's *God of the Witches,* and Elworthy's *Horns of Honour*. In that amusing little book, *Dorset Up-Along and Down-Along,* an account is given of this custom:

> The Bull, shaggy head with horns complete, shaggy coat, and eyes of glass, was wont to arrive, uninvited, at any Christmas festivity. None knew when he might or might not appear. He was given the freedom of every house, and allowed to penetrate into any room escorted by his keeper. The whole company would flee before his formidable horns, the more so as, towards the end of the evening, neither the bull nor his keeper could be certified as strictly sober. The Christmas Bull is now obsolete, but up to forty years ago he was a recognised custom. In some parts of West Dorset this creature was known as the Wooser, and there are those who tell us that he has his origin in devil-worship.

"The Kalands of January" was New Year's Day, which would of course, have fallen within the traditional Twelve Days of Christmas.

In all this period there is only one influence that I can think of which might have affected the Wica, beside their having received a name. That is when the Romans turned Christian, and all the disasters began to happen to the Roman Empire. A number of the more conservative type of Romans believed that all these disasters were a punishment for their deserting the old gods who had always given victory to Rome. They wished to ask pardon of these gods, but the Roman government and the priests had destroyed all the temples, or converted them to other uses. They would know of this little fertility cult of Britain and Western Europe. These were their own gods under other names, and so many of them would begin attending witch meetings, as the only way in which to enter into communion with their own old gods. Some of these at least would have belonged to the Dionysiac cults, others may have been, like Lucius Apuleius, initiates of Isis; and it is quite possible that they taught their Mysteries to the witches (for they seem to have possessed some at least of them, if we take the evidence of the villa of the Mysteries of which I have already spoken).

It is said that after the Norman Conquest, when there were numerous Saxon risings in out of the way parts, the Norman troops sent to suppress these were often led by "French-speaking witches." This can mean that the local witches were better educated than most, and spoke French; but it is more likely that Norman witches came over at the Conquest, fraternised with the dwellers on the heaths, the "heathens," the British people of the outlands who hated the Saxon usurpers, and found out what was going on. Hereward the Wake is said to have killed one of these witches who was helping to hunt him in the Fen country.

It was often said that the Normans kept witches as courtesans in their castles. I should imagine that this was quite likely. A Norman castle held a number of fighting men but not many women. As there was a sort of alliance between the castle and the people of the heath, it is probable that some soldiers did have British sweethearts. Being non-Christians they would not have a Christian marriage; but we must remember that outside the great families few had. William the Conqueror himself was the love-child of Robert the Devil, also called Robert the Magnificent, and a tanner's pretty daughter, Arlette or Harlotta, from whose name some say the word "harlot" comes. Many of the great men of the time were proud of the title of "Bastard." (When King Louis of France wished the Duc de Maine, one of his illegitimate sons, to succeed him, he had enquiry made, and it seemed that more than half of the kings of France had been born out of wedlock; so the Comte de St. Simon tells us. It was the Regent d'Orleans who put the legitimate heir on the throne, by force.)

When, on his gaining the realm of England, William the Conqueror was asked by Pope Gregory VII to do homage to him as King of England, he replied, "Fealty I have never willed to do, nor will I do it now. I have never promised it, nor do I find that my predecessors did it to yours"; a reply that must have increased his popularity with the witch cult as much as it pained the pious. His successor, William Rufus, lived to pain them even more, for he was an open pagan; and it may be noted in this connection that Rufus, although not the eldest son, inherited the throne because he was the Conqueror's favourite. Had the Church had its way, Rufus would never even have been born; for Pope Leo IX had curtly forbidden Baldwin, Count of Flanders, to give his daughter Matilda in marriage to William the Norman; but the couple wed in defiance of him. Historians have often puzzled over the reason for the Pope's action, as they have over the reason for the Conqueror's father being nicknamed "Robert the Devil." If William and his family were, to say the least of it, half-pagan, the puzzle is solved.

Chapter VII

Magic Thinking

Perhaps at this point it would be a good idea to ask the questions: "What is Magic? Why do people believe in it?"

Professor Nadel, formerly Professor of Anthropology and Sociology at the Australian National University, Canberra, gave a most interesting talk on the Third Programme of the B.B.C. on the 4th of January, 1956. He said, "In a word, magic attempts the physically impossible, and if this is so, then inevitably the believers in magic must be confronted again and again with evidence proving the failure of their magical efforts." He gives as evidence that rainmakers throw up water into the air so that it falls like rain, and when the rain does not come they see their charm does not work. But there is nothing "physically impossible" about rain falling. The Professor has started with a wrong definition. If magicians tried to make the rain fall upwards, for instance, they might be accused of attempting the physically impossible. What, however, they are trying to do in this instance, is to cause a natural phenomenon to occur as and when they wish it to do so. Modern science is constantly attempting the same thing.

I define magic as attempting to cause the physically unusual. Aleister Crowley defined it as "The Science and Art of causing Change to occur in conformity with the Will." S. L. MacGregor Mathers (Frater D.D.C.F. of the Order of the Golden Dawn) defined it as "The science of the control of the secret forces of nature."

Unfortunately, professors and others seem to get their ideas of magic from Grimm's Fairy Tales, where someone waves a wand and immediately the impossible happens. I doubt if the Grimm brothers had ever heard of rain-making; if they had, they might have described it something like this, "The magician threw a bowl of water into the air, so that it fell down in drops, waved his wand, and immediately rain descended from the cloudless sky." Now, although some curious things can be done with the right sort of wand, actually nothing is ever done like this.

Magic is, as I understand it, the art of getting results. Take a very crude example. If I make a wax image of a man in the proper manner, stick pins into it and roast it in the traditional way, and tell the man what I am doing, and he dies of fright; I contend that he died as the result of a magical act. If I tell him that I am doing this, without actually doing it, and he dies of fear, he is dead all the same, is he not? Now, if I, using the wax image as a point of focus, project what I am doing into his mind, without letting him know by word or deed, and he dies, I contend that his death is still the result of a magical act. In my Museum in the Isle of Man I have Australian Pointing Bones, Malayan Keris Majapahit, etc., which are used to kill by pointing. There seems to be incontestable proof that many people die annually as the result of their magical use; cases where the man has been taken to hospital and examined, and not the slightest trace of poison or anything which could cause death has ever been found. Though they often are frightened, everything has been done to reassure them, and they are sometimes quite happy, and show no signs of fright at all (and fear does cause certain psychological signs and has certain effects on the human body). They may not show these effects; but in a day or two their hearts stop beating, and the post-mortem cannot find the cause of death. (I should perhaps add, for the benefit of the nervous reader, that I am referring to happenings in Australia and Malaya, and not in the neighbourhood of my Museum!) Those interested may find further details in a little book called *Deadly Magic: including the Australian Pointing Stick,* by Colonel F. J. Hayter.

I have read that many people describe magic, or "attempted magic," as being performed by imitating the result required, i.e. "showing the Power what to do," and repeating a rhyme to make it work. I gather that they believe the imitation causes the effect to occur, when "triggered off," as it were, by a rhyme. I prefer to think that doing the imitative act, making the model of the thing, etc., are simply useful means of focusing the mind. This is reinforced and driven into the unconscious mind by a repetition of words (the Spell). This need not be in the form of a rhyme at all, but rhythm or alliteration are an aid to memory; that is, you cannot drive a thing into your unconscious and fix your mind pinpointed on your object if you have to stop and think what the next word is, and the act of reading distracts your attention, however slightly. In fact, you want something which almost says itself. I cannot for the moment think of a spell in limerick form, though doubtless they exist; but they almost say themselves, and the impact of the final rhyme should be very effective. Also, I think that the "spell" should have a decided reference to the work in hand, though some people say this is not necessary, and that words in an unknown tongue, especially "Enochian," as used by Dr. Dee and Edward Kelly (and later Aleister Crowley), or a string of words of unknown meaning, "the barbarous names of evocation," have the best effect; though to use them effectively you must learn them by heart that they may "say themselves" at the proper instant without any effort of memory. There is the witch practice of raising the power to the utmost and then clearly stating what is required, ending with a formula of which I may give the last two lines. It "says itself," ending like hammer blows with "As I will, so mote it be, chant the spell and Be it Done!" A magical practitioner who discovered this ending said to me sadly, "I like that so much more than our formulae. I am so tired of bleating, 'I demand this' and 'I demand that', ending tamely with 'If it be Thy Will' and 'Thy Will be done.'"

Mrs. Nesbit wrote many years ago that to work magic you must express your wish in original rhyme made up at the moment, and the worse the poetry the better the results; but I do not think she meant this to be taken seriously! (As with H. G. Wells' idea in one of his humorous stories that all ingredients in magical compounds must invariably be the worst, instancing that if an egg is called for in the recipe it must be addled.) However, this latter is not so silly as it seems, with regard to some kinds of magic. The late Aleister Crowley contended that sudden feelings of revulsion could have a great effect on some natures, and there is no doubt that he made the most extraordinary experiments in these directions. The "great Tantric secrets" which he used in his secret Order, the O.T.O. (Ordo Templi Orientis, or Order of Oriental Templars) were of this nature, and there is no doubt that he occasionally produced results, though I think this was because he himself had naturally exceptional powers; but he was fascinated by these, which I can only describe as revolting, practices, because they suited his nature. As he said to me once, "The witch practices are fine for people who like that sort of thing, people of that nature; but I like something I can wallow in and keep it up for eight hours at a time"; and I think he could. But he had to take an increasing amount of dangerous drugs to do so, and though he used these intelligently, and could stand heroic quantities, he suffered for this in the end. However, he was an old man when he died, and his intellect was unimpaired.

I wish here that I could nail the silly lie that Aleister Crowley was a "Satanist." Crowley, like most intelligent people, did not believe in Satan. (I might add that neither do I.) The statements I have read in "popular" articles about him, that he had "made a solemn pact with the Devil," and "sold his soul to Satan," are either sheer ignorance or journalistic invention. Crowley was born of parents who were narrow and exclusive Plymouth Brethren. As a boy, he revolted against the strictness of his upbringing until, as he says, "I practised wickedness furtively as a magical formula, even when it was distasteful; e.g. I would sneak into a church—a place my mother would not enter at the funeral service of her best-loved sister. (Church of England, because I confidently supposed that Anglicanism was a peculiarly violent form of Devil-Worship, and was in despair at being unable to discover where the Abomination came in.)" In 1898, when he was twenty-three, he joined the Hermetic Order of the Golden Dawn, which claimed descent from the original Rosicrucians. In this Order he learned magical practices which enabled him, in Cairo in 1904, to contact a powerful discarnate entity called "Aiwass," who dictated to him the two hundred and twenty verses of *Liber Legis, The Book of the Law.* Upon this document Crowley based his *Magick,* and indeed the rest of his life. It was from *Liber Legis* that he obtained his famous dictum, "Do what thou wilt shall be the whole of the Law. Love is the Law, Love under Will." This was not, however, an invitation to universal licence, and people who think it was thereby reveal the fact that that is what they would like to do if they could do what they would. Crowley maintained that "Every man and every woman is a star," and, like the stars in the heavens, each had a proper course appointed to them. This course he called the True Will; and he maintained that if everyone did their True Will there would be no trouble in the world. "The sun moves in space without interference. The order of Nature provides an orbit for each star. A clash proves that one or the other has strayed from its course." Therefore, he said, the proper task of man is to discover his True Will and do it; and he recommended his Magick as a means whereby one could discover one's True Will. He said further that the great aim of Magick should be to obtain the Knowledge and Conversation of one's Holy Guardian Angel, who would show the way. All other aims of Magick were side-issues, valuable only as they conduced to the great aim, the Great Work; and if they were pursued as ends in themselves, they became Black Magic. He took the title of "The Beast

666" because he believed that the Apocalypse, in which this interesting character is described, is a prophecy of the ending of one great Age and the beginning of another, and that he was the symbolical "Great Beast" who was to be the herald of the New Age, which he called the Aeon of Horus. Many other occultists, including those of such extreme respectability that they almost curl up and die whenever Crowley's name is mentioned, agree that we are now in the transition period between two great Ages, the Age of Pisces and the Age of Aquarius, and that this breaking-up of old forms of civilisation to make way for new ones is the reason for the world-wide strife and upheaval experienced in this century.

It will be seen that these matters bear no relation or resemblance whatsoever to the popular conception of "Satanism" so beloved by the writers of sensational fiction. And as there is nothing secret about these teachings of Crowley's (they being set forth plainly in all his major works), I can only conclude that the aforesaid writers and journalists either cannot understand the Queen's English, or else they continue to propagate this myth because they find it pays them better to titillate the public with thrills of delicious wickedness than to tell the unvarnished truth.

Crowley was a poet of remarkable power and invention, and many of his rituals were composed in verse; probably for the reasons set forth above. I sometimes wonder if the origin of poetry was from magic; some formula, possibly a blessing, more likely a curse, would be found efficacious. The Druids of ancient Ireland were said to have excelled in the use of poetry for magical purposes; legend tells that one of them composed such a lampoon on a mean and inhospitable king that it brought the king's face out in blisters, and there are a number of other Celtic stories of magical effects wrought by Druid songs. As we know in schools, the most prosaic lessons get repeated in a sort of sing-song, and they often fall into some sort of rhythm, the end words being distorted until they rhyme. This is employed instinctively when witches start repeating spells not laid down in rhyme. In the old days alliteration was also much used, but this was more frequent among practitioners who worked alone. Alliteration is difficult to write, and more difficult to remember. To say aloud "So mote it be," does not come with the same decisive hammer stroke as it does if it is the last line of a rhyme.

Between blessing and banning, it appeared to our ancestors there were many formulas which produced mysterious results if said with the correct intonation, which "tuned in" to the vibration they sought. You may say, "Oh, we know that some special tones have effects on you, that's not magic!" Exactly; but I understand magic is knowing that certain things have certain effects, and how to make use of these effects to render people more sensitive to certain other influences. Combining half a dozen or more of such influences—say dancing, chanting, incense, etc.—has effects which some people would say "work like magic."

One of these stories which is popular with writers of fiction is that of the person who finds a spell in some old book or manuscript and says it for fun, and a demon or spirit appears, or something happens. This I think is highly unlikely, because the most important part of any operation is the *belief,* nay, the firm *knowledge,* that it *can* be done and that you *can* and *will* do it. You may realise that it will not happen at once, and that perhaps you have not got the operation right, so that you may have to vary the spell to obtain the right one. In my own experience, the most important thing is *who* you are working with. You must be in absolute sympathy with them, and it is very seldom that you are in sympathy with people at once. You can only obtain this by working with them for some time. Of course, you may, and very often do, feel instinctively "I can work with that person," and the trap here is that this may be just physical attraction. However, if this is felt by all the persons concerned, it is more than likely that practising together will induce the magical sympathy. One must always remember what magic is and how it works. It is not a case of pressing a button or on turning a tap. It is *work,* and often hard work. For most things it would be easier to produce the results by ordinary methods of working in the usual mundane way; and it is, above all, not a way to make money. But there are just certain things which cannot be obtained by ordinary methods, and then *it works.*

The plain fact is that under modern conditions magic is not the help that it was at one time. Its uses become fewer and fewer. To the primitive man it was almost everything; the difference between a good life and starvation. And it also gave the feeling of safety and protection for which nowadays council houses with subsidised rents, family allowances, doles, free medical attention, false teeth and spectacles, are such a poor substitute.

For one thing, although the voters may think these things are wonderful, they do not give that spirit of wonder and romance which magic still gives even in these prosaic days; that curious mingling of excitement and calm which its votaries feel. Again, in these "ghastly, thin-faced times of ours" we are debarred from the emotional release that people used to obtain from the big dances. They were natural and simple, and "delivered the goods," shall we say? That is, they made people feel things that no modern artificial entertainment can give, and made their lives worth living. As De Lancre said of the Basques, "They talk of nothing but the last Sabbat, they look forward to nothing but the next." We are debarred from nearly all of this realm of natural joy nowadays. Instead, we get the movies, the Palais de Danse, and television.

In my own belief, there are some things that can be done by magic, and some that cannot, and I doubt whether rain can actually be caused to fall by magic. But it must be remembered that I know one type of magic well, and am therefore inclined to believe that all types work in much the same way; I may be mistaken on this point. Those spirits which magicians and Qabalists attempt to invoke or evoke may exist, and if they do, I suppose they could affect the weather. One class of such spirits are those called "elementals," that is, spirits inhabiting the "four elements" of the ancients, earth, air, fire and water. I do know that there are people who appear to believe that they can affect the weather. However, the witches tell me, "In the old days people would want the witches to 'make rain' or 'make dry weather', and of course we couldn't; but if we said so our influence was gone. Well, we were usually weather-wise, and we could sometimes get clairvoyantly what was going to happen. So it was a case of putting them off until we knew what was wanted would happen naturally. Then it would be safe to do some rite." It was no laughing matter, because in Africa the witch-doctor is sometimes killed (to encourage the others) if rain does not come. The African practice is to say, "The Gods withhold the rain because someone has done something wrong; someone is making evil magic, or has committed incest. We must hold a big meeting and smell them out, and they must be killed." I think the British witches had in self-defence to invent some story; the Gods were wrathful because the Church had stopped the big dances in the proper places, or something of that sort. Possibly it was not very ethical; but the priests, and even more so the Puritans, were always blaming every misfortune, from twins to swine fever, on to "the malice of witches," and, of course, claiming all good weather and all other good things as answers to their own prayers. There were no weather bureau records kept in those days, so, as nowadays, people were always saying that the weather was so much worse than it was when they were young, and there was much more swine fever about, and that they got more toothache and bellyache and rheumatics than they had done thirty years ago, and it was all the malice of those wicked witches. It is a pity that no one ever thought to ask, before they got out the thumbscrews and the faggots, "If you really believe all this, why don't you put up big prayers in church to amend these things?" And when they said, "But we do, regularly," to ask further, "Then do you really believe the witches are stronger than your God?"

Just sixty years ago, Hiram Maxim tells us *in Li Hung Chang's Scrap Book,* the celebrated Chinese statesman, Li Hung Chang, was in England on a diplomatic mission, and the weather was exceptionally dry. He was amazed to find that we were praying for rain in the churches, having thought that we believed in nothing but trade and big guns, and he asked a Bishop, "Does your God answer your prayers, for I see the ground seems all dried up?" He was told, "Sometimes God answers our prayers; sometimes, in His wisdom, He withholds these benefits, in His infinite goodness." And Li Hung Chang said, "That is very funny. All same like Chinese joss."

Another awkward situation for a witch was when someone in a high position would send for her and say, "I want some strong and secret poison, or I'll have you burnt." Now, the witches were great herbalists, and working with herbs you naturally know that certain things are very good medicine, but too large a dose will kill. Henbane, for instance, is good for asthma, but it is very strictly on the poison list. My wife was formerly a nurse at St. Thomas's Hospital. In the course of her training, many things relating to the proper handling of poisonous substances were impressed on her. "No nurse may give more than six drops of this; a doctor may give up to ten drops of that, and no more; everything of this nature must be kept locked up; the lethal dose of this so-and-so." In other words, in the language of journalese "This woman was given a course of secret instruction, in which she was taught the use of poisons." The interpretation of the use of words in journalese and propaganda is an important branch of anthropological research into such questions as these we are dealing with. As I have stated, witches did know poisons, and I expect that in early days they were pressed to supply them, like Shakespeare's "poor apothecary" in *Romeo and Juliet.* Quite possibly some of the earliest witch burnings were cases of those who refused. There is not the slightest doubt that many people who were famed as magicians, alchemists and astrologers did supply poisons, and it is more than likely that some astrologers helped their predictions that some important person would die with a "little dose." All druggists sold poisons as a matter of course. Italy was famous for poisoning. There are letters extant from the pious King Philip of Spain, the husband of "Bloody Mary" and of Armada fame, in which he discusses sending messengers to Italy for the best poisons. He wanted various people murdered, as executing them for no crime would cause scandal, and if they were knifed in the back the murderer might be caught, and say who employed him; King Philip disliked that sort of publicity. In Italy in the seventeenth century a woman named Tofani is said to have invented a tasteless and colourless poison which claimed over six hundred victims, in the way of unwanted husbands, too long-lived relatives, etc. before she was finally executed. It was sold in bottles marked "Manna of St. Nicholas of Bari," after the miraculous oil which was supposed to flow from the tomb of that saint. It was the day of the "Bravo" who would murder anyone at a price fixed according to their rank. There is a story told about a famous Spanish grandee who was dying; the priest was hearing his last confession prior to giving him absolution, and asked, "Have you forgiven your enemies?" "But I have no enemies, Father." "But my son, think, you are a great statesman; surely you must have made some enemies during your long career?" He was told firmly, "Father, I am a Santiago de Santiago. Do you think any man ever lived a day after he became my enemy? I have no enemies, father." Murder was the custom of the age, especially among the upper classes; so if a witch was ever forced to supply poison by threats of burning, let us not think too hardly of her.

Charles Godfrey Leland, in his *Gypsy Sorcery*, says (p. 178):

> It may be truly said that the Holy Fathers and Inquisitors first systemised and formulated Black Magic. Under such authority belief in it flourished, filling the people with abject fear or unholy curiosity. The formidable Council of Constance, and the Formicarium, gave the list of witch crimes as 'Second Sight; Ability to Read Secrets and Foretell Events; Power to Cause Diseases, Death by Lightning, and Destructive Storms; to Transform Themselves into Birds and Beasts; to Bring Illicit Love; Barrenness of Living Beings and Crops; and the Devouring of Children'.

This Council had apparently never heard the yarn of witches flying on broomsticks, or they would doubtless have added that as well. Now, this Council was assembled by the Emperor Sigismund, and lasted from All

Saints Day, 1414, to late in 1418, three and a half years. It was primarily to put an end to the schism caused by the number of rival Popes. At this time there were three: Balthasar Cossa, called Pope John XXIII; Pedro di Luna, called Pope Benedict XIII; and Angelo Corrario, called Pope Gregory XII. Expecting trouble, one Archbishop alone brought six hundred horse soldiers with him. Others did much the same, so finally regulations were made limiting Cardinals to ten, Bishops to five, and Abbots to four horsemen, because of the extreme shortage of provender caused. It was this Council which gave John Huss a "safe conduct" to come before them and explain his views. He was foolish enough to trust them, and was promptly burned alive. John Wycliffe's religious ideas were condemned, and as he was dead his bones were ordered to be dug up and desecrated. Jerome of Prague, who had come with Huss, was so terrified at Huss's terrible fate that he recanted his "errors." He was excommunicated, anathematised, and then burned alive. The Council deposed all three Popes and elected a new one, Cardinal Colonna, as Pope Martin V, and made arrangements not to have more than one Pope at a time in future. Such was the type of Council whose decisions encouraged people to believe in black magic and witchcraft and all kinds of superstition.

For instance, in 1571 a travelling conjurer exhibited several quite simple card tricks in Paris. He was tortured until he confessed that he had attended a witches' Sabbat. He was then burned and as the result of what he said a number of people were burned on the same charge. Actually, it seems likely that what he said was dictated under torture, and possibly a number of innocent persons were burned in consequence. Between 1580 and 1595 over nine hundred people were burned alive in Lorraine alone, and a vast number fled the country, because of a witchcraft scare.

At the same time, an interest in occultism as apart from the old pagan tradition of witchcraft was more or less secretly followed by many of the nobility and even by Princes of the Church. For instance, in spite of the fact that in 1423 St. Bernardino of Siena had preached against Tarot cards at Bologna, calling them an invention of the Devil, in 1484 the famous miniaturist Antonio Cicognara was commissioned to paint a most beautiful pack of these cards for presentation as a gift to Cardinal Ascanio Sforza. Some cards from this magnificent pack were put on show in America in 1954. It is true that the Tarot cards could be used merely for gaming, but their greatest use, as occult students know, is for divination.

The sinister Queen Catherine de Medici (she who had the Protestants massacred on St. Bartholomew's Eve) was noted for her interest in the occult arts. It was whispered that her favourite son, King Henri III of France, was devoted to black magic. This may, of course, have been merely a political rumour spread to discredit him, as he was highly unpopular; but it seems quite likely that Queen Catherine did in fact instruct him in her occult practices, and after his death his curious magical instruments were publicly exhibited.

He was eventually assassinated, and supplanted by Henri IV, a prince who took life and religion much more light-heartedly than Queen Catherine or her son. He was originally a Protestant, but on being advised that he would be more acceptable as king if he changed his religion, exclaimed, "Paris is worth a Mass," and became converted. However, he too died at the hands of an assassin, leaving his son, Louis XIII, still a minor, and his Queen, Marie de Médici, who ruled as Regent. Once again the shadow of sorcery fell across the French Royal House. The Queen Regent, to the despair and chagrin of the nobles came utterly under the domination of two base-born Italian adventurers, Leonora Galigai and her husband Concini, for whom Leonora, the stronger personality of the two, lost no time in obtaining the title of Maréchal D'Ancre. Leonora, while nominally the Queen's Lady-in-Waiting, actually exercised such influence over the Queen that she and her husband practically ruled France, and amassed an enormous fortune. She seems to have been one of those strange personalities who, like Rasputin, possessed the power of casting a kind of hypnotic glamour over others. Soon her husband Concini was loaded with honours, while the sixteen-year-old King was kept virtually a prisoner. Again, like Rasputin, it was rumoured that the serpent-eyed Leonora practised black magic, and that it was this which gave her extraordinary ascendancy over the Queen.

The young king, becoming desperate, conspired with some of his nobles to assassinate Concini, and one of them shot the Maréchal dead. He was hastily interred, but the Paris mob, by whom he was hated for his oppressions, dragged the body from its grave and hung it on the gibbet which Concini had erected on the Pont Neuf, to intimidate all who ventured to oppose him; and so bitter was the rage against the Maréchal that after the symbolic hanging his body was cut in pieces and actually sold to anyone who wished to buy. That, at least, is one explanation for this scene of macabre horror; but another is, it is said, Concini being esteemed as a powerful sorcerer, such grim relics were believed in themselves to possess some magical virtue.

The King, having regained his liberty, sent a company of archers to arrest Leonora Galigai and take her to the Bastille. She was brought to trial, accused of sorcery. It was deposed that some books in Hebrew had been found in her apartments (which may possibly have been grimoires), and one of her servants said that he had accompanied her to a church in order to make a sacrifice of a cockerel there at midnight. Every man's hand was, of course, against the fallen favourite; but it does seem that the Maréchale associated with an Italian Jewish doctor named Montalo, who was a reputed sorcerer, and that she consulted a fortune-teller and carried charms upon her person. She was, of course, found guilty, and condemned to be beheaded and burned on the Place de Greve, on the 8th July, 1617.

Her reply to the charge of sorcery is memorable. "My sorcery," she said, "has been the power which those who are strong of mind are bound to possess over the feeble-spirited." (*"Mon sortilège a été le pouvoir que doivent avoir les âmes fortes sur les ésprits faibles."*) Seeing her portrait (and she was certainly not remarkable either for beauty or pleasantness of expression), and recollecting these words, one feels a little sorry for Queen Marie de Médici.

Leland says,* "There is a strong tradition that the Popes have been practising witchcraft ever since the tenth century, and that Pope Sylvester II confessed to this on his death-bed." Here, however, Leland fails to appreciate the distinction between ceremonial magic and witchcraft proper, as so many writers do. Both Catherine de Medici and Leonora Galigai may have been sorceresses; but they were far too good Catholics to be pagan witches. *Ceremonial magic, black or white, the magic of the grimoires, is something quite different from witchcraft, and has behind it quite a different set of ideas.* Some of these ideas date back to Ancient Egypt, and examples of them may be found, in the papyri of that land; but in the form in which they were known and practised in the Middle Ages they were definitely Christian in outlook and phraseology. However, this was but a cast which they had been given in translation, for they are based upon the Jewish secret tradition, the Qabalah. To explain here the ideas of that great tradition would be a hopeless task; it requires a book to itself, and some good

* Op. Cit. p. 188.

preliminary elucidations of it may be found in *The Mystical Qabalah,* by Dion Fortune, and *The Kabalah Unveiled,* by S. L. MacGregor Mathers. Briefly, it may be said that ceremonial magic of this type works upon the premise that spirits, evil or good, may be commanded by the knowledge and use of those Holy Names, whether of God or of the angels and archangels, which that particular spirit is bound to fear and revere, by reason of its occult affinity and subjection to them. When evil spirits are evoked, they are commanded and constrained by the Holy Names of God to do the magician's will. Hence the saying "A name to conjure with." The word "conjure" really means "to swear with," or "to take oath with." It is not always evil spirits who are called forth; but nevertheless the beings who answer the magician's call or conjuration are generally considered as being tricksy, if nothing worse, and the magician is enjoined in the grimoires, or books of magic, to stand within a circle about which are written sacred names and sigils, so that the circle constitutes a kind of astral fortress. If a visible appearance of the entity evoked is desired, then a triangle is drawn outside the circle, and the spirit is constrained to appear within the triangle. One often sees fanciful representations in art of a scene of ceremonial magic which show the robed magician standing *outside* the circle, and the demon or spirit appearing *within it.* This is, according to the practice laid down in the grimoires, quite absurd.

Those familiar with the legends of Ancient Egypt will remember the belief of the Egyptians in the "hekau" or "words of power" by which discarnate entities, and even gods and godlings, might be compelled. Isis is said in one legend to have acquired her power by obtaining and using the *secret name* of the Supreme God Ra. This, of course, leads us back to yet more primitive beliefs, such as that which makes some savages reluctant to tell anyone their real name, in case it might be used to make magic against them. They prefer to be called by a nick-name.

The Qabalistic magic of names seems rooted in the Hebrew legend that King Solomon by his great wisdom discovered the Words of Power, the Secret Names of God, and bequeathed his knowledge to his son Rehoboam. This is the alleged origin of what might be called the classic grimoire, "The Clavicule (or Key) of Solomon," which purports to be the actual document which King Solomon left as a legacy to his son. There are a number of different editions of this work. Its companion-piece is a work called "The Lamegeton, or Lesser Key of Solomon" (sometimes called

"The Goetia"), which purports to be an account of the seventy-two rulers of evil spirits whom the good King Solomon, for the benefit of mankind, bound in a brazen vessel and cast into the sea. By the folly of later generations this vessel was fished up again and the fiends allowed to escape; but the seals which Solomon compelled the demon princes to give him are contained in the "Lemegeton," and by these curious sigils, and the magical procedure and Names of Power given with them, they may yet, says the book, be bound to do the will of the magician.

I know personally a man who told me that he recently succeeded in evoking to visible appearance one of the spirits of the "Lemegeton." This spirit has appeared to him on more than one occasion, and spoken to him. Whether, of course, the appearance would have been visible and audible to a third person I do not know. The appearance of the spirit was somewhat different from that laid down in the grimoire; though according to Aleister Crowley, who also practised the evocation of these spirits, this is not unusual. The interest, I think, lies in what the spirit is alleged to have said. It gave its name in what later proved to be the correct Hebrew spelling, and told the operator that creatures of its kind were not necessarily either "good" or "evil"; they were just *different.* That is, they were on a different plane of evolution to that of the human race, and consequently it was misleading to classify them by human standards as being either "good" or "evil" spirits. For this reason also, intercourse between them and humans was not always healthy. The spirit did not seem to be particularly malignant. Its appearance was that of a being the height and build of a tall, strong man, but covered with what looked like shining scales, and having a head with what seemed to be either small, faun-like horns or high, pointed ears.

The two grimoires mentioned above are the source-books for most of the other magical books of this and later periods, which either copy and adapt them, or at any rate closely resemble them. Some light upon how such books came into Christian hands is thrown by the preface to a manuscript copy of the "Key" in the British Museum (Lansdowne MSS. 1203): "This Testament was in ancient time translated from the Hebrew into the Latin language by Rabbi Abognazar, who transported it with him into the town of Arles in Provence, where by a notable piece of good fortune the ancient Hebrew Clavicule, that it to say this precious translation of it, fell into the hands of the Archbishop of Arles, after the destruction of the Jews in that city; who, from the Latin, translated it into the vulgar tongue, in the same terms which here follow, without having either changed or augmented the original translation from the Hebrew."

During the Middle Ages many learned Christians, notably Pico de Mirandola, studied the Jewish Qabalah, ostensibly "to bring about the conversion of the Jews"; but actually to gain knowledge of its magical practices, which they then proceeded to give a Christian veneer to, so that later grimoires not only use the Hebrew Qabalistic Names of God and of the archangels to constrain the spirits, but also the names of Jesus, Mary, and the Apostles.

The Wica seem to have been taught certain beliefs, most probably by the Kabalists, which they have incorporated into their own.

One of these beliefs is that there were two parties, or sects, in ancient Israel, which might be compared to our modern English "High Church" of Charles I's time and the Puritans, and the Kings of Israel did what they believed or found politically convenient. That is, they built "High Places" and "Groves" and worshipped there.

Then the next King would give in to the Puritan Party and would cause them to be destroyed. Then his son and heir on succeeding would promptly reinstate them.

During their periods of power, the puritanical sect seem to have been able to interpolate various sayings into the "Sacred Writings" which favoured their aims. Finally in the reign of Josiah, who was particularly superstitious and credulous, the High Priest Hilkiah pretended to find a new roll of the Mosaic Law, which during all the three hundred years the Temple had been built, no one had ever heard of.

While it was perfectly possible for interested parties at times to add a few lines to the end of an existing Roll, it is perfectly impossible that there could be any unknown roll in the archives at a period when interested priests of both sides were continually going through the Rolls, seeking to find some passage which would back up their opinions.

But the High Priest managed to frighten the King in order to force him to disgrace his party's opponents.

As is told in II. Kings, XXII. II. the King was terrified and rent his garments, and said, "Go ye, enquire of the Lord . . . concerning this book that is found: for great is the wrath of the Lord that is kindled against us, because our fathers have not hearkened unto the words of this book." So it is obvious that this Roll consisted of threats of the vengeance of the Lord against those who worshipped in the old manner, Astroth in the Temple, where Solomon placed her, the way which Hilkiah and his party wished to suppress.

Being thus frightened, King Josiah did as the New Roll commanded, giving full power to the Puritanical faction, and he performed all the destruction as told in II. Kings, XXIII. "And like unto him was there no King before him, that turned to the Lord with all his heart, and with all his might, according to all the law of Moses: neither after him arose there any like him."

Now the Kabalists very plausibly say, "The Bible is full of stories of people who did the will of the Lord and prospered. And the country prospered also. And of those who worked against the will of the Lord, and met sudden death in consequence, and the land also suffered from the Wrath of God."

And they say this is a case in point, because of Hilkiah's "Pius Forgery" and of the Kings favouring the Puritanical party. As we are told in the next verse, II. Kings, XXIII, 26. "The Lord turned not from the fierceness of his wrath, wherewith his anger was kindled against Judah . . ." and in verse 27, ". . . I will cast off this City of Jerusalem which I have chosen, and the house of which I said, 'My Name shall be there.'" And verse 29 tells us how Josiah was promptly killed at Megiddo by Pharaoh who laid the whole country under heavy tribute of gold and silver, and took the King's son prisoner to Egypt where he died. Another son, Jehoiakim, succeeded, but Nebuchadnezzar later took him and all his family and all his mighty men and all his artisans, and all his treasures to captivity in Babylon.

Some at least of the Kabalists believed that the true story behind all these curious happenings was that Hilkiah and his party were secretly bribed by Babylon with promises of lavish tythes and unlimited power over the people to cause religious disunion in the land so that it might easily become prey to Babylon. Some of them think that the forged book was afterwards written into Deuteronomy, Chaps. 4, XXVI, XXVII.

Others think it was discreetly "abolished" as soon as it had done its work. It will be readily understood that the Wica are naturally interested in stories like this which showed the "dirty work" of the people who oppressed them, and the Kabalists, who secretly worshipped the Goddess.

Chapter VIII

Magic Thinking (Continued)

Now, these ideas and procedures, while ancient enough (the magical works of Solomon are mentioned by Josephus), are as things of yesterday compared with the ideas behind witch practices, which, as I have been trying to show, date from the Stone Age. Though the basic idea of "the magic of the name" may be primitive, and though similar techniques—though, of course, using different God-Names—were known to the Ancient Egyptians, the ceremonial magic which has come down to us from the Middle Ages is a highly sophisticated tradition, which requires a certain amount of education in order to work it. It also needs elaborate preparations and paraphernalia; and it is definitely Judeo-Christian in language and outlook. The witch tradition, on the other hand is not Christian or Jewish; it could be worked and was, by people who could neither read nor write; and its paraphernalia are of the simplest. The witches' circle is not cast to keep the demons out, because no demons are evoked; it is cast to keep the "power" *in*. They share a belief in "the power of the name" to the extent that they do not like their Gods to be named unnecessarily, nor for Their names to be divulged; but this belief as we have seen, springs from a very primitive level of human development and instances of it can be found in almost all human societies. The witches' practices of ritual dancing, "initiative magic," etc., are much more primitive in form than the solemn and elaborate rites of the ceremonial magician. Ceremonial magic was a pursuit of "clerks" and noblemen; the witch belonged essentially to the people, though the tradition might be handed down here and there in an ancient and noble family.

However, some practitioners of ceremonial magic, though they may not have belonged to witch covens themselves, nevertheless knew of their existence, and sometimes got witches to assist them as clairvoyants. In return, they would help and shelter the witch in times of persecution; and the witch, when poor, would obtain good, well-made magical weapons and implements from the magician. I have described in fiction the working of such a "gentlemen's agreement" in my novel, *High Magic's Aid.*

One thing, however, I must emphasise. I know of no grimoire which enjoins the magician to hail Satan as God, or to worship the Powers of Evil. Debased, stupid and blasphemous as the ideas contained in the more unpleasant grimoires may seem to us today, they are not the practice of "Satanism" as described in sensational fiction. Their basic idea is to invoke God and His angels to compel the demons to serve the magician, sometimes for thoroughly ungodly ends. In the higher type of grimoire, however, the practitioner is solemnly warned against using the knowledge contained in it for evil, and told that if he does so the evil will rebound on himself.

Pope Honorius III, who preached the Crusades, is alleged to be the author of a famous grimoire to evoke spirits, the use of which was reserved exclusively to priests. We have a copy of *The Grimoire of Honorius* in the Museum. It is much the same as all grimoires; it is diabolical in the sense that it tells you how to evoke demons and force them to work for you. Personally, I doubt whether an evil spirit could be induced to do good for anyone. It has a preamble purporting to be a Papal Bull of Honorius III addressed to the priests of the Church, entrusting them with the methods of controlling devils. Whether this is authentic or not, the grimoire is evidently intended for the use of priests, because some of its requirements could only be carried out by an ordained priest. For instance, it specifies that the operator "should rise in the middle of the night on the first Monday of the month, and say one Mass of the Holy Ghost. After the consecration, he takes the Host in his left hand, and, being on his knees, he speaks thus: (and here follows a long prayer to Jesus Christ to "vouchsafe to Thine unfortunate servant, who now holds Thy Body in his hand, the strength and power to apply his strength against the rebelled spirits"). This is followed by the sacrifice of a black cock, after sunrise, and the next day, at daybreak, a Mass of the Angels is celebrated. A feather of the sacrificed cock is to be on the altar, and beside it a new knife. Taking the consecrated wine, the master then writes with it certain figures on a piece of virgin paper which is resting on the altar. When the Mass is over, the document is wrapped in a piece of new violet-coloured silk, together with the Oblation and a part of the consecrated Host. The sacrifice of a male lamb, and the recital of various psalms and litanies are called for, ending with the Mass for the Dead, and detailed instructions are then given for the evocation and control of devils.

According to Leland, a printed edition of the Grimoire of Pope Honorius was published in Rome in 1629. "It is not Kabalistic, and is permeated with Christian ideas, and is accompanied by a copy of a Papal Bull permitting its use."

It is noteworthy that Pope Honorius III in 1223 wrote to the Archbishop of Canterbury urging him to give an English benefice to Michael Scott the wizard. The Archbishop offered Michael the Archbishopric of Cashel in Ireland; this he refused because he had no knowledge of Irish. It was a great position, and much to his credit that he refused it because he thought himself unfitted for the post. Michael Scott was evidently highly esteemed at the Vatican, as in 1227 Pope Gregory IX, the successor of Honorius, again made overtures on his behalf.

In 1611 a priest named Father Godfrey was arrested on a charge of corrupting several women, and of being present at several witches' Sabbats. The Abbe of Poponsa, who wrote an account of the trial, says, "The process contained many depositions upon the power of demons. . . . Several witnesses said that after being anointed with oil Godfrey transported himself to the Sabbat (no broomstick?) and afterwards returned by the shaft of the chimney to his chamber. One day when these depositions were being read to the Parliament and the imaginations of the judges excited by a long recital of supernatural events, there was heard an extraordinary noise; then a tall man in black suddenly appeared in the fireplace. The judges, thinking it was the Devil come to rescue his disciple, all fled, except Councillor Thornton their reporter, whose gown got caught in his desk. Terrified at being, as he thought, caught by another devil, he tremblingly made the sign of the cross, with his eyes starting from their sockets, as the tall man approached, bowed, and apologised, explaining that he was the chimney sweep, who, having swept the chimneys of Monsieur des Comptes, whose chimneys adjoined the Tournelle, had by mistake descended into the Parliament Chamber." Now, this points, incidentally, to very big chimneys which intercommunicated, so it is quite possible that at times people who wished to go in and out unobserved might do so via the chimney, thus getting into the house next door. It is possible that Godfrey did this, though it is no proof he was going to a Sabbat; he might simply have been calling on one of the women whom he was accused of debauching. Highwaymen and others are well known to have been captured hiding in chimneys. It was probably a well-known practice for athletic people to use them, and may even account for the "Father Christmas" legend. As they burned firewood, and not coal, it would not be too unpleasant climbing about these chimneys.

Priests did use magic in those days. Leland gives the spell pronounced by Sir John Rowell, priest of Corstophine in Scotland, against thieves who had raided his poultry yard, calling upon these demons to torment them: "Gorog, Harog, Sym, Skynar, Devetinus, the Devil that made the Dyce, Firemouth, Cocodame, Tutuvillus, Browney and Syr Garnage." He does not give the date, but it was probably before Mary Queen of Scots passed the first law against magic and witchcraft in Scotland, in 1563, "That na manner of person nor persones of quatsumever estait, degree or condition they be of, take upon hand in onie times hereafter to use onie maner of witchcraft, sorcerie or necromancie, under the paine of death, als weil to execute against the user, abuser, or seeker of the response of consultation."

At first sight it seems curious to some that the Church did not object to ceremonial magic, while they persecuted the witch. I think the only answer is that the Church practised this kind of magic itself, and it knew that witchcraft practised a different form of magic because it was a separate religion, and that it involved the carrying on of a tradition of practices by certain families and groups of people who could only obtain knowledge of these practices by secret initiations or family teachings; and the Church hated and dreaded these traditions as belonging to a deadly rival.

Totemism existed among Stone Age people, and they handed down secret traditions from one generation to another. It is most probable that the Mysteries of Egypt, Sumeria, Eleusis, Samothrace, the Cabiri, Bacchus, etc., were merely elaborations of these primitive traditions. It would appear that throughout the ages there has been a fusion of occult beliefs. It has long been an article of belief promulgated by various mystic societies, offshoots of the Blavatsky tradition, that the secrets of wonderful sciences have been handed down from generation to generation, to modern times, by a series of "Adepts," of the Theosophist persuasion. While I doubt this latter part, I think that a secret tradition has been handed down; but it depends on how you define an "Adept." This is usually taken to mean some wonderful man, and they give the names of Francis Bacon, the Comte de St. Germain, Roger Bacon and others. But even allowing that these were "Adepts," they cannot say from whom they received their "Adeptship," and to whom they passed it in turn, and I would like authentic information on this subject. However, if it is the case that certain knowledge was passed on by quite ordinary people, as a secret and sacred, I think it is most probable. There were many such lines of transmission, whose possessors met and discussed their traditions, and from finding themselves in contact, or even in conflict, with each other, these people received each other's ideas. Greek and Roman writers, and even those of a later date, have said "That when the ancient mysteries are spoken of, it should be understood that one and the same series of ceremonies are intended, one and the same initiatory processes and revelations, and what is true of one applies with equal certainty to all. Thus Strabo says the strange orgies in honour of the mystic birth of Jupiter resembled those of Bacchus, with those of Ceres, Rhea, Venus, and Isis. Euripides says the rites of Cybele are celebrated in Asia Minor, and are identical with the Greek mysteries of Adonis, Dionysus, and the Cretan rites of the Cabiri." Now, we have a great deal of proof that these ancient mystics were in possession of much occult wisdom, and magical or semi-magical practices, and that when the Mysteries were destroyed in about the Fourth Century, and prohibited from functioning in public, it is only natural to expect that they would go underground, and continue in the lower ranks of society, which everywhere are the most conservative. The origin of the word "pagan" is from the Latin word "paganus," meaning a villager or peasant; and the word "heathen" is Anglo-Saxon, meaning "a dweller on the heath."

Rites which were intended to be performed in a huge temple might, slightly modified, be performed on a deserted heath, which meant that people would have to go some distance to attend. Now, the most convenient place for many people to attend secretly was often a crossroads, where people could come from all directions, and this is the more appropriate as crossroads are sacred to Diana in her form of Hecate, the Goddess of Witchcraft. It is noteworthy that early mentions of witchcraft often say that witches assemble at the crossroads, and that the witch Goddess is the Goddess of the Moon and Night. Though she has many names, she is closely identified with Diana, for is she not the consort of the old Hunting God? Lewis Spence, in *The Encyclopedia of Occultism*, speaks of Bensozia, "Chief Deviless of certain Sabbatic meetings held in France in the 12th and 13th centuries. She was the Diana of the ancient Gauls, and was also called Nocticula, Herodias, and the Moon. He says one finds in the manuscripts of the church at Couserans that ladies of the 14th century were said to go on horseback to the nocturnal revels of Bensozia. All of them were forced to inscribe their names in a Sabbatic catalogue along with those of witches proper, and after this ceremony they believed themselves to be fairies. There was found at Montmorillon in Poitou, in the eighteenth century, a portion of an ancient temple, a bas relief with the figure of a naked woman carved upon it, thought to be the original deity of the Bensozia cult." Violet Alford and Rodney Gallop, writing in *Folklore,* Vol. XLVI, 1935, on "Traces of a Dianic Cult from Catalonia to Portugal," say:

> The church porch at Moissac (on the Garonne near Agen), shows a carving of a naked woman, a toad serving in lieu of a fig-leaf, and a devil by her side; another, on a wall at Castel-gaillard, shows a woman galloping on a lance. Du Mège wished to transport this to Toulouse Museum, but the inhabitants of the village refused to let it go, saying that if they were deprived of it hail would destroy their harvest, and the river would come down in flood. (*De Mège, Archëologie Pyrénénne, Toulouse, 1858*).

There is no word in French exactly corresponding to our "witch," which in the original Anglo-Saxon possessed two forms, "wicca," (masculine), and "wicce," (feminine). The French used the word "sorcier" for both sorcerer and witch, the feminine form being "sorcière." "Sorcellerie" can be usually translated as "witchcraft." The ladies who went on horseback as stated above presumably came long distances. Being forced to write their names, I take simply to mean that they were told, "If you want to come again, you must be one of us, that is, be initiated, and then you will be a fairy." Now, in France, as in Scotland, a large number of people spoke of "fairies" when they obviously meant witches. It was a more polite term, and in Scotland any communication with "fairies" was taken as an admission of dealing with witches, that is, with the "heathen," the People of the Heaths, who practised the Old Religion and worked magical rites. To sum up, there were great festivals in honour of the Naked Goddess of the Moon, to which, while the common people may have walked, and would all have been neighbours and known to each other, the nobles (for I think it unlikely that these ladies came without male escort) came on horseback. As there was persecution about, they had to be vouched for when they came for the first time, and their names recorded, so that they could come again as members of the cult who had done some act of worship to the Goddess; then, if they were spies, they would have trouble with the Church, because they had become "fairies," that is, witches, and adored the Witch Goddess.

The "Romance of the Rose," composed at the end of the thirteenth century, has this half-jesting, half-serious account of these "night-riding witches":

Maintes gens, par lor folie,
Cuident estre par nuit estries
Errans avecques dame Habonde;
Et dient, que par tout le monde
Li tiers enfant de nacion
Sunt de cest condicion,
Qu'il vont trois fois en la semaine,
Si cum destinée les maine,
Et par tous ces ostex se boutent,
Ne clés ne barres ne redoutent,
Ains s'en entrent par les fendaces,
Par chatieres et par crevaces,
Et se partent des cors les ames,
Et vont avec les bonnes dames
Par lius forains et par maisons:
Et le presevent par tiex raisons,
Que les diversités veues
Ne sunt pas en lors liz venues.

The above verse, in its quaint old French, is an allusion to the well-known Decree of the Council of Ancyra, referring to "Certain wicked women, reverting to Satan, and seduced by the illusions and phantasms of demons, (who) believe and profess that they ride at night with Diana. . . ." This decree was echoed in an episcopal statute of Auger de Montfaucon, 1279–1304, which says, *Nulla mulier se nocturnis equitare cum Diana paganorum, vel cum Herodiade seu Bensozia, et in numina multitudinem profiteatur.*" It will be noted as a curious fact that the Church here appears to be maintaining that the stories of riding on horseback to the Sabbat to worship the Witch Goddess were all "illusions and phantasms of demons," and people are enjoined not to believe in them. This was in fact the official teaching of the early Church for many years, until it was realised that this attitude was untenable, when it was conveniently discovered that this decree of the Council of Ancyra was in fact apocryphal, and instead the people were warned that the Sabbat was real after all, and that it was a deadly sin *not* to believe in it! Many documents illustrating this *volte-face* on the part of the Church are quoted in H. C. Lea's *Materials Toward a History of Witchcraft*, to which I refer the reader for the details of this rather amusing sidelight on the infallibility of the Church's teaching about witchcraft. (See Appendix 4.)

"Dame Habonde" was Abundia, the Goddess of Fertility, and "Bensozia" was "Bona Socia," "The Good Neighbour." All these terms are titles of the Witch Goddess, and euphemisms for her real name, even as her followers, the witches, are referred to as "les bonnes dames." Other terms for the Goddess were "La Reine Pedauque," the Queen with the Goose-Foot (the "goose-foot" being itself a euphemism for her sign, the Pentagram); and "Frau Hilde" or "Holda" in the Teutonic countries. Dr. W. Wagner's *Asgard and the Gods: the Tales and Traditions of Our Northern Ancestors* says of Holda "... that those who were crippled in any way were restored to full strength and power by bathing in her Quickborn (fountain of life) and that old men found their vanished youth there once more." This is precisely the witches' Goddess of Rebirth and Resurrection; and it is the same tale which was told about the magical cauldron of the Ancient British Goddess, Cerridwen. The inner meaning in both cases is the same; the Goddess's gift is rebirth in a new body, reincarnation. "With sturdier limbs and brighter brain, the old soul takes the road again."

Incidentally, this may be the inner meaning of the old British tale of Avalon, the Place of Apples. Every old Celtic tale speaks of the afterworld as a place of apple-trees, but nobody seems to know just why. If the reader cares to make the experiment of slicing an apple across, he will see the answer: the core forms the sign of the Pentagram, the symbol of the Goddess of Rebirth and Resurrection. "Avalon" was the place where souls went to rest between incarnations on earth. To this day, in the witch ritual, the Priestess first stands with her arms crossed on her breast and her feet together, to represent the God of Death, and then opens out her arms and stands with feet apart to represent the Goddess of Resurrection. In this position the human body resembles the figure of the Pentacle, or Pentagram. Because it was the place from which the old and weary soul was reborn in a young body, with its strength and courage renewed; Avalon was also called in the Celtic "Tir-nan-Og," the land of Youth.

Wagner, in *Asgard and the Gods* (1880), points out that Holda resembles another Goddess of Resurrection, Ostara, who, according to the Venerable Bede, gave her name to our festival of Easter. She was the Goddess of Spring, but her legends are nowhere recorded,

> One monument alone, and that a newly-discovered one, remains of the old worship, the Extern-stones, which are to be found in the Teutoberg Forest at the northern end of the wooded hills. It is stated in the chronicle of a neighbouring village, dating from last century, that the ignorant peasantry were guilty of many misdemeanours there when doing honour to the heathen goddess Ostara. . . . The rocks may perhaps have been called Eastern or Eostern-stones, and may have been dedicated to Ostara. There, as elsewhere, the priests and priestesses of the goddess probably assembled in heathen times, scattered Mayflowers, lighted bonfires, slaughtered the creatures sacrificed to her, and went in procession on the first night of May, which was dedicated to her. . . . Edicts were published in the eighth century forbidding these practices; but in vain, the people would not give up their old faith and customs. Afterwards the priestesses were declared to be witches, the bonfires, which cast their light to great distances, were said to be of infernal origin, and the festival of May was looked upon as the witches' sabbath.

If animals were slaughtered at these festivals it was probably for the mundane purpose of providing something to eat, which the bonfires served to cook; because no witch meeting was, or is, complete without a convivial meal of some kind. When people had come some considerable distances to a meeting-place, they wanted a substantial meal, and the meat and drink were part of the attraction of the witches' sabbaths. The Church tried to dispel this dangerous attraction by spreading the story that the meat and drink of the witches were actually all kinds of horrible and disgusting substances, in order to make the Sabbat sound repulsive, so that people would not wish to go to it. But the very monstrosity of these stories defeats its own ends; because what people on earth would get out of their warm beds at night and go long distances for the exquisite pleasure of eating muck and kissing a billy-goat *a tergo*? The common people went to the witches' Sabbats for one natural and understandable reason; because they had a jolly good time there.

I think it is worth noting that, while most of the pictures illustrating the works of the opponents of witchcraft seem at first sight to be works of phantasy and imagination, if not of madness, on going through a number with a witch, we both noticed various things which were right.

Actually, it was as if the man who made the drawing had been present and seen something he did not understand, or possibly had talked to someone who had seen it. (Of course he may have been present at the trials.)

Most of these things I may not speak about. But I may mention this. I was puzzled, at first, by the great number of these pictures which showed the skeletons of animals, usually with some fragments of flesh still on them. They are generally depicted as if they were alive and moving. I used to think these were simply to make the picture horrible until I was present at a witch party in a wood when they "Barbecued" a whole sheep over a bonfire (and mighty good it was too). This was roasted whole, on a huge iron spit, and when done the flesh was sliced off the bones. It was a weird sight, with the flames lighting up the trees, and I suddenly saw the framework of the sheep, through the bonfire, its ribs bare, the bones of the four feet hanging down. The flickering of the fire and smoke made it seem to move as if it were alive, and it was exactly as the old "Witch pictures" showed it, excepting this had no head, and it is quite possible that in the old days they may have barbecued it with the head on.

It is noteworthy that Joan of Arc at her trial freely admitted dancing round "the Fairy Tree." One of her companions who thus honoured "the fairies" was burned as a witch in Joan's lifetime. In the beginning of her career there was a plot among the men of the French army to assassinate her because she was a witch. All through her history she seems to have been advised and guided by a number of persons. Some have thought that this must have been a powerful secret society. Of course, she said that they were "saints," St. Michael and St. Catherine, both of whom are old divinities in Christian disguise; St. Michael taking the place of the Sun-God, and St. Catherine that of Cerridwen, the Celtic Nature-Goddess; hence the popularity of these two saints as the patrons of churches and chapels built on hill-tops, the old "High Places." It will be remembered how carefully Joan dodged the question, "Did St. Michael appear to you naked?" It is evident from her trial that Joan did not like telling a direct lie, but that she was an adept at evasion; she could dodge about like a lawyer. A careful perusal of her answers as given in the record of the trial yields some intriguing points, and I recommend it to the interested scholar.

For one thing, upon Joan's own admission, her compliance with the requirements of the Catholic Church with regard to confession, attendance at Mass, etc., was the very minimum possible; and when she wrote any letter to her colleagues the contents of which were "for show" only, and which she did not wish them to believe, she would put "Jesu Maria" and the sign of the cross at the top of it. A curious use of the cross for a devout Catholic to make!

That which particularly scandalised the priests who tried her was her persistent adoption of male attire. Now, there is a tradition in the witch cult that a priestess may impersonate either the God or the Goddess, but that a male priest may only impersonate the God. So Joan in male attire may well have been impersonating the God of the witches, as Margaret Murray believes; especially in view of the curious device which she adopted as her personal standard, namely an upright sword with its point encircled by a crown, and with a fleur-de-lys on either side of it. This figure is identical with the Ace of Swords in the old mystical symbols of the Tarot cards, which are still used by occultists, and are the ancestors of our present-day playing-cards.

Much ingenuity has been exercised by occultists and others to account for the origin of these cards, and it is at least a curious parallel that according to an old Irish "Book of Invasions" which is considered to date from the 12th century, the four magical talismans which the Tuatha de Danaan, the ancient Irish Gods, brought to Ireland with them were the Sword of Nuada, the Lance of Lugh, the Cauldron of the Dagda, and the Stone of Fal, which are analogous to the Sword, the Wand, the Cup, and the Pentacle comprising what A. E. Waite called "the Four palmary symbols of the Tarot." And the Sword of Nuada, "from whose stroke no one ever escaped or recovered," is none other than the sword of the Old God of Death Himself, which is yet borne symbolically by His representative in the rites of witchcraft.

The meaning of the Ace of Swords in the old Tarot symbolism was "Triumph," and, as the Old God's own symbol, it was, if Joan was His living representative, perfectly appropriate, the two fleur-de-lys being, of course, the national emblems of France.

The Church tried and condemned Joan for heresy, partly because that was what they were interested in stamping out, and partly because her heresy was easy to prove. Today, if a man has committed a dozen murders they seldom try him for more than one at a time; it is only if they cannot get the desired verdict that they bring forward the next crime most easy to prove. So it was with Joan; her heresy was clear, and they got her put out of the way as they wanted. It was unnecessary to proceed with the question of fairies and witchcraft. Twenty years after, when the king was firmly on the throne, he was so annoyed by the jeers of other crowned heads at his having been put on the throne by a witch that he ordered a retrial, with much faked evidence. Joan became a national heroine and, as Bernard Shaw says, would be much amused to hear that she was a Christian saint.

In all the witch trials it seems that a lot of the answers given were quite true, if you realise the fact that "the Devil" was simply a man, often wearing a mask. He was the High Priest, who even at some rare ceremonies nowadays wears a helmet with horns, which are probably the remnants of the mask. It seems that at some witch ceremonies in Australia actual masks are occasionally worn; but as these ceremonies are said to have been held in "studios" this may be just artistic licence, though I think it is probably an attempt to revive the ancient practice. For instance, Jeanne Belloc, in the reign of Henri IV of France, was indicted for witchcraft in her eighty-fourth year. She said she first attended a Sabbat in 1609, where she was presented to the Devil, who kissed her, a mark of approbation which he bestowed on the greatest of sorcerers (witches) only. She said the Sabbat was really a kind of masked ball, to which people often came disguised as dogs, cats, donkeys, pigs and other animals, though others were without disguise. If you take this as a meeting of the People of the Heath and other believers who wore animal disguises to obtain religio-magical good luck and fertility for their domestic animals, as the prehistoric people of the caves used to do, and at the same time enjoy themselves, and that she, as an eminent cult member, was naturally introduced personally to the leader, who kissed her, just as might happen today, her account is quite understandable.

There is even a story from Scotland of a young witch who became impatient of the "Devil's" attempts to play music for dancing upon a "trump" (a kind of Jew's harp), and snatched the instrument from him, fetching him a playful smack on the cheek with it saying that she could play it better than he. This story alone should dispose of the idea that the "Devil" who presided over the Sabbats was any kind of supernatural being. Imagine Milton's Satan being smacked across "the chops" by a Scottish serving-wench!

Gomme, in *Folklore as a Historical Science* (p. 201 *et seq*), stresses the importance of the act of initiation as applied to the witch cult. "It emphasises the existence of a caste apart from the general populace. The existence of this caste long before, where they did practise their powers, carrying back this act of initiation age after age. It is clear that the people who were from time to time introduced into the witch caste carried on the practices and assumed the functions of the caste even though they came into it as novices and strangers. We thus arrive at what might be termed an artificial means of descent into a peculiar group of superstitions. This was influenced in the Middle Ages by beliefs of the carrying on of traditional practices by certain families and groups of people who could only acquire such practices by initiation and family teaching." This is, of course, exactly what happened. It is a family group, if you like; but not all of the family belongs to it, only those who are initiated, and people of non-witch families are at times introduced and initiated. While it is unusual for members of the cult today to think of themselves as a "caste," they certainly regard themselves as a kind of "family" apart. At a witch meeting, where I was present, a visit to a nudist club was discussed, and a woman said, "I wouldn't like that." I said, "Why not?" And the reply was, "I don't care *here,* of course; but I wouldn't go before other people." The exact "caste" feeling!

Returning to the statement that all the Mysteries are one, I think that this plainly means that there are certain what might be termed "natural" forms of religion which are felt to be true by peoples of European stock. Peoples of Eastern and African stock also have their own "natural" forms, which may be different from those of Europe. Christianity, in the form we know it at least, is an Eastern religion which was originally imposed from above by force upon Western Europe, and while it has many good points, it is not of the real form natural to the people of these countries. This is, I believe, one reason why the witch cult has survived the most cruel and determined persecutions that mankind has ever known.

Plato says, "Of what the disease of the spirit consists, from what cause it is dulled, how it can be clarified, may be learned by philosophy. For by lustrations of the Mysteries the soul becomes liberated and passes into divine condition of being, hence discipline willingly endured becomes of far greater utility for purification. . . . On entering the interior part of the Temple, unmoved, and guarded by the sacred rites, they genuinely receive into their bosoms divine illumination, and divested of their garments they participate in the divine nature." The same ideas are found in the Speculations of Thales. Proclus, in his *On the Theology of Plato,* says, "the mind is affected and agitated in death, just as in initiation into the Mysteries, and word answers word, as well as thing to thing; for to die, and to be initiated, is the same. With hymns, dances, and sublime and sacred knowledge crowned and triumphant, they walk the regions of the blessed."

It is an old saying that "The difference between orthodoxy and heterodoxy is that orthodoxy is my doxy and heterodoxy is someone else's doxy." John Calvin's doxy (a most ill-favoured hag) was embodied in his famous dictum, "All pleasure is sin." Nowadays most people modify that a little, saying "My pleasures are innocent, everybody else's pleasures are sin." Witches cannot sympathise with this mentality. They are inclined to the morality of the legendary Good King Pausol, "Do what you like so long as you harm no one." But they believe a certain law to be important, "You must not use magic for anything which will cause harm to anyone, and if, to prevent a greater wrong being done, you must discommode someone, you must do it only in a way which will abate the harm." This involves every magical action being discussed first, to see that it can do no damage, and this induces a habit of mind to consider well the results of one's actions, especially upon others. This, you may say, is elementary Christianity. Of course it is; it is also elementary Buddhism, Hinduism, Confucianism, and Judaism, to name only a few.

So many Gods, so many creeds,
So many paths that wind and wind,
When just the art of being kind
Is all this old world needs.

Leland says, in his *Gypsy Sorcery* (p. 435),

> There arose a class of judges and Inquisitors like Bodin in France and Sprenger in Germany who composed lengthy treatises upon the manner of discovering witches and putting them to the test, and generally presiding over witchcraft trials. The cold-blooded cruelty of these textbooks can only be accounted for by the likelihood that their authors felt themselves justified through motives of fidelity to the Church of Christ and religion. The awful terror disseminated, especially among the more intelligent by the possibility of a charge of witchcraft being brought against them at any moment, brought about an intolerable state

> of things. The intellectual or rich might be arraigned at any time by any rascal who liked to bring a charge. It is curious that the more serious part of the population did not attempt to stop this terrible state of affairs; but they could not, because the whole system was countenanced by the Church, in whose hands all the persecution lay.

We can understand what all this meant to the witch; what it would have meant to the Founder of the Christian religion, we may well wonder.

CHAPTER IX

Why?

Someone asked me the other night, "Why do women take the chief place in witchcraft?" I had to say, "I don't know." No one knows. To say that it has always been so is not an answer. The easiest thing is to say it is a survival of matriarchy. It may well be, but I doubt if it is the true answer; because we do not know exactly what was the origin of matriarchy. I think the best explanation is because women represent the Goddess; and this probably originated when the cult of the Goddess was superimposed on the original cult of the Old God of Hunting and Death.

It must be clearly realised that not all women are regarded as representatives of the Goddess. It is only those who are recognised as being young and lovely, loving and generous, motherly and kind. In fact, those who possess all those qualities which can be summed up in the one word "sweetness." They should be Man's Ideal; in that way they may be worthy to have the spirit of the Goddess invoked to descend upon them.

The poet sings:

O Woman! In our hours of ease
Uncertain, coy, and hard to please,
And variable as the shade
By the light quivering aspen made,
When pain and anguish wring the brow,
A ministering angel thou!

Now, that is not quite the witch ideal. She should be steadfast, trusty and easy; otherwise she is not fit to have the Goddess descend upon her. If she is cross and selfish and ungenerous, it is certain she will never receive that divine blessing. Our Lady of Witchcraft has a high ideal set before her; she must be fresh and kindly and always the same to you. In any case, she will always receive the honour and respect which witches give to every woman, but to receive the high honours she must be worthy of them.

Among the virtues she must have is the realisation that youth is among the requisites necessary for the representative of the Goddess, and that she must be ready to retire gracefully in favour of a younger woman in time. She will then become one of the Elders, whose decisions are powerful in council.

But as the Old God told the Goddess, "Age and Fate wither all things, and against them I am helpless. But when men die and come to me I give them rest and peace so that they may return."

So a true Priestess realises that gracefully surrendering pride of place now is one of the greatest virtues, and she will return to that pride of place the next time, in another incarnation, with greater power and beauty. In a sense, the witch religion recognises all women as an incarnation of the Goddess, and all men as an incarnation of the God; and for this reason every woman is potentially a priestess, and every man potentially a priest; because to the witch the God and the Goddess are the Male and Female, the Right and the Left, the Two Pillars which support the Universe and every manifestation of male and female is a manifestation of Them.

There are many types of beauty, and beauty of the spirit is greater than that of the body. The purifications you undergo in the cult increase that secret beauty. The Mysteries in ancient times must have been a garden of fair faces. One may love black eyes more than brown, some blue more than grey, and there is the wonderfully rare green eye. To some white skin is wonderful, others prefer suntan or even brown; but they are all different facets of the same gem.

[See publisher's note.*]

The great religions, Christianity in its different forms, Mohammedanism, and to a great extent Buddhism, and Communism *in excelsis* (for Communism is a religion, like that of the early Hebrews, "Fight furiously to get the greatest amount of plunder for the tribe, sacrifice your lives in thousands, so the Temple will be rich and the survivors may take part in the riches"); all these are religions designed to control the masses so that they will work hard in order that the governing classes may create a society which is wealthy and powerful.

---

* [The reader should be made aware that in the following several paragraphs the author offers sweeping statements that include bigoted and offensive views on an array of topics. The publisher has chosen to preserve these paragraphs in the text as it reflects the author's views in the mid-1950s when this book was written.]

Call these governing classes kings, priests, Nazis, or Communist Commissars, it makes no matter; they are all the same, though some are more ruthless than others. Whatever labels they put on their policies, they are essentially the same, and entail the eternal "moral policing" of their subjects; and you must understand that any force which in any way obstructs or interferes with this constant "moral policing" will at once be opposed by the Powers that Be of these "religions." For none of them can stand the permission to have one's own secret thoughts, those sweet dreams of the All-Mother and Eternal Bride, who is gentle and loving, kind and generous. Beauty and sweetness are a terror to all these organised tyrannies; so they must be debased and hidden as much as possible.

The Communists and Nazis, being utterly ruthless, forbade not only freedom of speech and action, but also cosmetics and pretty clothes. Other religions, being less powerful, attempt to prevent beautiful clothes. What monstrosities women have been persuaded to clothe themselves in, in the name of "modesty"! The religions actually "work" the fashion shows in Paris and elsewhere to force women to wear long and voluminous skirts to hide their legs, and all sorts of devices are put through to prevent the figure being displayed. Curves must be covered up or flattened out, and girls made to look as much like boys as possible. "*Vive Homosexuality!*" is the cry. As long as we can keep men's minds away from anything sweet and lovely!

Our young men and maidens must be guarded against anything which makes them think "thoughts." So art must consist of children's scribbles with an obscene meaning. In fact, it is better for people to be sniggeringly obscene, rather than that they should be natural and blessed with the Blessing of Pan. So their sense of the beauty of sex and nature must be systematically destroyed, and they must be taught that "Marriage was ordained for the pro-creation of children only," thus reducing human love to the level of cattle-breeding.

For if they think of beauty, they will never be great Commissars. They will never be ready to betray their country at the command of "the Party." And above all, they will never work at a soulless job, or such vocation as that of a fomenter of strikes, or a Nazi executioner, or one of the Dominican "Hounds of God" who led the Inquisition. They would never have helped Savonarola destroy all lovely things. They would never be Puritans, as those who made such a desert of England, and from whose excesses we still suffer; (the days when a ship's captain returning from a long and perilous voyage on a Sunday, kissed his wife, and spent the rest of the day in the stocks being pelted by the rabble for the awful crime of "Sabbath breaking").

Be they Red Commissars in Europe or MacCarthyite "investigators" in America; Gestapo bosses in the Twentieth Century or witch-hunting priests in the Middle Ages; spiritually they are all of the same kindred. The same black poison corrodes them all; the warped lust for power, welling up from fears and repressions in the depths of the unconscious mind.

There was no room for this sort of spirit in the witch cult, nor in the mystery religions which were its predecessors in the days of Bronze Age matriarchy, so long as they remained true to their traditions. The purpose of initiation was to give the neophytes esoteric instruction which would rid them of their fear of the unknown and help them to find a philosophy which made sense of the Universe, notably the doctrines of reincarnation, karma, and the immortality of the human soul; and in the sacred orgies they lost their repressions and found ecstasy and the Blessing of Pan.

Just where the puritanical, patriarchal religion originated we do not know. Robert Graves, in *The White Goddess,* has suggested that they came from the East. But certain it is that in prehistoric times they began to infiltrate, undermine, and sometimes attack the older forms of religion. *Why* this happened is an even more difficult question. The answer may lie in the ancient esoteric teaching that human affairs follow a certain cosmic cycle. Perhaps it was necessary for the human race to descend into the "Kali Yuga," or Dark Age, as the Easterns call it, or the "Age of Pisces," the Sign of suffering and self-undoing, in order to learn some important lesson.

The Jewish puritans in Biblical times, who set out to destroy the "High Places," seem to have started the idea, "Beauty is Evil"; I suppose because those whom they were seeking to destroy, the priestesses who worshipped the Queen of Heaven, were lovely; and perhaps because their young men were rebellious, asking, "Why should we destroy things which are beautiful and enjoyable?" So the people had to be conditioned to think of ugliness as holy; as later the Christians declared, "Dirt is holy, cleanliness is of the witch and the Devil." They spoke of the dangerous enemies of good Christians, who lay in wait in the dark to seize their souls for the Devil, and they proceeded to describe these enemies as wood nymphs, loreleis, and witches, as in the legend of Tannhauser, with eyes like stars and teeth like pearls, their lovely white shoulders and breasts gleaming in the starlight (the stories of the hideous, foul old witch came much later). So the early Christians set their converts on to loot and destroy pagan temples and villas, and in due course the Puritans set the rabble on to destroy any beautiful Christian church, smashing stained glass windows and defacing any beautiful carved work they could get at. So when it came to the ears of a shocked priest or minister, "There are some left who worship beauty, who say that love and death are as one, for love is stronger than death, it follows you into the next world, to adventures beyond space and time; who say that goodness is also happiness and that happiness is goodness"; such a cult was marked for destruction.

As I have said, there are certain religious ideas which seem to come naturally to people, and I can only conclude that it is because there is a certain fundamental need for them. For instance, among the American Indians the boys spend a long period in the woods undergoing a course of fasting, purging and flagellation. This is undergone to bring the initiate into direct touch with the divine "Something." The Greeks called it the Noumenon behind the manifested world of phenomena. We may call it the deeper layers of the unconscious. This rite is what changes a child into a man, and hence is called a "Rite de Passage." When he leaves the class of boys and becomes a warrior, he thus gains a guardian spirit, or a contact with the Gods, which becomes a guide for his whole life. In Europe, Asia and Africa, at periods when there was no possibility of intercourse, practically all primitive peoples had much the same initiation ceremonies, and these were initiations into priesthoods, into magic powers, secret societies and mysteries. They were usually regarded as necessary for the welfare of the tribe as well as for the individual. They usually included purification and some tests of courage or fortitude—often severe and painful, instruction in tribal lore, sexual knowledge, in the making of charms and in religious and magical matters generally, and often a ritual of death and resurrection. This is practically what the American Indians' practice consisted of.

When you enquire the reasons for these resemblances, at the bottom you always find the Cult of the Great Mother of all Living, the Moon Goddess. We may know her best as Ishtar of Babylon, but she was worshipped under many names in the various countries where she ruled; Attar, in Mesopotamia; Ather, in Arabia; Astar, in Abyssinia; Atargatis in Syria, and Astarte or Artemis in Greece. For she is the force which expresses itself in the giving and taking (or receiving again) of life, and she is also the "love force," the Witch Goddess who introduces herself in these words:

No other law but love I know,
By naught but love may I be known,
And all that liveth is my own,
From me they come, to me they go.

She is the Great Mother of All, the giver of fertility and the power of reproduction. All life comes from her; all life-giving crops and fruits, animals and people are her children. She is the Bringer and the Taker Away, the Goddess of Life, Death and Rebirth; but all in a sweetly loving way. Laughingly she has been described as "The Mother who lovingly spanks and kisses her children."

The celebrated "Dance of the Seven Veils" was originally a religious ceremony, the story of Tammuz and Ishtar, which formed a prominent part of the ritual of the story of the Great Goddess. This was observed by the ancient Jews, but puritans among them strongly objected to its being observed in the Temple of Solomon, and it was condemned by the Biblical prophets. Yearly Tammuz, or Adonis (from "Adonai," meaning "Lord"), died and went to the Underworld, and winter came and the fruits of the earth failed, and neither man nor beast nor plants could propagate, nor could they wish to propagate, all being sunk in hopeless inactivity.

On cuneiform tablets is written the story of "The Descent of Ishtar into Hades":

Since the Lady Ishtar descended into the Land of No Return,
The bull does not spring upon the cow,
The ass does not bow over the jennet,
No more man bows over woman,
The man sleeps in his chamber,
The woman sleeps alone.

We may think differently, but to the ancients the power and desire for fertility were gifts of the Gods. When the Goddess was absent from the earth in the Land of No Return, all natural desire was likewise absent from the earth. So all mankind mourned, while the Goddess went to the Other World to rescue her love, and at each of the six gates she had to pass the guardians deprived her of some clothing, symbolised by the veils. When she was naked at the seventh gate she was deprived of her jewels. Thus ritually naked, she shone forth in magical power as Queen of the Underworld, and rescued Tammuz and brought him back again to the world of men.

Some think that the loss of her clothing and jewels represents the waning of the moon, until she rises again in her beauty and power.

Magic and inspiration are her gifts. She is the Goddess of Magic and Magicians. Aphrodite taught her son Jason "to draw down the dark Moon, invoke Hecate; for she herself had not the power of magic."

The Rites of Hecate were performed at night; they were to turn aside evil. She is Dea-Triformis of the cross-roads, the Queen of Ghosts, and she sweeps through the night followed by a dreadful train of spirits and baying hounds. She is queen of all that lives in the hidden parts of the psyche, in the unconscious mind, as we would say. She is often represented in ancient art as three figures in one, Artemis, Selene and Hecate. Artemis is the waxing moon, Selene the full moon, and Hecate the dark moon. They each usually carry a large knife (the witches' Athame), a torch, and a whip or scourge. The greatest of magic power lay in Hecate, the dark moon, whose rites were always held at night.

On the thirteenth of August there was a great festival to Artemis in Greece and to Diana, the Queen of Heaven, in Rome, to prevent the coming of autumn storms which might spoil the coming harvest. Nowadays in these countries the same day, the thirteenth of August, is set aside for prayers to the Virgin Mary, Queen of Heaven, to turn aside storms till the harvest is gathered in.

Women of all Western Asia and many of Southern Europe wear a crescent as an amulet to secure the Moon Mother's aid in time of childbirth. Today these women may tell you the Moon Mother is the Virgin Mary; as they say this they will bow to the moon in the sky. And to most of us it is considered lucky to see the new moon if it is not through glass, because the latter implies that you are in a house and not, as you should be, outside to pay reverence to the new moon. Old accounts of primitive people describe them as crowding out of their houses to welcome the new moon.

There is a curious superstition that the moon sends children, not directly, but by a giant moon-bird, to the different women. Possibly this is the origin of our idea of storks bringing babies. I remember a large flight of storks over Jerusalem when I was there (their wings make an extraordinary noise), and people saying, "There will be many babies born in the next day or so."

Sometimes the crescent moon was conceived of as a magical boat sailing upon the waters of space, which brought new souls to be born on earth, and bore away the souls of the dead to the Other World. The Three Queens who bore away the dying King Arthur to Avalon were the Triple Goddess in her Moon-boat.

Almost everywhere in the non-Christian world the moon is served chiefly by women, though men take a subordinate part in the rite. But women have the magical power to work the fertilising activities of the moon, including rain-making and the care of a sacred fire, which must not be allowed to die. When a man is rain-maker, he usually holds the office by marrying a moon-priestess. In many parts of Africa, the rain-maker has to have a certain woman to aid him in pouring out water. The King of Dahomey is the incarnation of the Moon God and chief rain-maker, but he cannot do this alone, he must be helped by the priestess of the Moon God. In many of the African tribes, however, the ritual of rain-making must be carried out by naked women, who, taking water from sacred springs, throw it over themselves.

We should remember that one of the charges against mediaeval witches was that they went naked to pools and streams and threw up water to bring rain and storms.

Until quite recent times, peasants in Germany, the Tyrol, Russia, Rumania and Hungary, when rain was needed, led a naked girl to a stream and sprinkled her with water, or sometimes all the girls of the village would go naked through the village singing, everyone sprinkling them with water.

The fertilising power of the moon was thought to lie in her light, so this was reinforced at times by torches, candles and fires burned in her honour, which were used as fertilising magic, being carried round newly-planted fields in modern times, as torches were carried in Hecate's honour in ancient times.

Diana the Huntress was also the mother of all animals and humans, and was depicted with many breasts, like Diana of Ephesus. She is shown with a crescent head-dress, and often with a lighted torch. The torch was very prominent in her worship.

It is noteworthy that the 2nd of February is celebrated as Candlemass in honour of the Virgin Mary, Moon of our Church; but before it was celebrated on that day with torches in honour of the triune Moon Goddess of the Celts, Brigit, Bride or Brigentis, and on this day her new fire was kindled and blessed. It is traditionally one of the witches' Sabbats, and is celebrated with fires by present-day witches.

Now, the moon goddesses of the East, as among the Celts and in Rome, were served by priestesses who tended the sacred fire, emblematic of the power of the sun and the moon. Sometimes these priestesses were called "Vestal Virgins"; but usually considered as wives of the king, and often he gained his power by marrying one of these priestesses. In early Rome many of the kings were sons of a Vestal Virgin; that is, one whose woman's nature had been dedicated to the Goddess, and not to ordinary married life. On their consecration, Roman Vestal Virgins received the name of Amata, or "Beloved," which was the name of the wife of the legendary king of Rome, Latinus, from which the name "Latin" is derived. Together with the perpetual fire in the temples of the moon goddesses there were usually phallic symbols to represent her divine fertility. In Rome these were known as "Priapus," and Robert Graves, in his book, *The White Goddess,* considers that the famous "Palladium," on the safe keeping of which in the temple the safety of the country was thought to depend, was not a "respectable" statue of a clothed divinity, but a phallic image. In many countries these "Vestal Virgins" were as the sacred prostitutes in the Temple of Jerusalem, the "Temple Maidens," who gave themselves to strangers for hire, the money going to the Temple. Thus "Virgin" was used in its ancient meaning, which was simply "unmarried." That is, they were pledged to the service of the God.

Now according to modern ideas, this was very shocking; because we are conditioned to think so. In modern times, for about the last two thousand years, enormous numbers of women have been "pledged to the service of the God." They are expressly called "the Brides of Christ"; they must live in convents in a life of utter misery, all their natural instincts stultified. It is inconceivable that any Deity should condemn millions to such a life of long-drawn-out repression, unless you understand the idea behind it all, that is, "The Gods are not all-powerful, they need the aid of men and women. If sufficient nerve power is raised by the worshippers the God will become all-powerful."

One of the earliest attempts to do this was the "Sacred Marriage." The love was not merely for the satisfaction of those who took part; their powers were dedicated to a higher purpose, that of giving great power to the Gods, and at the same time bringing the Gods into communion with their worshippers.

People do at times attempt to produce a good effect by using evil means, and there seems to be evidence that some of the priests also used homosexuals for the same purpose (and to make money for themselves); but the main fact remains clear. It was believed that the Gods needed man's aid to perform the blessings required by the tribe or nation, and that it was a religious duty to assist the Gods in this good work. This could be effected by personal self-sacrifice, or vicariously by the sacrifice of others. When the whole nation believed in this, they saw no reason why this service of the Gods should not give pleasure to men at the same time.

At one time it was considered that education could only be obtained by long and frequent thrashings; now it is considered that if the lessons are made interesting and pleasant, better results are obtained. The ultimate aim is the same, a good education. The best way to produce it is simply a matter of opinion. Though I have heard the unpleasant way denounced, I have never heard the pleasant way described as "wicked."

When the puritanical party won in Palestine the pleasant way of "raising power" was stopped, and large numbers of the people believed that all the tribulations and foreign captivities were the result of depriving the Jewish tribal God of His "Power," and of his Goddess-consort, so that He could no longer protect the people. See Jeremiah, Chap. 44, v. 15–19, referring to "the remnant of Judah, which are gone into the land of Egypt to sojourn there": "Then all the men which knew that their wives had burned incense unto other gods, and all the women that stood by, a great multitude, even all the people that dwelt in the land of Egypt, in Pathros answered Jeremiah, saying, 'As for the word that thou hast spoken unto us in the name of the Lord, we will not hearken unto thee. But we will certainly do whatsoever thing goeth forth out of our own mouth, to burn incense unto the queen of heaven, and to pour out drink offerings unto her, as we have done, we and our fathers, our kings, and our princes, in the cities of Judah, and in the streets of Jerusalem: for then had we plenty of victuals, and were well, and saw no evil. But since we left off to burn incense to the queen of heaven, and to pour out drink offerings unto her, we have wanted all things, and have been consumed by the sword and by the famine. And when we burned incense to the queen of heaven, and poured out drink offerings unto her, did we make her cakes to worship her, and pour out drink offerings unto her, without our men?'"

It is evident from the above verses that the chief part in this cult was taken by the women. I was digging with the Wellcome Expedition in 1936–1937 which excavated the Biblical city of Lachish. We found the Temple of Jehovah, and in it the remains of a very beautiful ivory statue of the Goddess. According to an article in *The Observer*, dated July 10th, 1955, "Unearthing the Holy Land's Past," by T. R. Fyvel,

> On the site of a Cannanite temple (approx. 1750 B.C.) standing on the seashore of Western Galilee, a team under Dr. M. Dothan uncovered a "high place" about fourteen metres in diameter. . . . A striking find was an exquisite stone mould, the first of its kind seen in Israel, of a horned goddess with high conical cap and long hair and a provocative look—it might be Ashera of the Sea, or Astarte.

A bronze cast made from the stone mould illustrates the article; it shows a tall, slim goddess, naked except for her ritual ornaments, and with a delightfully mischievous expression.

However, after the triumph of the puritanical party in ancient Palestine, the documents which we now call the Bible were carefully edited and expurgated to remove all favourable mention of the Goddess-Consort and her rites.

Many years later, under the influence of St. Paul and others of his kind, large numbers of people dedicated their lives to unpleasant tortures, as hermits. These becoming uncontrollable from their eccentric conduct, and leading to riots and bloodshed, they were later regimented into convents and monasteries. The religious heads knew the idea behind this, though I doubt if the rank and file realises it nowadays. But undoubtedly much of the strength of the early church lay in the great reserve of "power" which is being continually raised in these establishments all over the world (by abstaining from all acts of sexual intercourse); by the constant direction of the thoughts to the will of the Church and its aggrandisement; and sometimes by actual tortures, such as the wearing of painful belts and spiked bracelets, and by flagellation. At the same time such power is being raised in a most wasteful way, and as there does not seem to be any reasonable formula to preserve and contain it, it is continually leaking out and being dissipated. Hence the frequent curious stories of peculiar psychic phenomena in monasteries and convents, such as that of the "possessed nuns" of Loudun; all such, of course, being attributed to the ubiquitous "Devil," or to "miracles." The only Christian order which consciously makes use of this power nowadays is the Jesuits, and it is noteworthy that practically every state in the world has at one time or the other had laws against this Order, because they were always influencing things too much in their own favour.

St. Clement of Alexandria, who, before turning Christian, was initiated in the worship of the Goddess Cybele whose symbol was a crescent moon in perpetual union with the sun, says the following confession of faith was made:

> *I have eaten from the timbrel,*
> *I have drunk from the cymbal,*
> *I have borne the sacred vessel,*
> *I have entered into the bridal chamber.*

Now, it seems obvious that "I have eaten from the timbrel and drunk from the cymbal" means that a sacred meal, or a species of Eucharist with food and drink that had been blessed was eaten out of the "working tools" of the cult, and this meal is known to have consisted of a cake of barley, and of wine. It is noteworthy that the witches' "sacred meal," "Cakes and Wine," consists of cakes (any sort) and wine, which are blessed and then eaten and drunk out of the "working tools," and this blessing has at least a phallic or fertility significance. "I have borne the sacred vessel" may be something similar to the witch custom that everyone should have one of the "working tools," usually the Athame, in their hands all the time when the hands are otherwise unoccupied. Perhaps in St. Clement's time the "entering into the bridal chamber" involved more than a fertility blessing. I mention this to show how the ancient mysteries were all connected together.

In these mysteries, to demonstrate the truth that God is Male and Female, and that true blessedness consists in their union, it was customary for women at their initiation into the mysteries of the Great Goddess to sacrifice their virginity by entering into a sacred marriage, *hieros gamos,* which was consummated sometimes with a phallic image, sometimes with a stranger, and sometimes with a priest. This was to make the act impersonal. The priest was considered an incarnation of the God; so was a stranger. He might even be the God himself. The two were strangers to each other, who had never met before, and would probably never meet again. Now, allowing for the fact that early Protestant writers were prejudiced, there seems little doubt that until the time of Henry VIII at least, there were certain convents where the nuns were regarded as the brides of the priests and were regularly used as such. It was not simply a case of loose living. It was sincerely believed that the Sacred Marriage should be regularly and reverently performed, to bring power and blessings on the community, as had always been the case. The early Protestants did not realise this. There had always been two schools of thought in the Church with regard to this, and, owing to their streams of abuse the old custom was discontinued. At least, it was only practised in strict secrecy; but the knowledge of its existence at one time was widespread, and during the French Revolution many unfortunate monks and nuns were ill-treated to make them admit these practices. It is probable that it was this which inspired "Les Noyades," when, as Swinburne sang:

In the wild fifth year of the change of things,
When France was glorious and blood-red, fair
With the dust of battle and deaths of Kings.
A queen of men with helmeted hair.
Carrier came down to the Loire and slew
Till all the ways and the waves waxed red:
Bound and drowned, slaying two by two,
Maidens and young men, naked and wed.

That is, many priests and nuns, among others, were stripped, bound face to face, and ceremonially drowned, in what was called "Civil Marriage." While this was, of course, done in mockery, it illustrates what all the peasants knew, viz., that there was a Sacred Marriage, which they believed was still practised by the priests and nuns, and it amused them to kill them while they were celebrating it, even though involuntarily.

As Charles Seltman so truly says in his *Women in Antiquity* (p. 30),

> There are occasions when nakedness becomes essential as an act of worship within a religion which has passed well beyond the primitive and magical. The idea is there in the Moslem rite of removing the shoes and washing the feet before entering a holy place; carried further, it was more reverent still to discard all contamination of clothes and to enter the shrine in cleanliness and purity, fearing no harm from evil spirits, because God is in His House. Accordingly, cult nakedness can be both cathartic and prophylactic, both cleansing and protective. Yet it was not only within the shrine, but at times in processions of a religious kind that

> such a custom might exist. Thus it is evident from Attic painted vases of the 8th and 9th centuries B.C. that women mourners, and even the widow herself, walked naked in the funeral cortege of any Athenian citizen. Coming nearer home, we observe Pliny's remark that in religious ceremonials in Ancient Britain the women and girls went completely naked after having stained themselves all over with a brownish sun-tan lotion. These considerations may justify the view that every little naked Mesopotamian terracotta does not necessarily represent Ishtar, but is rather a permanent substitute for the female votary. The figurine would thus represent the woman in the act of worship, all clothes discarded and with her hands pressing or supporting the breasts.
>
> Periodically fertility rites were practised by the women of Mesopotamia and all Hither Asia and the borderlands of the Midland Sea (Mediterranean). Writers equipped with quite another set of morals have often assumed that women were in some sense "stained" by such orgiastic rites, but we now perceive things more clearly and must concede that the women, like the later Thyiads at Athens and Delphi, thoroughly and passionately enjoyed the fertility rites and felt sanctified by them. Indeed it is evident that such were the distinctions and privileges of the women in Babylon that we cannot fail to be astonished at the contrast of their lot with the grim lot which was to befall human females three millenia later.

With reference to this passage, witches have pointed out to me the two sets of gestures made with the hands which are so often portrayed in artistic representations of the female form, of this period. One, the hands on the solar plexus, is so like a certain witch gesture; and they think the other, the exhibiting of the two breasts with the hands, represents the full moon and probably the sun as objects of worship, that in this way the woman symbolised the Sun God and the Moon Goddess, and this is why so many of the figures of this period are of women. Men would be present at the rites, and also be totally naked, but they could not represent the Goddess, and so would not have figurines of them dedicated to the Gods. This again is in accordance with the witch custom. The High Priestess stands for the Goddess, but at times can represent the God if necessary (that is, if a man of sufficiently high rank in the cult is not present); but no man can ever represent the Goddess. In fact, through all antiquity the attitude towards women seems to have been much as in the witch cult. Woman was a privileged person, as long as she was worthy. That is, she had to be kind and charming and generous. The spirit of chivalry is essentially a pagan one. It was the fashion for Victorian writers to take the view that woman in ancient times was underprivileged, that she had to till the fields while her lord and master went off to the wars. Nowadays we realise that war creates necessities, and in time of such necessity women had to become land-girls, and rather enjoyed it. We tend to hush up the fact that this newly-won liberty has brought back what the Victorian writers dared only to express with hints, namely that when women get free some of them do what they like, in spite of all the Church's teachings. All religious bodies professed to be extremely shocked at the Kinsey Reports, saying that only in America could such things take place, and that it could only happen in non-religious communities. The curious thing about the Kinsey Reports was the percentage of pre-marital and post-marital sexual intercourse among women of all ranks, incomes, and religious families, was approximately the same. That is, about thirty-four per cent of all women questioned admitted this quite freely. Now, when you consider that women who are practising Christians are, to say the least, apt to be shy at admitting their, shall we say, laxness, we can only conclude that the true proportions are very much higher. A much-publicised report by the Marriage Guidance Council gives about the same ratio from England.

Swinburne's famous verse tells us his opinions:

Thou hast conquered, O pale Galilean;
The world has grown grey at thy breath.
We have drunken of things Lethean,
And fed on the fulness of death.

Which is a poetical way of saying that the Church has taken all the pleasures out of our lives, and has done this simply to enforce their dictum that "Love is Shame." However, a large number of women in Christian countries nowadays assert their right to love without being in the least ashamed of it. To the extent, at least, that they will tell the Marriage Guidance Council and similar bodies all about it; for remember, the Marriage Guidance Council cannot use any Inquisitional methods; they simply ask, and only the people who feel no shame, or are even rather proud of it, will tell frankly of their sexual experiences.

Now, accepting these reports at their face value, can we not assume that public opinion is slowly changing on these matters? When I was young, there were whispers of "awful women" who got divorced, or worse still, who lived with men to whom they were not married. There were tales of people who had met them by chance and discovered their guilty secret, and when this was known the culprits were forced to leave the neighbourhood, hanging their heads in shame. Nowadays they stay and brazen it out. All their friends know they are not married, and no one seems to think anything about it.

Contrary to the reports of the Church, witches do not believe in or encourage promiscuity. To them sex is something sacred and beautiful, which should not be allowed to become sordid or cheap. (They also recognise a fact which many Christians seem to have forgotten, namely that there are six other Deadly Sins beside Lust.) In a rare old book in my possession, *Receuil de Lettres au Sujet des Malefices et du Sortilege... par le Sieur Boissier* (Paris, 1731), there is quoted much valuable evidence from a big witchcraft trial at La Haye Dupuis in 1669, which illustrates the attitude of the witch cult in this respect. One witness, Margeurite Marguerie, said that when a male witch was not at the Sabbat his partner did not join in the dance, and it is said further, "As for the dance, it is done... back to back and two by two, each witch having his wife of the Sabbat, which sometimes is his own wife, and these wives having been given to them when they were marked (i.e. initiated: my note) they do not change them; this kind of dance being finished, they dance also hand in hand, like our villagers...."

Boissier is a valuable witness, as he is writing about things which occurred in the living memory of his own time, and he is by no means prejudiced in favour of witches, because his book ends with the reproduction of a letter to the King of France from the Parliament of Normandy, in protest against the King having commuted the death sentences passed in the above case into sentences of banishment and suspended further proceedings, pointing out at great length that such clemency to witches offended God and endangered Christendom. (Much to his credit, Louis XIV took no notice of this pious prayer.) Incidentally, the evidence which Boissier quotes also shows that those who attended the Sabbats were naked; that for the most part, the witches were those who came from witch-families, and had been taught by their parents; that those who wished to slip out of their houses unseen to attend the Sabbat were in the habit of doing so via the huge, old-fashioned chimneys; that there were three "marks" given to the witches at three different times, but only the older ones had all three, which was "to make them magicians" (i.e. the modern "Three Degrees"); and that the witches, in order to scare people away from their meeting-place, impersonated the Wild Hunt; all of which I had written of in my previous book, *Witchcraft Today,* as having been told me by present-day survivors of the witch cult, before Boissier's somewhat rare book came into my possession; and before I had even heard of it. I may therefore refer those who have challenged my statements on the above points to the evidence quoted in Boissier's book.

We may get a better perspective of these secret Sabbats and merrymakings by looking at the social conditions in which they flourished. Charles Seltman, in *Women in Antiquity* (page 163), says, speaking of Christianity:

> As an historical religion, with a founder in time, the Faith has a meaning; but not so if it escapes—as it was already doing by the mid-first century of our era—from the formidable example and precept of its Founder. Such evidence as we have makes it most improbable that He would have consented to the defamation of half—the female half—of humanity. . . . Yet it was this line which led, through fear of women and sex, to a terrible escape into vowed celibacy and chastity. In the framework of the mediaeval and modern world most monks and nuns were quiet people dedicated not only to their ideals, but to a proposition called 'holiness'. But the large monastic movements too often enabled a small number of fanatics to gain control over the well-equipped machinery of the Church. Many of these creatures were single-minded, dedicated, truculent, and not quite sane, for they believed themselves to be the consecrated instruments of God, and they had that fear and hatred of women of which such men alone can be capable. People in the Middle Ages were, in fact, going slowly mad, because of the appalling code adopted concerning women. The atom bomb today is said to be driving us towards insanity; which state, however, is nothing compared with the wild thought induced by a faith founded upon a "Heaven and Hell conception" of the physical universe.

As G. Rattray Taylor, in "Sex in History," says (page 19):

> The Church never succeeded in obtaining universal acceptance of its sexual regulations, but in time it became able to enforce sexual abstinence on a scale sufficient to produce a rich crop of mental disease. It is hardly too much to say that mediaeval Europe came to resemble a vast insane asylum. A condition, one might add, in which various small

groups of more or less enlightened people strove hard to keep the flickering flame of sanity and human progress alive.

The proceedings of the Court Christian, the Church Court, in many cases overruled the law of the land. Chaucer tells us of the Archdeacon's Court, which concerned itself with sexual offences, witchcraft, defamation, wills, contracts, intestacy, lack of sacraments, and many other "manner of cryme which needeth not rehersen at this time, of unsure and symmonye also," and tells of the Bishop's Apparitor or Summoner, "For smale tythes and smale offringe he made the people piteously to singe. He is a runner up and down with mandements for fornicacioun."

As J. W. Jedwine tells us in *Tort, Crime and Police:*

The Church Courts have all the sexual offences and the Courts fine women 'for being violated'!!! i.e. women raped by force, as in the case of a city being taken in war. Later the women are stripped and then publicly whipped for this offence and the man pays money to the Church, while any who have sheltered a woman who has sinned are punished by the Church as backsliding Christians—"Robert Donalson and Margaret Masoun are decernit to pay XI s. for 'nocht reveling of the barne born in their hous be Janet Masoun gotten adulterie be Jhon Beatoun of Pitlichie and also to mak perfect humiliatioun.'" (Registers of St. Andrews Kirk Session. Scottish Hist. Soc. p. 796).

The Summoner was assisted by spies and mischievous persons who encouraged litigants to seek the Court Christian rather than the common knowledge of their neighbours. The records of the leet Jurisdiction of Norwich (Seld. Soc.) give ample evidence of this. . . . The court which claimed these rights as of things belonging to religion might be a court belonging to an undesirable alien; for instance, the English Priory was not infrequently the cell of a French Abbey (see Y.B. 17 Edw. III, 14,18). . . . In the Orkneys, the proceedings of making a vow to St. Magnus was to cast lots whether the vow should be to go south on a pilgrimage, or set a slave free, or to give the money to St. Magnus's shrine. It generally ended in the money being given to the shrine. . . . There had been in King Stephen's day a disputed claim between St. William of York and Henry Murdoc, who was the candidate of the Cistercians and of St. Bernard and Rome. St. William in 1153 was restored to the Archbishopric of which he had been deprived; Osbert of Bayeux, who had been an Archdeacon to Murdoc, poisoned St. William in the Eucharistic chalice, and claimed immunity as a clerk from the common law!!!

Now, I think we should try to consider the "Why?" of this fantastic state of the law. Why should any man get away with a cruel and cowardly murder? (A layman might be excused for thinking that poisoning the chalice of the Holy Communion was also something in the nature of a sacrilege.) I think the only answer can be that there was such a general hatred of the priesthood, or what it stood for, that no priest could feel safe if tried by any ordinary legal tribunal. (Of course, in the case of Osbert of Bayeux there might be the complications due to a Norman murdering a Saxon.) But there was always the strong claim of the Church that all clerks (i.e. priests or lesser orders) were above the law and could break it with impunity. The Select Pleas of the Crown (S.P.C., p. 121) show that in 1220 a man charged with assault and killing in the Park of Lord Warenne claimed clergy, as he was an acolyte, and so got off scot free. *The Ancient Laws of Wales,* edited by Aneurin Owen (A.L.O.W. v. II, 92), says

> If a scholar commit a theft and is degraded, he is not also to be killed, since there ought not to be two punishments for one cause.

From this it appears that occasionally the courts could deal with a criminal clerk by unfrocking him, but could do no more. In any case, it seems a clear verdict of "Not Guilty, but don't do it again."

Les Très Ancient Coutumier de Normandie (T.A.N.C. Chap. 72), the Constitutions of Richard III (Coeur de Lion), says, "Priests and Clerk are not to be hung; clerks in prison are to be handed to the Bishop." Of course, if the said clerk had done anything the Bishop objected to, woe betide him; but in practice, handing him over to the Bishop meant simply letting him go free. Incidentally, this custom became known as Benefit of Clergy, and amounted to, in fact, that anyone who could read must be adjudged a cleric. The test was a small verse of the Scriptures, which the accused was supposed to read in open court. I say "supposed" because it became a by-word that all criminals learnt it off by heart, and it was known as "The Neck Verse," as it saved them from hanging. The Church clung obstinately to this privilege and the first attempt to mitigate this evil was that all who pleaded "Benefit of Clergy" were branded on the thumb to prevent them claiming it twice. Then willful murder was removed from their benefits. In a later age, those who removed the penal laws against witches thought that for priests and bishops to commit murder was "not quite nice." For manners and opinions were changing slowly.

It is difficult for us to understand the mentality of those days. Those who think of the Middle Ages as a period of Romance, all tournaments and feasting and romantic love affairs, must remember that this did exist in the days of such monarchs as Good King Rene of Provence, the patron of the Troubadors; but Pope Innocent III's Crusade against the Albigenses crushed most of it out. The women of the privileged classes, as we call them nowadays, could have a fairly good time, and so could the lowest classes of all, if they did not mind hard work and were fond of children. Peasants can be very happy under conditions of dirt and in surroundings which would make social reformers shudder. But it has been said that between these two classes the only available careers for women in those days (Charles Seltman, op. cit.) were "The bourgeoise wife-cook-housekeeper, the prostitute, the nun, and the witch." This opinion is interesting. That is, apart from the nobles and the drudges (wives, serving-maids, peasants) who were bound to labour all the days of their lives, and the nun who was bound to an even worse fate, the only free women, people who could use their brains, were prostitutes and witches. Now, there were prostitutes in swarms in every town, and they accompanied all armies in well-organised hordes, cheerfully going over to the enemy if their protectors were vanquished. The Church at times persecuted them, but usually they let them alone as long as they paid tithes on their earnings.

It is curious in these days to find witches regarded as a class or profession. Ever since the "burning time," witches always do everything they can to be inconspicuous, but in the early times it was different, before the reign of ecclesiastical lynch-law began; most of them were, as nowadays, married women and happily married, and they had a distinct status, being respected and somewhat feared, though also loved for their services to the community as doctors, midwives, and turners-away of evil generally.

The village priest was often regarded in much the same way; he may have bothered people about tithes, he was, all the same, undoubtedly a good influence; nor, as in the case of the village priest of Inverkeithing in 1282 or the Basque priests about whom De Lancre wrote in 1613, was he above occasionally taking part in the rites of the Old Religion himself. It was the monks from the Abbey, who never did anything for the good of the country folk, who were much loathed. They were always coming round for tithes on everything, taking things by force and never giving anything in return, and made the Church much hated. It was hated also for its constant attacks on "reasonable" women, that is, those who did not fall into the categories of wife-housekeeper-drudge or nun. Women, they thought, should breed numbers of children to be monks and nuns, with enough married ones to carry the breed on, or they should be nuns and give up everything. As Simone de Beauvoir, in *The Second Sex** says,

> It is Christianity which invests women anew with frightening prestige; fear of the other sex is one of the forms assumed by the anguish of man's uneasy conscience. . . . Evil is an absolute reality; and flesh is sin. And, of course, since woman remains always 'the Other', it is not held that reciprocally male and female are both flesh; flesh is for the Christian, the hostile 'Other' is—precisely Woman. In her the Christian finds incarnated the temptation of the world, the flesh and the devil. All the fathers of the Church insist on the idea that she led Adam into sin. We must quote Tertullian (end of the 2nd century A.D.): 'Woman! You are the gateway of the devil. You persuaded him whom the devil dared not attack directly. Because of you the Son of God had to die. You should always go dressed in mourning and in rags'. . . . Christian literature strives to enhance the disgust that man can feel for women. Tertullian defines her as 'a Temple built over a sewer'. . . . St. Augustine (A.D. 354–430) called attention with horror to the obscene commingling of the sexual and excretory organs: *'Inter faeces et urinam mascimur.' That is, "Between urine and filth we are born."*

Many theologians considered (and for that matter, apparently some of them still do) that original sin is involved in the very law of generation: "Concupiscence is a vice . . . human flesh born through it is sinful flesh. The union of the sexes transmits original sin to the child, being accompanied since the Fall by concupiscence" (St. Augustine).

Some of the followers of St. Augustine even said that the Almighty was wrong in commanding Adam to "be fruitful and multiply" by the means provided, and that the sin of Adam lay in obeying the Almighty's will, suggesting that if Adam had only had the delicacy to refuse to have anything to do with these disgusting methods the Almighty would have been forced to invent a more decent way to carry out His plans. The Church has ever been curiously reluctant to credit the Great Architect of the Universe with knowing His job.

---

* French Edition, 1949, English Trans. 1953.

While the Church was influenced by people with this mentality, one can understand the "Why" of many of its actions. When the witch cult, on the other hand, regarded St. Augustine as being a singularly nasty-minded old man, and believed in the divine purpose and sanctity of its Horned and Phallic God and His Moon Goddess consort, one can also understand the "Why" of its beliefs and actions, and the origin of the centuries-long conflict that was joined between them, and which is not resolved yet.

Chapter X

Curious Beliefs about Witches

Probably it was the Church's influence which caused the most curious stories to be circulated about witches, and possibly the one which was most successful in causing fear and hatred of the craft was the story that they made wax images, and stuck pins in them, to kill the original.

To attempt to kill by this method is a very ancient practice and is almost worldwide. Ancient Babylonian inscriptions give the formula for making wax, clay, or pitch figures which were slowly burned while sacred formulae were recited to torture and kill the original of the image. The Koran tells that an attempt this way was made on the life of the Prophet. It is an historical fact that the Bishop of Troyes was tried in A.D. 1318 and condemned to death, the evidence showing that having quarrelled with the Queen of France, he made a wax image of her and after doing various indignities to it, burned it, so the Queen died. In 1663 an attempt was made on the life of Pope Urban by stabbing his image with a knife while it was slowly melted before a fire. Similar attempts were made on the life of King Louis XIII of France.

It is curious that the Church does not seem to have objected to this type of murder if it was practised by priests or laymen. Only the witch was signalled out for abuse, Why? The reason seems clear to me. The Church knew very well that priests' magic at best was a "hit or miss" affair, but witches' magic worked, and so might be dangerous.

When I wrote my first serious book on the subject, *Witchcraft Today,* speaking of the use of the wax image, I said:

> Up to now I have not found anyone who knows the exact rite used. I have not the slightest doubt that some still know it though they won't admit so. I particularly want to obtain possession of it because I think it is apt to be more or less unchanged from the days when the cave man practised it.

Since then I have been lucky enough to see one made, but unfortunately, or rather fortunately, this was not to kill anyone, as I think the method used could kill. It also bore out what a witch told me long ago, "Before you can do any harm to your enemy by means of a wax image you must be in a genuine and spontaneous rage, as you would need to be before you knocked him down physically."*

In this case a certain man, whom we may call X, attempted to gain some property by blackmailing the owner, saying in effect "If you don't give it up, certain facts will be known which will be extremely unpleasant for you and your friends." The owner consulted lawyers, but was told, "If this was spread about it would be unpleasant. X would not say it himself, or we might get him for slander. He would get other people to spread the yarn. You must judge if it is not better to let him have the property than let your friends suffer. It is only a matter of three thousand pounds."

The owner objecting to being blackmailed, went to a witch who knew the blackmailer well, and did not approve of his doings. So at the next meeting, she brought this case up as all had had unpleasant experiences with X. It was agreed that he might be dealt with, but only in a way which would cause him no harm. So I was able to see exactly what was done. Of course I may not tell what this is, but I can say I consider it to be a very ancient practice, a way of directing a curse, something which I suppose has been found out by trial and error, that doing something in a particular way will have a particular effect. In this case the power was directed to prevent the offender speaking, by pinning his lips together, and to prevent his moving in any way against the owner, by binding the figure tightly.

Of course the unbeliever will say it was pure coincidence that X stopped all threats immediately, sold his house and left the district.

I think this might be taken to show how a witch's ethics are at least better than, say, the Bishop of Troyes.

To be truthful, I know the Chief Witch *was* in a rage, and I believe if the others had allowed her, the man might have been seriously injured, if not killed. But this I think also shows what I have so often said. "Witches may be angry and forget their teaching, but the others will not let them do any harm."

For, if there is anyone present who does not agree to all that is attempted, they can spoil the charm. This may explain the charge found in

* I have this wax image on exhibition in my Museum of Magic and Witchcraft.

witch trials, "That you were present and consented to the killing of A," or whatever the charge against the principal was.

Now, because I have told of the one case at which I was present when the witches' "Poppet" was used, please don't think that witches are always doing this sort of thing. It is the first case I have seen in nearly twenty years.

It is the usual point of view of certain critics to say, "They know how to make 'wax images', that *proves* they are *always doing it.*" Presumably they feel that if they only could do it themselves, nothing could prevent them using it on all they disliked.

Long ago, certain people had a similar feeling, and the horrible fact was true that they had only to accuse anyone of witchcraft, to have them burned. Anyhow, the fact remains, there are very few witches who know how to do it, the rank and file certainly don't. I was talking to a couple who had been present when the "Poppet" was made, and both said, "We saw it done, but still don't know how to do it," and that's exactly my position; I feel there is something which escaped me, and "she who did it" won't tell me.

It is quite probable that people who are not witches know the secret. J. M. MacPhearson's *Primitive Beliefs in the North-East of Scotland,* p. 203, tells of an old lady in Inverness "who took umbrage at her Minister because he refused her Holy Communion. She adopted the ancient method of making an image. The Pastor fell into bad health, gradually growing weaker. Then the image was discovered, the spell broken, and he recovered." This old lady must have been a devout Christian to desire Communion so much.

He also tells us (p. 204), of the Fishermen of Prestonpans who used to set sail on Sunday evenings for the fishing grounds. A clergyman of the town prayed against their Sabbath breaking, so "to prevent any injury accruing from his prayers, the fishermen make small a image of rags and burn it on top of their chimneys." In this case the Minister's prayers were such as would cause evil.

The use of an image to protect one against evil, is common knowledge among witches, especially to cure illnesses. When the patient was at a distance an image was made, the "link formed" and remedies were applied to it.

The fact is, people all over the world know the art of making images, from Babylonia, India, Ancient Egypt, Greece, Ceylon, Africa. There is the idea that what was done to a man's image was done to him, by a sort of homoeophathetic magic. Sorcerers attempted it on a large scale. When we burn someone in effigy, we are really attempting to bring at least bad luck to him.

It was believed that Nectanebus, the last native king of Egypt, about 358 B.C. kept his independence in this way. He had wax models of Egyptian ships and fighting men made, also those of any likely enemies. When any attempted to invade Egypt, he placed their models in vats of water, opposed to the Egyptian models, and by his conjurations the ships fought on the water, the enemy was vanquished and their ships sunk. And this caused the real ships to sink likewise.

As his successors did not practise this art, Egypt lost her independence.

With all this rage for "Disarmament" nowadays to make a few such "Wax Ships" might be a good precaution. And what about wax atom bombs? But don't ask witches, they don't know this art; it is sorcery.

The question seems to me to be, "Why is it thought that it is so wicked for a witch to make an image, when there seems to be no objection to other people doing the same?" One obvious answer is "The Witch's Poppet works while other people's don't." Though it seems to have worked excellently for the Bishop of Troyes and the Old Lady of Inverness. But, and a very big but, if witches could kill their enemies so easily, why was there not a notable number of deaths among their "Oppressors"? If there had been, surely it would have been broadcast as an example of the malice of witches.

For the witch persecution was the one thing which would be apt to raise them to the state of "genuine and spontaneous rage" necessary.

I don't want for a moment to convey the impression that witches are more ethical than other people, and I think that when first attacked they hit back, but the actual "initiated witches" as distinct from the "Congregation" were few. The Church as a whole was a strong clever force, and knew how to strike swiftly, and to a certain extent to protect itself against magic. It is a tradition among witches, that thousands of people were tortured and burnt for every one witch; and every time a witch struck back, many thousands more were martyred. The witches met and decided, "We can't fight against this terror every time we strike, so many thousands were massacred, the only way any of us can survive, is to go underground, never hurt any, however much they have wronged you, then in time we will be forgotten." They did so, and with a bit of skilful propaganda, made witchcraft a figure of fun, an old woman with a black cat, flying on a broomstick, and so, slowly, they were forgotten, all laws against them having been repealed, as soon as it was known how harmless they were. Still, a witch was burned alive in Mexico in 1955, and the "powers that be" expended much money and influence in suppressing this fact, regarding it as an act of savagery. Well, the Mexican witch may not be the same as the British one, and she may have been doing some harm, or she may not have been a witch at all; the real charge against her seems to be that she had been performing a ceremony in honour of the old gods.

Because it is the unfortunate result of the Church's propaganda that the word witchcraft is used by the Press, when they mean a curious case of poisoning, a case of a Poltergeist, an Australian Blackfellow using a pointing bone, a Voodoo sacrifice, a bit of "queer work" by an African Witch Doctor, alleged Devil Worship in Paris or elsewhere, or even the curious case of where some schoolboys had a nature class in an abandoned summerhouse, who put the specimens they collected before them on a round table. A caretaker's wife seeing this circle, howled "Black Magic" and "Witchcraft," rushed off to the Vicar who it is said, asked permission of his Bishop to exorcise the place. The sensational Press had their usual orgy of screaming headlines, but when the truth came out were discreetly silent.

The truth is, at one time, we had more humour. When a very celebrated French Naturalist describing some animal said, "This is a very wicked animal; if you attack it, it defends itself." He was much ridiculed for saying this.

Why? When it is thought that if a Witch is attacked, she must not fight back, yet the howl is ever, "She is so wicked." Perhaps it is because the persecutors think she is harmless, so she is fair game. As people always speak of a witch as she, I do the same; though, of course, I mean by the term both male and female.

But to return to the making of the wax image.

I think that the binding of this figure illustrates one of the uses to which a witch puts her cord. From ancient times "Cords, Threads or Clews" have been mentioned as used by witches, for evil or good, and often they are described as coloured. Greek witches are always described as using coloured cords.

Modern witches do the same; I have asked the reason, and they say it's just because they are pretty. This may simply mean that as witchcraft is a religious rite, they have everything as "nice" as possible, or there may be some reason which is now forgotten. It has been suggested to me that it might be merely that white cords would soon show dirt, but I don't think this is right, or they would use black, or dark coloured ones, though Italian witches use black cords or thread when making an evil charm.

In this Museum I have a dried-up lemon stuck with black pins and bound with black thread. This was made to part two lovers whose union the parents did not approve of, and black cords are said to be employed for "killing spells."

Incidentally, the witch used white cords to bind the blackmailer, but this was not to injure him in any way, simply to prevent him harming others, and was the only cord she had handy.

It is said that Babylonian witches snared people's souls by tying knots in a cord, saying a spell at each knot. It was an old charge against witches in Europe, that they tied knots to ruin people, though my friends deny knowing this art. But there is not the slightest doubt that (so called) witches in the Isle of Man and elsewhere used to sell knotted cords to sailors, to give them favourable winds, it being usually said that untying the first knot made a light wind, which soon died away, untying the second brought a strong wind, which presently failed, untying the third knot brought a storm which generally sank the ship.

This I think shows how everything a witch did was distorted. Sailors are not bigger fools than other people. It is obvious that no one in his senses would untie the third knot if he believed it would raise a storm, and any canny Captain would buy a number of cords and only untie the first two. I say "so-called witches," for everyone who sells charms and spells has not been initiated. And it is an old witch law that "you must never work magic for money." Though, of course, as with every religion, not all adherents always obey the teachings.

Returning to the subject of "Cords." The Inquisition originally charged witches with "Raising Storms, Human Sacrifice, and Wearing Girdles," which has always seemed to me to be a curious combination especially at a time when girdles were an ordinary article of attire.

Now, the Inquisition may have been composed of sadistic scoundrels; they were, however, certainly not fools. When they made this charge, it had a real meaning to them.

It must be remembered that the same charge was made against the Templars. The *Chronicle of St. Denis* states emphatically: "In their girdles was their mahommerie," i.e. their magic. Some witches believe that this means that the Inquisition knew that both Templars and witches used them to work magic.

In the Chronicle of Cyprus, it is mentioned as a curious fact that a Templar's servant removed (stole?) his master's girdle; as soon as he knew, the Templar killed him with his sword. It also tells that an eavesdropper heard a Knight Templar instructing some novices, telling them to guard these cords well, wearing them concealed beneath their clothing as through them they might attain great prosperity. I cannot imagine anything that could be done with a cord, to gain great prosperity except to use it in the witches' way to "work magic."

Some authors confound the cord with the "Witches Garter." This is a badge of rank which is seldom used nowadays as far as my experience goes, but a number possess them and occasionally wear them.

The garter was occasionally employed in the old days as a sign of recognition. It would not be much use nowadays when, if anyone wanted to pretend to be a witch, it is the first thing they would think of.

Dr. Margaret Murray thinks the cord was used as a means of execution of traitors; of this I have no knowledge, though the cases she quotes appear to me to be mercy killings, a man being taken, and subjected to the usual prolonged tortures, strangled himself or was strangled to gain a merciful death to go to the realms of the Goddess, the land described by the poets, "where the young men are walking with the gold light low on their limbs, and the young girls with radiance on their faces and bosoms, and the young blossom bursting from the apple-boughs, and all that is young there glorying in the morning, and it is morning there for ever, in the land of youth." The land where the Wica believe they will go for rest and refreshment till by the power of the Goddess they will be ready to be reborn on earth again.

T.C. Lethbridge says (p. 125) in *Gogmagog:*

> Witchcraft only came into full being when a pastoral stage of existence replaced hunting as a mode of life. In order to secure this end, ritual dances were performed, ritual licence and feast took place, and at intervals victims were put to death by fire. It is known that the chief object of adoration is a goddess, but I have never seen her name disclosed, although something resembling "Adraste" has been suggested. The leader of the ceremonies, however, seems frequently to have been dressed up to resemble a bull, goat, or horse. . . . Now, this ritual bears a

> close resemblance to that deduced for our Gog and Magog religion. Is it the same or not?
>
> (p. 127). The popular picture of witches, which still remains with us today, is the result of long and furious propaganda by their enemies. It must be far from the truth. A faith, which needed so much venom from ecclesiastical authority to suppress it, must have had many good points in order to make it a serious rival. It is clear . . . it had a firm belief in immortality.
>
> (p. 131). The question of the Druids. Their name is certainly connected with the Celtic root 'dru' for oak. They are reported by contemporaries as priests of the sacred oak in the sacred grove. . . . If we can show early examples of the use of the sacred groves, or rites connected with the oak, it will go a long way to show that a priesthood of the Druidic type existed in Britain before the iron-age Celts arrived. These Celts may have been the first to call them Druids, but they would have been Druids none the less.
>
> (p. 136). It is not unexpected to find evidence for the existence of two beliefs side by side and in the same individual. Not only is there the Biblical testimony for it among the ancient Hebrews; but if Dr. Margaret Murray is right, which I feel sure is the case, the ruling families of England, down to Plantagenet times, were devotees of both religions. . . . The rites of the older faith, now regarded as superstition, are practised all over the country today. It did not mean the people were not Christian; but that they could see a lot of sense in the old beliefs also. The idea of transmigration and subsequent rebirth on earth may have had a wider appeal to Celtic warriors than that of twanging a harp in the sky, or resting on the bosom of Abraham. . . . Many of the rites of Isis became Christian ceremonies; many pagan gods and goddesses were canonized as Christian Saints; Brigid became St. Bridget, Ma and Matrona became St. Mary.

Now, everything Mr. Lethbridge says is exactly what the witches have told me, excepting that they deny ever having used any kind of living sacrifice, human or animal. Mr. Lethbridge believes that the Goddess was at first a ferocious personality, a Goddess of death and destruction, but who distributed the apples of life and was of a maternal character; who later turned into a milder Moon Goddess to whom blood offerings were no longer made.

Mr. Lethbridge naturally accepts the evidence he meets with; I do likewise with regard to the traditions and rituals which have survived, and I find a hatred of any blood or burnt sacrifice. It is quite possible that this hatred comes from a time when such things were done. (Even though modern witches attribute it to objections to the goings on of Aleister Crowley.) Also, I think there is much evidence that there was "Hunting Magic" originally, and I presume it was the same people who as they gradually turned to cattle-keeping would perform pastoral rites, though this is only my theory.

The first of May (May Day) is celebrated in Europe and America, but no one seems to know exactly why. It is not a Christian festival. Formerly it was celebrated with processions and rejoicings. It is conjectured to be the remnant of some ancient fertility rite that once marked the coming of Spring. But Spring begins in March; others say it had to do with a Roman goddess, Florilia; if so, we should expect to have something which suggests her worship.

Others say it was the Celtic Beltane, when sacrifices were made to the God Baal, or Beal. Now, the Roman Apollo was sometimes called Belinus, the god of Tyre was Baal; the Phoenician's god was Baal; and the great Irish god was Beal. All of these names meant the Sun; although their festivals were in the Spring, they do not seem to have all been on May Day.

The witches have one of their most important festivals in honour of their Goddess on that day; however, as they worship the Moon, their day begins at sundown. So according to our reckoning, they keep the night of the 30th April. Now, is there anything which might lead us to think that the witches' festival was the origin of May Day. Was it celebrated in England? We read, "It was a time of pleasure and love-making. Young people went out the night before April 30th and spent the night drinking, making music and in love." They broke branches from flowering trees and after a night of abandon, returned home at dawn, "Bringing in the May."

The puritan Philip Stubbs wrote in 1585: "I have heard it credibly reported . . . that of fourtie, threescore, or a hundred maides goying in the woods overnight, there have been scarcely the thirde part of them returned home undefiled." He was a Puritan and probably exaggerated yet there must have been something that he was complaining about; he also disliked the May Pole, and says: "They dance about like as the heathen people did at the dedication of the idols whereof; this is the perfect pattern, or rather the thing itself." I take this to mean that he recognised what the May Pole represented.

The Puritans passed a bill through Parliament calling the May Day celebrations a "Heathenish Vanity." The dances were condemned as pagan and a device of the devil.

Thomas Hall, one of the Puritan writers, said: "If Moses was angry when he saw the people dance about the Golden Calf, well might he be so to see people dancing the morrice about a post in honour of a whore." May we not assume that he knew that May Day was in honour of some goddess, whom the people still venerated, but her name is never mentioned. Why? And, if so, may she not have been the goddess of the Witches, whose name I am forbidden to mention, as I tell in *Witchcraft Today.*

I wonder why it was chosen as a holiday for labour demonstrations by the very serious body, the Socialist International, as long ago as 1889. Did they know the Goddess promised freedom to all her children?

Chapter XI

Who Were the Gods of Britain?

Britain has been very unlucky in the matter of history. While she has some of the most wonderful ancient monuments in the world, they mostly date from a time when writing was uncommon, and what was written was not usually inscribed on stone, though there are Ogham inscriptions in South Wales and at Silchester in Hampshire. Caesar tells us that the Druids used Greek characters in writing, though there are two so-called "Tree Alphabets" which were also used by them. But owing to the Roman invasion tending to break up the British tribes, the coming of Christianity which destroyed so much of the old traditions, then the Saxon invasions and the consequent several hundred years' fighting which they led to, the destruction of the libraries such as that of Bangor Abbey which was burnt by the followers of St. Augustine, and the abominable damp English climate, we have hardly any written records surviving; while the Roman extermination of the Druids and the general break-up of Ancient British tribal life have eliminated most oral traditions also.

There are also such historical incidents, deeply distressing to the anthropologist, as that which records how certain Bishops complained to Henry VIII, in the days when he had been newly dubbed "Defender of the Faith," that there was a "heathen priest" in Wales named Darvell Gadarn after the huge "idol" of the same name, made of oak which he served, and to which the people were in the habit of offering sacrifices of cattle. In order to save the people's souls from Hell, the Bishops had the "priest" and his "idol" brought to London and there burned together. This was a terrible loss to our knowledge, as the "idol" may well have been a relic of immemorial age, and probably represented Hu Gadarn, Hu the Mighty, the ruler of the Celtic Hades.

Ireland was more fortunate, as there the Druids stayed on at the king's courts as wise men and magicians, and it was never conquered by the

Romans or the Saxons. Also in later years, many Irish priests wrote down the traditions of the country, partly to explain the coming of St. Patrick; but they included many tales of the ancient days. So there is a fairly good account of the ancient Irish Gods, their names and attributes, even though a Christian gloss has been put over the whole.

Another source of information about the Ancient Gods is the mediaeval romances such as the "Morte D'Arthur," the Grail stories, etc., in which the Gods and Goddesses appear under strange disguises; the Moon Goddess, for instance, appearing as "Morgan Le Fay," or the Old God appearing as a "fairy knight," as in "Sir Huon of Bordeaux."

Arthur himself seems to be a form of the Old God of Death and the After-World; for it is evident that even in Shakespeare's day he was regarded by the common people as the Ruler of the After-World. It will be remembered how Shakespeare makes Sir John Falstaff's landlady, when describing his death, say that "He made a good end, and was gone to Arthur's bosom if ever a man was." King Arthur was, in some districts, regarded as the leader of the Wild Hunt, which definitely identifies him with the God of the Witches. T. Crofton Croker, in his *Fairy Legends and Traditions of the South of Ireland,* tells us,

> Popular legends are full of accounts of wild huntsmen, and such restless personages. King Arthur, we are told, used to hunt in the English woods: no one could see the monarch himself, but the sounding of the horns and the cry of the hounds might be plainly heard; and when any one called out after him, an answer was returned—'We are King Arthur and his kindred'.

The epitaph on King Arthur's tomb at Glastonbury as given by Sir Thomas Malory is an illustration of the ancient belief in reincarnation: *Hic jacet Arthurus, Rex quondam, Rexque futurus,* i.e. "Here lies King Arthur, who was king before and who shall be king again." In his novel, *Wife to Mr. Milton,* Robert Graves describes how John Milton, the poet, believed so strongly at one period of his life that King Arthur would reincarnate and again lead the British nation that he was in the habit of casting astrological figures in order to ascertain the most favourable time for such a child to be conceived as would provide the spirit of Arthur with a vehicle for reincarnation, and then having intercourse with his wife at the time the figure indicated, in an attempt to beget a son who should be King Arthur reborn.

It is apparent from the foregoing that King Arthur was regarded both as a hero who would some day reincarnate, and as a God. It would seem that the *Dux Brittanorum* who rallied the broken British nation against the Saxon invaders after the withdrawal of the Legions had come in the minds of the people to be associated with the attributes of an ancient God. This is a familiar occurrence to students of comparative religion, who will remember how divine myths of various kinds, such as miraculous birth, etc., come to be incorporated into the lives of famous men as time passes and their stories are told and re-told. Those heroes who passed into the realms of the Gods became like unto them, even as in Ancient Egypt the soul of the just man became as that of Osiris.

A certain amount has been written by various authors about the old legend of the Wild Hunt; but its connection with the witch cult does not seem to be generally realised. However, I stated in my book, *Witchcraft Today,* that modern witches had told me that they were in the habit, in old times, of going to their meetings riding on horseback, dressed up in strange clothes and shouting wildly, in order to scare people away. This strange cavalcade would, of course, have been taken by the country people to be the Wild Hunt, with its phantom horsemen, to look upon which was death. Some persons cast doubt upon my statement about this matter; but, as I have previously mentioned, confirmation of my informants' statements came to me from a rare old book, *Receuil de Lettres au Sujet des Malefices et due Sortilege . . . par le Sieur Boissier* (Paris, 1731). In this book Boissier repeats the evidence given at a witchcraft trial in France in 1669, some of which is to the effect that the witches were holding a meeting at a cross-roads near an old grange when someone came along the road, whereat "The Devil caused six horses to appear, upon which six witches mounted," and with whoops and wild yells galloped past the intruder, which effectively scared him away. Of course, he would have taken them for the famous phantom train, legends of which are found all over Europe.

But *why* should the witches impersonate the Wild Hunt? Did it have any other significance to the cult, beside the joke of scaring people? I think it did, and that the legends of the Wild Hunt are the remains of one of the oldest traditions of the Ancient Gods.

Its leader goes by various names in different countries, and in different districts of the British Isles. But under whatever names he may be known, he is always the Old God of Hunting and Death. One of the most famous of his names is Gwyn ap Nudd, and Charles Squire has this to say about him in his *Celtic Myth and Legend, Poetry and Romance:*

> Gwyn ap Nudd has outlived in tradition almost all his supernatural kin. Professor Rhys is tempted to see in him the British equivalent of the Gaelic Finn mac Cumhail. The name of both alike means 'white'; both are sons of the heaven-god; both are famed as hunters. Gwyn, however, is more than that; for his game is man. In the early Welsh poems, he is a god of battle and of the dead, and, as such, fills the part of a psychopompos, conducting the slain into Hades, and there ruling over them. In later, semi-Christianised history he is described as 'Gwyn, son of Nudd, whom God has placed over the brood of devils in Annwn, lest they should destroy the present race'. Later again, as paganism still further degenerated, he came to be considered as king of the Tylwyth Teg, the Welsh fairies, and his name as such has hardly yet died out of his last haunt, the romantic vale of Neath. He is the wild huntsman of Wales and the West of England, and it is his pack which is sometimes heard at chase in waste places by night.
>
> In his earliest guise, as a god of war and death, he is the subject of a poem in dialogue contained in the Black Book of Caermarthen. Obscure, like most of the ancient Welsh poems, it is yet a spirited production.... In it we shall see mirrored perhaps the clearest figure of the British Pantheon, the 'mighty hunter', not of deer, but of men's souls, riding his demon horse, and cheering on his demon hound to the fearful chase. He knows when and where all the great warriors fell, for he gathered their souls upon the field of battle, and now rules over them in Hades, or upon some 'misty mountain-top'.

Gwyn's father, Nudd or Llud, is the same as the Irish God Nuada, the owner of the Great Sword "from whose stroke no one ever escaped or recovered," i.e. the Sword of Death, which was one of the Four Talismans of the Tuatha De Danaan, the Children of the Goddess Dana, the Great Mother of Gods and Men. He may well be merely a younger version of Nudd, as Horus was of Osiris.

One of Gwyn's especial haunts was Glastonbury Tor, which in early times was surrounded by almost impassable swamps. It will be remembered how the witches claim Glastonbury as one of their sacred places. As "Avalon," the Place of Apples, with their symbolism of rebirth, it would naturally be sacred to the Old God of Death and Resurrection. I have already mentioned the Sacred Well there, which was already ancient when Christianity first came to Britain.

It occurs to me as a possibility that the famous "Glastonbury Thorn" may well be the last remaining relic of a sacred grove, as it is mentioned in the early Grail romances, which speak as if a number of such trees existed there. All such relics of the olden time would, of course, be Christianised after the conversion, or nominal conversion, of England, and legends made up to account for their existence.

Indeed, wherever we find a really old Christian sanctuary, we may be almost certain that it is built upon a still more ancient shrine of paganism. It was the deliberate policy of the early Church to do this, as they knew that the people would continue to go to their traditional sacred sites anyway, whether they were Christian or not, so they might as well be Christian. There is extant a letter from St. Gregory, then Pope, to Abbot Mellitus in A.D. 601, in which the Pope directs that existing pagan temples are to be "purified" and changed into Christian churches, so that "the nation, seeing that their temples are not destroyed, may remove error from their hearts, and knowing and adoring the true God, may the more familiarly resort to the places to which they have been accustomed." (Quoted by the Venerable Bede in his "Historia Ecclesiastica.") Sometimes, as we have seen, the old temples and sites were deliberately defiled and razed, but when this was too dangerous, as it tended to arouse popular feeling, it was found a better policy to adapt them quietly and subtly to the new religion.

Hence it is that the Celtic Elysium, Avalon, became the focus of Christian legend; although, as I have mentioned before, there is nothing basically impossible in the tale of Joseph of Arimathea, if he were really in the tin trade, having come there after the Crucifixion, when probably his position in his native country would have been at least difficult, if not dangerous. He would, like so many others after him, have come to Britain as a political refugee, hoping to be able to make a living by some trade he knew.

A legend of Glastonbury Tor illustrates the struggle between the pagan and the Christian elements at Glastonbury. It relates how an early Christian hermit, St. Collen, who dwelt in a cell near Glastonbury Tor, one day heard two men who were passing his cell talking about Gwyn ap Nudd, and saying that he was King of Annwn (the After-World) and of the fairies. St. Collen put his head out of his cell and told them to hold their tongues, saying that Gwyn and his fairy host were nothing but demons. The two men retorted that soon Collen would have to meet the Dark Ruler face to face. Later, someone came knocking at Collen's door, and on Collen calling out "Who's there?" he got the reply, "I am the messenger of Gwyn ap Nudd, King of Hades, to bid thee come by the middle of the day to speak with him on the top of the hill." The saint refused to go. The messenger came again with the same message, but he still refused. Then the messenger came a third time, and on receiving a third refusal he told the saint that if he continued not to comply after being summoned three times it would be the worse for him. So the saint decided to go, but as a precaution he took a flask of holy water with him.

The saint toiled up the green slope of the great Tor, and to his surprise he found it crowned by a splendid castle, which he had never seen before. Handsomely dressed courtiers were walking about, and a page conducted the saint to where Gwyn himself was sitting on a golden chair before a richly-spread table. Gwyn, in contrast to the saint's discourtesy, invited him to share his feast, adding that if there was anything he especially liked he had only to ask and it should be bought for him. But the saint, feeling himself to be the victim of magical illusion and glamourie, said, "I do not eat the leaves of trees." He evidently knew the traditional spell of *fith-fath,* or shape-shifting, by which a common thing could be made to look like something "rich and strange." However, Gwyn continued to speak the saint fair, and asked him if he did not admire the courtiers' livery, which was red on one side and blue on the other. "Their dress is good enough for its kind," said the gruff saint. "What kind is that?" asked Gwyn. "The red shows which side is being scorched, and the blue shows which side is being frozen," replied the saint; implying that they were either demons or damned souls in hell. And therewith Collen laid about him with his flask of holy water, and the King of Annwn, together with his castle and his weird companions, vanished into thin air.

As usual, the heathens are shown as being kind and polite, and the "saints" as churlish and destructive.

St. Collen is by no means the only person to have witnessed strange things on Glastonbury Tor. There are tales today of people who have seen strange lights and fairy-like forms upon the Tor, and I have met local people who have solemnly assured me that the Tor is hollow—perhaps a "folk-memory" of the Hollow Hill where the Old God reigned.

Gwyn's "Fairy Host" the *Sluagh,* as it is called in Ireland, is traditionally composed of those whose souls are too good for hell, but not good enough for heaven; or else of the souls of unbaptised persons, i.e. pagans. It may be noted, however, that the name "Gwyn" means "white," and in the doctrine of the Druids the Higher Realms of the After World (what Spiritualists would call the "Higher Planes") were called the Realm of Gwynfyd. Curiously enough, white was once popular as a colour of mourning for the dead. Henry VIII is said to have worn white mourning for Anne Boleyn, and there is a beautiful portrait extant of "Marie, Reine d'Ecosse, en Deuil Blanche," Mary Queen of Scots wearing white mourning for her first husband. White was the colour of mourning in Spain until 1498, according to Cobham Brewer. Its signification was *hope* for the soul of the departed. One wonders if it might be a distant relic of paganism, with its hope for the soul in the After-World, and the promise of re-birth, as opposed to the grim Christian doctrines of the Last Judgment, and of Heaven being reserved for a chosen few, while the greater part of mankind were menaced with Hell and Purgatory.

Gwyn's divine father, Nudd, or as the Romans called him, Nodens, had a famous temple at Lydney on the Severn. He was regarded as a healing God as well as a God of the sea, or, as he was called, "The God of the Great Deeps," and the Romans equated him with Silvanus, who was the King of the Wood. This seems to be a curious complexity of attributes; however, not all deeps are those of the sea.

Late and post-Christian as are the Welsh poems and stories translated by Lady Charlotte Guest in the "Mabinogion," they yet give a few vivid glimpses of the leader of the Wild Hunt, who appears therein as "Arawn, the King of Annwn," accompanied with his white fairy hounds with the red ears which are so often a feature of Celtic myth. In North Devon these spectral hounds are called "Yeth Hounds," i.e. Heath or Heathen Hounds, and on Dartmoor the "Wish Hounds." One wonders if this might not be a corruption of "Witch Hounds."

In Scandinavian and Teutonic countries the leader of the Wild Hunt is Odin or Woden, and Dr. W. Wagner, in *Asgard and the Gods,* has a very intriguing comment to make about it; he says,

> The Wild Hunt generally went on in the sacred season, between Christmas and Twelfth Night. When its shouts were particularly loud and distinct, it was said that it was to be a fruitful year. At the time of the

> summer solstice, and when day and night became of equal length, the Wild Hunt again passed in the wind and rain, for Woden was also lord of the rain, and used to ride on his cloud-horse, so that plentiful rains might refresh the earth.

Now it will be noted from the foregoing quotation, firstly a connection in the popular mind between the Wild Hunt and fertility, and secondly a connection between the appearances of the Wild Hunt and the equinoxes and solstices, which are four of the witches' Eight Ritual Occasions.

From Ireland comes another legend which connects a kind of Wild Hunt or fairy cavalcade with fertility, and also with a witches' Sabbat. T. Croften Croker, in his *Fairy Legends and Traditions of the South of Ireland,* relates how around the Lake of Killarney there is a legend of a great chieftain of a bygone age, called "The O'Donoghue." He ruled in the time before history, and his reign was distinguished by abundance, wisdom and prosperity—a kind of Golden Age. One day, he left the world of men and walked into the Lake of Killarney, after uttering to his assembled court a prophecy of the times which were to come after him.

He is supposed to rise out of the waters, mounted upon a white horse, and ride upon the surface of the waves, accompanied by a beautiful fairy train, to the sounds of enchanting music. It will be noted that his appearance is connected with fertility and good fortune, and that the occasion of it is May Day, one of the old Sabbats. It is not difficult to see in the figure of "The Good O'Donoghue" one of the ancient Gods.

There is, however, another aspect of the beliefs regarding the Wild Hunt which illustrates the other side of the Old God's character, namely that of the God of Death. That is the tradition which connects the appearance of the Wild Hunt with some national calamity. This especially seems to apply to the appearance of "Le Grand Veneur de Fontainebleau" in France, and Herne the Hunter in Windsor Park in England. Wagner, in *Asgard and the Gods*, says of the former that his shouts were heard beside the Royal Palace the day before Henry IV was murdered by Ravaillac. Obviously, the Old God of Death had come for the soul of the doomed King. "The Raging Host also passed over the heavens twice, darkening the sun, before the Revolution broke out. The populace everywhere believes that its appearance is the foreshadowing of pestilence or war, or some other great misfortune."

With regard to Herne the Hunter, Eliott O'Donnell, in his book, *Haunted Britain,* speaks of

> . . . the fearsome spectre of Herne, his head crowned with gigantic stag's horns. Sometimes he is seen on foot and sometimes mounted on a huge black horse. When the latter, he is accompanied by his hounds, which follow him in his mad career around the park.
>
> It is open to conjecture whether the Phantom White Stag, which is also rumoured to haunt the Park, is the quarry of Herne, since, so far as is known, it has never been visualised chased by the Hunter's hounds. Its appearance is said to predict some event of national importance and, according to a rumour circulated at the time, it was seen in the Park immediately prior to the outbreak of the First World War.

This stag could be a kind of *alter ego* of Herne himself.

I have heard somewhere, too, that Herne and his phantom band were seen just before the fatal illness of King George V.

Christina Hole, in *English Folklore,* says,

> Before any calamity affecting the royal family or the nation, the apparition of Herne the Hunter is seen with horns on his head, together with the ghostly form of the blasted oak (Herne's sacred tree: my note). Sometimes a white stag appears also, issuing from a hollow which is associated with fairies. All three phantoms are said to have been seen in the park before the economic crisis of 1931.

Herne the Hunter, with his helmet crowned with stag's antlers, his wild band of followers, his association with "fairies," and the huge oak tree, now apparently destroyed, beneath which he used to appear, is the British example *par excellence* of a surviving tradition of the Old God of the Witches.

The dual nature of the Old God will be noticed. He is the giver of fertility, both of the ground and of humans and animals; but he is also Lord of the Gates of Death. This dual nature has caused some students of comparative religion to equate him with Janus, who was in very ancient times the consort of Diana, and who was depicted with two faces. There is also an obvious resemblance to the Indian Shiva, who is the Phallic God as well as the Destroyer, and who is the consort of the Great Mother Goddess, Shakti.

The witches explain this duality by a ritual in which they invoke the Old God: "Thou art the Opener of the Doorway of the Womb; and yet, because all things that are born must also die, that they may be renewed, therefore art thou Lord of the Gates of Death."

In the Magical Legend of the Witches, which I gave in *Witchcraft Today* and which is reprinted as an Appendix to this book, the Old God explains to the Goddess that Age and Fate (i.e. Karma) against which he is powerless (because they are Cosmic Law) cause all things to wither and die: "But when men die at the end of time, I give them rest and peace, and strength so that they may return," i.e. be reborn upon the earth, or reincarnated.

In two of the English countryside's most famous "hill-figures" we may perhaps see these two aspects of the Old God manifested. "The Giant of Cerne," cut upon the hillside at Cerne Abbas in Dorset, ithyphallic, and with uplifted club (also a phallic symbol), shows him as the God of Fertility; and he is still regarded as such by the local people. It is said that if a childless woman wishes to become fruitful she may do so by spending a night lying upon the Giant's phallus at the proper season of the year; and there is a story that when a local clergyman was incensed by the Giant's naturalistic appearance, and, being unable to put breeches upon him, proposed that part of the Giant's anatomy to which he objected should be ploughed up, he was prevented from carrying out this project by the indignation of the local people. Happily, the Giant of Cerne now belongs to the National Trust, and is, we may hope, safe from such vandalism.

There is another story from Cerne to the effect that about the time of the first World War a community of nuns came to live there, and were softened by the sight of the gloriously shameless Old God. So the Mother Superior directed them to go up on the hill with vessels of holy water and sprinkle this work of the Devil in order to exorcise its disturbing influence. On their return, passing through the village, they were told, "It baint no use you going up there this time o' year. You got to go up in May if you wants babies."

The other figure is, of course, the "Long Man of Wilmington," in Sussex. This figure was re-cut in late Victorian times, having been allowed to become overgrown until it was merely an outline visible when dew or hoar-frost was upon the grass. However, when towards the end of the last century there took place a renaissance of interest in archaeology, the re-cutting was carried out at the insistence of Dr. J. S. Phené. Naturally, in those days they would not have cut "The Long Man" in quite such a naturalistic form as that of the Giant of Cerne! However, apart from this the old outlines were, I believe, followed as closely as possible.

The figure appears as usual, upon a hillside; this time with outstretched arms which appear to be holding two long wands. Sir Flinders Petrie thought that it might have represented the Sun-God opening the gates of dawn. I think that Petrie was very nearly right, but that it really represents the Old God as Lord of the Gates of Death, which he is represented as holding.

At the time of writing, traces of yet other "giant" figures cut in the earth have been found on the slopes of the Gogmagog Hills at Wandlebury, a few miles from Cambridge, by Mr. Thomas Charles Lethbridge, Honorary Keeper of Anglo-Saxon Antiquities at Cambridge University Museum. Examination of this site has only just commenced, and it will be some time before any final conclusions can be reached; but enough has already been uncovered to show that one of the figures is a naked Goddess. To the north of the figure, on the brow of the hill, is an ancient earthwork which Professor Grahame Clarke of the Cambridge Department of Archaeology believes may have been the scene of fertility rites, traces of which apparently survived until Elizabethan days, as a University edict of that time forbade students from attending "festivities at Wandlebury." Something similar happened at Cerne, where there is a small earthwork on the brow of the hill, just above the figure, which is known locally as "The Giant's Frying Pan." Here the Maypole used to be erected every May Day, until Cromwell and his Puritans put a stop to it. It is very probable that this figure represents an ancient British Goddess, and I believe that close by it, over her head, has been found the shape of a crescent moon, and beside her part of the figure of a horse, or some kind of beast. The Moon, of course, would be a clear link with the Mother Goddess. There are probably yet more figures of this type existing in the British Isles which modern techniques of archaeology, especially aerial photography, may yet uncover, and from which we will learn more of our Ancient Gods.

A remarkable Neolithic figure of the Great Mother was found at the old flint mine known as Grime's Graves in Norfolk. Jacquetta and Christopher Hawkes, in their book *Prehistoric Britain,* describe it thus:

> Enthroned on a ledge sat the chalk-carved image of a fat and pregnant woman, looking down on a phallus, also cut in chalk, and a great pile of deer-horn picks that had been laid as offerings at her feet. Here, in fact, was the shrine of a fertility cult, but one apparently intended to serve a curious and unexpected purpose. This particular shaft had failed to strike the usual rich flint-bed, and it seems reasonable to suppose that the shrine was set up to counteract the sterility of this pit and ensure the abundance of the next. But this was only one manifestation in the peculiar conditions of a mining community of a fertility cult that was generally practised among the Neolithic people—female figurines and phalli have been found at several causewayed camps and in a tomb, where presumably the rites were directed to more hopeful biological ends—the fecundity of men and beasts.

Precisely the same concept may be found among witches today. Their Goddess is the Mother of Fertility in *all* its forms, whether it be the fertility of the earth, of cattle and human beings, or the material prosperity of some venture, or those more subtle forms of fertility which germinate in the mind and bring forth poetry and the arts. This latter is not merely a modern refinement. One of her Celtic names was Cerridwen, and this name is found in such place-names as Liskeard in Cornwall, which is "Lys Cerrid," the Court of Cerrid. She it was who, in Bardic mythology, was the owner of the Magic Cauldron in which was brewed the "Awen," the Draught of Inspiration, and in which old men became young again. This, as time passed, became Christianised as the Holy Grail. A gulf of time separates the Great Mother of Grime's Graves from the White Lady of the Bards, but the archetype is the same. Her "Cauldron" is the Womb of the Goddess, the Mother and Lover of all men, because she is incarnate potentially in all women.

I must not, however, give the impression that the people of Ancient Britain worshipped only one God and only one Goddess, who were exactly the same in all parts of the country. In very early times the country was split up into many different tribes, which, of course, lived in localities differing from each other as to the type of country they were. For instance, the sea-faring people would conceive their God as a God of the Sea; those who depended upon agriculture would pay most reverence to that aspect of Divinity which manifested as the green and growing things of Nature returning each year, or the fertility of cattle; and the hunters would have a Hunting God. Also, these tribes had different dialects, and even different languages, and so the names of the Gods would vary from one part of the country to another. As Charles Squire, in his *Celtic Myth and Legend, Poetry and Romance,* says:

> The Celts, both of the Gaelic and British branches, were split up into numerous petty tribes, each with its own local deities embodying the same essential conceptions under different names.

And this statement, I think, is more or less true of all peoples.

But the two great realities with which all ancient people were faced were essentially the unchanging, unending ones of Life and Death; and these it was, together with that third elusive thing, magical power, which the Gods held in Their hands. Consequently, wherever men have formulated for themselves figures of Divinity, these have ever been the archetypes: the Lady of Life, the Lord of Death and What Lies beyond; and between them the web of magic has been spun.

Nor are the Great Ancient Ones mere concepts lingering in the leaves of old books and the minds of old scholars. The people remember; nay, the very land itself remembers. Christina Hole, in her book, *English Folklore,* quotes a story told by R. M. Heanley in the *Saga Book of the Viking Club,* January, 1902. She says:

> In September, 1901, he (Heanley) saw a Kern Baby made of barley straw placed opposite the gate of a wheat-field. The farmer's wife told him it was there to avert storms. She said that prayers were all right so far as they went but the Almighty must be 'strange and throng' with so much corn to look after, and she added: 'We mustn't forget owd Providence. Happen it's best to keep in wi' both parties'. In many country districts the word Providence is not used in its ordinary religious significance but denotes the Devil, or rather the old gods with whom he is so often confounded.

Dr. Evans in the *Folklore Journal* for March, 1895, tells how, on a Good Friday morning in the late nineteenth century, an old man said to him, "I be a-going to the King-stones, for there I shall be on holy ground." He was referring to the Rollright Stones on the border of Oxfordshire and Warwickshire, which were traditionally the chief meeting-place in not so Ancient times of the neighbouring witches.

Accounts of the Irish and Welsh Pantheons are, as I have said, fairly plentiful, though the latter are of late date, and we may feel confident that the Ancient Gods of Wales are also those of Ancient Britain. The Irish Gods resemble them closely, with slightly different names owing to the difference in language. But in England almost all accounts have been destroyed by successive waves of invasion, and by the activities of the Christian hierarchy, so that little remains beside the elusive traces in folklore, the great figures cut on the hillsides, and the beliefs preserved in the witch covens.

The Great Mother in Ireland was called Dana; the Welsh version of this name was Dön. Dön had a daughter called Arianrhad, which means "Silver Wheel," so we may consider her as being a Moon Goddess. But she was also the Goddess to whose castle the souls of heroes went when they died, and the constellation Cassiopeia was called Lys Dön, the Court of Dön. There were, however, places in Britain called Caer Arianrhod. In Cardigan Bay, in Wales, there is said to be a city sunken beneath the sea which is Caer Arianrhod, the bells of which can be faintly heard swinging with the tide.

Arianrhod had a brother, who was also her consort, called Gwydion, and he was "The prime enchanter of the Britons." The stories in the "Mabinogion" treat of these Gods and Goddesses, but in a late and confused fashion, and are evidently post-Christian because they contain references to such things as the saying of Mass. We can, however, distinguish the outlines of divine figures shining through these mists of obscurity, and make out something of what the Ancient Britons believed about them, their relationships and functions, and the meaning of their myths. Arianrhod, for instance, is said to have given birth to twin Gods, Llew, the Sun-God, and Dylan, the God of the Waves, and to have miraculously conceived these children by leaping over a wizard's wand. This is interesting, because it shows the early meaning of the wand as a phallic symbol, and its relationship to the broomstick which witches carried as such. Christina Hole, in her *English Folklore,* says, "Gypsies leapt over broomsticks at their weddings, and there was a form of marriage over a broomstick which was fairly common at one time, though it was not always considered binding if either party wished to default afterwards." Actually, I think this is more a Tinker than a Gipsy custom. At least, this is what Gipsies tell me. In Yorkshire an immoral woman is called a besom. Mothers were usually careful to prevent their daughters from stepping over a broom, and mischievous or spiteful people sometimes laid one where the girl would walk over it by accident; the reason being that if she strode over a besom or broom-handle she would become a mother before she was a wife. The ivy-wreathed thyrsus carried by the Bacchantes probably had essentially the same meaning. One sees pictures on old Greek vases of Bacchantes waving a branch with a bunch of leaves on the end of it, which are reminiscent of the pictures of witches with broomsticks.

Llew, the Sun-God, is the same as the Celtic Lugh whose festival, the Lughnassad is, as we have seen, that "Lammas" which is one of the witches' Sabbats. It is a curious thing how, in spite of all the propaganda for "staggered holidays," Lammas-tide at the beginning of August is still the period to which the working-class population most stubbornly clings as its favourite time for taking a holiday. They don't quite know why, they just feel that "it's the proper time"; and no other time seems quite the same. Folk-memory dies hard.

The Wizard God whose wand brought Llew and Dylan into the world was Math, the brother of the Great Mother, Dön. His name meant "treasure" or "wealth," and he taught his arts to his nephew Gwydion, who then became the Druid of the Gods. Gwydion may be the same as the Teutonic Woden or Odin. Math may have been the original of Merlin.

The great Sea God was Manawyddan, the son of Llyr. His Celtic name was Manannan MacLir, the God of the Isle of Man. He it was who owned the original "Davy Jones's Locker." An old Welsh poem tells how:

The achievement of Manawyddan the Wise,
After lamentation and fiery wrath,
Was the construction of the bone fortress of Oeth
and Anoeth.

This is described as being a prison, in the shape of a beehive, made of human bones mortared together, divided into innumerable cells forming a kind of labyrinth; here he imprisoned "those found trespassing in Hades" (presumably the wicked, or else those who were not under the protection of the Gods by having gone through the Mysteries). This gruesome tale was gradually transmogrified into the sailors' tradition of "Davy Jones's Locker." The Celtic mind was apt to associate the After-World, not only with the "Hollow Hill," or "Avalon," the Place of Apple-trees, but also with a beautiful land "Under the Waves," or across the sea in the West, though this last conception would, of course, be more common among people who lived by the sea, and their Sea-God Manannan or Manawyddan, with his beautiful wife Fand, would be the rulers of it.

It must be remembered that the words "Hell" and "Hades" do not convey to the early peoples the connotation which they have today. "Hell" is called after the Goddess Hel who was the Scandinavian and Teutonic Goddess of the Dead. Her realms were not a place of fiery punishment, but simply the place people went to when they died. Similarly, "Hades" takes its name from the Greek God who was the Ruler of the After-World, and it has the same meaning as the former.

Perhaps the Irish Gods, the Tuatha de Danaan, are those whose figures appear more clearly in "the sunset of old tales." The Gaelic Moon Goddess was called Brigit or Bride, and she was also the Goddess of fire and poetry, which the Gaels deemed a type of supersensual flame or light. We talk of people as being "enlightened," or "fired with enthusiasm." Bride is depicted crowned with the crescent moon, and with a flame of pale fire arising between her hands. One of the Gael's most poetic conceptions was the Love God, Angus Og, Angus the Young, who bore the Cup of Healing in his hands. Another was that of the God called The Dagda, the father of Angus. He was an Earth God, apparently, and had a magical harp, the tune of which, as he played it, caused the seasons to change and follow upon each other in their order.

To give a complete account of the ancient Irish and Welsh pantheons would be too much of a digression; the interested reader may find fuller accounts of them in *Celtic Myth and Legend, Poetry and Romance,* by Charles Squire; *Myths and Legends of the Celtic Race,* by T. W. Rolleston; *The Candle of Vision,* by "A. E."; and the works of Fiona Macleod (William Sharp). But I think enough has been said to indicate that they were not mere "fertility demons" (whatever those may be), or tribal fetishes, but an Olympus of gracious beings which was undoubtedly the product of a poetic genius of which our race may well be proud—for there is plenty of Celtic blood in the English people.

I mention this point because of a rather amusing incident which occurred at a lecture I recently attended at Caxton Hall. The lecturer was speaking upon the subject of the Celtic Gods, when a gentleman in a biretta got up and condemned him roundly for not disparaging them, saying that they were "the Devil." Being ever willing to learn something new, I enquired of the owner of the biretta if he would be kind enough, as there were a considerable number of Celtic Gods (not to mention Goddesses), to indicate to me which particular one of them was the Devil? As I understood there was only one devil, and he couldn't be them all at once. I regret, however, that I received no intelligible reply, or I would gladly pass on the information to the reader.

Chapter XII

Signs and Symbols

A frequent allegation is made against witches by the sillier type of writer that they seek to desecrate Christian churches, and to wreck Christian graveyards. Did these people but know it, there should be few in this country more interested in the preservation of our old cathedrals and churches than the members of the witch cult, because it is in those very cathedrals and churches that some of the most interesting secret signs of the cult are to be found.

We must remember what the conditions of the country were when our oldest places of Christian worship were built, for the elucidation of this paradox. We have already seen how it was the accepted practice of the early Church to build their places of worship upon pagan sites; but by whom would the actual building of such churches have been carried out? The answer is, by the average British craftsman, who at that time might *or might not* have been himself a Christian; who had, however, in the matter of building places of worship, no other master but the Christian Church to provide him with employment. On the other hand, the Church itself employed the best craftsmen it could obtain; if it had stayed to make enquiry into their private beliefs, it might never have got its church or cathedral erected at all.

We have often heard the wealth of carving upon ancient churches and cathedrals described as "quaint" or "curious" or "grotesque"; but few of the general public have realised just how "curious" some of these carvings were. Experts upon church architecture, staggered by the subjects of some of them—even allowing for the coarse humour of olden times—have advanced various unconvincing explanations for their existence, such as that "the ecclesiastical authorities wished the church to be a sort of universal picture-book of contemporary life for a congregation which could not read," or that "the carvings were intended to convey pictures of vice as cautionary tales, to be avoided." Just how unconvincing these explanations are the reader may judge as we progress; but even were they true of the more Rabelaisian and scandalous representations, they cannot account for the presence of symbols which are definitely pagan.

Two of the most interesting of the latter are those known as the "Sheila-na-Gig" and the "Green Man." The former is a crude figure of a naked woman, with the sexual organs deliberately emphasised. Its intention is not obscenity, but simply a representation of the female principle of fertility. In its rough and primitive way, it is a figure of the Great Mother, like the little Palaeolithic figurines from the caves, previously mentioned. The name "Sheila-na-Gig" means "Sheila the Giddy," or "The Merry Sheila," according to Payne Knight, who was one of the first writers to notice these curious figures; Dr. Margaret Murray, however, gives the meaning as "Woman of the Castle." It is, of course, an Irish name, because these figures were at first mainly discovered upon old Irish churches, though examples occur in Britain also, as we shall see, and upon the Continent.

In the Museum of the Society of Antiquaries in Dublin, according to T. Clifton Longworth, there are several examples of the Sheila-na-Gig, removed from ancient churches. One of these came from Rochestown, Co. Tipperary; another from White Island, Lough Erne, Co. Fermanagh; and a third from County Cavan.

In his book, *The Devil a Monk Would Be,* Longworth describes and illustrates a Shiela-na-Gig from Kilpeck Church, about nine miles from Hereford. He says of this church that it is "one of the most remarkable Norman churches in this country. It displays a wealth of fantastic figures of men and beasts and much beautiful Celtic plaited work and interlaced carving, so that all antiquarians are agreed it must have been built under Irish influence. Among the quaint carvings high up near the roof is a crude example of the Sheila-na-Gig." (The influence, however, could have been Welsh or Scottish.) He goes on to say that there is a similar carving on the West Front of Southwell Minster, but that it is in such a lofty position that the details are difficult to make out; and that there is another in York Minster.

To Longworth, these carvings are "gross obscenities." The student of ancient cults may, however, look at them with different eyes. Crude and primitive they are, certainly; but as sacred in their own way to the men who carved them as, for instance, a statue of the Madonna to the Catholic.

Indeed, the Vesica Piscis which surrounds the figure of the Mother of God in many pictures and carvings is simply a formalised representation of the same idea; the gateway of birth.

One of the most remarkable Sheila-na-Gig figures to be found in this country is that preserved in the Lake Village Museum at Glastonbury. It is known as "Jack Stag," but the figure is obviously female, though much worn and weathered by time. It used to stand upon the top of the old Market Cross, which was demolished in 1808, and replaced by the present rather graceful, though modern, structure. The connection of Glastonbury with the Old Religion has already been noted.

M.D. Anderson, in *Looking for History in British Churches** says:

> Strange as it seems, the mediaeval clergy did not prevent the intrusion among the designs used to decorate churches of some crude symbols derived from the old fertility rites. In an article in the *Anthropological Institute Journal for 1934 Dr. M. A. Murray illustrates several examples carved upon English churches of the emblem known as the Sheila-na-Gig (Woman of the Castle) and notes its affinity with the Egyptian goddess Baubo. At Whittlesford (Cambs) the Sheila-na-Gig is carved over a window of the church tower, accompanied by a sinister, human-headed quadruped.*

Baubo, in the sacred legend of Isis and Osiris, endeavoured to comfort Isis, heartbroken over the death of her husband Osiris; but all her efforts failed until at last in desperation she suddenly whipped up her skirts and showed her naked body to the goddess, who burst out laughing at the sight. Exactly the same incident occurs in the sacred legend of Eleusis, only this time the jesting lady is named Iambe, and the mourner to whose face she brings a smile is Demeter, sorrowing for Persephone. It is reasonable to suppose, therefore, that this legendary incident contains some religious teaching. I suggest its underlying meaning may be that the bereaved one takes comfort and smiles at the sign of the Gate of Rebirth, the promise that the lost beloved will be reborn in another reincarnation, and that they will remember, know and love each other again. It is also evidently associated with the ancient idea of ritual nudity, especially in the latter's connection with fertility.

In the Notes at the end of the above-mentioned book the author states that further examples of possible fertility figures carved on churches are discussed and illustrated in *Man,* XXX and XXXI; also an

---

* John Murray, 1951.

article by Dina Portway Dobson on Anglo-Saxon sculpture in *Bristol and Glos. Arch. Soc. Trans.*, L.V.; and that examples of the Sheila-na-Gig on roof bosses may be found in C. J. P. *Cave's Roof Bosses in Mediaeval Churches.*

It does indeed seem strange that the mediaeval clergy did not prevent the intrusion of these pagan images. Were some of them secret sympathisers with the Old Religion, with a foot in both camps? Or was it that the builders of these ancient churches were at least as much pagans as they were Christians?

It may be objected that no one but a believer would build a church; we have, however, the examples of Voltaire and Sir Francis Dashwood to the contrary. The church built by the latter at West Wycombe has some curious features, which may be indicative of his private beliefs. It will be remembered that he was also the founder of the notorious "Hell Fire Club."

The form of the Christian cathedral is, after all, based upon that of the old sacred grove. The vaulted arches of the naves of our great cathedrals reproduce in stone the form of overarching trees, and at the end of them the East Window, usually in the form of a circle, represents the Sun in its rising. The twin towers which are so often a feature of the fabric hark back to the memory of Twin Pillars; and the soaring spire is a phallic symbol. Someone informed G. K. Chesterton of this latter fact once, and, he tells us in one of his essays, "For a moment I was in the mood in which they burned witches!" But no amount of emotional tantrums on the part of the devout will alter the facts of religious history. Chesterton felt that to believe that a church spire was a phallic symbol was to belittle the church; the witch whom he wanted to burn would not think so.

Nor, possibly, would some of the old-time priests. Not all of them were witch-hunting fanatics. On the contrary, many of them were gifted with sufficient tolerance and wisdom to permit the Old Religion and the New to flourish peacefully side by side, and even to appreciate that "There is no religion higher than Truth." Take, for instance, the famous Horn Dance celebrated at Abbots Bromley in Staffordshire, which is clearly a survival of the rites of the Old Religion. According to M. D. Anderson, the six sets of reindeer's horns and the hobby-horse used in this dance are still kept in the church when not in use, and originally the dance took place *in the church itself*; later, the music was played from the church porch while the dancers performed in the churchyard, and nowadays the dance takes place through the streets.

Dancing in churches was by no means an unheard-of thing; it was often made a concomitant of Christian festivals. The original "Christmas carollers" were dancers. An old direction from Sens lays down that the leaders of the clergy "on the second day of Christmas shall execute a dance in the choir of the church or around it, holding staffs in their hands." The boy choristers known as *seises* dance before the High Altar of Seville Cathedral during Mass to this day, I believe. However, the Synods of Rouen, 1214, of Liege and Exeter, 1287, and the Theological Faculty of the University of Paris, 1444, all condemned the practice of church dancing. The last-named conclave called it "this filthy custom," saying that "it had been taken over from the heathen and commemorates them." It was the Reformation which put an end to almost all church dancing; the practice was forbidden in Protestant Germany and Protestant England in the middle of the sixteenth century. But we may in imagination, when seated in an ancient church or cathedral, see the merry carollers, or the dancers of the Feast of Fools in their animal masks, treading their gay round between the great branching pillars which arch themselves above into the dim, carven roof like so many tall trees turned to stone; and then, as time rolls back, see the carven stone again become branches and leaves, and the glories of the East Window transform into the rising sun, as the dancers greet the dawn in the sacred grove.

We have seen that the old naked Goddess of Fertility is to be found carved on British churches, whether secretly placed there by her devotees, or under the tolerance of a parish priest who either worshipped her in secret himself or else turned a blind eye to her pagan presence; and the Old God is also to be found there. His guise is that of the "Green Man," or "foliate mask," as it is sometimes called. This is the figure of a man's face, usually elvish-looking and with pointed ears reminiscent of horns (one very old example, at least, is actually horned). The face appears as if looking through a screen of foliage, usually, though not invariably, of oak leaves, and leaves are represented as curling from the half-open mouth. This mask has been named the "Green Man," because it has been suggested by students of folklore that it represents the figure known as "Jack in the Green" who used to take the leading part in the May Day festivities. It will be remembered that May Eve is one of the witches' Sabbats, and the old custom was to stay out all night gathering green garlands to deck the procession which was held on the morrow, when the phallic "Maypole" was erected—often, as we have seen, upon an old pagan site—and the people danced around it. Some of the green branches used to be arranged upon a kind of wickerwork frame, crowned with a garland of flowers, and inside this erection the man representing "Jack in the Green" used to parade, being almost invisible beneath his green canopy. The foliate mask is suggested to represent this figure peering through the foliage; the inference being that he is a form of "the spirit of vegetation," the green leaves returning in the spring.

"Jack in the Green" very probably did represent this; but in her article in *Folklore* (1939) upon the "Green Man," Lady Raglan gives an illustration of a very much older form of the foliate mask which she calls a "Janiform bust," from Rome, of which she unfortunately does not give the date, stating merely that it is from classical times. It is a bust showing two faces, one a young man, the other an old bearded man. On each side of the pedestal are the words "SACR. DIAN." Both faces are adorned with leaves; the face of the young man (or god?) has leaves springing from its mouth. The hair stands up around both faces, and upon the forehead of each it forms two points reminiscent of horns. The ends of the hair, and the beard and moustache of the older face, fall into leaf-like shapes.

Now, we have seen that Janus or Dianus was a form of the God of the Witches; the two faces depict his dual nature. As the witch ritual says, "Thou art the Opener of the Doorway of the Womb; and yet, because that which is born must also die, that it may be renewed, therefore art Thou Lord of the Gates of Death." Being the consort of Diana, he was the King of the Wood, and as the Phallic God, he was the renewer of life. It is evident that the bust which Lady Raglan illustrates depicts him as the renewer of life in spring; the green leaves take life from his mouth. Closely akin to him are Faunus and Silvanus, and Pan, who was hailed in Hellas as "Pamphagë, Pangenetor," "All-Devourer, All-Begetter"; and as "Chairë Soter Kosmou," "Beloved Saviour of the World," yet from whose name was derived "panic" as a term of terror. Priapus, too, was the Phallic God and the God of Gardens. The concept of fertility, of eternal, ever-renewing, upspringing life, is the basis of them all.

May we venture to suggest that the foliate mask is not merely derived from the figure of "Jack in the Green," but that both are derived from the same source—the Old God of Fertility?

The Old God makes an actual appearance as "The Green Man" in the old romance of "Sir Gawaine and the Green Knight." The figure of the "Green Knight," weird and fantastic yet courtly and kind in a way that puts Sir Gawaine to shame, is typical of the Old God; and it is to be noted that his "wife" in the story is Morgan Le Fay, the Lady of the Moon, who appears sometimes as an old hag, and sometimes as an enticing young woman.

Morgan the Goddess
Therefore it is her name.
Wields none so high hautesse
That she cannot make full tame.

The romance was written somewhere between 1360 and 1400, and at its end are the words "Honi soit qui mal y pense," which is the motto of the Order of the Garter founded in 1349. The story turns upon the possession of a girdle of green silk (The Witch Cord, or Girdle?) the love-gift of Morgan Le Fay, which the lords and ladies of King Arthur's court later adopt as the sign of their fellowship and the remembrance of the courtesy of the Green Knight and his Lady. It will be remembered that the Order of the Garter was founded ostensibly as a memorial of King Arthur's Round Table by that King Edward III who gave refuge to Lady Alice Kyteler when her coven in Ireland was persecuted by the Bishop of Ossory. It is notable that Edward III later went out of his way to be as obnoxious to the said Bishop as he could. It may also be noted that when he commenced the project of founding the Order of the Garter he is said to have instructed his secretary, William of Wykeham, to make enquiries into the tradition of the Order of St. George and the Garter. It is difficult to see how enquiry could have been made into the tradition of an Order which did not yet exist, so the Garter must have an earlier meaning.

"Sir Gawaine and the Green Knight" is an English "Mystery Legend," and as such I recommend its study to the interested scholar. It happens, too, to be a very good story.

Lady Raglan tells us that she first noticed the "Green Man" on the chancel arch of a church at Llangwn, Mon. Here in this church it is, "as in so many others where we have found it," the only carving in the church.

She later found two more of the same kind, one on the font at Stow Minster in Lincolnshire, the other on what had been the capital of the pillar in the nave of Melrose Abbey. Since then Lady Raglan and the Rev. J. Griffith have found examples in twenty-three counties of England, as well as in Midlothian. In many of the cathedrals and minsters there are several examples, as at Southwell, Exeter, Lincoln, Wells and Ely.

There are also examples on the Continent (e.g. the Church of the Dominicans at Ghent, and the church at Semur-en-Auxois). It was a great witch joke, against the Christians, that they could publicly worship their own gods. These heads were deliberately made so as not to be recognised for what they were. We have two specimens in this Museum, one of massive oak, the other a rare specimen of wrought iron. I know of a similar wooden one from an old church which has been destroyed that is now preserved in a witches' meeting place.

"I have already mentioned that in many churches it is the sole decoration, and surely if we were about to choose one carving only for the decoration of our church, we should select the person or the symbol that was in our opinion the focal point of our religious ideals. Mr. C. J. P. Cave, who has photographed hundreds of roof bosses in cathedrals and churches, says that in the majority the only alternative to these leafy faces or foliate heads, as he calls them, is oak leaves, and I also have noticed this predominance of oak. It is, however, by no means invariable. . . . It is possible that there is no special meaning in the choice of foliage, but I think it is significant that oak predominates." (Oak, of course, was the Druids' sacred tree.) There is Hernes oak at Windsor.

St. Bernard, we are told, when contemplating the decoration of the Cluniac churches was aghast at the "fantastic monsters" in the cloisters, and blushed for these "absurdities." He declared that they were dangerous, attracting the soul and hindering meditation upon the will of God. Perhaps he had some inkling of paganism among them.

One of Lady Raglan's illustrations, from the font of St. Woolo's Church, Newport, Mon., shows a foliate mask which is definitely horned, and has great whorls of foliage coming from its mouth. Another mask, from the cloisters of Mon Majour, near Arles, France, which also illustrates this article, shows high, pointed ears, reminiscent of horns, and a beard and moustache, as well as the usual foliage. There is a mask similar to this on the outside of Salisbury Cathedral, near one of the entrances.

A very lively misericord from Lincoln Cathedral, which Lady Raglan illustrates, shows not only oak leaves as foliage adornment, but also acorns. Another, from the Chapter House at Southwell Minster, has foliage which looks like hawthorn in flower. It was necessary for the person taking the part of "Jack in the Green" in the May Day procession to make a small hole in the erection of green boughs that covered him, to be able to see his way, and this little figure from Southwell Minster appears to be doing exactly that.

It is notable that a number of these foliate masks have the tongue protruding. Lady Raglan suggests that the original "Green Man" may have been the Divine King, and was perhaps sacrificed by hanging, the green garland itself being later hung up in his place, as at Castleton in Derbyshire, where it is suspended on the church tower after the May Day procession is over. However, it occurs to me that the motive of the protruding tongue may be the schoolboy one of derision (perhaps at the solemn edifice in which he finds himself?) as the examples she shows look quite cheerful and far from dead. To stick out the tongue was originally a phallic gesture.

Lady Raglan says,

> The fact is that unofficial paganism subsisted side by side with the official religion, and this explains the presence of our Green Man in a church window with the Virgin beside him and below him the sun. This extraordinary figure may be seen in mediaeval stained glass at the church of St. Mary Redcliffe at Bristol. He is crowned, and it would seem that to the artist who made the window, and presumably also to the priests who ordered it, he was equally venerable with the Virgin.

It would certainly appear in this instance that he was regarded as a sacred being, and some at least of the worshippers may have accepted the picture of the Virgin as a representation of the Great Mother upon which the priests had put clothes.

On a roof boss at Pershore (Worcs.), too, the foliate head wears a crown.

In the Notes at the end of M. D. Anderson's book, *Looking For History in British Churches,* it is stated:

> Examples of the foliated mask can be seen (on bosses): Beverley (Yorks), St. Mary's; Boxgrove (Sussex); Canterbury Cathedral; Congresbury (Somerset); Ely Cathedral; Exeter Cathedral; Kings Nympton (Devon); Hereford Cathedral; Norwich Cathedral; Patrington (Yorks); Pershore (Worcs); Sherborne Abbey (Dorset); Tewkesbury (Glos); Warmington (Northants); Winchester Cathedral; and Worcester Cathedral. All these examples are illustrated in Mr. C. J. P. Cave's book on Bosses. The foliated mask also appears frequently in misericords as, for instance, at King's Lynn, St. Margaret's; Coventry, Holy Trinity; Wingham (Kent); Lincoln Cathedral.

I have found, too, a beautiful example of the "Green Man" among the elaborate decoration of an illuminated manuscript in the British Museum (B. M. Egerton M.S. 3277, f. 126 b.). This is a page from a Psalter and Book of Hours, illuminated, perhaps, by an East Anglian artist, for Humfrey de Bohun, 7th Earl of Hereford (d. 1373), and his daughter Mary (d. 1394), first wife of Henry IV. A reproduction of this page in colour appeared in the Christmas number of *The Sphere* in 1954, as one of the illustrations to an article, "The Beauty of Mediaeval Illuminated Manuscripts," by Julian Brown.

Another form in which the Old God managed to get himself into the fabric of an English church is that sculpture described by Baring-Gould as being carved in granite over the porch of Sheepstor church in Devon, namely a skull with ears of corn issuing from the mouth and eyes. When in their ceremonies there was no man of sufficient rank present to represent the God, in the old days the witches symbolised his presence by a skull and crossbones placed upon their altar at the Sabbats.

It occurs to me that this practice may be the origin of the many legends of "Screaming Skulls." The general form of the "Screaming Skull" legend is that a skull is preserved in some old house, and that any attempt to remove it is immediately followed by unearthly screaming, and sometimes by storms and "Poltergeist" disturbances. Legends of this type exist at Ambleside in the Lake District; at Wardley Hall in Lancashire; at Bettiscombe farmstead near Bridport in Dorset; at Warbleton Priory, Sussex; at a farmhouse at Chilton

Cantelo, in Somerset; at Tremarrow, in Cornwall; and at Burton Agnes Hall, between Bridlington and Driffield. This curious pattern of "haunting" looks as if either the realms of spookery are somewhat uninventive, and the inhabitants thereof keep repeating themselves, or else that there existed an ancient custom of keeping in various places, with great reverence, a skull, which was regarded with such superstitious awe that supernatural disturbances were expected to follow its removal; and that in later days, when the original reason for this reverence and awe had been forgotten, romantic stories were invented to account for it.

While upon the subject of sculptures of the Old God in churches we must not forget the famous "Lincoln Imp," who squats upon a spandrel on the north side—the "Devil's side"—of Lincoln Cathedral. He is unequivocally horned and hairy, but bears a human face with a broad grin, which consorts well with his nonchalant attitude of one leg crossed over the other. A better figure, for the period, of the Old Horned God it would be hard to find.

Another way in which the British craftsmen of old days preserved the signs and symbols of the Old Religion was by their so-called "Masons' Marks" with which they used to mark the stones they worked. When I wrote my little historical novel, *High Magic's Aid,* I had the dust-jacket of it adorned with a few witch signs. I have recently been given a cast of a "Mason's Mark" from a stone in the archway of the south door of the very old church at Bramber, in Sussex. It is identical with one of the signs given on the dust-jacket of *High Magic's Aid.*

The sign of the Pentagram, too, is found as a "Mason's Mark." One such is upon the south doorway of Nutfield Church, in Surrey, and is illustrated in *Old English Churches,* by George Clinch, F.G.S. (L, Upcott Gill, 1902.) Graffiti, I have been told, are often found within old churches near the north door—the pagan "Devil's Door." I have tried in this chapter to cite enough examples of pagan signs in churches to prove my case. It is my hope that it may be taken as a first rough sketch of an interesting line of research, which other students will take up.

Not only, however, did the mediaeval craftsmen work the symbols of their private beliefs into the fabric of the buildings which they helped to erect; they also included criticisms, scathing to the point of obscenity, of the ecclesiastics they were working for. T. Clifton Longworth, in his book, *The Devil a Monk Would Be,* gives descriptions and photographs of the most extraordinary carvings, mostly satires on the clergy, including the well-known one of a fox-priest in a pulpit preaching to a congregation of geese, and similar subjects. Can we really believe that these carvings were executed by devout Christians? The carvings are a mute witness of something at least curious in the relations between the working man who made the great cathedrals, and their ecclesiastical masters; many of them have now been removed or covered up, though others are still *in situ* in odd corners of the most dignified and sacred edifices.

For instance, Longworth gives an illustration of a carving in St. Davids cathedral which shows a cowled fox giving the Host to a human-headed goose; and he states there are few ancient sets of misericords which do not include the figure of a fox in the pulpit preaching to geese.

In Worcester cathedral a vested fox is shown giving absolution to a kneeling sheep; and in Chester Cathedral a fox in clerical habit is shown at a sly assignation with a young woman in a wood. Do not these show a spirit of "Anti-clericism" to say the least! "Another scene portrays a devil wheeling a barrow load of monks to hell; they are accompanied by a fox with a stolen goose in his mouth."

Many of the queer old carvings in mediaeval churches are, of course, simply examples of the Rabelaisian humour of the times; but it is a humour which, we may feel, has a distinct tang of paganism in it. Further details of such carvings may be found in Longworth's book, already mentioned, and in *Les Licences de L'Art Chretien,* by Dr. G. J. Witkowski (Paris, 1921). Many of them are of such a nature as to be unsuitable for description in a book intended, as this is, for the general reader; and as ornaments in a church they are, to put it mildly, surprising. Anyone who reproduced them nowadays, or even described them in plain language, would soon find himself in jail for obscenity, together with his unfortunate publishers and the booksellers who stocked his works; yet we are seriously asked by some commentators to believe that they were authorised by Bishops and clerics to improve the minds of their congregations! Some people have no sense of humour.

May we theorise that some, at least, of these extraordinary sculptures were the wordless protest of the members of the Old Religion, who were allowed to adorn no places of worship save those of the Christian Church; and who, not being permitted to carve shrines for the Old Gods, yet placed their emblems where they could in places where they were now compelled by law to worship, even though such emblems might be no more than a scratched pentagram or a "Mason's Mark"?

"The Promised City." This is a phrase which strikes a note in many people's minds, arousing thoughts of a Heavenly Jerusalem, built of precious stones. Where one wears gorgeous robes and a golden crown, and does nothing but play a Golden Harp all day (and presumably, all night) long and is not forced to do any work. All races seem to have visions of something similar to this. The Chinese have tales of such a city; it is the basis of all their secret societies.

The Christian type is descended from the days when Christianity was a Secret Society, organised in small cells. They obtained their recruits by promises of "Be faithful, and you will eventually be taken to this Heavenly City; if not now, well, at the end of life. Continue to be obedient to us, and when you die you will go to Glory. But to the average man this is "Cloud Cuckoo Land"; he wants somewhere where he can go at once, if only temporarily. Somewhere where he can throw off all the cares and frustrations of this life, even if it is for a few hours only.

The truly religious of all faiths possibly attain this, or something like it, by prayer. The opium smoker and the taker of hashish can usually attain this at will; at least at first (provided they can get what drugs they require). Some drunkards do so for a short time, but "pink elephants" have a way of spoiling this type of Promised City. The anarchists of the 19th century thought they could attain it by abolishing all Governments, when each man could do as he wished. But, unfortunately, so many of them wished to call attention to their views by following the example of the Irish dynamiters, throwing bombs in crowded places, and murdering kings and presidents. So the non-anarchists did as they wished, and executed a few anarchists. The late Aleister Crowley taught his disciples to bleat, "Do what thou wilt shall be the whole of the law." Too late they found that this meant in practice, "Do what Aleister Crowley wills shall be the whole of the law."

Much as the late Henry Ford is said to have declared, "Every purchaser of our next year's model can have a car of whatever colour he chooses, provided he chooses black." Sprague de Camp wrote a very funny story of a "Heavenly City" where everyone became what he wished to be. His hero found himself there dressed as a dashing cavalier of the d'Artagnan type, but with vague ideas of how a cavalier should dash because most of his neighbours were dressed in plate armour, or else as Wagnerian heroes, in bear-skins, with huge swords. Most of the girls were movie producers' ideas of Egyptian princesses; all the men were handsome, all the women surpassingly beautiful. But the trouble was where to stay, and where to eat. Because the very few people who imagined themselves hotel-keepers thought themselves of the Western kind, who ran their hotels with a six-shooter in each hand, with which they settled all complaints. And the only people who fancied themselves as barmen thought of themselves as "keeping order" by throwing bottles at their customers' heads. Also there were many cowboys who imagined themselves shooting out the lights, but nobody who thought of "mending them." There were large numbers of Interplanetary Patrol men, but no Interplanetary traffic, because, though there were many designers of Interplanetary spaceships, there was no one who fancied the donkey work of building them.

There were numberless harem beauties. No one, however, regarded himself rich enough to keep a harem. There were beautiful spies, and bearded communists everywhere. In fact, it was the very place to keep away from. Because of the fact, what you wish must always be conditioned by the doings of the people around you. Now this was very clearly pointed out by some of the early Christian writers, who believed that, among the most wonderful joys of heaven was looking over the walls at the people you saw being tortured in Hell. The Inquisition also saw glimpses of the Promised City, and disliked what they beheld. For they complained bitterly, "The Basques, man, woman and child, talked of nothing but the Last Sabbat, and thought of nothing but the next one." And they pointed out the truth, that in all men there is the dream of a secret place where they can be happy, if only for a time, where for a short while at least they may know "the Joy that passeth all understanding." Where there were no ill effects, as by the use of drugs. It is no "Religious Ecstasy" which may only be experienced, if at all, once in a lifetime; but somewhere on this earth as the Basques did of old, "You may wish to talk of nothing but the last meeting, and long for nothing save the next." It is what the "Wica" suffered torture and death for rather than give up. It is the foretaste of the "Promised City" which we may now enter today—the "Witches' Circle."

Chapter XIII

The Black Mass

I have previously, in the chapter headed "Magic Thinking," remarked that there was (and is) a type of magic which is Judeo-Christian in phraseology and in theological outlook, and that this type of magic was practised by priests among others; namely, that magic which seeks to invoke God and His angels (in the case of the Qabalah), or God the Father, Son and Holy Ghost, Christ, the Virgin, and the Saints (in the case of Christianised rituals), to give the practitioner power over demons, in order to compel the latter to carry out his wishes. I have also pointed out in what way this type of ceremonial magic differs from witchcraft. Nevertheless, many writers about witchcraft accuse witches of performing perverted Christian ceremonies, notably a mockery of the Mass, which they call "the Black Mass." Hence, in this chapter I propose to enquire into what the Black Mass really was (and for all I know, is); who were the people who really performed such a ceremony; and what was the psychology of that state of mind which gave rise to it.

The Grimoires have been often described as books of Satanism, and consequently people who have never seen one have been led to believe that these books enjoin the worship of Satan; nothing could be further from the truth, as the most cursory examination of them will reveal. (We have a considerable number of them in this Museum, both printed and in manuscript. The general reader will be able to find extracts from the most important grimoires in *The Book of Ceremonial Magic*, by Arthur Edward Waite). The theology of the grimoires is of the most orthodox. God and His angels, Christ and the saints, reign above; the devil and his angels reign below. The former are *invoked*, that is prayed to attend; the latter are *evoked*, that is forced to appear, by the power of the former. This conception was elaborated in former times in the most meticulous way. For instance, about 1583 Johann Weyer published, in his *Pseudomonarchia Daemonum*, a detailed account of the hierarchy of hell, which was divided into Kings, Marquises, Dukes, Princes, etc., etc., each of which had legions of minor devils subject to him, to the number of seven millions odd. He seems to have believed this, but H. C. Lea suggests that Weyer's motive in publishing this treatise was to illustrate the follies of superstition then current among priests about the powers of demons. In a note, Mr. Lea's editor, Professor Arthur C. Howland, says,

> It indicates a curious state of mind that the invocation of these spirits is addressed, in the name of the Trinity, to Jesus Christ, praying him by the merits of the Virgin and saints to grant divine power over all malignant spirits, so that whomsoever the adept calls shall at once appear and perform his will, without injuring or frightening him.
>
> I suppose the reasoning of this was that if, as universally believed God had granted the power to Solomon over evil spirits, there was no reason why he should not do so to any one else who sought it. Besides, this was virtually what the exorcists were doing every day. The theologians universally held that there was no sin in commanding demons, though it was heretical to supplicate them, and thus this formula eluded the laws against magic and sorcery. In fact, it was only the assumption by a layman of the power of the clerk.

In later times, however, after the Reformation, this kind of magic was also condemned, as we read that according to the secular jurists, the possession of books of ceremonial magic of this nature was evidence sufficient to bring one to torture and the stake. But in earlier times, as we have seen, the distinction was drawn; the ceremonial magician, who was often a priest, was more or less licit in the eyes of the Church because he "commanded demons"; the witch, however, who prayed to the Old Gods, was condemned, as this was held to be "supplicating demons."

Much has been made in recent years by such writers as Hugh Ross Williamson and H. T. F. Rhodes of the concept of "Dualism," meaning that idea which divides the Universe between a good God and an evil God, or "Satan," between whom eternal war is waged. Valuable as the researches of both these authors are, I must beg to differ from them upon some important points. They hold the idea that this Dualism is an important factor in the development of the witch cult, and with this I cannot agree, because both have the orthodox conception that Satan was the deity the witches worshipped, and from what I know this is not so. The people who ascribe powers to Satan which are almost the equal of those of God are Christians, whether orthodox or unorthodox. The paganism from which the witch cult is descended did not do so.

What did paganism teach about the origin of evil? This, of course, depends upon what one means by "paganism." The only kinds of paganism with which we are concerned here are those which may have had some influence upon the witch cult. Druidism, the religion of the Celts, had no doctrine of an evil deity opposed to the God of Good. There is no evidence that the religion of the Great Mother Goddess or the old Hunting God had any conception of a supernatural author of all evil. And what of the Mystery Cults of the ancient world; have we any way of ascertaining what the Mysteries taught about the origin of evil?

Fortunately we have. In the 4th century A.D., when paganism was engaged in a fierce struggle with the new creed of Christianity, Sallustius, who was a close personal friend of the Emperor Julian (called the Apostate because he tried to restore the old religion), wrote a treatise called Peri Theon kai Kosmou, *About the Gods and the World.* It is probable that this treatise was a kind of manifesto of the highest type of paganism prevailing at that time, and it is evident that its author was an initiate of the Mysteries.

The treatise is printed in the third volume of Mullach's *Fragmenta Philosophorum*; apart from that, before Gilbert Murray published a full translation of it as an Appendix to his *Five Stages of Greek Religion,* the only edition of it which was generally accessible, and that rarely, was one published by Allatius in 1539. Professor Murray says of it that it "may be said to constitute something like an authoritative Pagan creed."

With regard to the myths of the Gods, Sallustius says, "For one may call the World a Myth, in which bodies and things are visible, but souls and minds hidden." Hence myths are a means of teaching people divine truths. "... The myths state the existence of Gods to all, but who and what they are only to those who can understand."

Sallustius' strong belief not only in the survival of bodily death, but in the continued activity and interest of those souls who have passed beyond earth in benefiting humanity, is evidenced by his remark, "May these explanations of the myths find favour in the eyes of the Gods themselves and the souls of those who wrote the myths."

He says, "It is proper to the First Cause to be One—for unity precedes multitude—and to surpass all things in power and goodness. Consequently all things must partake of it. For owing to its power nothing else can hinder it, and owing to its goodness it will not hold itself apart. . . . After this inexpressible Power come the orders of the Gods. Of the Gods some are of the world, Cosmic, and some above the world, Hypercosmic."

Sallustius positively denies the existence of a Power of Evil, or even of evil spirits, in the sense that they are "devils." He says,

> The Gods being good and making all things, how do evils exist in the world? Or perhaps it is better first to state the fact that, the Gods being good and making all things, there is no positive evil, it only comes by absence of good; just as darkness itself does not exist, but only comes about by absence of light.
>
> If Evil exists it must exist either in Gods or minds or souls or bodies. It does not exist in any God, for all God is good. If anyone speaks of a "bad mind," he means a mind without mind. If of a bad soul, he will make soul inferior to body, for no body in itself is evil. It he says that Evil is made up of soul and body together, it is absurd that separately they should not be evil, but joined should create evil.
>
> Suppose it is said that there are evil spirits: if they have their power from the Gods, they cannot be evil; if from elsewhere, the Gods do not make all things. If they do not make all things, then either they wish to and cannot, or they can and do not wish; neither of which is consistent with the idea of God. We may see, therefore, from these arguments, that there is no positive evil in the world.
>
> It is in the activities of men that the evils appear, and that not of all men nor always. And as to these, if men sinned for the sake of evil, Nature itself would be evil. But if the adulterer thinks his adultery bad but his pleasure good, and the murderer thinks the murder bad but the money he gets by is good, and the man who does evil to an enemy thinks that to do evil is bad but to punish his enemy good, and if the soul commits all its sins in that way, then the evils are done for the sake of goodness. (In the same way, because in a given place light does not exist, there comes darkness, which has no positive existence.) The soul sins therefore because, while aiming at good, it makes mistakes about the good, because it is not Primary Essence. And we see many things done by the Gods to prevent it from making mistakes and to heal them when it has made them. Arts and sciences, curses and prayers, sacrifices and initiations, laws and constitutions, judgments and punishments, all came into existence for the sake of preventing souls from sinning; and when they are gone forth from the body Gods and spirits of purification cleanse them of their sins.

Then Sallustius goes on to explain the inner meaning of religious rituals, in his section headed, "In what sense, though the Gods never change, they are said to be made angry and appeased." He says,

> It is impious to suppose that the Divine is affected for good or ill by human things. The Gods are always good and always do good and never harm, being always in the same state and like themselves. The truth simply is that, when we are good, we are joined to the Gods by our likeness to them; when bad, we are separated from them by our unlikeness. And when we live according to virtue we cling to the Gods, and when we become evil we make the Gods our enemies—not because they are angered against us, but because our sins prevent the light of the Gods from shining upon us, and put us in communion with spirits of punishment, and if by prayers and sacrifices we find forgiveness of sins, we do not appease or change the Gods, but by what we do and by our turning towards the Divine we heal our own badness and so enjoy again the goodness of the Gods. To say that God turns away from the evil is like saying that the sun hides himself from the blind.

"This solves the question about sacrifices and other rites performed to the Gods. The divine itself is without needs, and the worship is paid for our own benefit. The providence of the Gods reaches everywhere, and needs only some congruity for its reception." (Compare with the witches' idea that man had to do some-thing to "build a bridge," so to speak, between himself and the Gods). He continues, "From all these things the Gods gain nothing; what gain could there be to God? It is we who gain some communication with them."

"Nor," he says, "need the fact that rejections of God have taken place in certain parts of the earth and will often take place hereafter disturb the mind of the wise; both because these things do not affect the Gods, just as we say that worship did not benefit them; and because the soul, being of middle essence, cannot always be right. . . ."

He reveals very clearly his belief in the doctrines of Reincarnation and Karma when he goes on to say,

> It is not unlikely, too, that the rejection of God is a kind of punishment; we may well believe that those who knew the Gods and neglected them in one life may in another life be deprived of the knowledge of them altogether. Also those who have worshipped their own kings as Gods have deserved as their punishment to lose all knowledge of God.

This belief is further elaborated when he speaks of the transmigration of souls.

> If the transmigration of a soul takes place into a rational being, it simply becomes the soul of that body. But if the soul migrates into a brute beast, it follows the body outside, as a guardian spirit follows a man. For there could never be a rational soul in an irrational being.

(Note the belief in what today would be called "Spirit Guides"; also, he evidently does not think that a human soul could literally transmigrate into an animal, however brutal and debased it had become, and believers in reincarnation today generally take this view also.)

> The transmigration of souls can be proved from the congenital afflictions of persons. For why are some born blind, others paralytic, others with some sickness in the soul itself? Again, it is the natural duty of souls to do their work in the body; are we to suppose that when once they leave the body they spend all eternity in idleness?

"Souls that have lived in virtue are in general happy," he says, "and when separated from the irrational part of their nature, and made clean from all matter, have communion with the Gods and join them in the governing of the whole world." Here he is evidently speaking of those who have progressed to the point where they will have no further need for reincarnation on earth. But he does not use the promise of Heaven or the threat of Hell as a means of making people good, for he continues:

> Yet even if none of this happiness fell to their lot, virtue itself, and the joy and glory of virtue, and the life that is subject to no grief and no master are enough to make happy those who have set themselves to live according to virtue and have achieved it.

Now, the thing that will, I think, strike most the consciousness of the reader who is well versed in the teaching of the higher types of spiritualist and occult circles generally is not the antiquity of this teaching of Sallustius, but its startling modernity. It might have been spoken yesterday. Further, it might have been spoken at a witch meeting, at any time, as a general statement of their creed; and it will be seen that there *is no room in it for any "worship of the Evil Principle."* Of course, not all of Sallustius' teaching stands up so well to the passing of time; for instance, he had the idea that the earth was the centre of the Cosmos; but the spirit of his teaching, the spirit of the Mysteries of his day, which is also the spirit of the beliefs of the witch cult, is timeless.

Very truly does Professor Murray say,

> In part instinctively, in part superficially and self-consciously, each generation of mankind reacts against the last. The grown man turns from the lights that were thrust upon his eyes in childhood. The son shrugs his shoulders at the watchwords that thrilled his father, and with varying degrees of sensitiveness or dullness, of fuller or more fragmentary experience, writes out for himself the manuscript of his creed. Yet, even for the wildest or bravest rebel, that manuscript is only a palimpsest. On the surface all is new writing, clean and self-assertive. Underneath, dim but indelible, in the very fibres of the parchment, lie the characters of many ancient aspirations and raptures and battles which his conscious mind has rejected or utterly forgotten. And forgotten things, if there be real life in them, will sometimes return out of the dust, vivid to help still in the forward groping of humanity.

To return to the theory advanced by Hugh Ross Williamson and H. T. F. Rhodes that the concept of Dualism has influenced the witch cult, the suggestion has been put forward by these writers, especially the latter, that the sect of Christian heretics known as the Cathari or Albigenses was closely associated with the witch cult, that these heretics held the conception of Dualism, and that they celebrated a kind of "Vain Observance" of the Christian Mass as a form of defiance, or perhaps of inverted salutation, of the God of the Christians, whom they regarded as the Evil Principle; and that this was the origin of the "Black Mass" that the witch cult is alleged to perform.

The works of Mr. Rhodes and Mr. Williamson are scholarly and of great interest; but I submit that upon this point they have been misled. I propose to examine, therefore, who the Cathari really were and what they really taught.

The Catharist heresy is thought to have made its first appearance in the early part of the 10th century A.D., in the Balkan peninsula. From there it spread rapidly, as usual along the trade routes. By the 11th century it had spread across Macedonia, Thrace, Asia Minor, Greece, and through Bosnia and Dalmatia into Italy, and thence into France, and through Hungary into Germany. By the beginning of the 12th century it had developed into a complete system of faith and conduct which differed in important ways from orthodox Christianity.

It stemmed originally from Manichaeism, and seems to have been preached in the Balkans by Paulicians, a heretical Christian sect which was descended from the Manichees, who held the philosophy of Dualism. One of the reasons for its popularity was that these preachers held their services in the common tongue of the people, as opposed to the orthodox practice of holding services in Latin. It was opposed to Papal Christianity, and, like so many religious movements, proclaimed itself to be "the only true Christian Church."

In some respects, the Cathari were ahead of their time. They believed that all men would eventually be "saved," and denied the doctrines of "Hell" and "eternal damnation," saying that these were incompatible with the goodness of God. They also realised that the cruel God of the Old Testament was an unworthy representation of the Deity, and indeed went so far as to say that he was so full of bad passions and injustice that he must be the Bad God, and not the God of Good. They did not regard Jesus as God Incarnate, but as a good man whom God had sent upon a special mission to earth; not to redeem people by vicariously dying for them, but to teach them the way to live.

They believed in reincarnation, and held that by this means all would eventually become perfect, but that men could shorten the number of incarnations they would have to undergo by making an effort to live as Jesus taught.

They absolutely denied the validity of the sacraments as administered by the Roman Church, saying that no sacrament could be valid unless it was administered by a priest who was a good and holy man, and hence fit to administer it, and unless the recipient of it was in such a state of spiritual awareness that he could fitly receive it. This was absolutely contrary to the Roman teaching that so long as a man was an ordained priest his moral character mattered nothing; the sacraments he administered were automatically valid. It was this denial of the orthodox Church's claim, especially with regard to the Mass, that caused the Cathari to be so bitterly persecuted and so savagely put down.

But the most individual and curious of their teachings was that based upon the concept of Dualism. They said that the material world, being imperfect, could not have been created by the Good God, who was perfect. Hence it must have been created by the Evil God! They held the concept that there was not one God, but two; one good and the other evil. They said that the Good God had no concern with the world of matter at all, save to redeem men's souls from it as soon as possible. Only the Good God's world—the Heaven-world—was real and eternal. The world of matter was evil, illusive, and transitory. (One may detect in the Catharist teaching some strange echoes of Buddhism, and the life of the Cathar "Perfecti" reminds one irresistibly of the Buddhist *Sangha*; sufficient, indeed, to make one wonder if Catharism could be the remote descendant, curiously transformed, of one of those Buddhist missions dispatched by King Asoka to, among other places, the Near East, whence the Catharist heresy first arose and where it lingered longest.)

The Cathari accounted for man's place in nature, and his possession of a material body, by asserting that the Evil God had seduced a large number of the angels of heaven to separate themselves from the Good God, and that they had thus "fallen," and become ensnared in the Evil God's realm, the world of matter. The Good God had permitted them to exile themselves, but had decreed that the snare of the Evil One should become the instrument of their redemption, by means of reincarnation, until they won back again to their original state of blessedness and purity. These fallen angels were the human race. Hence, the Cathars said, mankind's proper course was to separate themselves as much as possible from the world of matter, and strive only to return to their original purity. From this doctrine they took their name; theirs was the religion of *catharsis,* a Greek word meaning "purification."

From this doctrine, too, they derived their teachings of an extreme asceticism. They might own no property; but held all material goods in common, and laid out such wealth as they had upon relieving the sick and poor. They built no churches; all the Vatican's pomp and display, they said, was a delusion of the Evil God. They met where they could, sometimes in the open air. Their services were very simple, and their main sacrament, the *Consolamentum,* was intended to bring about the union, or rather re-union, of man with his Higher Self. This they called "the Baptism of the Holy Ghost," and one who had received it was from thence-forward vowed to a life of the most extreme asceticism, and complete withdrawal from all earthly ties. These ascetics were known as "Perfecti," and they seemed to have lived much as the early Buddhist monks, and, like them, to have been regarded with much reverence by the common people, who contrasted their lives of poverty, celibacy, good works, and continual prayer, fasting, and preaching with those of the ordinary clergy, who were often luxurious, lecherous and venal.

There were few Perfecti, because there were few men or women (for the Cathars admitted both sexes), who could stand such a life of complete poverty and self-abnegation; there were, however, many "credentes" or "believers," who followed and supported them. These credentes were permitted a certain amount of worldly ties, but it was understood that they should endeavour to progress towards the reception of the Consolamentum, and complete emancipation from the material world.

The Cathars held seven things to be mortal sins: the possession of property; communication with worldly people, except to convert them; telling anything but the truth, at whatever cost; the slaying of another human being, upon any pretext, including those of war or judicial execution; the killing of any animals, other than reptiles or fishes; the eating of animal flesh; and sexual intercourse, whether the latter were for procreation or merely for gratification of desire, because this was the means whereby the Evil God maintained his world of matter, and kept human souls imprisoned in it.

It will be readily seen that this is a very different creed from that of the witch cult. There are some superficial resemblances, in that both believed in reincarnation, met in the open air or in obscure places, and that the Catharist Perfecti had a girdle consisting of a sacred cord; yet the main doctrine of the Cathari is diametrically opposed to the witch cult's main tenet, namely the worship of fertility, and hence the sacredness of sex.

How, then, did the Cathars come in any way to be associated with witches? The old proverb says that "Misfortune makes strange bedfellows." In order to discredit them, the official propaganda of the Church spread abroad the same stories of "hideous orgies," "obscene rites," etc., etc., about the Cathari as it did about the witches, the Stedinger, the Waldenses, and the Knights Templars; about anyone, in fact, with whom it disagreed. Martin Luther, for instance, is seriously stated by some of those writers who profess to expound "the horrors of the Sabbat" to have been the result of his mother's liaison with an incubus demon!

The preaching of the Cathars was a considerable thorn in the side of the Church, especially when they denied the validity of the Church's sacraments. This struck right at the heart of the Church's authority, and so influential did the Cathars become in Southern France, in that region known loosely as Languedoc, that, having failed to overcome the heresy by means of missionaries, Pope Innocent III, in 1207, preached a Crusade against the "Albigenses," as they were called (after the French town of Albi, which was one of their centres). All who would join the crusade were promised the same remission of sins as they would gain by crusading in Palestine.

The nobles of Languedoc, however, resisted the invaders by force, and sought to protect the Cathars by giving them refuge in their castles; but they were overwhelmed by the superior numbers of those who had answered the Pope's call, anxious for blessing and greedy for loot. The crusading army was under the supreme command of Arnauld, the Papal Legate, and when it stormed and captured the town of Béziers he was asked what was to be done with the inhabitants, and how the faithful were to be distinguished from the heretics. He replied, "Kill them all; God will know His own." The charitable request was complied with; the inhabitants of Béziers were massacred and the town was pillaged and burnt. Similar treatment was meted out to Carcassonne. Remembering Béziers, the bulk of the inhabitants fled, though some of them were captured, and of these fifty were hanged and four hundred burned alive. The town was pillaged, but not burnt as it was needed to lodge the army.

These horrors were but the first of many; the Holy War dragged on its wretched course for nearly twenty years, with war's usual consequences of devastation and ruin. As a direct result of the struggle against the supporters of the Cathars, the Inquisition came into existence, when in 1232 Pope Gregory IX transferred all inquisitorial powers upon the Order of Dominicans, and a few years later extended the same powers and privileges to the Franciscans. This episode in history has been described by Paul Daniel Alphandery, Professor of the History of Dogma at the Sorbonne, as "A reign of terror which wasted Languedoc for a century." The Inquisitors took over where the crusading army had left off. When they had run their course, Catharism in Languedoc was virtually dead; so was Languedoc. Its wealth, culture, organisation, and self-respect were destroyed.

Another direct result of the struggle with the Cathars was the definite adoption by the Church of the Dogma of Transubstantiation. Controversy upon this point had been carried on for some centuries, but it was not until 1215 that the word "Transubstantiation" was adopted and the doctrine defined by the Fourth Latin Council. Also, the Church very definitely took the stand, as before stated, that the moral character of the priest who performed the Mass mattered nothing; so long as he was a priest, the Mass was valid, and transubstantiation took place.

Now I am going to advance what I am well aware is a highly controversial view, which I fear may offend some people. *That view is that the root of the practices known as the "Black Mass" is to be found in this latter belief, when it was held by spiritually ignorant people and unworthy priests.* It has nothing to do with the witch cult or the Cathars, and never has had anything to do with them.

The Black Mass was—and I hope I am right in speaking of it in the past tense—a Mass which was performed by an ordained *priest,* with various magical ceremonies added, in order to use, or rather pervert, the power of the Eucharist to some magical end. We have seen an example in the extracts from the *Grimoire of Honorius* which I have quoted in the chapter headed "Magic Thinking." I know that various alleged examples of "Black Masses" are to be found in the confessions of witches, extracted under torture; *but what reliance can be placed upon such evidence when they were told what to say and tortured until they said it?*

Of course, it will here be argued, by those who complain that I have gone out of my way to claim that there is nothing diabolical about witchcraft, that I am a special pleader. If they will not listen to me, perhaps they will listen to the words of a man who officiated as confessor to those who were condemned for witchcraft at the height of the persecution in Germany in the 17th century; a man who, far from being a witch or favourable to the witch cult, was in fact a Jesuit Father; a man who was, furthermore, one of those noble and courageous characters who shine brightest in the darkest periods of history; Father Friedrich Von Spee, S.J.

When Phillip von Schornborn, Bishop of Wurzburg in 1642, was a young man, he asked Father Von Spee why his hair had turned white before its time; Von Spee answered that it was caused by the agony of mind that he felt when, in the course of his official duties, he had had to accompany to the stake those who were condemned for witchcraft; because "he had not discovered in a single one anything to convince him that she was justly condemned. They had in their confession, out of fear of greater torture, confessed what was required. But when they recognised that they had nothing to fear from the confessor, they had with heartrending despair deplored the ignorance or wickedness of the judges and in their last necessity called on God to witness their innocence. This had so shattered his nerves that he became grey before his time." (H. C. Lea [Op. cit.] who quotes Leibnitz as his authority for this story).

Father Von Spee was not the only member of his Society who deplored the horrors and injustices of the witch-hunts; he was supported by two more Jesuits, Father Paul Laymann and Father Adam Tanner, and by a Protestant Doctor of Holy Writ, Johann Meyfarth. The latter said that in his youth, by the will of God, he had been present at a number of scenes of torture inflicted upon alleged witches, "and he would give a thousand dollars if he could banish it from his memory." All of these Churchmen wrote books protesting against the use of torture to extract confessions of whatever was required, at a time when to raise one's voice against the prevailing persecution was to court its immediate fury against oneself, and their works had considerable influence upon the restoration of sanity and humanity to a country in the grip of an hysterical reign of terror.

Von Spee, in his book *Cautio Criminalis, seu de Processibus contra Sagas* (First Edition, Rinteln, 1631), says:

> Judges and Inquisitors should follow not only the laws but natural reason. It is incredible how this is everywhere disregarded when almost all rage against the accused and hold as valid and true whatever bears against them, while whatever favours them is cast aside. When they can convict they triumph; but if innocence is demonstrated they are wroth.

He continues with a scathing exposé of the methods of the witch-hunters, in which he spares neither the religious nor the secular power. He says,

> That inquisitor is not incorruptible who sends agents to places to inflame the minds of the peasants about witches and promises to come and destroy them, if a proper collection is made for him; when this is done he comes, celebrates one or two autos de fé, excites the people still more with the confessions of the accused; pretends that he is going away and has another collection made; when he has exhausted the district, he moves off to another and repeats the same.
>
> ... The process is that the inquisitor summons the woman before him, tells her she knows of what she is accused and the proof is as follows and she must purge herself and answer. As I have very often found, she does this and explains away everything to the minutest point, so that the futility of the accusation is manifest. She might as well be speaking to a stone. She is merely told to return to her cell and think whether she will persist in denial, for she will be summoned again in a few hours. In the

> meanwhile an entry is made in the protocol that she denies and is sentenced to torture. No mention is made of her disproof. When brought back she is asked if she persists in her obstinacy, for the decree of torture is issued. If she still denies, she is carried to the torture. Where has there been anyone who, no matter how she has cleared herself, has not been tortured? Even if there is no legitimate proof, many judges enter of the record that they proceed according to what is alleged and proved.

Remember, this is not a mere conjectural account. Father Von Spee was an eye-witness of the things of which he writes. And yet the pitiful farragoes of hideous nonsense to which condemned witches "confessed" are taken seriously by people otherwise possessed of their wits as "evidence of the evils of witchcraft"!

Von Spee goes on,

> What is to be thought of torture? Does it bring frequent moral peril to the innocent? In reflecting upon what I have seen, read and heard, I can only conclude that it fills our Germany with witches and unheard-of wickedness, and not only Germany but any nation that tries it. The agony is so intense, that to escape it we do not fear to incur death. The danger, therefore, is that many to avoid it will falsely confess whatever the examiner suggests or what they have excogitated in advance. The most robust who have thus suffered have affirmed to me that no crime can be imagined which they would not at once confess to if it would bring ever so little relief, and that they would welcome ten deaths to escape a repetition. . . . I confess that I would at once admit any crime and choose death rather than such suffering, and I have heard many men, religious and of uncommon fortitude, say the same. . . . There is a frequent phrase used by judges, that the accused has confessed without torture, and thus is undeniably guilty. I wondered at this and made enquiry and learned that in reality they were tortured, but only in an iron press with sharp-edged channels over the shins, in which they are pressed like a cake, bringing blood and causing intolerable pain, and this is technically called without torture, deceiving those who do not understand the phrases of the inquisitors. . . .
>
> The law prescribes that no one under torture shall be questioned about accomplices by name; but this is disregarded and names are put in the mouths of the accused for denunciation. This is not only customary in many places, but special crimes, places and times for the Sabbath, and other details, are suggested in the questions. . . . Some executioners, when preparing the accused for torture, will tell them what accomplices

> to denounce and warn them not to refuse; they will also tell them what others have said about them, so that they will know what details to confess, and thus make all accord. Thus the protocols are made to agree, and the evidence of guilt is perfect. . . . *All that Remy, Binsfield, Del Rio and the rest tell us is based on stories extorted by torture. (My italics.)*

Nicholas Remy was the author of *Demonolatria* (Lyons, 1595); Peter Binsfield was the author of *Tractacus de Confessionibus Maleficarum et Sagarum* (Trier, 1589); Martin Del Rio was the author of *Disquisitiones Magicae* (Louvain, 1599–1601). All of these books were accepted as standard authorities upon witchcraft, *and by such modern writers as Montague Summers they are so accepted still.* By "and the rest" I presume that Von Spee includes all the other anti-witchcraft writings, including the *Malleus Maleficarum.*

"What are the arguments," says Von Spee, "of those who believe that what is confessed under torture is true? It is marvellous that the learned writers who teach the world about witchcraft base their whole argument on this deceitful foundation."

It is indeed; and it is even more marvellous that in this twentieth century they continue to obtain credence.

Where, then, did the stories of the Black Mass come from? The inquisitors and executioners who put them into the mouths of alleged witches must have got the basic idea for them from somewhere. I suggest that it was in fact widely known and whispered about that this type of perverted Mass was performed for magical ends, though decent Churchmen abominated it; and that superstitious people regarded the consecrated Host as a powerful implement of magic. This is proved by the charms containing pieces of consecrated Hosts which we have in this Museum; by such stories as that told by Montague Summers, who does not seem to realise the real significance of it, of ignorant country people who regarded the Ablution from the chalice which had held the Eucharistic wine as a remedy for the ailments of their children; and by innumerable instances in the various grimoires of magical implements, etc., which have to be consecrated by having a Mass said over them. The first reformed Prayer Book of Edward VI (1549), has a rubric which runs as follows: "And although . . . the people these many years past received at the priest's hands the Sacrament of the Body of Christ in their own hands . . . yet as they many times conveyed the same secretly away, kept it with them, and diversely abused it to superstition and wickedness . . . it is thought convenient the people commonly receive the Sacrament of Christ's Body in their mouths at the priest's hands." The purpose was not, as the legend of "Satanism" insists, deliberately to insult the Host, but to use it for magic; and it will be noted that the rubric condemns those who do so, not as "Satanists" nor even as witches, but simply as being superstitious and wicked.

It was people of this mentality who were the clients of priests who were prepared, for a consideration, to say a Mass for magical purposes. One such practice, for instance, was that of saying the Mass for the Dead in the name of a living person, to cause them to die. So many of the Church Councils fulminate against this practice, that it must have continued through many centuries.

If the practice had ceased, there was no reason to continue forbidding it.

I believe that the Catholic Church permits priests to say Masses for some particular "intention" of one of their congregation, and, of course, in the hands of any upright priest such a practice is safe from abuse. No decent priest would say a Mass for an "intention" that was obviously bad. But has it always been free from abuse? Especially in mediaeval—and even later—times, when superstitions of all kinds held sway over men's minds to an extent which we find difficult to understand or even credit? And when it was firmly believed, by both priest and people, that however bad a man was, so long as he was an ordained priest transubstantiation of the elements of the Mass would automatically take place at his word?

Have we any real evidence about the Black Mass which is worth more than the paper it is written on? There is very little, only one case being worth examination, because it does seem that the people who carried out the investigation had no axe to grind; indeed, as the investigation proceeded they were more concerned to hush up the scandalous details than to produce more. I refer to the famous "Affaire des Poisons" in the reign of King Louis XIV of France.

The prime motive of this investigation was not to uncover "Black Magic" or "witchcraft" at all, but to put a stop to the many cases of mysterious deaths by poison which were reaching the proportions of a national scandal; and it had no theological or heretical implications, but was simply a straightforward piece of police detective work. It was carried out by the lieutenant of the Paris police, Nicolas de La Reynie.

The witch-hunting mania in France was by then practically a spent force. Indeed, as I have already mentioned, Louis XIV had some years previously, in 1670, commuted the sentences passed on a number of people for witchcraft into banishment for life, and refused the request of the Parliament of Rouen that those condemned should be put to death. However, belief in the efficacy of the "occult sciences," such as alchemy, astrology and divination of all kinds, as well as ceremonial magic, was widespread. Medical science was still comparatively in its infancy, and this added to the peculiar terror of death by poison, because those medical tests by which poisoners today can quickly be detected had not yet been devised. Consequently, frightened people mistook natural deaths for the results of poison, and conversely deaths which were really by poison could not be proved.

In 1676 all Paris had been shocked by the trial and execution of a young and beautiful Marquise, Madame de Brinvilliers, for having poisoned her father and her two brothers, and having attempted the life of her sister. It was revealed during the course of the trial that she had, in fact, poisoned a number of others "for practice," before commencing the attempt upon her father, which was so cunningly carried out that his death appeared to be the result of a protracted illness. She had obtained her supplies of poison from one Saint-Croix, her lover, who pretended to be an alchemist.

Because of the high rank of the murderess, and the atrocious details of the case, the mind of the entire fashionable world was for some time occupied with nothing else; all gossip and speculation ran upon poison; it was widely rumoured that Madame de Brinvilliers was not the only purveyor of silent death who moved gaily in high society, but merely one who had had the misfortune to be found out.

France in those days possessed, at Versailles, the most brilliant court in Europe, centred around "Le Roi Soleil." Louis XIV; a monarch who could say *L'état, c'est moi,* which was little more than the truth. Inevitably, around this centre of luxury and magnificence, clustered a swarm of hangers-on; a demimonde which lived by supplying the luxuries, and sometimes the vices, of high society. Among these were pretenders to occult arts of all kinds; apothecaries who would compound cosmetics, perfumes, love-potions and poisons, as well as medicines; so-called alchemists who did a little coining on the side; card-readers, astrologers, palmists, and clairvoyants, or "sybils," as they were called; and midwives who, when discreetly consulted, would undertake to procure abortions or dispose of unwanted children, as well as carrying on the more respectable part of their calling. The Court of Versailles was a hierarchy with the Sun-King at its summit, while on its lowest levels moved some of the worst vermin of Paris.

A highly fashionable pastime was to have one's fortune told by the cards; a "sybil" who had the art of engaging conversation and a spice of showmanship could make a fortune out of telling other people's—provided, of course, that she could tell what her clients most wished to hear, or at least give them some idea of how to bring their desires to pass. Most of the fortune-tellers were shrewd psychologists; some were much more.

One evening towards the end of 1678 a lawyer named Perrin was one of a merry dinner-party at the house of Madame Vigoureux in the Rue Courtauvilain. Everyone was very gay and a little drunk, and in the mood to laugh at anything. In particular, they were kept in fits of mirth by the sallies of a plump, fashionably dressed widow, Marie Bosse, who was one of the most successful fortune-tellers by cards, and much patronised by high society. Oh, she told them, if they could only see the people who came to consult her! Duchesses, marquises, grand seigneurs, all came to her little house. Only three poisonings more, and she'd be able to retire with a fortune!

The company were convulsed with laughter. But it so happened—upon such little things does history sometimes depend—that as the Widow Bosse made her remark Perrin's eyes had been upon the face of his hostess, Madame Vigoureux; and he had seen, just for a fleeting moment, an expression upon it which made him wonder if the joke was really so funny; if, indeed, it was a joke at all.

He thought the matter over, and spoke about it to his friend, Captain Desgrez, who happened to be the police officer who had arrested Madame de Brinvilliers. Desgrez sent the wife of one of his men to have her fortune told by the Widow Bosse. She had been primed to complain of a husband whom she wanted to get rid of. It only took two visits for the woman to get hold of a phial of poison.

La Reynie, Desgrez' superior, gave orders for the arrest of the Widow Bosse and the little coterie of so-called "midwives," fortune-tellers and charm-sellers who were her closest acquaintances. Without knowing it, he had commenced to uncover a scandal the reverberations of which were to echo through every rank of the hierarchy of Versailles until they reached the throne itself.

La Reynie soon discovered that La Bosse, La Vigoureux, and their accomplices were small fry. The big fish was the woman who directed their organisation, Catherine Monvoisin, commonly known as La Voisin. She has been described as one of the most amazing criminals in history, a description with which I agree. She has also been described as a witch, a description with which I definitely disagree, for reasons which I will set out further on.

La Voisin was no back-street fortune-teller. To her house in the Rue Beauregard came the elite of Paris, who queued to consult her, whether by cards, by hand-reading, by physiognomy, or by astrology, "occult sciences" at which she was considered an adept. She kept a retinue of servants, and an equal retinue of lovers, whose presence her husband, a brow-beaten nonentity, had to suffer. She received her clients dressed so magnificently that it was said the Queen of France had no finer robe than the one she wore when delivering her oracles; it consisted of a mantle of crimson velvet sewn with two hundred and five double-headed eagles in gold thread, and trimmed with costly fur; a skirt in water-green velvet, trimmed with French point lace; and shoes sewn with golden double-headed eagles to match those on the mantle. The whole had been specially woven for her, and had cost her fifteen thousand livres. After her clients for the day had been dismissed, she herself gave lavish evening parties.

She had even, in 1664, been to the Sorbonne to engage in a debate with the doctors there upon the truth of astrology, and claimed that they had not been able to controvert her in argument.

Among her many friends was a young courtier named Louis de Vanens, a great amateur of magical sciences, and a young man of culture and good looks. He had also had the good fortune to be one of the intimate circle of friends of the most powerful woman in France, the King's mistress, Madame de Montespan.

Late, in the course of his investigation, La Reynie was to write among his notes: "*Revenir à La Chaboissière (le domestique de Vanens) sur le fait qu'il n'a voulu être écrit dans son interrogatoire, après en avoir entendu la lecture, que Vanens s'était mêlé de donner des conseils à Mme. de Montespan, qui mériteraient de le faire tirer à quatre chevaux.*" "Return to La Chaboissière (Vanens' servant) upon the fact that he did not wish to have written down in the statement of his interrogation, after having it read over to him, that

Vanens had given such counsels to Mme. de Montespan that he deserved to be torn in pieces by four horses."

But as yet, Madame de Montespan's name had not entered into the story. It was the discovery of the widespread trade in poisoning, abortion, and the murder of unwanted children that caused La Reynie to urge the King and his ministers to set up the famous "Chambre Ardente" to put a stop to the evil once and for all. This tribunal was so called (i.e. "The Burning-Chamber"), not because it imposed sentences of burning, but because it was the custom for such extraordinary tribunals to sit in a chamber hung with black and lit with burning candles and flambeaux.

When La Voison's house in the Rue Beauregard had been searched, an upper chamber had been found above the cabinet in which she gave her famous consultations, which was obviously used to carry out abortions; and behind the cabinet, in a hidden recess, a furnace was discovered containing the remains of burnt human bones. La Voisin eventually confessed that she had burned in the furnace, or buried in her garden, the bodies of over two thousand, five hundred infants.

The figure seems incredible; yet her confession was not extracted under torture. La Reynie was not permitted, as he himself records with some indignation, "to put her to the question." On the contrary, the problem soon became, not how to make La Voisin talk, but how best to silence her and hush up the whole affair. The more La Reynie probed into the ramifications of this 17th century version of "Murder Incorporated," the more worried not only he, but the King and his ministers, became. Duchesses, marquises, grand seigneurs, had indeed consulted the like of Marie Bosse and La Voisin, and gone away with a little phial of poison. A number of nobles fled the country, and it was rumoured that the King had assisted their flight, rather than see them exposed to the public scandal of a trial.

La Voisin's guilt, however, was plain; her handsome income had for years been derived more from crime than from the profession of the occult arts, though she had also commanded high fees for her practice of the latter. She was condemned to death, and executed on the 20th February, 1680.

La Reynie continued his investigations into the ramifications of the trade in poison; many of the people whom he knew were guilty had been placed beyond his reach, because of their high rank; still he was determined at least to ensure that their creatures, the go-betweens and suppliers of poisons, should not escape justice, or be enabled to continue their profitable careers of crime. He had soon discovered that he was not only dealing with common criminals; when the police had searched La Voisin's house in the Rue Beauregard, they had found in the grounds a kind of pavilion which was fitted up in a peculiar manner. The walls were hung with black, and at one end there was an altar. Behind the altar stretched a black curtain with a white cross upon it, and instead of the usual white altar-cloth the top of the altar was covered with a draping of black, which concealed a mattress placed beneath it. The altar had a tabernacle surmounted by a cross, but the candles were black.

La Reynie had soon discovered that La Voisin had many acquaintances among the less reputable type of priest. In spite of the fact that she had made an outward show of piety—she had actually been arrested as she left the Church of Notre Dame de Bonne Nouvelle, where she had been attending Mass—the Missionaires of St. Vincent de Paul had long suspected her of evil practices, and had had her under surveillance, without being able to obtain any positive evidence against her. But after La Voisin was executed, her daughter Marguerite Monvoisin—now that her mother had no more to fear or hope for in this world—began to talk. She made her first important statement on the 12th July, 1680, having all this time been detained in prison as a material witness. What she said struck horror into La Reynie. He could not believe it; yet it was so supported by the statements of other witnesses, with whom Marguerite Monvoisin could have had no contact since she had been arrested, that he dared not discredit it.

As witness after witness confirmed Marguerite Monvoisin's story, La Reynie soon had no alternative but lay what he had discovered before the King, with the result that, on the 1st October, 1680, the sittings of the Chambre Ardente were abruptly suspended by Royal order.

Briefly, the story that Marguerite Monvoisin and the other witnesses told was this: in 1667 her mother had acquired a new and brilliant client at the Court, the young and beautiful Marquise de Montespan. At that time Louis XIV had as his reigning mistress Louise de la Vallière, a charming and sweet-natured young girl who seemed unsuited for such a position. Madame de Montespan was determined to oust her and take her place, and she consulted La Voisin with a view to obtaining her desires by magical rites. La Voisin put her in touch with two practitioners of ceremonial magic, Lesage and the Abbé Mariette, priest of Saint-Severin. Who put Madame de Montespan in touch with La Voisin is not known; though from the statement already alluded to, we may well conjecture that it was Louise de Vanens. A magical ceremony was arranged at a house in the Rue de la Tannerie. Lesage, Mariette, and Madame de Montespan met in a small room furnished with an altar. Mariette was in his priest's vestments, and Lesage apparently acted as assistant, chanting the *Veni Creator*. Madame de Montespan knelt before the altar, while Mariette read what was described as "L'évangile" over her. Then she recited the following conjuration: "I demand the friendship of the King and that of Monseigneur the Dauphin, and that I may retain their favour, that the Queen may be barren, that the King may leave her bed and her table and come to me, that I may obtain from him all which I ask of him for myself and my parents, that my followers and servants may be agreeable to him, that I may be cherished and respected by the great nobles, that I may be called into the counsels of the King and know all that passes there, and that, this liking increasing more and more, the King may leave La Vallière and think no more of her, and that the Queen being repudiated, I may marry the King."

Madame de Montespan was evidently a lady who knew what she wanted, and would stick at nothing to get it. It does not appear, however, that this was a Black Mass, but merely a magical ceremony done under the forms of orthodox religion.

At the beginning of 1668, she actually introduced Mariette and Lesage into the Royal Court itself, and they secretly performed a magical ceremony in the room of her sister, Madame de Thianges. It appears to have resembled the one already described; incense was burned, and conjurations recited to obtain the King's favour and get rid of Mlle. de la Vallière.

Shortly after this rite, Madame's dearest dream was realised; the King took her to bed with him, although to outward seeming La Vallière was still *Maitresse en titre.* Soon, however, it was evident that La Vallière's reign was over, and that the new favourite was destined to eclipse her completely. The Marquis de Montespan, Madame's husband, who had had the bad taste to object to the arrangement, was first made the object of public ridicule in a thousand epigrams and in Molière's comedy, *Amphitryon;* and then, when he still refused to behave according to the usages of polite society, exiled to Spain. Madame de Montespan acquired such an ascendancy over the King that she was known as "the Queen of the Left Hand." He presented her with the magnificent Château of Clagny; in the Royal Palace itself, she occupied an apartment of twenty rooms on the first floor; the

Queen occupied eleven rooms on the second floor; on State occasions the Queen's train was borne by a page; but it was the Maréchale de Noailles who bore that of Madame de Montespan.

In 1669 she gave birth to the first of the seven children whom she had by the King; and until 1672 her reign was absolute. In that year, however, the King began to give her cause for jealousy. She saw and felt her empire shaken, and she suffered agonies of fear and rage. For fifteen days she refused to see anyone; but at last she did see someone—La Voisin.

Her old acquaintances, Lesage and the Abbé Mariette, had in the meantime been chastened by a sojourn in prison for sacrilege, and Mariette had for the time being fled abroad. However, La Voisin introduced her to a practitioner of a darker shade than these two, who, she assured her, was prepared to perform even more powerful ceremonies; the Abbé Guibourg.

Guibourg was a sixty-seven-year-old priest, who alleged himself to be the illegitimate son of a nobleman. He had a number of benefices in Paris and the surrounding districts. His reputation was evil, and in the pursuit of black magic he was utterly ruthless. He had had several children by his mistress, a woman called La Chanfrain, and he was said to have used some of them as sacrifices in his monstrous rites.

It is said in *The Key of Solomon,*

> In many operations it is necessary to make some sort of sacrifice unto Demons, and in various ways. Sometimes white animals are sacrificed to the good Spirits and black to the evil. Such sacrifices consist of the blood and sometimes the flesh. Those who sacrifice animals, of whatsoever kind they be, should select those which are virgin, as being more agreeable unto the Spirits, and rendering them more obedient.

It is evident, from the details given, that the purpose of Guibourg's ceremonies was to evoke demons and compel them to obey his requests; and we have seen that the disposal of unwanted children was part of La Voisin's trade. Madame de Montespan was a passionate, desperate woman, and not noted for softness of heart. Yet they were both mothers, and we cannot but wonder at the psychological processes which led the one to supply the sacrifice, and the other to watch it performed before her eyes.

Once again, I think, the explanation is to be found in a superstitious and perverted view of the sacraments. They salved their wretched consciences by the idea that, so long as the child had been baptised, it was a sinless creature which, when killed, would go straight to heaven. There is a story about La Voisin which illustrates this belief. La Lepère, one of La Voisin's midwife cronies, was once in the room in the latter's house where she gave her fortune-telling consultations, together with La Voisin's husband. La Voisin herself was in the room above, in the act of supervising either an abortion or a clandestine birth. Presently, she came downstairs with her face wreathed in a cheerful smile, exclaiming, "*Quel bonheur! L'enfant a pu ètré ondoy!*" ("How fortunate! The child was able to be baptised!") She is said to have been very particular that any child which she handled which was born alive should be baptised before it was "disposed of." A lurid light is thrown upon this belief by the slang name by which those midwives were known who were prepared, "for a consideration," to make away with unwanted babies. They were called "*faiseuses D'anges*," "makers of angels."

This trait of La Voisin's is, I think, a clear piece of evidence that she was not a member of the witch cult; *because no member of the latter would have entertained such a belief, nor would they have had any faith in Guibourg's consecration of the elements in the Mass as part of a magical ceremony.* Witchcraft, as I have already explained, is a religion as well as a system of magic, and no genuine practitioner will perform its rites for pay. La Voisin, on the contrary, was blatantly "in it for the money." All her magical practices seem to have been founded on perversions of the Church's sacraments, and without her acquaintances among the priesthood she could do nothing. A real witch would have had no need to call in renegade priests. Her fortune-telling was based on card-reading, astrology, palmistry, and physiogomy, and there is nothing esoteric about these things (except in connection with the Tarot, and that is not a secret of the witch cult).

Dr. Jules Regnault, in his book *La Sorcellerie, ses Rapports avec les Sciences Biologiques* (Paris, 1936), actually gives the words of Guibourg's abominable "blessing" of the destined victim, "*Notre Seigneur Jésus-Christ laissait venir à lui les petits enfants. Aussi j'ai voulu que tu viennes, car je suis son prêtre, et tu vas, par ma main que tu dois bénir, t'incorporer à ton Dieu.*" ("Our Lord Jesus Christ suffered the little children to come to Him. Even so I have willed that thou comest, for I am His priest, and thou goest, by my hand which thou should'st bless, to incorporate thyself with thy God.") Unfortunately, Dr. Regnault does not give his authority for this wording; which, if it is authentic, is a perfect illustration of the mentality behind the

Black Mass. It will be noted that in it Guibourg describes himself as the priest of Jesus Christ; not as either a "Satanist" or a witch.

It might well be felt that while such so-called "priests" walked the earth, there was little need to evoke demons. But was Guibourg any worse than Nicholas Remy, who, in his book, dedicated to Cardinal Charles de Lorraine, boasted of having been personally responsible for the deaths of nine hundred witches, and urged judges to be merciless in torture; or Arnauld, the Papal Legate, who presided over the Massacre of Béziers?

The root of all these horrors is the same; it springs ultimately from no doctrine, nor from any cult; it is simply the heartless cruelty of souls whose utter selfishness blinds them to all interests and feelings save their own. Nor is the advancement of any cult, nor the extirpation of any cult, the remedy for it; the only real remedy is the spiritual evolution of mankind as a whole.

Guibourg and La Voisin told Madame de Montespan that, in order to attain its object, the Black Mass must be said three times in succession. Accordingly, arrangements were made to say the first one in the chapel of the Château de Villebousin, in the hamlet of Mesnil, near Montlhéry. It was a requirement of this particular ritual that the woman on whose behalf it was being said had to lie on the altar naked. The spectacle of the most powerful, and one of the most beautiful women in France, lying naked on the altar of the Black Mass, has often seized the imagination of sensational writers and artists, and we have usually had the scene depicted with Madame de Montespan lying extended upon the altar. Actually, however, she lay across the altar, on her back, her body at right angles to its length and with her knees drawn up. A pillow supported her head, and she held in her extended arms the two candlesticks with their black candles. A cross was placed between her breasts, and the chalice between her thighs. Guibourg, the officiating priest, stood between her knees. We are told by Marguerite Monvoisin that he had a special vestment for this ritual, a white chasuble sewn with black pine cones.

The ritual apparently followed the orthodox wording of the Mass, but with the monstrous addition of the sacrifice of a baby, at which the following words were said by Guibourg on behalf of Madame de Montespan: "Astaroth, Asmodeus, princes of affection, I conjure you to accept the sacrifice which I present to you, of this child, for the things which I demand of you, which are that the affection of the King, and of Monseigneur le Dauphin, may be continued towards me, and that I may be honoured by the princes and princesses of the Court, and that nothing may be denied me of all that I ask of the King, either for myself or for my family and servants." This is Guibourg's version of the conjuration, which he gave to the Chambre Ardente.

H. T. F. Rhodes has made a number of speculative deductions from the details of the description of this Mass, in the course of which he says, "The dominant features of the two-faced Satan of the 17th century are those of the mother-goddess. It is only in the light of this fact that the black rites and ceremonies of the period can be understood. The name was Astaroth." But upon this point Mr. Rhodes has been egregiously misled. The "Astaroth" to whom Guibourg's conjuration was addressed was not a goddess at all, but a goetic demon. He is mentioned as such in the *Grimorium Verum,* the *Grimoire of Pope Honorius,* the *Sacred Magic of Abramelin the Mage* (which dates from 1458 and in which Astaroth and Asmodeus are listed as two of the Eight Sub-Princes of Evil), in the *Pseudomonarchia Demonum,* the *Dictionnaire Infernale* of Colln de Plancy, the *Dragon Rouge,* the *Goetia,* and in Francis Barrett's *Magus.* He is described as "a Grand Duke of Hell," and he is pictured in the *Magus* as a bearded figure with a fierce expression. He is said to appear in the body of an angel, mounted on an infernal dragon, and to manifest his evil nature by bringing with him a foul odour. His attribute is the ability of causing friendships with great lords. In the *Grimoire of Pope Honorius,* it says, "Those who would obtain the favours of rulers call him."

Asmodeus is a destructive demon mentioned in the *Goetia* and in a number of other grimoires. It has been suggested by S. L. MacGregor Mathers that his name is derived from the Hebrew word *Asamod,* to destroy or exterminate. The purpose of the Black Mass at which these two demons were evoked was firstly to regain the King's favour, and secondly to destroy Madame de Montespan's rivals; hence the purpose of choosing this particular evocation is perfectly clear.

Mr. Rhodes has been further misled when he says that the Mass was "offered" to Astaroth and Asmodeus. It was the blood sacrifice alone which was offered to demons; the Mass—Heaven help them!—was offered to God, in order to control the demons and make them obey.

Two more masses were performed, at fifteen-day and three-week intervals; the second took place in a tumble-down house at Saint-Denis; the third in a house at Paris, to which Guibourg was taken with his eyes blindfolded, and conducted thence again in the same way. And in due course, Madame de Montespan regained her ascendancy over the King.

In 1675, however, the King was seized with one of his fits of piety, and Madame de Montespan was banished from the Court. This time she went straight to La Voisin, who supplied her with "magical powders" which she was to get introduced into the King's food and drink. It was not the first time that this had been done. Some of the officers who served the King's table were in Madame de Montespan's pay. Marguerite Monvoisin stated, "Every time something new happened with regard to Madame de Montespan, and she feared some lessening of the King's favour, she told my mother, so that she might bring her some remedy, and my mother had recourse to the priests, by whom she had Masses said, and she gave some powders which the King was to be got to take." She said that these powders were made according to different formulas, but that all were intended as aphrodisiacs, and were composed of cantharides, the powder of dried toads, the blood of bats, "*et les plus ignobles ingrédients.*" These things were made into a paste which was placed underneath the chalice during the Mass, and blessed by the priest at the moment of the offertory. The paste was then dried and powdered, and secretly administered to the King in his food. The operative principle, of course, would have been such aphrodisiac substances as cantharides: an overdose of this, however, would have proved fatal, and in fact, according to medical records, Louis did sometimes show symptoms of being drugged with some such substance. At one time, he suffered from fits of dizziness and his sight became obscured; at another, he seemed to have a feverish, satyr-like desire for women. The other fantastic ingredients of La Voisin's "magical powders" might have served to dilute the dangerous drugs and make their action less violent.

Once again, La Voisin's designs worked, and the King summoned his mistress back to Court. But they had worked only too well; the King, recovering from his mood of religion, went to the other extreme, and the unhappy "Queen of the Left Hand" had a whole succession of rivals. She became so desperate that once again she resolved to try the Black Mass. This time the Masses were held at La Voisin's house in the Rue Beauregard, in the black-draped pavilion which the police discovered when they searched the place, after La Voisin's arrest. The usual three Masses were said, but Madame de Montespan was only present in person at the first one, at which a child was sacrificed. The other two were said on her behalf by Guibourg and La Voisin. It was the duty of Marguerite Monvoisin to help her mother to prepare the "chapel," and sometimes to act as assistant. Madame de Montespan was not the only woman who came to La Voisin's house to take part in a Black Mass, and apparently there was an alternative ritual. Dr. Regnault (Op. cit.) says:

"Notons toutefois que la messe dite pour Madame de Montespan ne fut pas tourt à fait complète. En raison de la situation de la courtisane, on avait choisi le vieux Guibourge, afin qu'il ne fût pas tenté de suivre le rite le plus courant qui consisterait à placer, après la consécration, l'hostie dans le vagin de la femme, en guise d' hymen, et à pratiquer le cöit dans ces conditions." According to a statement of Marguerite Monvoisin, however, Guibourg did practise this ritual; but it is not clear whether or not he practised it with Madame de Montespan. The purpose, however, was not a ceremonial desecration of the elements, but a perversion of the ancient Sacred Marriage.

Once again, Madame de Montespan regained the favours of the King; her rivals were disregarded, and she seemed to reign more brilliantly than ever, Queen in all but name of the most magnificent Court in Europe. But in spite of the luxury with which she was surrounded, she was an unhappy, tormented woman. Apart from the precariousness of her position, which might any day be menaced by the rivalry of another, perhaps younger and prettier face, it cannot have been pleasant to live with the memory of the sights and sounds of the Rue Beauregard, or of the chapel in the lonely château, or the old ruined house at Saint-Denis. Saint-Simon tells us that towards the end of her life she would not sleep except in a room well lit with many candles, and with the curtains of her bed wide open, and that she paid a number of serving-women solely to sit up with her at night and watch while she slept. She had, he says, a great fear of death.

She had no need to fear blackmail; such was her position that no one would have dared it; but she must have dreaded discovery. In 1677 her old friend, Louis de Vanens, had been arrested, on charges connected with coining, which he had been concerned with under the cover of an "association of alchemists"; and the police were beginning urgently to probe the scandal of secret poisonings. It seems unlikely that she was completely ignorant of La Voisin's participation in the latter.

At the beginning of 1679 her rival appeared upon the scene, a beautiful young girl of eighteen, Mlle. de Fontanges. Fair-haired, gentle and charming, she is said to have borne a strange resemblance to Louise de la

Vallière, the King's old, and some said his only real love, whom Madame de Montespan had driven from the Court so many years ago. The King fell in love with her.

Madame de Montespan was beside herself with rage and fear. No longer did she seek to regain the King's favour. She went to La Voisin, and offered her one hundred thousand ecus to poison both the King and Mlle. de Fontanges. La Voisin, dazzled by the sum she offered, undertook to do it. She was actually engaged on a scheme to kill the King when she was arrested.

Even that blow did not soften Madame de Montespan's determination to poison the Duchess de Fontanges. Her actions at this time show such desperation that it might be conjectured that she was almost out of her mind; for she promptly entered into negotiations with La Filastre, one of La Voisin's gang of expert poisoners, and despatched her to Normandie and Auvergne to obtain more subtle poisons. Upon her return to Paris, the woman was arrested; and it was her declarations which, when conveyed to the King by La Reynie, removed the last doubt from his mind of his ex-mistress's guilt, and caused him to order the immediate suspension of the Chambre Ardente, on the 1st October, 1680.

Although in March, 1679, in the same month that La Voisin was arrested, Madame de Montespan had fallen from favour, she was still treated publicly by the King with polite gallantry. However, when he proclaimed Mlle. de Fontanges a duchess, with a lavish pension, Madame de Montespan had a violent scene with the King, in which she reproached him bitterly, and their relationship grew increasingly cold.

It might be thought a curious coincidence that the outbreak of the scandal of the "Affaire des Poisons" should coincide with the King's tiring of Madame de Montespan. However, had he merely wished to get rid of her, there was no necessity to have made a scandal that rocked the entire French nobility, and startled Europe; and in fact, when the discoveries of La Reynie's investigation were placed before him, the King and his two ministers, Colbert and Louvois, far from proclaiming the fallen favourite's shame to the world, made desperate efforts to conceal it. It took four days of pleading on the part of La Reynie to persuade the King to permit the Chambre Ardente to resume its sessions, and he then did so only that the affair might somehow be concluded. In the meantime, all the dossiers of evidence that implicated Madame de Montespan had been sequestered from the rest, and given in a sealed casket to the clerk of the Chambre Ardente, to be put away; they were not shown to the judges. All those who could bear witness against her were imprisoned for life, by *lettre de cachet,* and La Reynie regretted that in this way many of the worst criminals, including the Abbé Guibourg himself, escaped the public execution that he would have given them by law.

On the 14th June, 1709, Nicholas La Reynie died; and on the 13th July, 1709, the King sent for the sealed casket. It was brought to him at the Palace, and he is said to have burned its contents with his own hand, in the fireplace of his private apartment. La Reynie, however, had made extensive notes—indeed, he had been bound to do so—of the case in all its ramifications, and it is these notes, together with letters between him and the King and his ministers, which tell the story. It is an uncommonly ugly story, but it has for that very reason the appearance of truth. If Louis XIV had wished an invention against Madame de Montespan, he would hardly have made one which was so humiliating to himself; and, as Nicholas de la Reynie wrote in his notes, after carefully comparing all the evidence about the Black Masses which Guibourg and Marguerite Monvoisin had given, "Guibourg and la fille Voisin agree with each other upon circumstances so particular and so horrible that it is difficult to conceive that two people could have imagined them and concocted them all together, unknown to each other. It must be, it seems, that these things were done, to have been said."

Madame de Montespan had one more terrible scene with the King, in which he may have taxed her with her guilt; we can scarcely know for certain what passed, for no one else was present except Madame de Maintenon, who kept a discreet distance. She was the governess of Madame de Montespan's seven children by the King, and ultimately became his mistress when the young Duchesse de Fontanges died the next year, at the age of twenty-two. Poison was strongly suspected as the cause of her death, though it may have been natural.

After this scene, the King had no further relations with Madame de Montespan; to lessen public scandal, however, she was permitted to remain at Court. In 1691 she retired to a convent, and the King gave her a handsome pension. Towards the end of her life, she became very repentant, and it is said that, in spite of the terrors of death and of the dark from which she suffered, when death finally claimed her she met it calmly. She died in 1707.

I have treated this story at such length because, as I have mentioned, it is the only account I know of the Black Mass which is supported by anything worth calling evidence. The conclusions which I have drawn from it may not be acceptable to all. Nevertheless, it is as clear as daylight (except to those of whom the old proverb says, "There are none so blind as them that won't see"), that the people who were practising the Black Mass in the 17th century were not witches, but priests. Guibourg was not alone in his infamy; we have also the names of the Abbé Davot; Dulong, the Canon of Notre Dame, and Brigalier, a Royal Almoner; the Abbé Guignard, and the Abbé Sebault; Barthelemy Lemeignan, the vicar of Saint-Eustache, and another priest called Tournet: and a Bishop, Gille-Lefranc. H. T. F. Rhodes—upon the *facts* in whose book I cast no doubt, disagreeing only with the deductions he draws from them—tells us that between 1673 and 1680 at least fifty priests were executed for sacrilege, and that the majority, if not all of these, were associated with La Voisin.

Do not let me give the impression that by stating these facts I am attempting to cast a slur upon the Catholic clergy as a whole. In every religious community there are good and bad; but unfortunately the bad often make more noise in the world than the good. While witch-hunting butchers such as Institoris and Sprenger were at their hateful work, hundreds of kindly and decent parish priests were at theirs; and against the memory of Guibourg we should place that of Tanner, Laymann, and Von Spee, who risked their lives in their attempts to secure justice and humanity for those accused as witches.

Chapter XIV

Some Allegations Examined, Part I

In the year 1951 the British Government of the day added an important chapter to the long history of legislation affecting witchcraft, and also, incidentally, to that relating to religious and personal liberty. They passed the Act of Parliament known as the Fraudulent Mediums Act.

This Act is, I believe, a unique piece of legislation in that it legally recognises the possibility of *genuine* mediumship and psychic powers, and imposes penalties only on those who fraudulently pretend to the possession of such powers in order to make money. The Spiritualists hailed it as their charter of freedom, and it was those M.P.s who were sympathetic to Spiritualism who backed the Bill in the House and secured its passage.

It is interesting to note how the laws relating to witchcraft have reflected the opinion and intellectual climate of the times. As we have seen in the early days in Britain when the hold of Christianity upon the mass of the people was not strong, the Church could only impose penances and fines for what, in later years, became capital offences. Then the Church, growing stronger, began to persecute the poor and helpless among the "heathen," but let the great nobles alone. However, as the Church's power grew it began to fly higher. The first big trial of a person of high rank was that of Dame Alice Kyteler, and even then they only seized her servants, torturing and burning them; she herself escaped. Presently, however, not even the highest in the land were immune, and the full fury of persecution raged, with the law reflecting the Church's doctrine that witchcraft was the direct concern of Satan.

Still, with the rise of rationalism in the eighteenth century public opinion would no longer support the death sentence on witches. It was not due to a new spirit of clemency in the Church, but to an increased growth of rationalism among the people, that the prosecution of witches began to dwindle and finally ceased. In 1736 James I's Witchcraft Act of 1604 was repealed, and replaced by an Act which said in effect that there was no such thing as witchcraft, and that anyone who *pretended* to occult powers was *ipso facto* a fraud, and should be prosecuted as such. It was under this Act, coupled with the Vagrancy Act, that spiritualist mediums were prosecuted up to 1951.

In 1951, as we have seen, it was repealed in its turn and replaced by the Fraudulent Mediums Act. This again reflected the change in intellectual climate, from the rather materialistic rationalism of the 18th and early 19th centuries to the present-day investigations into parapsychology, psychic research and study generally as pioneered by such bodies as the Society for Psychical Research and such philosophers as Carl Gustav Jung, together with the rise of such movements as Spiritualism and Theosophy. Once again the spirit of the age has changed, and the change is reflected in its laws.

Now to those religious bodies who have for centuries been preaching that all such things were the direct intervention of Satan in human affairs, and consequently that no ordinary person should be allowed to investigate them for himself and make up his own mind about them without "theological guidance" (such as is contained, for instance, in the *Malleus Maleficarum*), the Fraudulent Mediums Act of 1951 was gall and wormwood; and we know from experience that these interests do not take this sort of thing lying down.

It may, of course, be the sheerest coincidence; but towards the end of 1951 a number of very strange things began to appear in certain sections of the Press, and they have kept on appearing at intervals ever since. The general trend of these stories has been that Britain is being riddled and undermined by "Black Magic," and that the public should be aroused to a state of alarm about it.

The first article was published in a sensational newspaper in 1951, saying, "There are many men and women in Britain today who delight in wickedness and who, subscribing to the cult of Black Magic, take part in unbelievable debauchery." Their reporter gave his findings as follows:

"1. Black magic is *not* practised by a few crazy individuals. *It is the cult of many organised groups.*

"2. Most of the men and women involved are not only sane—*they are highly intelligent.*

"3. They include people who are nationally and internationally famous. A revival of witchcraft is sweeping the country, and people must be warned against it." The reporter also said: "I have in my possession a dossier, the result of many years' work by an investigator, a Mr. A., who is out to expose these malignant people and their teachings and practices. This dossier gives the most detailed information on the activities of many well-known people."

His article concluded, "I urge the authorities to keep a closer watch on strange and crazy-sounding societies. Many of them are far more sinister than they appear to be."

Now, when statements are made which are deliberately calculated to alarm the public about something, and which urge the authorities to take action, I think it a pity that it is not disclosed just who is responsible for such statements, and what evidence there is to support them. However, in spite of the fact that we were assured that Mr. A. was not a crank, the public have never been given the opportunity of judging this for themselves. We are not told what qualifications he possesses, nor was his true name mentioned.

Further, if this paper really possessed a dossier "giving the most detailed information on the activities of many well-known people" who were practising Black Magic, *why weren't the facts published?* Why, instead of making use of this spicy scoop, did the writers fail to produce their informant Mr. A., or the dossier? I think it is time the public were told. If there is anything evil going on, why not inform the police?

I wonder if these newspapers have stopped to reflect on what may be the effect of statements that many people "who are nationally and internationally famous" are involved in black magic. Is not this calculated to undermine the confidence of the ordinary man and woman in the, shall we say, "governing classes" of this country? Let those who think I am exaggerating remember how the ordinary Russian's faith in the Czar and his family was undermined by the horrible stories that were told about their subservience to the "Black Magician," Rasputin. I do not suggest that the papers which have printed such statements as that which I have quoted are deliberately aiming for this object; but I do suggest that this vague smear-and-scare campaign is potentially more dangerous to Britain than the alleged activities of all the so-called black magic groups put together.

We have heard a very great deal about "The Black International of Satanism." Between the covers of a thriller such things are no more sinister than the activities of Dr. Fu Manchu; but when they are presented as sober fact, which British citizens should get alarmed about, I think it is time to ask either for some of that awkward thing, evidence, or for a halt to be called until it can be produced. Personally, in the course of a long life, the greater part of which has been devoted to an interest in folklore, anthropology, psychic research, magic, and knocking about in some of the odd places of the world in general, I have never come across the slightest evidence that any such "Black International" exists outside works of fiction, and consequently I do not believe that it does.

What we do come across, time and again in history, is the tragic results which have accrued from listening to people's irresponsible imaginings and taking them for truth. Apart from the millions who perished in the witch persecutions, there were such affairs as the "Popish Plot," in the days of Charles II, when Roman Catholics all over England were persecuted, and some lost their lives, on account of sensational rumours spread in the first instance by a man called Titus Oates, who was ultimately proved to be an impostor; but Titus Oates was severely punished for his lies.

At the end of October, 1952, an article entitled *Witches Devil-Worship in London* appeared in the Press. This repeated the tales about "obscene ceremonies, involving priestesses, blood sacrifices of cats and goats, and ritual dances to the rhythm of drums," and told how "Surrounded by black draperies, with the signs of the Zodiac glowing in the light of candles, these worshippers of the Devil perform their incantations while herbal incense burns." Once again the allegation was repeated that some of those who took part in these things were "highly intelligent men and women, some nationally and internationally famous—but all slightly unhinged."

In 1953, two more articles about *Black Magic in Britain* appeared in the October and November issues of a psychic periodical, now defunct. Among all the usual sensationalism, tales of "pacts with the Devil," blood sacrifices, "black rites," "orgies," etc., etc., appeared this significant passage:

> Spiritualists recently rejoiced that they had at last been granted their "freedom charter." One of the last things the Labour Government did was to place upon the Statute Book the Fraudulent Mediums Act which replaced the centuries-old Witchcraft Act and Vagrancy Act, under which mediums were open to prosecution every time they held a seance or conducted a service in a Spiritualist church.
>
> For many years Spiritualists in and out of the House of Commons had been campaigning for the withdrawal of these two Acts, but some people who had a little more vision warned that abolition would open the door for all sorts of occult practices, some of which were undesirable to say the least. That is exactly what has happened.

Some of the stories retailed in these articles were identical with those which had been told in 1951. Further, we were informed that "A journalist who was carrying out an investigation of certain occult practices was forced to drop his story as being 'too hot to handle' when he found the identity of some of the people involved." "High officials of political parties," we were told, consulted occultists.

Once again, the smear-and-scare campaign's usual technique; not one scintilla of evidence is produced to support the allegations made, while the hint is dropped that the full truth cannot come out because people in high positions are preventing it. What nonsense—*what dangerous nonsense!*

In September, 1954, a wonderful two-page spread came out. "Men eavesdrop on the Devil." But alas it did not come anywhere near living up to its title. (Otherwise, what an interview it might have been!) In fact, the Devil, as far as I can make out, was never there. The reporters watched the so-called "Black Magic" ceremony, though actually they revealed that the whole proceedings had been "made up" in the house of a black gentleman who we will call Mr. X., purely to make a story, and that some girls had been invited who did not know they would be photographed by concealed cameras.

All these preparations were said to be made to prove that people in Britain were interested in Black Magic. A ceremony was said to have been performed to release a young man from a Black Magic spell cast on him some time before; this was enlivened by playing a gramophone record of an old jazz number. The article was written to suggest that something wicked was going on. Personally I cannot see it is so very wicked to attempt to release someone from a Black Magic spell. But a reporter said: "I have seen a black-magician kneel before a candle and pray to the devil." Now, I think this was a very rude allusion to their host's colour. And, anyhow, the Devil, possibly being frightened of the reporters, did not come. The other reporter said he had seen this magician massage a blonde girl's back. That apparently was all that happened.

Except the utterly priceless comment of this reporter: "It is disturbing to get confirmation that there are adults in Britain who still wish to flirt with Black Magic." "What," it may be asked, "do these wonderful revelations amount to after all?"

In 1955, these sensational papers promised us "The shocking inside story of Black Magic in Britain." This was to be the real MacCoy at last.

Oddly enough, no reference was now made to the dossier which, it will be remembered, contained detailed information about "unbelievable debauchery" in which "people who are nationally and internationally famous" took part in the course of their participation in the rites of black magic; notwithstanding that the same reporter was still responsible for the articles. On the contrary, the chief "confessor" proved to be a black woman of obscure origin who lived in Birmingham.

"Made in Birmingham" has, alas, too often turned out to be the hallmark of "antiques" of doubtful provenance, and the "witch cult" of the sensational Press proved to be no exception.

In letters of about two inches high, the words "Black Magic in Britain" leapt at us from the page. "You are about to be frightened" we were told. (The British nation—so notoriously timid!) "*The Sunday Pictorial* begins today (it was the 22nd May, 1955) to publish a startling dossier with the prime idea of scaring anyone who may be tempted to flirt with black magic . . . the dossier you are about to read concerns the devil on our doorstep—here in Britain." (Where was the previous dossier? In the waste-paper basket?)

"Because devil worship is practised in secret, because its followers look no different from the man or woman next door, this investigation has taken many months . . . enough has been discovered to prove to you that devil worship can wreck the health, corrupt the mind and degrade the body of those it ensnares.

"Its crimes—as we will show—include blasphemy, desecration, moral perversion.

"Our investigators have found the evidence of a nation-wide chain of witchcraft groups called Covens.

"Its members are sincere in a satanic belief that theirs is the ancient religion of Britain. They claim it is older than, and superior to, Christianity.

"Time and again I have been warned during this investigation:

"'The public will never believe you if you print the facts. The truth is inconceivable.'"

The writer goes on to quote—inevitably—the Rev. Montague Summers, "a retired Roman Catholic priest," and a famous sensational writer.

"In his (Summers') warnings he wrote of 'fearful forces of evil, forces of power which seem illimitable.'"

But no one took any notice of Montague Summers. Except, of course, the sensational Press; and now look what a glowing reward had come to them!

Four months ago, it is stated, news had been received from the Midlands that "For the first time a person who had been vitally involved in a thriving black magic circle was prepared to make a full statement." They had found a black woman who claimed to have been a High Priestess of a local witch coven. . . . She told of her training, her initiation, of secret meetings at night. She told of visits to graveyards at midnight to "claim souls of the newly-buried for the devil." She told how strong men and women had been made sick by spells. How at ceremonies lasting into early dawn orgies were practised while everything decent in life was mocked. . . .

"The word of one woman," it was considered, "was not enough. An all-out attempt was made to find more evidence. At various times, in the last five months, many members of our editorial staff have worked on this probe into evil. We have travelled thousands of miles—backwards and forwards to the Midlands, to the South Coast, to Belfast, to Oxford, and to the extreme west coast of Eire. The results have been strange, exciting, and at times terrifying. The hunt has included visits to lonely graveyards. Chases in fast cars. Mysterious telephone messages. . . .

"How do covens get their recruits? Likely members are wooed with promises of power and thrills; too late they find they have acquired a passport to debauchery. In some covens each member is expected to introduce nine new initiates a year. . . . How can one get free from this evil grip? Seek out your Doctor or Clergyman. Tell him what has happened—in confidence. Or write to us."

Now, it might have been legitimately expected, after five months of investigation which, if we were to believe the above account, must have rivalled the adventures of Bulldog Drummond, that the sensation seekers would have had something to tell its readers. However, the curious thing about this series has been that *at no time has the result of this five months' investigation been made public.*

It was admitted that "The word of one woman was not enough." *Yet the word of one woman was all that we were ever given.* Not one word of corroboration of this woman's story was, as we shall see, ever printed. Nor did any other member of the sensation seekers' staff apart from this particular reporter, ever give their views, or their story. We were never enlightened as to what was found on the South Coast, in Belfast, Oxford, or the extreme west coast of Eire, nor the purposes of the "chases in fast cars," or what the "mysterious telephone messages" were all about.

In the same article we were told about the way in which a woman associated with the "devil-worshippers" created a flash of light by placing her finger-tips together, and of another woman who was able, by some occult power, to make her head and feet luminous. As a member of the Society of Psychical Research, I should have very much liked the opportunity to meet both these ladies; but nothing more was ever heard about them.

Personally, after a close study of the peculiar technique of the sensational Press, I find the things they leave unsaid very much more intriguing than those they say. We shall see later on how one piece of evidence about witchcraft in Britain, which I provided for them and was prepared to guarantee as genuine, they flatly refused to print, upon the most feeble excuse I have ever heard.

In the next Sunday's issue was given the confession of a witch. "She confesses today," we were told, "in the hope of saving others." She stated: "This is my confession. I write it to convince you that I have been caged by fear. Fear of black magic and the Devil. Perhaps you do not believe that here in Britain, in the twentieth century, it is possible to be involved in the evils of witchcraft. I can assure you from my own terrible experiences as High Priestess in a Black Magic circle, that this is true. . . ."

She tells us that she was one day introduced to a man who came to have a dreadful significance in her life. Wherever she moved to, he followed her; he began to talk to her of strange religious theories, and slowly a relationship of teacher and pupil came about. Most of her lessons were by telephone, sometimes twice a day, and often the calls lasted half to three-quarters of an hour. "Eventually I was so gripped by the voice on the 'phone that I lived only to hear it twice a day. One day in 1945 when he did not phone me as he had promised to do I even tried to commit suicide." The man, she tells us, taught her various remarkable things; how to call upon "the elements," and ask them to send their spirits to her, how to make any man enslaved to her (wasn't she rather slow not to have used this latter knowledge upon her teacher, to make him 'phone her as promised, instead of trying to commit suicide when he didn't), how to build a temple in her mind, and how to use obscene language. This is, incidentally, the first time that I have ever heard the latter quoted as being part of the equipment of a magician, and I cannot quite see of what practical use in magic this accomplishment would be.

Further, Mr. X. taught her "to call upon Hell—'Oh, Hell, help me!'" (Not, as one might have supposed, upon the receipt of his telephone bill, but as a form of prayer.) She was also taught to pray "directly to Michele, a nickname of the devil."

"I was told," she continues, "that when I had found nine pupils I could be initiated into the full Black Art. . . . This day came on February 15th, 1948. . . . In a large private flat. There were about fifty people present. There was a small altar. . . . A young cockerel was killed and the blood poured into a glass to be given to those to be initiated . . . beside myself.

"The candles were on a slant, almost upside-down, burning." (This in itself must have been a rather remarkable magical feat—I wonder if the sensational Press's reporter has ever tried burning candles upside down? They go out at once). "A cross was placed upside-down in a tumbler containing water. . . . The first initiate drank the blood of the sacrificed chicken, and was informed that she had drunk the blood of the devil. Twisted prayers were said. She signed a pact bearing blood giving her soul to the devil in return for power. . . . I was initiated as a High Priestess, after my long training. My mother was an Egyptian, and I was told that Egyptian blood was most suited to this position of authority. . . . The ritual was a complete mockery of Christian worship."

She goes on to describe how, "veiled, wearing my robes," she took part in further ceremonies as High Priestess. There was, she says, a beating of drums, music playing soft and low, apparently provided by some kind of band, and a kind of call would be given. "It is a most peculiar call, a kind of shrill sound that would go right through you, as if someone were in agony." Then she would be pushed through a curtain by one of the officiators, to go and stand on the left-hand side of the altar. (What a disrespectful way to treat a High Priestess! Or was poor Mrs. Jackson's veil so thick that she couldn't see where she was going? In which case, how can she have seen the things she describes?)

"The Priest would walk slowly through the crowd up the room and kneel in the centre of the circle. . . . Chanting would begin." There were "twisted prayers" and "mock hymns." Then the music and drumming would begin again and "fanatical dancing" would ensue, working up to a pitch when "men and women tore their clothes off."

"Drinks were given to anyone and everyone. It was right to use obscene language—the worse the better. Often these meetings lasted into the early hours of the morning."

All this in a Birmingham flat—meetings at which about fifty people at a time took part! What a pity that the comments of the occupants of the adjacent flats are not recorded—still, perhaps that accounts for the obscene language!

She continues: "Members of the circle were tested as to their allegiance. My first test was an instruction to go to a churchyard at midnight. There I was told that I should find the new grave of a certain person who had been buried that day. I was to pray aloud to Michele to take the soul of the dead person. For proof that I had carried out the task, I was to bring back clay fresh from the graveside."

Personally, this hardly strikes me as a very convincing test. I cannot see what was to prevent the person who was being "tested" from bringing back clay fresh from their own back garden, and spending the night in their bed. However, this is probably merely my natural depravity; the devil-worshippers of Birmingham were far too honourable and upright to do such a thing.

She concluded her article, "I do want . . . to emphasise now the reality of the sinister growth of witchcraft in Britain today. . . . I believe that eventually unless this vast wave of wickedness is checked, black magic could bring about the absolute moral corruption of this country."

Now, this description bore absolutely no resemblance whatsoever to any meeting of a British witch coven I had ever seen or heard of. But there was one thing to which it did bear a very strong resemblance.

Allowing for exaggerations, it could easily be a description of a Voodoo rite, as practised in New Orleans or Haiti. "Michele," for instance, is a very curious appellation for the God of British witches; because it is obviously intended for the French name "Michel." Voodoo arose among French-speaking blacks, and the names of their deities are almost all French or given a French turn of speech; for example, Ogoun Feraille, Mam' Erzulie, Baron Samedi, etc. Anyone who is sufficiently curious may meet with corroborative evidence of the resemblance of the rites she describes to Voodoo in a classic book upon the subject, called *Divine Horsemen; the Living Gods of Haiti,* by Maya Deren. Here and in other books upon the subject one may find accounts of the blood sacrifices of chicken, the dressing-up in robes and veils, the handing out of drinks to the devotees, the drumming and "fanatical dancing," the altar resembling a Christian one, and in particular the curious rite of going to a churchyard to contact the souls of the newly-dead, which is typical Voodoo. *But it is not witchcraft.*

It is possible, of course, that a black woman, as she tells us she is, would use the word "witchcraft" thinking it the English word for "Voodoo"; but was there no one on the sensational Press staff who knew the difference?

She states, "My mother was an Egyptian, and I was told that Egyptian blood was most suited to this position of authority." Why? What has "Egyptian blood" got to do with a position of authority in a British coven? Are we to deduce from this that the Egyptians are witches? They were all Mohammedans and Copts when I was out there. But black blood is considered preferable for the High Priestess of a Voodoo society. American and West Indian black people believe all magic came from Egypt, so a person who was half Egyptian would have some magical authority among them. In this way only could be explained her extraordinary statement that she was made the High Priestess on her initiation.

By no means do I wish to appear to defend the practices she has described. On the contrary, I think them thoroughly undesirable, stupid and nasty; but to say that they are "witchcraft" and that the people who carry them on are "witches" organised into "witch covens," is ridiculous and untrue.

Why could not the sensational Press honestly say, "We have reason, from statements made to us, to believe that Voodoo practices are carried on in England. We think that this should be investigated and any excesses restrained"? Why was witchcraft brought into it?

In spite of the fact that they had taken this lady's word alone was not enough to ensure the acceptance of the sensational stories she told, the next issue still bore no corroborative evidence. Her story was continued, with screaming headlines as usual.

She says, "I knew my confession might put me in danger . . . Three days after that confession appeared I was attacked in the street near my home. . . . On the crown of my head is a patch completely denuded of hair. . . . The hair was slashed off by my attackers. Until it is proved to me otherwise, I shall believe that the purpose of this attack was to frighten me into ending my story in the sensational papers."

They now stated that she had found a warning sign, made of graveyard chippings and twigs, on her doorstep before the attack occurred. This sounds to me like an *ouanga*—a West Indian Voodoo sign.

However, the story of the alleged attack sounds very odd. According to her, it took place at 1.30 a.m. She was, she tells us, going in fear of vengeance—yet here she was walking the back streets of Birmingham alone at 1.30 a.m., a thing I would not much care to do myself. Further, she must have been in the habit of doing this, or how would the attackers have known where to find her?

On August Bank Holiday Monday, 1951, she says, she was lying ill in bed at her home, in Birmingham, when "half an hour before midnight, I was told that someone was at the door for me." Knowing, she says, that this meant she was wanted to preside at a ceremony, she stopped only to pull on a dressing-gown over her nightdress, and went down to a waiting car. It drove her to the Bull Ring, the city market place, and from there a van took her to a house.

"I slipped a robe on top of the things I was already wearing. . . . I walked through the curtains into a big room. The room seemed full of a sort of pink glow, and at first I could just distinguish shapes that I knew were people. Then, as my eyes got used to the lack of light, I noticed the markings on the floor. . . . Facing the room now I saw, immediately in front of the altar, a star drawn on the floor and, close to it, a dragon."

Now, this is another typical Voodoo touch. It is the custom in Voodoo to draw various designs on the floor, called "vevers," to invoke the

Voodoo deities, each deity having a special "vever" of its own. These are pictured and described in Maya Deren's book, already mentioned.

"Now the ritual began. . . . Three young men brought in a young girl. They led her to the point of the star nearest a statue. The men were cowled and masked." The leader "spoke a parody of the Lord's Prayer, then he called on the covens. . . . 'We have a virgin in our midst who is to be initiated.' Chanting began and the young girl—she seemed to be about seventeen—was brought to the statue. She was made to repeat certain declarations. . . . Other parodies of religion followed . . . distortions of a Mass were carried out. . . ." And this, she continues, was followed by the usual drinking and dancing.

"When dancing began, everybody was served with drink—whisky, rum, gin, whatever they wanted. As soon as a glass was emptied it was refilled." The hospitality was certainly generous; one cannot help wondering who paid for it all. The black lady became ill and was allowed to go home, after giving her vow of silence to all present, and her handprint being taken in the blood of a cockerel on a sheet of paper. Before this, she says, she had been "reprimanded" because she refused a drink. Reprimanded! A High Priestess! And a vow of silence demanded from her, accompanied by ugly mumbo-jumbo, before she was "told" she could go home!

Surely, if she had really been a High Priestess, she would have been in charge of the proceedings, and it would have been her place to reprimand, not to be reprimanded? I'd like to see anyone reprimand a witch High Priestess.

She continues: "Then after something that happened on November 23rd, 1953, I suffered a severe nervous breakdown." She had tried, she says, to break away from the black magic circle in 1952, but all kinds of misfortunes had beset her until she "came down to living in utter degradation in a laundry van." So, apparently, she went back to the cult, until the above date, when she attended her last ceremony. That night, she says, she was taken by car to "a lonely graveyard."

"We all got out of the car except the driver. We walked to an open grave and stood around it. A man pulled a book out of his pocket and began a ghastly warped version of the funeral service. Afterwards all raised their arms towards the dark sky. With fingers outstretched they asked Michele (the devil) to take the soul of the dead woman and give back the wisdom of the ages in return. That was the last ceremony I attended. . . . Then I began to receive strange telephone calls ordering me to attend meetings. These requests stopped when the Press investigations were discovered."

It would appear that upon the occasion of the ceremony described above "Michele" was being sadly cheated; for if the grave was open late at night, as she says it was, surely it must have been empty? If "Michele" didn't know this, then he was a poor hope for bestowing the wisdom of the ages.

The next instalment, we were promised, was going to be entitled "The Search for the Truth"; but it never appeared, a circumstance with which I think I may have had something to do. *No corroboration whatsoever of the black lady's story was then, or at any other time, ever published.* Nor were the circumstances in which she came to tell it to the sensational Press, ever revealed.

In fact, after publishing another completely uncorroborated and even less convincing story from an anonymous woman in an unknown part of England, the whole series fizzled out.

Later, however, it had a very surprising sequel, and as very much less publicity has been given to this sequel than was accorded to the original story, I think public attention should be directed to it.

On May 25th, 1956, a series of articles entitled "Evil at Work" began in a picture paper. The first one, referring to the writer's investigations in Birmingham, contained this remarkable statement:

"Senior officers at Birmingham police headquarters told me they would be glad to investigate any complaint received, *but that so far no responsible person had given information.* (My italics)."

They authorised this statement: "We cannot say no such thing is going on, but we feel sure that if it was we should have received complaints."

But they admitted that on one man's premises they found a purple robe, incense, and bottles containing some of the objects usually associated with witchcraft. "There was some suggestion that he was trying to set up as a sort of witch-doctor to the more primitive among the coloured population," I was told, "but we dealt with him by bringing a false pretences charge relating to a cheque offence. That showed him to be a common criminal. That deflated him."

It would seem to have deflated the sensational Press, too. Does this mean that, after the screaming headlines in which the alleged horrors taking place in Birmingham had been proclaimed to the nation, the senior officers at Birmingham police headquarters did not regard either the sensational Press or the black lady as being "responsible persons"?

Well—they said it! I didn't!

Chapter XV

Some Allegations Examined, Part II

I am sorry to say that some of my witch friends did not treat *The Sunday Pictorial's* revelations with the sobriety and concern evinced by the Bishop of Exeter, the Rev. F. Amphlett Micklewright, the Rev. Gordon P. Owen, and Mr. Stanley Maxted, all of whom had been uttering solemn warnings about the seriousness of the *Pictorial's* discovery.

A reporter asked me what I thought of the lady's story of being attacked and having a piece of her hair cut off. I pointed out to him that the description of her injury—slight abrasions to the scalp and a patch of hair cut off—was also perfectly consistent with an injury that was self-inflicted. He said, "*How do you know?*" I replied, "When an injury is self-inflicted, they are always careful never to do anything that really hurts; they'll slash hair, tear clothes, break their spectacles, put mud on themselves, but never anything that is painful. In England, when anyone wants to scare a person they slash their face, cosh them, or give them a black eye. Abroad they knife them."

And indeed, what was to stop her alleged assailants—two men in a deserted street at 1.30 a.m., as she described them—from beating her unconscious and half-killing her, if they had chosen to? Yet all they did was to cut off a piece of her hair!

However, in the next issue of the paper referred to, dated June 12th, 1955, instead of the article "The Search for the Truth" which had been announced, and which we had expected to involve the "chases in fast cars," "mysterious telephone messages," and all the other thrills we had been promised, there appeared a fierce denunciation of myself, under the title "This Man's Whitewash is Dangerous. No Witchcraft is Fun."

It commenced, "Dr. Gerald Brosseau Gardner is an authority on witchcraft." (I am obliged for this entirely unsolicited testimonial; but I don't know why they gave it to me, as they wouldn't take any notice of anything I told them about it.) "It is through him," it was stated, "that many people get their first mistaken ideas about witchcraft." (That's odd, if I'm an authority.)

The article went on, "He is a self-confessed witch and a practising devotee of a witch coven in Britain. But he is also a whitewasher of witchcraft.

"He puts around the, to my mind, dangerous idea that witchcraft is not evil.

"He seems to overlook that what may begin as an innocent dabble in search of excitement may lead eventually to devil worship."

Now, this is nonsense. There is nothing very "innocent" in "dabbling" in the kind of thing these papers had been describing, rites at which, *upon their first initiation,* people had been alleged to drink the blood of sacrificed animals and sign pacts giving their souls to the devil in exchange for power. People who are prepared to do that are not "innocent"; they know perfectly well what they are doing, and if that is what these papers call "an innocent dabble in search of excitement," I beg to differ.

However, you have to believe that there is such a being as the devil, and that he can give you power, before you are likely to do such things. So how can this result from joining a cult which specifically denies the existence of any such being?

In fact, with a singular lack of logic, the article continues:

"In books Gardner has written and in his lectures, he goes out of his way to dismiss the idea that witchcraft in Britain is in any way diabolical.

"He claims that this is a stupid notion deliberately fostered by the Church and is absolutely untrue.

"Nowhere in Gardner's book *Witchcraft Today,*" says the reporter wistfully, "could I find descriptions of horrible and degrading ceremonies. . . ." I commiserate with him. He must have been very disappointed.

"And yet," he goes on, "when I challenged Gardner last week" (Really? I hadn't noticed it!) "he admitted that most people would be shocked by witchcraft ceremonies which include:

"ONE: Men and women dancing in the nude.

"TWO: Praying to a horned god.

"THREE: Stimulation through wine, music and drumming.

"He agreed that in ceremonies in some parts of the world it is necessary to have a nude girl on an altar."

I have no recollection whatsoever of making the statement that most people would be shocked at witchcraft ceremonies; in fact, I don't think any *normal* people would be shocked at them. There are a large number of *nudist* clubs in this country today at which dances take place regularly; and the sky hasn't fallen yet on that account! "Stimulation through wine, music and drumming" takes place at all the most respectable night-clubs. Is anybody shocked? With regard to the second abomination, "praying to a horned god"—*Why not?* He only wears a helmet with horns on it. Is it not a little refreshing these days to find people who worship anything other than money and their own advantage? Or whose ideas upon life and religion are not entirely conditioned to what J. B. Priestley has so cuttingly described as "Ad-Mass"?

"I drew Gardner's attention," says that same colleague, "to another book published under his name and privately printed which is on sale in London.

"In this book, which is sold as fiction, is a detailed description of initiation into the witch cult. The ceremony is performed in the nude. Afterwards, the candidate, blindfolded and feet tied together, is scourged. Finally, after giving an oath never to reveal the 'secrets of the Art', the candidate is touched with a 'magical' sword. He said: This description of initiation was 'broadly correct.'" Of course it is not.

In spite of all the agonised appeals of these papers for members of witch covens to go to their doctor or clergyman, or to the papers themselves, *how many did?*

We may be sure that if any people *who were initiates of any genuine witch coven* had come forward and begged to be released by the kind offices of these papers, the fact would have been blazoned abroad. So I repeat, *how many did?*

The answer is, *None.* That fact in itself is evidence that the followers of the Old Religion are happy in their faith.

With regard to the description of a witch initiation given in my book, *High Magic's Aid,* which is what the reporter is talking about, I am very sorry to disappoint this earnest young man; I can assure him that I did not wilfully lead him up the garden path on this point; but my novel is "sold as fiction" because it *is* fiction, fiction moreover about events which were supposed to be happening in the year 1206. And the details which it contains, as an historical novel, *are* "broadly correct." At least, I exercised my best endeavours to make them so.

Nevertheless, evidently thinking that he was on to something good, the reporter proceeded to quote a large chunk of what he called "one of the lurid passages" from my novel, which described one of the Great Sabbaths as held in the old days. He did not, however, quote it quite in full; in fact he cut out what he would probably call the most "lurid passage," so I will re-quote it here in its completeness. It concerns a man, not a member of the cult, but who nevertheless has been to one of the Great Sabbaths to which half the countryside came in those days, talking to a woman who is an initiated witch in the year A.D. 1206.

"'Tell me the truth', he said suddenly, 'this altar used at your gatherings. . . . In Spain I saw the living body of a woman, and they practised abominations on it'.

"'Yes,' she replied simply, 'At the Great Sabbath the living body of a priestess *does* form the altar. We worship the divine spirit of Creation, which is the Life-spring of the world, and without which the world would perish. Are we then so abominable? We count it not so. To us it is the most sacred and holy mystery, proof of the God within us whose command is: Go forth and multiply'.

"'Tis a phallic religion', said Thur, 'and the broomstick symbolises the phallus.'"

"Surely," says our indignant reporter, "even Gardner can see that the type of person likely to be duped and snared into witchcraft in Britain is likely to prefer this foul bait to the whitewash of his other book? And, indeed, to expect it from the coven he joins? There is no doubt at all that there are satanic devil-worshippers in Britain who are ever ready to provide this type of sexual perversion to capture the men and women they wish to make their slaves."

What type of "sexual perversion"? The worship of "the divine spirit of Creation, which is the Life-spring of the world, and without which the world would perish"? Is that "sexual perversion"?

The worship of the witch cult is, and always has been, that of the principle of Life itself. It has made of that principle, as manifested in sex, something sacred. *Which is the perversion?* This, or that outlook which seeks to make humans ashamed of their naked bodies, and fearful of sex and "original sin" and something unclean? Our psychiatrists' consulting-rooms are full of the miserable neurotics who have been produced by the latter; more, far, far more, than have ever been crazed by alleged "black magic." The Press would not need to search five years before it could find one of them.

There is still, in the collective unconsciousness of men's minds, a realisation of the rightness of the Old Sacred Marriage. I remember listening to a radio programme once, in which people from an audience were asked to come up to the microphone and answer questions. I believe, though I cannot be certain, that the compère was Wilfrid Pickles. One man was asked if he could tell the audience of some dream that he would like to fulfil. He thought for a bit, and then said, "I'd like to take part in one of those things they used to do in the old times, what they called the Sacred Marriage; provided the woman in it was my wife." Other people in the same programme have said how they would like to go out in the moonlight and dance naked, or dance barefoot on grass. What made them say these things? If it is not folk memory, or hereditary memory, what is it?

When the Church made marriage a Sacrament, they were right; but when they added that it was ordained for the procreation of children and for that alone, they were a thousand thousand times wrong.

Let me make it clear, however, that the witch cult does not hold sex sacred as an end in itself, but as a living symbol and manifestation of the Great Source of All Things which men call God. Further, the Great Sabbaths as described in the quotation I have just given were suppressed by the Church many centuries ago.

Before the quotation referred to, these papers said, "Gardner admitted, too, that some witches find great power in new spilled blood."

It will be noted that the reporter does not say that I said witches used blood in their rites. He could not do so, because I had specifically denied it, both verbally and in print. What I had actually told him was that any witches who had read his books knew about the use of blood by such practitioners as Aleister Crowley, but that they did not do it themselves. In fact, Crowley's book, *Magick in Theory and Practice,* in which he discusses blood sacrifices, has been widely read since its publication in the 1920's, and has, to my knowledge, been in at least one Public Library, where the librarian described it as being "very popular." (So much for "dark occult secrets"!)

Of course, the reporter may have misunderstood what I said to him; but upon his own admission he had read my book, *Witchcraft Today,* in which I made the same denial, not only once but several times.

However, to clear up any possible misunderstanding, now or in the future, I will say it yet again: witches do not use the blood of sacrificed animals, birds, or any other living things in their rites. As I have previously stated in Chapter VII, blood was sometimes used in ceremonial magic, but this is a different thing from witch rites. The ceremonial magician was generally a man who worked alone or with one or two assistants. If he wanted to raise power quickly, and was not too scrupulous as to how he did it, this might be one of his methods; on the other hand, witch rites are worked by a number of persons, who especially if they are of witch families, may have inherited psychic or mediumistic faculties, and the power they generate is like that of a spiritualistic circle. The methods they use do not need such rites as blood sacrifices, even if they were willing to use them.

As this article constituted a personal attack upon myself and my views, I have deliberately reproduced here just as much of it as I could. Actually, of course, this reporter's interview with me had put him in a cleft stick; he had asked me, as an authority on witchcraft, what I thought of the black lady. I had given him the opinion which I have repeated here. He had either to print that opinion, which would have spoilt the whole stunt, or else attempt to silence me and discredit what I said about witchcraft, and he chose to do the latter.

During the next few weeks, the number of motor coaches which arrived at the Museum were almost more than we could cope with. I got as many copies as I could of the papers' attacks, and put them there for people to see; and to my huge amusement many people wanted to buy them, and several of them were stolen. I must give the papers the credit of having spelt my name rightly, and adorned some of their articles with an excellent photograph of me; but I had never thought it was so good that people would want it for a pin-up. However, devotion to truth compels me to record the fact!

Not only did I achieve the status of a pin-up, but fan-mail started to come my way; our local postman had to give me a mail-bag all to myself one day, and the daily deluge of letters kept up for weeks.

Many of the letters were evidence of the interest taken by people in all walks of life in what is generally known as the supernormal, and of their dissatisfaction with orthodox approaches to life and religion. Often, the writers gave personal experiences, and interesting scraps of folklore and tradition. I can only remember one letter which was hostile; this was from a clergyman, who said that I was quite as bad as the spiritualists and the Christian Scientists!

Chapter XVI

Some Allegations Examined, Part III

It will be remembered how the newspaper reporter had told me that they would give a witch a chance to reply to what had been said, provided she wrote something that was worth printing. I therefore got a woman friend who is a member of a witch coven to write a short article, and send it to someone to post for her to the paper's office in London. However, they flatly refused to print it.

I think, however, that the reader should have the opportunity of judging the witch's reply, so I reproduce it herewith. Fortunately a copy of the article had been kept, and I submitted it to the Editor of the Spiritualist newspaper, *Psychic News,* in which it appeared as follows in the issue dated July 23rd, 1955, with only very minor changes of wording from the original:

Witchcraft in Britain

> "They (the witches) are sincere in a satanic belief that theirs is the ancient religion of Britain; they claim it is older than, and superior to, Christianity."
>
> That paragraph appeared in a series of articles on witchcraft printed by a Sunday newspaper. It is perfectly true. I am a witch, and that is what I believe.
>
> The only word I would disagree with is the word "satanic." Whether or not my religion is superior to Christianity is a matter of opinion, but that it is much older is a matter of fact, as eminent anthropologists will tell you.
>
> So why do people persist in accusing me of worshipping the Devil? The idea of the Devil is something belonging to Christianity; the scapegoat which men have invented to excuse their own follies and crimes. I don't believe in the Devil, so how could I worship him?

Whom, then, do the witches really worship. They worship the ancient Gods of this land of Britain, whose tradition is rooted deep in British soil. The Old Gods are not dead, as I know by experience.

During the last war a witch coven invoked the Old Gods to protect this land from Hitler's threatened invasion, even as their forefathers had done against Napoleon and, earlier still, against the Spanish Armada—or so the tale is handed down to us.

I have seen them invoked for many purposes and have invoked them myself; but I have never seen them invoked for a bad purpose. And these purposes have been so often achieved that to call it coincidence, as many will, would, if they knew all the details, require a greater effort of credulity than to believe that there's something in it.

You want to know how these ceremonies are performed? Well, I can tell you this, that they are not performed with ridiculous obscenities so often attributed to them.

How many witches are there in Britain? Very few genuine ones, and most of these come from witch families in which the tradition has been handed down.

We believe in reincarnation and that those who in former lives have belonged to us will be drawn back into the cult.

We have no need to "dupe" or "snare" anyone into witchcraft. Our own will come to us. We know when people want to join us whether they belong or not. Sensation-seekers hoping for foul and erotic rites please note—we don't want you!

Out in the wilds, as far as we can get from so-called civilisation, we gather to celebrate our rites. Perhaps around an old time-worn stone circle, or upon a hill-top, or in the depths of a forest.

There—not in luxury flats, as has been described, we feel close to the unseen powers of the universe; we can sing the old song in a lost language, dance the old dances, and do other things of which I may not tell you (though they are neither evil nor obscene). And the Old Gods come.

I have been possessed by the Goddess of the witches; it felt as if I were being burned with cold, white fire. Another girl I know has had the same experience, and her face changed so that she looked like another person.

I have had the experience, too, of going out of my body and visiting a person at a distance of hundreds of miles; I was able to identify later, in the flesh, the things I had seen in this "astral" visit. (Incidentally, it is this power which gave rise to the old idea of witches flying through the air!)

And I have seen in the course of a ceremony the power rising from the body of the high priest like thin, feathery spirals of smoke.

I have seen spirits, too, who have come to join in the rite; but they have been spirits of men and women—not demons—and I have felt that they came as friends.

One of our rites consists of calling upon the Lord of the Gates of Death to permit our friends, who have passed into His realm, to return for a while to speak with us.

If I say that they have returned, and that I have spoken to them and they have answered me, you may not believe me; but it is the truth, and I know others who have had the same experience.

Do you really think that if witchcraft was merely a tissue of obscenities and absurdities, or a mocking of the Christian religion, that it would have lasted from generation to generation, from century to century?

Why then, if witchcraft is not evil, is the Church opposed to us?

My answer is, because they are afraid of us.

They know that in centuries of persecution they have not succeeded in stamping us out; nor will they ever do so, and they know, too, that they have lost their hold on the people, who have become dissatisfied with Church dogmas. Hence they fear us, as they have always feared us—as a rival.

One day, I believe, the people of the world will turn back from the road of scientific, orthodox civilisation which has proved so stony and return to the life and religion of nature.

When that day dawns, the wise Old Gods will be there—waiting.

The paper who promised to give a witch the chance to reply never even chose to reveal the fact that a reply had been offered, let alone received.

Instead, in the next instalment of their series, on June 19th, 1955, they published a story which they alleged had been sent in to them by a woman reader living with her family somewhere in the South of England. She says:

A year ago I would have laughed if anyone had told me such things existed....

I got my rude awakening last summer when I couldn't sleep one night.

I could hear an odd sort of noise.... I wondered if my neighbour had left her wireless on. Soon I found out that it wasn't the wireless but a sound of the most peculiar moaning gibberish coming from the nearby wood. I thought it might be someone drunk or even hurt, and I thought I wouldn't do any harm if I investigated; so I slipped on my coat and

> went across from my bungalow to the open common. What I saw, I now realise, was a meeting of a coven of witches. The ritual was one which makes the ex-witch's story of her experiences told in the paper, seem like a Sunday-school treat. . . .
>
> . . . That night I felt a force of real evil. . . . I have certainly never known such terror, and I can honestly say I have never known a minute's freedom from fear since.

"They were horrible, quite horrible," she says, but we are never told why. Believe it or not, that is all the description of what she is alleged to have seen that is given.

The paper's informant went on to say that two representatives of the alleged "coven" called on her afterwards.

"They warned me," she says, "after haranguing me for a long time of the virtues of these 'nature rituals', that if I breathed a word of it to anyone my family and I would be penalised terribly.

"They even threatened to use my young son in their ceremonies. So I have never said a word to anyone, not even to my husband. Often I have heard them since on the common. I have thought of going to the vicar and risking their powers. But I know he wouldn't believe me. . . . We can't move away from here because of my husband's work. And he would never believe about witches. I daren't tell him to go out and see for himself when I hear them, in case they hurt him." And she never told the police!

"There!" says one particular paper, "Here is Mrs. Vacancy Blank, of Somewhere-on-the-Map, to *prove* what we say!"

"Yes," says one particular anthropologist, "and you've got to admit she's a first-rate witness. On her own admission, her husband and the vicar, who know her personally, won't believe a word she says on the subject. And why not give her name and address?"

"*Your* books," says the newspaper ponderously, "in the wrong hands can be dangerous."

By June 26th, 1955, the witch-hunt had worked its way from the front page to the back, where it was asked in the "Crime Strip,"

> Who were the ghouls who desecrated the graveyard at the West Wycombe home of Sir John Dashwood, Bart., last week on the night of Midsummer Eve—the most important day in the calendar of black magic?

> There was fantastic damage, gravestones uprooted, urns overturned. Was it the work of people celebrating the Black Mass?
>
> Why are those who practise the Black Art so keen to visit the Dashwood home? Because in the mid-eighteenth century a Sir Francis Dashwood formed the notorious "Hell Fire Club." Police are puzzled by the thoroughness of the damage. Four grown men were needed to lift some of the smashed stonework.

This feature was headed "On Witches' Night."

Now, this interested me. I had heard a lot of stories of what happened at Black Masses, but this was the first time I had ever heard that such athletic proceedings as the smashing of gravestones were part of the ritual.

So, in spite of the fact that Midsummer Eve has actually no particular connection with black magic, I went to West Wycombe to see what had happened.

However, I could not find anybody on the spot, including the Curator of the "Hell Fire Caves," who believed that a Black Mass had taken place there. The damage was simply a piece of silly vandalism, and I satisfied myself that, although it might have taken four men to replace the stones from where they had fallen, a child could have tipped them over from their original positions. A couple of mischievous schoolboys could have accounted for all the damage done.

The next week this paper carried an account of four other graveyards in which headstones had been thrown down and smashed, and said, "People living in the area are asking. 'Was it a gang of Teddy Boys? Or was it a coven of witches performing one of their Black Magic rituals?'"

The responsibility for this latter statement rests squarely upon the paper in question and to plant suggestions like this is to risk a dangerous chain reaction. There seems, unfortunately, to be a certain element among adolescents which delights in senseless damage. However, when we had read previously of thousands of pounds worth of damage being caused annually by hooligans, nobody had thought to whisper with bated breath "Was it witches?" This spicy addition to the thrills of vandalism was calculated to give its perpetrators an extra zest. One can well imagine what went on in what for the sake of argument may be described as their minds; vandalism, as psychologists know, is an attention-seeking device: "Now we're really making the headlines—they think it's the Black Mass! What a laugh! Let's smash some more!"

After this, all was quiet until the beginning of this year, 1956. Then a certain section of the Press got hold of a black magic yarn which was potentially more serious than anything they bad touched yet: The Charles Walton murder case.

The things that have been said about this case have been the deciding factor which induced me to write this chapter. After all, newspaper sensations are a very easy target for criticism, so easy that they are hardly worth shooting at. A new one appears regularly every week, duly makes its contribution to the gaiety of nations, and then comes in very useful for wrapping fish. However, when things are said which may affect the investigation of an unsolved murder, the matter becomes more serious. To unmask irresponsible sensationalism is then a public duty.

This mysterious and terrible crime, which shattered the peace of a beautiful, secluded little village in the Cotswolds in 1945, has been the subject of wild speculation, and dark hints of "witchcraft" and "ritual murder." Stated briefly, the facts of the case are these:

On February 14th, 1945, a farm labourer named Charles Walton, aged about 74, was found murdered on Meon Hill in Warwickshire. The murderer has never yet been caught, nor the mystery of the crime solved.

According to the account published in the *Stratford-on-Avon Herald* at the time, Walton was an inoffensive old man, having a good reputation with his neighbours. In spite of the fact that he suffered from rheumatism, and walked with the aid of two sticks, he still did small jobs, such as hedge-trimming, for a local farmer, Mr. Alfred John Potter, of the Firs Farm. He lived with a niece, Miss Edith Walton, of Lower Quinton.

On February 14th, 1945, Miss Walton returned home from work at about 6.0 p.m., and found that her uncle had not come home. His usual time of return was about 4.0 p.m. Fearing that her uncle, infirm as he was, had met with some mishap, she enquired of the neighbours, and one of them, Mr. Harry Beasley, went with her to look for him. They searched, but failed to find him; so they went to the farm and enquired of his employer, Mr. Potter. Mr. Potter knew where Walton had been working; the old man had been engaged in trimming a hedge on the slopes of Meon Hill. He led Miss Walton and Mr. Beasley to the spot.

They found Charles Walton there dead. According to the evidence given at the inquest, the body was lying "close against the hedge, in a bit of a ditch." He had been murdered with terrible ferocity. A bloodstained walking-stick was lying nearby, and bruises on the head suggested that he had been struck down with it. The killer had then slashed his throat with the hedging tool the old man was carrying, and finished his ghastly work by pinning the body to the ground with the two-tined pitchfork which was also part of Walton's hedging equipment. The two tines of the pitchfork passed on either side of the murdered man's neck. The billhook with which the throat had been cut was left embedded in the chest.

Professor J. M. Webster, of the West Midlands Forensic Laboratory, giving evidence at the inquest, said that the cause of death was shock and haemorrhage, due to grave injuries to the neck and chest caused by a cutting weapon and a stabbing weapon. He said that the cutting weapon had been wielded three times. So severe was the slash across the throat that all the great blood vessels of the neck were severed.

Cuts on the hands showed that the old man had attempted to defend himself.

Ex-Supt. Robert Fabian, in his book, *Fabian of the Yard,* describes how the Chief Constable of Warwickshire called in Scotland Yard to help in the enquiries, and how he and another officer, Sergeant Albert Webb, went to the scene of the crime to meet Supt. Alec Spooner of the Warwickshire C.I.D., and to commence their investigation. A plane from the R.A.F. airfield at Leamington took aerial photographs of the scene of the crime; a detachment of the Royal Engineers searched the fields with mine-detectors, looking for clues; four thousand statements were taken in the course of the investigation; but no arrest was made, and the crime remains upon the list of unsolved murders.

According to Ex-Supt. Fabian, Supt. Spooner called his attention, immediately upon his arrival in the Cotswolds, to the possibility of the belief in witchcraft being a factor in the murder. Supt. Spooner showed him a passage in a book, *Folk Lore, Old Customs and Superstitions in Shakespeare-land,* by J. Harvey Bloom, M.A., published in 1929. This book refers to the strong belief in witches and witchcraft, and says, "In 1875 a weak-minded young man killed an old woman named Ann Turner with a hay-fork because he believed she had bewitched him."

Fabian of the Yard was first published in 1950. And by 1952 a writer in a widely-read paper was saying,

> The manner in which the hay-fork was used was exactly similar to the murder in 1875, in nearby Long Compton, of Ann Turner, killed by a

> man "because she was a witch," and also to an earlier hay-fork stabbing when John Haywood attacked an old woman. . . .
>
> The murder of Charles Walton, still unsolved, may have arisen from an internal feud with a band of witches.

In its big splash in 1955, the sensational paper, too, had mentioned the Walton case, adding that "It happened on St. Valentine's Day, 1945—traditionally a day of sacrifice." The implication being, apparently, that Charles Walton was killed as a human sacrifice.

It was in February of this year, 1956, that the witch-hunters really "went to town" on this story. On February 15th, 1956, one paper ran a story, "Police Chief Goes Back on the Witches' Sabbath"; it described how Superintendent Spooner was in the habit of returning to the village every year on the anniversary of the crime, to see if there were any new developments, and added, "There was an identical killing 70 years before in a nearby village." It also added the remarkable information that the witches' Sabbath was when "The witch anointed her feet and shoulders with the fat of a murdered baby and then, mounting a broomstick, rode off into the night." Unfortunately it did not publish any accompanying photograph of this interesting scene.

However, on the following Sunday, the 19th February, 1956, a newspaper with close political affiliations to the *Daily Herald,* came out with a splendid headline: *Black Magic Killer—Woman Talks.* It said,

> A terrified woman, driven grey-haired by some of the most evil men in Britain, offered last night to help solve the murder of Charles Walton, who was impaled with a pitchfork in a lonely Warwickshire field on St. Valentine's Day, 1945. She will give the name of the alleged murderer to Det. Supt. A. W. Spooner, Chief of the Warwickshire C.I.D.
>
> This woman, who begged me not to reveal her name, has offered to tell Det. Supt. Spooner everything—provided she is protected from the vengeance of Britain's black magic cults.
>
> For twelve frightful years she took part with other members of the cults in grotesque rites that stem from Britain's mysterious past. Now she wants the police to stamp out these evil practices. And she wants them to solve the 11-year-old crime she claims was a ritual murder.

This paper's informant went on to tell a harrowing tale—which yet somehow seemed curiously familiar—of how as a young woman she had been to small religious meetings in London and Birmingham, where various "foul rites" took place; of how she was too frightened to go to the police; and how, when she tried to break away from the cult, her head was scarred with knives.

Walton's actual murderer, she said, was a woman who was brought by car to the Cotswolds from a different part of the country. The leader of the London branch of the cult had been present. The story of how the murder was committed had been told to her by the Midlands leader, who wanted to get "Number One in London" out of the way, so that he could gain national control of the cult for himself.

"The manner of killing," says the paper, "was identical with that in a murder of 1875 in nearby Long Compton, of a woman villagers thought was a witch."

In spite, however, of their informant's praiseworthy desire that the police should stamp out these evil practices, strangely enough it was this paper and not the lady herself, who gave this information to the police. They, of course, realised that they were legally bound to do so; but it seems very odd to me that anyone possessing such information, if it were genuine, should not have taken it straight to the authorities. Instead, however, this woman waited until a mention of the murder appeared in the Press, and then came forward; even then she did not go straight to the police, but to a newspaper.

The next day, February 20th, 1956, a paper gave further details of what the woman had said, under the headline: *Murder at Black Mass, says Woman:*

> A woman has come forward to say that a shepherd, killed eleven years ago, was murdered by a woman during a Black Mass at midnight. She says that she was once a member of a black magic society and that she knows the name of the killer.
>
> The body of the shepherd, 74-year-old Charles Walton, was found on St. Valentine's day, 1945, in the middle of a circle of stones in a field at Lower Quinton, Warwickshire. He had been killed by blows from a farm billhook and staked to the ground with a pitchfork. His neck was slashed in the shape of a cross. Villagers said it was a ritual murder. There was a similar murder on St. Valentine's Day, 1875, at Long Compton, also in Warwickshire. The accuser, an elderly woman from Birmingham, will probably be interviewed by police this week.

Now the reader with a long memory will doubtless be wanting to pause for some queries.

"Surely," he will be saying, "this isn't what I was reading just now? Walton's body, according to the evidence given at the inquest, was found lying 'close against the hedge, in a bit of a ditch.' And that ditch was on the slopes of Meon Hill. What's this about the body being found in the middle of a circle of stones?"

The answer is that when Ex-Supt. Fabian wrote his book, in which he mentioned this unsolved crime, he said that it was done "not far from the stone circle of the Whispering Knights," and that "it looked like the kind of killing the Druids might have done in ghastly ceremony at full moon." Since then every writer who has raided his book for "copy" has reproduced this statement without, apparently, ever bothering to check on it. Consequently they have been sadly misled; the Whispering Knights are not a circle, but part of a group of stones called the Rollright Stones: they are nothing to do with the Druids; *and they are twelve miles away from Meon Hill.* We can forgive Ex-Supt. Fabian for not being an archaeologist; but his definition of "not far from" as "twelve miles away" has proved a pitfall into which almost everyone who has written about this case has come a nasty cropper; and it looks as if either the papers or their informants were among them.

"Yes, and look here," continues that long-memoried reader, "she says that Charles Walton was killed at a Black Mass at midnight. But he went to work next morning as usual. His body was found in the evening."

Yes, I noticed that, too. To put it mildly, something seems amiss.

However, in another paper, in the issue dated March 15th, 1956, the same informant told quite a different story of the "Black Magic Murder." Their reporter had found her in a suburb of Wolverhampton, "an attractive woman with haunted eyes."

"Thirteen people," she says, "took part in the ceremony. One of them knew Walton. The rest came from various parts of the country.

"Walton was hedging that day in a field well away from houses and the road. The person who knew him approached him with two others. He was struck down. *It was exactly midday.* (My italics).

"Rapidly they mutilated his body, soaked some robes in his blood, drove in the pitchfork, and danced round the body." . . .

I should be greatly obliged if anyone could explain to me how thirteen people could dance round the body of a man which, according to the evidence given at the inquest by one of the three people who found it, was lying close against the hedge, in a bit of a ditch. Compared to the travelling circle of stones, this is a minor miracle. They should really have read the case up more before they started to tell this story.

Gradually, she told the reporter, she found out the story of the killing. She left the circle, and felt like going to the police (!)

"Within a few days the circle of silence was put on my doorstep. It was made of twigs and graveyard chippings. It meant 'Keep Quiet'.

"But I could not live with myself. I told one of the leaders that I would go to the police.

"That night, on my way home, I was grabbed and scalped. They took a complete circle of hair and skin from my head, using a doctor's scalpel."

Now, where have we heard something like this before? If we read on we shall soon see, as "Mrs. X," who claimed to be a former High Priestess of the black magic cult, described "some of the shocking rites performed by the Black Magic circle."

"At almost every ceremony I attended . . . there was wild singing and dancing, drinking and sexual depravity. . . .

"Animals were killed and their blood poured into goblets. The 'priests' prayed to the Devil for help. . . .

"The altar is a parody of a Christian altar. The Cross is placed upside down in a glass of water and the candles on a slant, almost upside down.

"Newcomers are initiated by being forced to drink the warm blood of animals. . . . Then they all drink glasses of spirits and dance round the altar. These newcomers wear white robes, which are soaked in blood. They have to sign a pact in blood, giving their souls to the Devil."

This description is almost exactly the same as that given by the black lady in 1955; so also is the story of her being attacked in order to intimidate her into silence, only now the alleged attack, which, it will be remembered, in the original case consisted merely of having a piece of hair slashed off, and which, according to the paper's account at the time, *was testified by a police surgeon* as having produced abrasions, bruising and swelling, and left "cut roots . . . on the left hand side area," is now described as a scalping, the removal of a complete circle of hair and skin, using a doctor's scalpel. It will be remembered how I had remarked upon the black lady's alleged attack as being possibly self-inflicted. Is this why the second story is different?

It follows that either there are two "Ex-High Priestesses" living in the Midlands, both of whom are selling the same story to the newspapers, or else that the lady who has named the murderer of Charles Walton, and the black lady are one and the same person.

Now, this is very intriguing. For if this is so, then it follows that this whole ugly smear, with all its sensational and horrible adjuncts, *rests entirely upon the uncorroborated word of one person*—a person, moreover, who, if we are to believe the newspaper accounts quoted, has been demonstrably wrong upon important particulars. A person, further, who has either been very badly misquoted or else has changed her story when it was realised that the first version would not do.

If I am wrong in this presumption (and it is a presumption which I think is justified in view of the remarkable similarity in the stories told) then it is very easily susceptible of proof, and I think the woman concerned should be asked either to explain the matters I have pointed out, or else "forever after hold her peace."

By now, however, the witch-hunting fraternity had fairly got the bit between their teeth. On March 25th, 1956, a paper came out with a front-page headline: "Black Magic: A Priest's Warning." The priest was Canon Bryan Green, the Rector of Birmingham, and by one of those funny coincidences which we keep coming across in these matters, Canon Bryan Green is a noted anti-Spiritualist. *Two Worlds,* the Spiritualist weekly, had this to say about him last August: "Though he is pathetically ignorant about Spiritualism, he does not hesitate to attack it—he does so periodically—with the usual nonsense that 'attempts to communicate with the spirits are dangerous and wrong.'"

This is what Canon Bryan Green had to say about black magic:

"I understand there has been a revival of Black Magic practices in Birmingham. I want to utter a condemnation and a warning.

"Nothing can be worse or more depraved than the deliberate distortion of the beautiful and natural gift of sex for sensuous and perverted feelings of gratification. And this is what Black Magic does.

"Moreover, it debases man's natural desires to love and trust God as his Heavenly Father and tries to get him to make the Devil his source of guidance. My warning is, — Keep clear of Black Magic. . . ."

What on earth Canon Green means by his first paragraph of his warning I find it hard to understand. Does he mean that it is wrong to get any gratification out of sex? And that if anyone does so, they are practising *Black Magic?* If so, I think he will find some difficulty in getting any doctors or psychologists to agree with him. With regard to his second paragraph, it seems to me that the most earnest believers in the Devil these days, and the people who are always boosting his supposed powers, are churchmen like Canon Bryan Green.

A paper's reporter mentioned the death of Charles Walton, and added that it was "believed to have been a ritual killing." By whom? We were not told; but "a student of pagan religions," who was "prepared to put his findings before the police," had given a warning—the "Preparations for a human sacrifice are well advanced as part of a ritual Black Mass to be performed by an unfrocked priest, regarded as world leader of the cult."

Personally, if information like that were in my possession, I would not waste time telling reporters what I was "prepared" to do. I would tell Scotland Yard immediately. If I couldn't prove it, they soon would—if it were true.

The reporter went on, "I have just completed an investigation on the people active in Black Magic. Many appear rational and intelligent. Some are well known publicly. They claim to be practising an ancient pre-Christian religion. But this is merely a cover for obscene, degrading practices."

Notice how the old smear-technique comes out again? People who are "well known publicly" are alleged to be practising black magic. No names are given, and no evidence brought forward to support what is said, so the smear can apply to anyone in public life, and any occult group which is not specifically Christian. Later on the paper became more specific. On the 3rd June, 1956, they said: "Peers on Yard Black Magic List." We were told that a man (anonymous, of course) had given Scotland Yard "a secret list of one hundred and twenty names of people said to be leading members of the Black Magic cult." (So it was not a "Yard list" at all, but a list compiled by an anonymous individual completely without credentials.)

"After the detectives had seen him last night," says their reporter, "the man told me: 'The list reads like pages taken from Debrett (the peers' and knights' Who's Who)! It includes two or three of the most famous names in the peerage and that of a former ambassador at the Court of St. James.

It also names a number of wealthy people, including one with two country mansions and a luxurious West End flat."

Sooner or later in these alleged investigations, we always seem to come to statements like this. It is always the wicked upper classes who are the mainstay of black magic, especially when the paper concerned is Left Wing in politics! If, however, this campaign originated as political propaganda, designed to foster class-hatred, it would indeed be singularly cheap and childish. I do not allege that it did so originate; my purpose here is to point out the singular persistence of this campaign, the remarkably flimsy basis upon which all this structure of rumour and fear has been built up, and the utter failure to bring forward anything worth calling evidence to support it. If there is any political slant, then I think it is a side-issue. The actual inspiration behind all the wild talk about "Satanism" was originally clerical, and it stemmed from the Roman Catholic Church. Its purpose was to combat the rising Spiritualist movement; it started back in the nineteenth century, and has been going on sporadically ever since, assisted by the anti-Spiritualist elements in the Church of England. Its methods have never been very intelligent, and they have always been fundamentally the same, namely to sell the idea to the public that any movement which attempts to make contact with God or with the world unseen, and which does not possess the permission of either the Vatican or the Church of England to do so, must have Satan behind it.

Now, with regard to the proposition that many people in high places are involved in black magic, I do not know whether it is true or not. I have tried for many years to find any traces and have failed, but I think it very doubtful, and I shall not believe it until I receive evidence; there is, however, one thing which I do know to be true. A good number of people of rank and education are Spiritualists, and they often occupy some public position. They do not always care for their belief to be known, but nevertheless they hold it and practise it. *Are these the people who are the witch-hunters' real quarry?*

I have already pointed out how there has been a veritable outburst of this kind of propaganda ever since Parliament gave Spiritualism legal recognition in the Fraudulent Mediums Act. Have there been any attempts to bring Spiritualism into the great witch-hunt?

The Spiritualist weekly, *Two Worlds,* noted some in its issue dated June 16th, 1956. By this time, a series on "Black Magic" had started in the *Sunday*

Graphic, and was being written by Dennis Wheatley, and on June 10th he said: "A more usual means of recruiting for the Devil is through the less reputable kind of spiritualist meeting or seance. Many people attend seances only in search of excitement. And at some seances the Black fraternity have what might be termed 'talent scouts.'"

On June 8th, 1956, the Rev. F. Amphlett Micklewright (who, it will be remembered, was one of the original backers of the campaign in the sensational papers) had said in an interview with G. W. Young, which was published in an article with the wonderful title, "Underworld of Black Mass Maniacs": "There is a sort of diabolism hanging on the fringes of freak religions, and some forms of spiritualism lend themselves to this sort of thing."

Commenting on these reports, *Two Worlds* said: "Well, what do you do—laugh it off or get angry? Should we protest when these circulation-boosters, reeking with dark hints and appetite-whetting chunks of sex and Satanism, dredge in putrescent inuendoes which could send the spiritually fastidious enquirer scuttling for terrified cover? Or do we smile and say, 'Well, people who believe that Spiritualism is a sort of antechamber to a gallery of the Black Arts are no good to us anyway?'"

Personally, I incline to the latter course; in spite of all the sound and fury of this campaign, the public are not so naive upon these subjects as they were in the nineteenth century, or even twenty years ago, and I have reason to think that the inspirers of it have found that out.

An attempt was also made to link spiritual healing with witchcraft, and both with black magic. A panel of ten doctors had been appointed by the British Medical Association to prepare evidence about alleged supernormal healing, to be given to the Archbishops' Commission on Divine Healing. Their report was published in May, 1956, and on May 11th, reporting it, the *Daily Mirror,* the week-day associate of the *Sunday Pictorial,* did so under the headline "These Cures by Witches Must Be Probed." Apparently one doctor had told the committee, "The practice of magic, both white and black, is widely spread in my Devon practice. I had one definite death from witchcraft, or I suppose I should say suggestion, while I was there." He also said, "The practice of charming away warts is extremely effective." Which of these matters was the "witches' cure" that "must be probed" is not clear. But by the 13th May, *Reynolds News* came out with a whoop: "Witchcraft Growing Warns Dean." The dean was the Very Rev. Hugh Heywood, Rural Dean of Southwell, Nottinghamshire, who had said in his Deanery Magazine that in parts of Western England the cult of the witch-doctor was growing, and added some remarks about healing by *radiesthesia,* which apparently he seemed to think was a form of witchcraft. It was all made to sound very sinister, and by June 2nd the *Daily Herald* was saying "The British Medical Association recently advised an inquiry into witchcraft in Britain."

On June 9th, 1956, *Two Worlds* reported the famous Spiritualist healer, Harry Edwards, as commenting: "It is not by chance the B.M.A. included references to witchcraft in their report to the Archbishops' Committee on Divine Healing. They are lining it up with spirit healing. It is one of their lines of attack for the future."

The *Daily Herald,* on June 2nd, 1956, promised us a story by a lady called Myrna Blumberg, who they claimed had become "an apprentice witch herself." This, I thought, should be good; and I awaited with great interest the account of Miss Blumberg's initiation. I wanted to see whether any human blood had flowed at the horrid scene, or whether they had been content merely with a couple of cockerels. I was also interested to know whether poor Miss Blumberg had had to throw over tombstones herself, and if so how many, or whether any male members of the staff of the *Daily Herald* had been gallant enough to come along and do it for her.

Well, Miss Blumberg certainly had the most remarkable initiation into witchcraft I have ever heard of; it consisted of hiring a car and a chauffeur and touring Devon! Her account of the various people she met who could charm warts and do other kinds of healing was most interesting. Nevertheless, after all the terrific tales we had been hearing, this was a distinct anticlimax.

However, she made up for it the next day, with the headline: "Black Witchery Can Lead to Murder." This article consisted of the inevitable interview with the Rev. F. Amphlett Micklewright, who said he was "convinced that under various guises there is as much witchcraft practised now as in the Middle Ages," and that he had been "close on the fringe of some of the most baleful things, distortions and perversions of old black magic," and of course uttered the usual solemn warning that "It's one of the most dangerous cults to dabble in"; a recital of various tales of curses being put on people, and a mention of the case of the murder of Charles Walton, in which it said "it was generally whispered that witchcraft played a part."

Miss Blumberg had interviewed Dr. Margaret Murray, who told her, "People write to me from all over the country as though I were an anti-witch and could break the spells they believe in. All I can do is to tell them to laugh it off."

Dr. Murray has my sympathy; they write to me, too. I do not always tell them to "laugh it off"; but that is the best advice in many cases.

Let's get this business of "bewitchment" and "putting curses on people" straight. There are two necessary prerequisites for "putting a curse on someone." The first is a genuine motive for doing so, and the second is the ability to do it. When those two things come together, and they sometimes do, you get an indubitable result. I know too many stories of this kind personally to say that it can never happen; but what I do say is that it is rare. In the first place, to do a thing like this requires a considerable expenditure of psychic force, which no one with real knowledge would do upon trivial grounds. Secondly, those who really know about these things would not resort to such an act unless in exceptional circumstances. Consequently, ninety-nine per cent of the people who think they are being "bewitched" are cases of sheer auto-suggestion, and I believe that such cases have been enormously increased by the newspaper scare campaign.

Nothing is more calculated to prey on the weak minds and send borderline mental cases over the edge than to read article after article in the popular Press boosting "the terrible powers of Satan," and alleging that Britain is riddled with black magic. If this book serves no purpose than to debunk this poisonous rubbish, it will have done a good job.

It was time that all this grim ghoulishness had some comic relief; and that was provided in abundance, for those who had a sense of humour, by a series on "Black Magic" in the *Sunday Graphic,* which commenced on the 3rd June, 1956. For after the author had been boosted in the advance blurb as "The man who knows, more than anyone about this strange, evil cult," he made, in his first article, this extraordinary admission: when, he says, he was an officer in the first World War, he was playing vingt-et-un, got fed up with losing, and called on the Devil to give him luck; he won the next game, and was so frightened that "I have never called on the Devil since. Neither have I ever attended any form of magical ceremony or seance, though I have interrogated many who have." And that, apparently, is the sum total of his practical experience!

Well, such candour is refreshing, and rather disarming; after that, I haven't got the heart to say very much about his articles! After all, "black magic" thrillers have provided me with many hours of innocent enjoyment.

By this time the cause of witch-hunting was rather scraping the bottom of the barrel for something fresh to say, and the papers had to eke out their yarns with hoary old legends about Aleister Crowley, and even with ordinary ghost stories. One of these was really pretty horrible.

"The Rev. Montague Summers told me," says the narrator, "of an exorcism he performed in Ireland, on a farmer's wife who, it was said, was possessed by an evil spirit. He arrived in the evening. On the table in the living-room was the remains of a cold leg of mutton—obviously for supper. At the sight of a priest the woman became so violent that she had to be held down. As he sprinkled holy water on her and commanded the demon to come forth, a small cloud of black smoke issued from her foam-flecked mouth. It went straight into the cold mutton, and within a few minutes everyone present saw that the meat was alive with maggots." I showed my secretary this tale, and she said, "Yes, that was a good story when I first read it, too. It had the Fourth Form scared stiff."

I said, "What do you mean?"

"Why," she said, "I've read that story years ago, when I was a girl at school. It's a book of fictional ghost stories called *A Mirror of Shalott* by Robert Hugh Benson. Admittedly, the venue has been changed from the West Indies to Ireland, but otherwise the story is just the same." So was Montague Summers leg-pulling or lying?

According to G. W. Young in *Reveille* on June 8th, 1956, the Rev. Amphlett Micklewright had told him of "wild orgies in places where the atmosphere was drugged with ether or chloroform, the smell being camouflaged by the burning of incense." It has evidently not occurred to these good folk to find out by practical experiment just what would happen if they sprayed a room with ether, and then introduced fire of any kind, such as candles or burning incense, into it. Still, perhaps that is just as well; the resulting explosion might well have proved fatal, and I should be sorry to see a grand police officer like Bob Fabian come to such a sticky end. (If anyone doubts my word on this, *don't try it yourself*—ask a hospital anaesthetist.)

If the drug sprayed were chloroform, the most likely result would be that those who inhaled it would be very sick; circumstances which are hardly inviting for even the mildest of orgies.

Ex-Supt. Fabian said further, "One of my most memorable murder cases was at the village of Lower Quinton, near the stone Druid circle of the Whispering Knights. There a man had been killed by a reproduction of a Druidical ceremony on St. Valentine's Eve."

Now, the Whispering Knights are not a circle; they are not Druidical; and they are about twelve miles away, as the crow flies, from Lower Quinton. Nor was Charles Walton killed on St. Valentine's *Eve*; and as no one knows for certain just what the Druid's ceremonies were, it is impossible to say that his death was a reproduction of one. Apart from these details, the description is accurate.

Let me make it clear, however, that I cast no doubt whatsoever upon Ex-Supt. Fabian's statement in the same article that people come to London from the provinces and pay heavy fees to take part in "revolting ceremonies" staged by "little Black Magic groups in London that rise, fester and disperse again like plague abscesses." Ex-Supt. Fabian has in his time been Chief of the Vice Squad which doubtless concerns itself with such things. Sexual degenerates with money can find those who are willing to provide the perverted satisfactions they crave. But this sort of thing is not witchcraft; I doubt if it is even really black magic, or any sort of magic. It is simply one of the rackets that the Vice Squad concerns itself with. Sometimes, doubtless, such things are done under the pretence of being "magical ceremonies" just as sometimes they are done under the pretence of being "private cabaret performances," or something similar; but they bear no relationship whatsoever to genuine witchcraft. Though, of course, sensational newspaper descriptions of alleged black magic rites involving orgies of sex and blood will have been eagerly lapped up by neurotic degenerates, and given them fresh ideas to emulate; a development for which responsibility does not lie at the door of the witches. And every time the sensational Press have big blurbs of "BLACK MAGIC" and BLACK MASSES, there are always some "bright young things" who say, "Let's have a go at this." I can confidently say this. Any "Black Magic "ceremonies ever held are just the result of sensationalism in the papers. I am speaking of the last fifty years, of course. Three hundred years ago it may have been different.

The articles by Dennis Wheatley finished on June 24th, with an injunction to readers to make the sign of the Cross if they were ever confronted with an evil manifestation.

Whether there was any relation between this newspaper campaign and the ugly outbreak of hooliganism which interrupted the Druid ceremony at Stonehenge at dawn on June 21st, 1956, is problematical; it may be significant, though, that the disturbance started, according to the report in *Picture Post,* with a cry of "You're pagan!" Throwing of thunder-flashes and smoke-bombs followed, a lady Druid's dress was set on fire, and the *Daily Telegraph* quoted a Ministry of Works custodian as saying that the crowd was "the most unruly I have ever seen in my twenty years here."

It is perhaps significant also that this disturbance of the traditional ceremony at Stonehenge, this insult to the Old Stones, has been followed by what I believe to have been the worst summer on record. It may be sheer coincidence, of course—but I know what our forefathers would have said!

But the first fine frenzy of witch-hunting had passed. On July 7th, 1956, *Illustrated* published the results of an investigation undertaken by its reporter, Norman Phillips, who came out with the rather disappointing verdict (in some quarters) that "Despite the headlines, solid evidence that black magic is practised in Britain is scant indeed"; that "there are not enough people in Britain who call themselves witches to form even one traditional coven of thirteen"; and that "witchcraft, as an organised belief, is as dated as the witch's hat in Britain." He asked, "Is black magic widespread in Britain—or are a few people making a mountain out of mumbo-jumbo for the sake of the curious?"

After what has been going on for the last five years, I think the reluctance of people to call themselves witches, especially to reporters, is hardly to be wondered at; but I think I have done something in this chapter to show that the answer to the last part of Mr. Phillips' question is emphatically "Yes!"

The last word to date has been said on this matter in the November, 1956, issue of *Prediction,* by their popular contributor Madeline Montalban, in an article discussing certain aspects of Karma:

> A recent case was that of a certain journalist who did a series of "black magic" articles for his newspaper.
>
> He drew a very small amount of his material from fact, a great deal from imagination and hearsay; and he presented the world with a sensational (and mostly fictitious) black magic scare.
>
> While he was doing this he came to see me, and I warned him against it.
>
> "Black magic may be wrong," I said, "but as you have had no kind of occult instruction, how are you to know what is black magic and what is not?

If you present this story as a warning to people, you create an interest in black magic that was not there before! You will also make a personal profit out of a sensation that may affect the weak-minded. And believe me, you'll suffer for it in the long run."

He did not see why he should. He was safe on his soap-box of "warning" the masses of the evils of black magic—though he got his information from unreliable sources, and was himself deceived.

Bit by bit his editor found the stories to be untrue; no reliable evidence was forthcoming, and the journalist "lost face." With that, he lost self-confidence, and others lost confidence in him.

This, in turn, brought about a series of personal misfortunes from which he has not yet recovered. When he last saw me he protested at the "injustice" of this and said: "I only wanted to bring the black magicians to justice."

That, of course, did not lie within his power.

The man did not understand his own unworthy motives. Accusing others of black magic always brings the accuser to trouble (note the witch-hunters of the past and the miserable ends they came to); and that unfortunate journalist now sees his world turned topsy-turvy. . . .

However, when he gets things into perspective, and realises that occult sins are punished by occult means, he will be wiser, happier—and luckier!

Considerations of space have precluded me from giving in this chapter the fully detailed debunking that the Great Witch-Hunt deserves. Also, I have deliberately confined myself to convicting the witch-hunters out of their own mouths, using only matter which the public can check on. I have, however, been assisted by private investigators, and I feel I must include one item which they turned up.

On a few occasions the ashes of fires had been found at the Rollright Stones, which might have been the work of tramps, gypsies, small boys or practical jokers; but which inspired a headline in *Reynolds News* on the 22nd April, 1956: "Witchcraft Fires on Pagan Hilltop." And on May 1st, 1956, another enterprising journal, which out of charity shall be nameless, came out with a story: "P.C.———Waits Up For Witches." It was a thrilling yarn of how "For eight hours last night P.C.———. . . kept vigil by the prehistoric Rollright Stones—on a witch hunt." ("Last night," of course, being May Eve.) "Each night this week," it stated, "he will resume his watch."

I am able to reveal that the police officer in question was, in fact, away that night upon an entirely different duty, in the company of another officer. Nor did he "keep vigil" the rest of the week either. The newspaper concerned, in spite of the detailed conversation with P.C.———which they reported, had in fact dreamed the whole story of the "watch for witches" up!

There are quite a number of anecdotes of this nature, and of some of the "investigators of witchcraft," which space in this book just will not run to; but I think enough has been said to enable readers to look with a somewhat more critical eye in the future at those big black headlines about "Black Magic and witchcraft."

Now, I propose to tackle boldly this alleged "witchcraft murder," the death of Charles Walton in 1945. What are the allegations in the case, and what are the facts?

1. It is alleged that authorities upon ancient religions have said that the circumstances of this crime show it to be a ritual murder.

   Fact: The only authority who has been willing to be quoted as saying anything about this possibility is Dr. Margaret Murray, who is one of the greatest authorities in the modern world upon this subject; and what Dr. Murray has actually said is this: The lack of a motive was puzzling. There was also the significance of the day—the 14th of February. In pre-Christian times February was a sacrificial month, when the soil was spring-cleaned of the dirt of winter. In the old calendar February 2nd was a sacrificial day, but the old calendar was 12 days behind ours, which means that February 14th corresponds to February 2nd. But I found nothing to support my theory beyond that. The pitchfork was never an instrument of sacrifice in this country, though it may have been in Italy—and there were Italian prisoners-of-war in the neighbourhood at the time." (Given in an interview with G. W. Young, published in Reveille, June 1st, 1956.)

2. It is alleged that British witches keep to the old calendar mentioned above, so that St. Valentine's Day, the 14th February, is a witches' Sabbath.

   Fact: The so-called "Old Calendar" is of no significance to present-day witches, because as I have already explained in the chapter dealing with the Celts and the Druids, the Sabbats relate to the Sun, the Moon, and the Zodiac. Hence St. Valentine's Day is not a witches' Sabbat, though it was originally a pagan festival. The witches' Sabbat in February is Candlemas Eve, the Celtic Oimelc, which occurs on February 1st, approximately 40 days after the Winter Solstice. As, according to Dr. Murray in the interview just quoted, this is the only possible connection between this crime and witchcraft in Britain, this is precisely the place where the connection breaks down. With regard to the Italian prisoners-of-war in the neighbourhood, the witch-hunters cannot have it both ways—if the killer was an Italian, then the crime is nothing to do with a British witch coven.

3. It is alleged that an identical crime was committed on the same day, February 14th, in 1875, at nearby Long Compton, when a woman named Ann Turner was killed with a hayfork, and that there was an earlier hayfork killing in the same neighbourhood, when a man called James Haywood killed an old woman; both the victims are alleged to have been suspected witches.

   Fact: There was no such crime on February 14th, 1875. What actually happened was that on the 15th September, 1875, a feeble-minded man named James Haywood attacked a 79-year-old woman named Anne Tennent, at Long Compton, with a pitchfork, and inflicted injuries upon her of which she died three hours later; he was testified at the inquest upon the victim to have been suffering from delusions that people were bewitching him. He was brought to trial at Warwick Assizes, found Not Guilty upon the grounds of insanity, and ordered to be detained during Her Majesty's pleasure. The crime was not identical with the death of Charles Walton. Poor old Anne Tennent was attacked in the road outside a village shop. Haywood was seen to stab her in the legs with the prongs of the pitchfork, and knock her down with the handle. She died of shock and loss of blood. A full report of the case may be found in the Stratford-on-Avon Herald for 1875, from which I have taken these details.

   It will be noticed that not only are the date and the victim's name wrong, but two murders have been made out of one. This is what is known as "conducting an investigation."

4. It is alleged that "nearby" the scene of the crime is an ancient stone circle known as the Rollright Stones.

Fact: The Rollright Stones are about 12 miles away, "as the crow flies," from Meon Hill. I should not personally define "nearby" as meaning "twelve miles away."

5. It is alleged that the Rollright Stones are a place where the Druids offered up human sacrifices.

   Fact: There is no evidence that the Druids ever had any connection with the Rollright Stones, which were already an ancient monument before the Druids ever came to Britain. Nor is there any evidence of sacrifices being offered there. And there is little evidence the Druids ever performed human sacrifices.

6. It is alleged that there is no other explanation of this crime than that it was a ritual murder.

   Fact: There is another possible explanation, and I think it is time it was given. That explanation is that someone killed Charles Walton because they thought he had the "Evil Eye" or possibly was a witch.

I am not saying that that is the only solution of this mystery; but what I am saying is that if *witchcraft enters into this crime at all,* then that is a far more likely explanation than the alleged "ritual murder."

The facts upon which I base this opinion are these: firstly, there is a strong local belief in witchcraft. J. Harvey Bloom, whose book, *Folk Lore, Old Customs and Superstitions in Shakespeare-land,* was published in 1929, relates how in 1912 he could only get people in the neighbourhood to tell him stories about witches "with much persuasion and some fear of the consequences." It is evident, from the folk-lore he recounts, that Meon Hill is a "witch district." For one thing, there is a local legend of the Wild Hunt. J. Harvey Bloom says, "Among the villages of the plain below the hill are many old folk living to tell those they can trust creepy stories of the Hell-hounds, Night-hounds, or Hooter, as they are variously named, that in phantom wise, with hounds and horn, pursue phantom foxes along the hill-tops at midnight. Many are the legends to account for uncouth sounds at night, which certainly do occur. One story is told of a local huntsman who would not desist from his favourite sport even on the Sabbath. On one Sunday judgment fell upon the ungodly crew; huntsmen, horses and hounds fell into a chasm that opened in the hill and were never seen again, though they still in ghostly wise hunt at midnight." (Note the folk-memory of the Wild Huntsman who comes out of the Hollow Hill.)

In his article in Vol. VI of *Folk-Lore* (1895), entitled "The Rollright Stones and their Folklore," Arthur J. Evans says, "Some say there is a great cave beneath the King Stone, and according to some the same exists beneath the circle too." This may be another folk-memory of the Hollow Hill that was the entry to the Old God's kingdom. It is noted in the Victoria County History of Warwickshire that the Rollright Stones were the traditional meeting-place of witches; and according to J. Harvey Bloom there is a proverb in the locality that "There are enough witches in Long Compton to draw a waggon-load of hay up Long Compton hill." We have already seen the bearing that this belief had upon the death of Anne Tennent.

However, we are more immediately concerned here with Meon Hill and its immediate neighbourhood. There are some earthworks upon Meon Hill, and Bronze Age articles have been dug up there, showing that it was anciently inhabited. It was at one time the scene of a "wake" or all-night fair, but the date on which this was held is now forgotten. According to legend, Meon Hill was made by the Devil. In a fit of annoyance at seeing Evesham Abbey built, he kicked a clod of earth at it, but at the prayer of St. Ecguuine the clod fell short, and formed Meon Hill. Legends of things being "made by the Devil" are usually a sign of pagan associations.

But how does all this have any bearing on the death of Charles Walton, that harmless old countryman so brutally and bloodily murdered on February 14th, 1945? For whoever killed him made certain that his blood should flow. Had robbery been the motive, a blow on the head with the stick would have sufficed. At the inquest, evidence was given that there had apparently been an attempt to go through his pockets, and his watch was missing. But the watch was only a metal one, and he had left his purse at home. Who was going to risk hanging to rob a farm labourer of a metal watch and possibly a pocketful of small change? Is it not likely that the searched pockets and the missing watch were blinds to conceal the real motive? Which was to get some charm he carried. (If this was of paper or parchment he may have carried it in his watch.)

Arthur J. Evans (Loc. cit.), speaks of "a very widespread superstition regarding witches, of which I found many surviving expressions in the neighbouring village of Long Compton. They say there that if you only draw her blood 'be it but a pin's prick', the witch loses all her power for the time." This belief was very prevalent in old times, and still exists among country folk. Dr. Margaret Murray told G. W. Young how at Swaffham in Norfolk, a farmer admitted slashing the forehead of a woman he believed had put a curse on him. Many cases of assault of this kind are on record. In the old times, if they struck the suspected witch an unlucky blow, and killed them—well, that was "just too bad." Their intentions had been entirely righteous, of course. It will be remembered how James Haywood, filled with superstitious fear, made sure that Anne Tennent's blood flowed when he killed her. Not satisfied with knocking her down with the pitch-fork handle, he stabbed her in the legs with the prongs; she died of shock and loss of blood.

It will be remembered that the area around Stratford-on-Avon is "Shakespeare's Land," and I believe Shakespeare makes one of his characters say, "Blood will I draw on thee, thou art a witch!"

Why should anyone have thought that old Charles Walton was a witch or had the evil eye? It appears that he had a local reputation as a seer of ghosts. This, before his death, had actually got into print. J. Harvey Bloom, that industrious collector of local folklore, says in his book (Op. cit.),

> At Alveston a plough lad named Charles Walton met a black dog on his way home nine times in successive evenings. He told the shepherd and carter with whom he worked and was laughed at for his pains. On the ninth encounter a headless lady rustled past him in a silk dress, and on the next day he heard of his sister's death.

According to *Fabian of the Yard*, however, Supt. Spooner told Robert Fabian this story, and said that it happened, not at Alveston, but on Meon Hill; and as in the *Stratford-on-Avon Herald's* report of his death it was stated that "Mr. Walton spent his whole life in Quinton, and was known to everyone," this version may be correct. To be thought to have second-sight in a place where they believe in witchcraft, is to invite suspicion.

Ex-Supt. Fabian testifies to the extreme and extraordinary reluctance of the village people to cooperate in his enquiries. When Ex-Supt. Fabian talks about such matters as black magic, Druids, and stone circles, I am prepared to question what he says; but when he speaks as a police officer he is speaking as an expert upon criminal investigation, and I accept his opinion. He says in his book: "We made our investigations in the village from door to door. There were lowered eyes, reluctance to speak except for talk of bad crops—a heifer that died in a ditch. But what had that to do with Charles Walton? Nobody would say."

What *could* it have had to do with Charles Walton—unless someone thought he was the cause of it? *Did* someone think that he had put the evil eye on it? Had the fear, hatred and superstition engendered by generations of pious witch-hunters settled so firmly into someone's mind that he suspected anyone possessing psychic powers of being a witch or having the evil eye liable to blast crops and injure cattle? And did they decide that the only way to avert the ill-luck was to kill him, making sure that his blood flowed freely? It is said that all authorities consulted said it was a witchcraft murder. The great authority consulted was Dr. Margaret Murray—she said it was *not.* And I don't know any who said it was.

She also said on television when I had the honour to appear with her: "It could not be a ritual murder, because any sacrifice on that date would only be for fertility, 'Good Crops.' And it must be a child of under seven years of age." We also discussed the idea of such a sacrifice, agreeing that it was always performed with much ritual, with a number of people present, and the police reports all proved that this was not the case. In this connection I might mention the black lady seems to have described what would have happened if it had been a Voodoo sacrifice. It is curious that the first story the papers told was that Walton was killed at a Black Mass at MIDNIGHT, a "wonderful story to conjure up scenes of horror," when people noticed that if Walton was killed at a Black Mass at midnight on St. Valentine's Eve, it was curious that so many people saw him alive and well the next day; so the story was hastily changed. She now said that "he was killed exactly at Mid-day on St. Valentine's Day." Now it so happens I was one of the people consulted at the time of the murder, as to the possibility of its being a ritual murder, or a sacrifice. I said it can't be a sacrifice because, what use is an old cripple for a sacrifice? All races I know of want something young and vigorous.

Because I was consulted I was told certain things not usually known, and I presume they are still police secrets, so I don't mention them. But I can say he was alive and well after mid-day, so this second story is all moonshine. I think he had some sort of charm (which if it was a written paper charm he may have carried in his watch). It is possible someone he knew said, "Don't put the evil eye on me, or cause any more accidents to happen to my animals" or something of that kind. They had words. Possibly

Walton said: "I'll put the eye, or the curse, on you." The murderer tried to "draw blood above the breath," as the old superstition is, to stop anyone "Ill wishing you." Walton fought, and the murderer realised that he may have hit harder than he intended, and thought "I will get into trouble; my only chance is to be sure he is dead." So finished him off with the billhook. Then he tore Walton's clothes open in front, got what he wanted, and fixed him to the hedge in a way which would stop the power of the "eye" from following him.

This is what I believe caused the police to think it was a "Ritual murder." In this connection it may be remembered that some time before, a police constable named Gutteridge was murdered by two men, named Brown and Kennedy, and they shot the dead man's eyes out, to prevent the eyes "following them."

I submit that if this was really a "witchcraft evil eye murder," then there is more to support this theory than there is to substantiate that of "human sacrifice." Although, if I am right, in one sense Charles Walton was a human sacrifice; he was a victim of the long campaign of witch-hunting that has been waged throughout the centuries; and the modern purveyors of fear and folly may well take it to their consciences.

Such writers need not flatter themselves that I have written this chapter to "confute" them; on the contrary, they are obviously people who have made up their minds upon the subject, and are not going to be distracted by mere proof. My purpose here has been to undeceive the public as to the reliability of the statements made, to expose the harm such evil nonsense can do, and to ensure that the man in the street will be more able in future to weigh up and criticise such stories, and evaluate them at their true worth.

Now there is one thing which I think should be remembered. These sensational stories may be said to only amuse people, that no one would believe them. But they have unfortunate repercussions. Spicy bits go to other countries and are copied and believed. The sensation about Witchcraft was started in May, 1955. On July 3rd, a poor woman, Josephina Arista, was accused of witchcraft and publicly burned at the stake in the little border town of Ojinaga, Mexico, according to *Fate*. The American Bureau of Information tells me they have every reason to believe it is true, though all sorts of influences are at work to hush the matter up, and the *Saturday Mail*, published in Glasgow, September 9th, 1956, tells of two women, Christina Trajo and Benita Sabina who, accused of being witches, were hacked in pieces and thrown on to a bonfire at Alfajayucan, Mexico, to purify their souls, on September 8th, 1956. Now I am perfectly entitled to express my belief: "That these three poor women met an agonising death as the direct result of these 'sensational writings'," and if journalists were less inclined to get "Spicy bits" at all costs, and verified what they wrote, those deaths would not have occurred.

Chapter XVII

The Future

Is there a future for the Craft of the Wica?

Yes, there could be. The great persecutions could not kill it because the spirit of wonder dwells in it. Its roots are set in the Ancient Magic, with its secrets of joy and terror which stir the blood and enliven the soul. It has suffered badly by reason of the modern disease of "meddle-o-mania" or "delirium interferens," which may be defined as a morbid desire to run other people's lives for them; so that people dare not initiate their children as they used to do in the good old days (and even dared to do in the bad old days, the "burning time"), for fear of finding some paid snooper from "the authorities" or a representative of the "Sunday Hysterical" on their doorstep. Yet, in spite of all, it survives; because there exists, even in the Welfare State, a spirit of romance, a love of the spice of life, and a dislike of smug respectability.

So I wonder, "What has the Craft to contribute to the future?"

For one thing, it may prick the bubble of myth that orthodox Christianity is the ancient faith of these islands and that there was no civilisation in Britain until the Romans came. The true Christianity, the faith which Jesus himself preached, may have come here once, but it was swiftly crushed. The various types of ecclesiastical domination which seized power and the wealth of the country are slowly rotting away. It is not only the old cathedrals, but the old dogmas, which are full of decay and the death-watch beetle; and we could better spare the old dogmas than we could the old cathedrals, for the latter were built by good men.

It is true that a number of people support the orthodox Churches with the mistaken idea that they are the only powers which can combat Communism. Now, they get subscriptions by pretending to try to do so; but of what do their efforts consist? Just think of the means the Church used to crush the witches, or the Templars or the Albigenses! It was the rulers of the Church who were responsible for introducing into the modern world the foul ideas of persecuting people because of their beliefs; of making "deviationist thinking" a crime; of conducting "purges" to "liquidate" minorities; of burning books, and suppressing freedom of speech and publication; of conducting "trials" where the accused had no hope of acquittal, whether they were guilty or innocent; of using torture to obtain "confessions" as required; of exterminating whole communities on the pretext that they were guilty of "acts of sabotage," or were about to "encircle" the State; in fact, there is not one hideous detail of the crimes against humanity committed by the jackbooted louts of Hitler and Stalin which was not taken from the blue-print provided by "Christian" orthodoxy. Only the names needed to be changed; all the rest of the plan for the suppression of human liberty was there, tried and proved. They sowed the wind, and men today are reaping the whirlwind of that sowing.

But we are today upon the threshold of a new Age. Call it the Aquarian Age, the Aeon of Horus, or what you will. The great, clean wind of a new Cosmic Power is blowing upon the world from the deeps of space. Already it has blown away many of the cobwebs of the past. Much prudery and false modesty, for instance, has gone by the board.

Many coastal resorts no longer trouble to provide changing huts on the beach.

One of the tolerant towns is Paignton in Devon. Many people bathe there regularly in the nude and are never bothered by police.

One housewife told me: "My husband and I go bathing in the nude together at every opportunity. We know a lot of young couples who do the same. There is nothing immoral about it if you have a clean mind."

Bustling Blackpool is equally broad-minded.

Publicity director Mr. H. Porter told *The Sunday Pictorial:* "We don't mind in the least if people expose their bodies to the sun, provided it is done in a reasonable way. Plenty of people slip off their clothes at the water's edge and run into the sea naked. Times have changed a lot in the last twenty years. Every year Britain is becoming less and less modest. We are no longer a nation of prudes and prigs on the beach. Nudists are no longer considered to be cranks by most people."

Bravo, Miss Audrey Whiting, who wrote this article! Get hold of your professional colleague some time, and talk some sense about prudery, priggery and hypocrisy to him!

People are no longer taught to look upon the transmission of the flame of human life through sexual union as something "dirty" and shameful. A new conception of the sacredness of human liberty has come into the world; and I want to emphasise that this conception of individual liberty is *new*. When Wilberforce tried to stop the slave trade, not so very many years ago, he was preached against by parsons up and down the country. The Tolpuddle Martyrs who dared to form the first trade union were denounced from many a pulpit. When Augustine saw the English children in the Roman slave-market he was greatly troubled at the fact that they had never been baptised, and prepared his mission to England right away. It never occurred to him to start a mission on the spot, and preach against the fact that here were human beings publicly exposed for sale. The pious Puritans of Salem in America, who started the witch-persecution over there, thought that it was wicked to own fine clothes and jewels; yet they never thought that it was wicked to own slaves, for it was one of their slave-women who was the first to be arrested and interrogated by torture. This concept of individual liberty is something that belongs to the New Age, not the Old. It has been slowly evolving since about the latter half of the eighteenth century, when the Aquarian spirit first began to breathe through human affairs. But it has had its heralds and forerunners, and some of these were among the witch-covens; and not a few of them are among the witch-covens still.

One of the ways in which the Craft of the Wica has served the Aquarian Age has been in the way in which it has kept alive the teaching of reincarnation and Karma. This was widely believed in the ancient world, not only by pagans but by many of the early Christians; but when the Church wanted to bring in the ideas of Original Sin, Vicarious Atonement, and Salvation by Faith, it realised that this old teaching of the Mysteries contradicted them, and must therefore be discredited. So in A.D. 553, the Church Council of Constantinople made the following official pronouncement, "Whoever shall support the mythical doctrine of the pre-existence of the soul and the consequent wonderful opinion of its return, let him be anathema." So all had to give it up except the "wise ones"! And that, of course, meant the witches.

However, a recent survey of religious beliefs in Britain surprised those who carried it out by the number of people it found who believed in some form of reincarnation. I wonder if this is entirely due to the teaching of the

Theosophical Society and similar bodies since 1875? Or did these teachings fall upon more receptive soil than they would otherwise have found, because the Wica had kept the old Mysteries alive, and so influenced the Group-soul of this country?

But all this belongs to the past, the reader may say. What of the future?

The Aquarian Age is ahead of us; but it is not yet fully arrived. We are in the transition period between two great Ages. Hence the world-wide turmoil of recent years. And there are those forces which would seek to work against the coming of the New Age, and delay it all they can for their own selfish ends. Strong though these forces are, they cannot prevent its coming; though they can cause prolonged suffering and destruction. The New Age is bound to come; but the choice of whether it comes in peace or in destruction rests with mankind. If man chooses to work in harmony with Cosmic Law, it can come in peace; if not, then his civilisation can go the way of Atlantis.

That which has influenced the Group-soul of this country once can do so again. I have already told of the belief of the Wica in the Ancient Gods of these islands. This is not mere superstition or a figure of speech. Initiates will understand me when I say that the Gods are real, not as persons, but as vehicles of power. Much food for thought upon this point will be found in such books as *The Mystical Qabalah,* by Dion Fortune and *The Art of Creation,* by Edward Carpenter; by those who care to seek. Briefly, it may be explained that the personification of a particular type of cosmic power in the form of a God or Goddess, carried out by believers and worshippers over many centuries, builds that God-form or Magical Image into a potent reality on the Inner Planes, and makes it a means by which that type of cosmic power may be contacted. Nor is the worshippers' belief vain; for though they may themselves have built the Magical Image, the Power which ensouls it is real and objective, if the building has been done in the right way.

Of course, the Craft of the Wica is not the only group which seeks to contact the Gods. There are other occult groups which use a similar technique, and their aims are the same, namely to bring through the Divine power to help, guide and uplift mankind at this dangerous and exciting turning-point in human history. But, so far as I know, these groups generally work with the Egyptian and Greek Gods and Goddesses, and I cannot think that these contacts are as powerful here as they would be upon their native soil; whereas the divinities of the Craft of the Wica are the Ancient

Ones of Britain, part of the land itself. (For a country exists not merely upon the physical plane, and man does not live by bread alone.)

Nor is the veneration of the Wica for the old sacred places such as Stonehenge and Glastonbury mere sentiment. Those who are sensitive to atmosphere will know that these places possess a life of their own, and, from what we have been told by seers, these too exist not only upon the material plane. They are focusing points for influence and the power from the Inner Planes, places where the Veil is thinner than elsewhere; and the "superstition" that it is dangerous to remove or injure the Old Stones is founded on fact.

I am quite aware that much of what I have written above, about "Magical Images," "Inner Planes," "the Group-soul of a nation," etc., etc., will sound like rabid nonsense to many. This consideration troubles me not at all, as in this chapter I have not written for the many but for the few who will understand. For remember, there are still many who believe in, practise and love the "Craft of the Wica."

As this book goes to press, a curious thing has happened, which I think is worth recording. The agent of a Sunday paper happened to get into touch with witches in the Midlands, and put this proposition to them: "Everything which is written about witches is by their persecutors. Now, if you will tell me your side of the case, it will be printed fairly and truly; and let the public judge." Further talk brought out that what he wanted was a beautiful young witch of high rank to tell the story, illustrated by nude photographs: that her full name and address would be given, so that, as he put it, the public could verify the facts. This proposal naturally was rejected as impossible, for it would result in the poor girl being persecuted for the rest of her life. Also, a woman is usually middle-aged at least, before she attains high rank. But after some discussion it was arranged that he should meet several witches, including a girl of twenty-five years of age, who was of high rank, that he would obtain all information to establish their good faith, and would be allowed to take part in an important rite, which would be held in the woods; and he, in return, promised to set out fully the witches' articles of faith. I am inclined to think that he was genuine in his belief. They were very excited about it, and had arranged to feature the rite in future numbers of the paper.

But when the article was published it had apparently been first submitted to various Churchmen. It started with a statement by the Bishop of

Exeter saying, "These are entirely evil things. To link such practices with Christianity is absolutely wrong." How he thought that anyone could link an ancient Pagan Cult, which was old hundreds of years before the advent of Christ, with Christianity, I leave it to the Bishop to explain. The article was of the usual "dirty smear" type. It said the proprietors of the paper had accepted the witches' offer in order to let the people of Britain know what was going on in their midst. Unfortunately the night of the witch-meeting was wet, so an abridged rite was held in a house. But a dozen very good photographs were taken. Only one of them was reproduced. The actual report of the rite was described quite well for someone who did not understand what he saw. To say that witches drink rum was probably a mistake, as it is a very strict witch law that no spirits may be drunk by them, and only two glasses of wine in the evening. Then part of the interview with a doctor was quoted, one practising in the Midlands, who firmly believes in the goodness and beauty of the witch-religion. He said given the opportunity, he thought witchcraft could again become a practicable and noble religion. The paper commented on this, saying "Condemned by the Church as a monstrous evil, how could any responsible human being believe in it as a religion?" Well, there are many things which the Church has condemned as monstrous evils, Protestantism, Nonconformity, Divorce, Vaccination and many other things which are now accepted as a matter of course. After all this, we were promised remarkable revelations the following week. But the story was then pushed into the back sheets. We were told the horrifying fact that a twenty-five-year-old High Priestess, Amanda, was initiated by her family into witchcraft when she was eight years old, and brought up in the belief that there was a Goddess who produced the sunshine and caused everything to grow. She worshipped the God and Goddess of Fertility, believing they had power to heal the sick, and to bring curses on the heads of those who do harm. We were told, further, that witches do not believe in the sacrament of marriage. (As it is only some of the Christian sects which do believe in the sacrament of marriage, there is nothing strange in witches disbelieving in it, holding the same view.) She was made High Priestess three years ago, because the Elders decided that she had "inborn Power." She was given a garter to wear above her knee as a symbol of her office. This, a necklace of lapis-lazuli and a silver bracelet, are all she wears at meetings of the Coven. This is all broadly correct, except that she was not given a garter when made a High Priestess. This is only presented to a woman when she is made a Priestess in charge of more than one Coven; and this is true in Amanda's case, to my knowledge. I was present when she received her garter.

But then the extraordinary statement was made that Amanda told the representative of the paper that "If they did not invoke the assistance of the God and Goddess, the Sun would not return each morning." Either this was a misunderstanding, a leg-pull; or of course, it may have been written in by the Editor. For no witch, and certainly not Amanda, ever believed in such a thing. But there is an ancient rite, which is still performed about the end of December, "the shortest day," when witches dance round with torches, in what is called the "Dance of the Wheel." Yet no one thinks of this as more than an old custom.

The article ends with, "Call it idiocy or evil, the Pagan Cult of Witchcraft is a fact that Christians in Britain have to reckon with." Now, it will be noticed that, even if the paper speaks the truth when it says its proprietors were approached with this offer, which they accepted, or whether the paper made the offer first, the fact remains that the bargain that if they would set out fully and fairly the witches' articles of faith, its reporter would be permitted to witness one of their ceremonies and would photograph it, was not carried out. The members of the paper have not made the least attempt to put on record the witches' faith. They broke their bargain shamefully. As always in the past, it is the wicked Pagans who tell the truth and who keep their word; it is the righteous, holy Christian who lies and cheats.

Now rumour hath it that the paper wished to keep to the bargain, but that strong pressure was put on its owners to kill the story! "The truth must not be known." If this is so, where is the alleged freedom of the Press? One can understand that the truth about a primitive belief which has been described as "a noble religion applicable to twentieth century life," had it become known, might have disturbed vested interests; though witches don't seek converts, converts might want to join the witches and, personally, I believe that this is well recognised, so it has been determined never to give them that opportunity. I have known many atheists who have entered the Cult and said, "It is so lovely to find a religion in which you can believe."

The Church, nowadays, gives people whist-drives and outings, it gives the girls wonderful white weddings. But it does not provide them with a faith in which they can believe. It is true that in early days some Christians were martyrs for their faith. But, remember, some nine million people were similarly tortured to death for witchcraft, even if they were not all witches. Does it not prove it was a faith people were willing to die for?

Yes, the witches died in thousands for their faith, happy in the conviction that they would go straight to a sunny place among their loved ones, and that rested, refreshed, they would in time be reborn on earth again, among their own people. It is this, and many other beliefs, that the paper agreed to put forward, but it seems some strong pressure was exerted to suppress its revelations; that at the same time "smear" suggestions were made about the witches without anything very definite being said, excepting that they (in common with the Puritans) do not regard marriage as a sacrament. Article 25 of the Thirty-Nine Articles which all clergymen have to swear to believe and to teach, says it is not a sacrament.

It is an old game to spread stories about a faith you dislike, so as to frighten people from joining it. I wonder how many Romans were scared off by the story that the Christians were cannibals, who ate human flesh and drank human blood at their communion services?

There was an old ideal, "The truth shall prevail." But the modern ideal seems to be, "See that the truth shall be unknown, so that it may *not* prevail."

Appendix I

The Magical Legend of the Witches

Now, G. (The Witch Goddess) had never loved, but she would solve all the Mysteries, even the Mystery of Death; and so she journeyed to the Nether Lands.

The Guardians of the Portals challenged her, "Strip off thy garments, lay aside thy jewels; for naught may ye bring with ye into this our land."

So she laid down her garments and her jewels, and was bound, as are all who enter the Realms of Death the Mighty One. (Note: there was a Celtic custom of binding corpses. The cord which had bound a corpse was useful in learning the "second sight.")

Such was her beauty that Death himself knelt and kissed her feet, saying, "Blessed be thy feet that have brought thee in these ways. Abide with me, let me but place my cold hand on thy heart."

She replied, "I love thee not. Why dost thou cause all things that I love and take delight in to fade and die?"

"Lady," replied Death, "'tis Age and Fate, against which I am helpless. Age causes all things to wither; but when men die at the end of time I give them rest and peace, and strength so that they may return. But thou, thou art lovely. Return not; abide with me."

But she answered, "I love thee not."

Then said Death, "An thou received not my hand on thy heart, thou must receive Death's scourge."

"It is Fate; better so," she said, and she knelt; and Death scourged her, and she cried, "I feel the pangs of love."

And Death said, "Blessed be," and gave her the Fivefold Kiss, saying, "Thus only may ye attain to joy and knowledge."

And he taught her all the Mysteries. And they loved and were one, and he taught her all the Magics.

For there are three great events in the life of man; Love, Death, and Resurrection in a new body; and Magic controls them all. For to fulfil love you must return again at the same time and place as the loved one, and you must remember and love them again. But to be reborn you must die, and be ready for a new body; and to die you must be born; and without love you may not be born. And these be all the Magics.

Appendix II

The Stedingers

THE FOLLOWING ACCOUNT, taken from *Memoirs of Extraordinary Popular Delusions,* by Charles MacKay, LL.D. (London, 1852), will serve as an example of the way in which not merely whole families, but whole communities of people, were exterminated in the course of the Church's campaign against the witch cult. MacKay states that his authority for this narrative is Entstehungsgeschichite der Freistädlischen Bünde im Mittelalter, by Dr. F. Kortüm (1827).

THE FRIESLANDERS, inhabiting the district from the Weser to the Zuydersee, had long been celebrated for their attachment to freedom, and their successful struggles in its defence. As early as the eleventh century they had formed a general confederacy against the encroachments of the Normans and the Saxons, which was divided into seven seelands, holding annually a diet under a large oak tree at Aurich, near the Upstalboom. Here they managed their own affairs, without the control of the clergy and ambitious nobles who surrounded them, to the great scandal of the latter. They already had true notions of a representative government. The deputies of the people levied the necessary taxes, deliberated on the affairs of the community, and performed, in their simple and patriarchal manner, nearly all the functions of the representative assemblies of the present day. Finally, the Archbishop of Bremen, together with the Count of Aldenburg and other neighbouring potentates, formed a league against that section of the Frieslanders known by the name of the Stedinger, and succeeded, after harassing them and sowing dissensions among them for many years, in bringing them under the yoke. But the Stedinger, devotedly attached to their ancient laws, by which they had attained a degree of civil and religious liberty very uncommon in that age, did not submit without a violent struggle. They arose in insurrection in the year 1204, in defence of the ancient customs of their country, refused to pay taxes to the feudal chiefs or tithes to the clergy—who had forced themselves into their peaceful retreats—and drove out many of their oppressors. For a period of eight-and-twenty years the brave Stedinger continued to struggle singlehanded against the forces of the Archbishops of Bremen and the Counts of Oldenburg, and destroyed, in the year 1232, the strong castle of Slutterberg, near Delmenhorst, built by the latter nobleman as a position from which he could send out his marauders to plunder and destroy the possessions of the peasantry.

The invincible courage of these poor people proving too strong for their oppressors to cope with by the ordinary means of warfare, the Archbishop of Bremen applied to Pope Gregory IX for his spiritual aid against them. That prelate entered cordially into the cause, and launching forth his anathema against the Stedinger as heretics and witches, encouraged all true believers to assist in their extermination. A large body of thieves and fanatics broke into their country in the year 1233, killing and burning wherever they went, and not sparing either women or children, the sick or the aged, in their rage. The Stedinger, however, rallied in great force, routed their invaders, and killed in battle their leader, Count Burckhardt of Oldenburg, with many inferior chieftains.

Again the Pope was applied to, and a crusade against the Stedinger was preached in all that part of Germany. The Pope wrote to all the bishops and leaders of the faithful an exhortation to arm, to root out from the land those abominable witches and wizards. "The Stedinger," said his holiness "seduced by the devil, have abjured all the laws of God and man, slandered the Church, insulted the holy sacraments, consulted witches to raise evil spirits, shed blood like water, taken the lives of priests, and concocted an infernal scheme to propagate the worship of the devil, whom they adore under the name of Asmodi. The devil appears to them in different shapes—sometimes as a goose or a duck, and at others in the figure of a pale, black-eyed youth, with a melancholy aspect, whose embrace fills their hearts with eternal hatred against the holy Church of Christ. This devil presides at their sabbaths, when they all kiss him and dance around him. He then envelopes them in total darkness, and they all, male and female, give themselves up to the grossest and most disgusting debauchery!"

In consequence of these letters of the Pope, the emperor of Germany, Frederic II, also pronounced his ban against them. The Bishops of Ratzebourg, Lubeck, Osnabruck, Munster and Minden took up arms to exterminate them, aided by the Duke of Brabant, the Counts of Holland, of Cleves, of the Mark, of Oldenburg, of Egmond, of Diest, and many other powerful nobles. An army of forty thousand men was soon collected, which marched, under the command of the Duke of Brabant, into the country of the Stedinger. The latter mustered vigorously in defence of their lives and liberties, but could raise no greater force, including every man capable of bearing arms, than eleven thousand men to cope against the overwhelming numbers of their foe. They fought with the energy of despair, but all in vain. Eight thousand of them were slain upon the field of battle; the whole race was exterminated; and the enraged conquerors scoured the country in all direction, slew the women and children and old men, drove away the cattle, fired the woods and cottages, and made a total waste of the land.

As it is stated that the clergy had "forced themselves into the peaceful retreats " of the Stedinger, it is clear that no clergy had been there before; in other words, the Stedinger were "heathens." It will be noted that they held their annual "parliament" under an oak tree, sacred to the Old God from time immemorial. The Pope was probably guessing at the name of their God, or merely inventing; "Asmodi" is Asmodeus, the evil spirit of the Book of Tobit, in the Apocrypha, and not a Teutonic name at all. The story of the "devil" appearing as a goose or a duck is, of course, nonsense; but the "pale, black-eyed youth," who presided at the sabbaths, and was greeted with a kiss, sounds like their human leader.

Had the valiant defenders of Friesland been Christians, their names would probably have been handed down to posterity as heroes;

For how can man die better
Than facing fearful odds
For the ashes of his fathers
And the temples of his Gods?

Thomas of Cantimpré, writing in the year 1258, admits that paganism was still existent in Germany in his day. He says, "Then there is the third species of demons called Dusii or Dusiones, of whom we hear much, to whom the Gentiles anciently consecrated planted groves; *to them the Prussian gentiles still consecrate woods, which they dare not cut down and never enter except to offer sacrifices.*" (My italics). *De Bonum Universale,* I. ii, c. 56. (Quoted in H. C. Lea's *Materials Towards a History of Witchcraft*). Many old writers mention these "Dusii," whom they liken to Faunus, Sylvanus and Pan. In other words, the old "King of the Wood," under whose sacred oak the Stedingers met.

Appendix III

Significant Dates in the History of the Witch Cult, with Special Reference to Britain

Later Palaeolithic Period (the Old Stone Age, when man used tools and weapons of chipped stone), the time of the cave paintings in France and Spain depicting round dances and a God, or a priest as a God's representative, dressed in animal skins and with a horned headdress; also of the making of figurines of a Goddess of Fertility, naked and with her feminine sexuality emphasised: about 12000 to 10000 B.C.

Britain became an island about 6000 B.C. It had previously been joined to the mainland of Europe.

Commencement of agriculture in the Near East (the discovery of farming and cattle-breeding, people having previously lived by hunting): about 6000 to 5000 B.C. (This meant that the concept of the fertility of the soil was added to that of the fertility of humans and of herds of game, with consequent additions to the rites and beliefs of religion and magic.)

From about 3000 B.C. people possessing Neolithic culture (culture of the New Stone Age, when men had ground and polished weapons of stone, and the knowledge of agriculture) began to settle in Britain. These people are said to have come from North Africa. They built the "long barrows," and may have had a cult of survival and the After-World akin to that of Osiris and Isis in Egypt, in its essential concepts.

As soon as mankind discovered agriculture, the worship of the Sun God and the Moon Goddess became important, because of the effect of the sun and the moon upon the seasons and the growth of crops. They were associated with survival and reincarnation, because primitive religion drew an analogy between these concepts and that of the annual death and rebirth of the sun, and the monthly disappearance and reappearance of the moon; also with the continual death and rebirth of the corn and other crops. This may be the origin of the old saying of Hermetic philosophy, "As above, so below."

Circa 3350 B.C. Sargon of Akkad recorded his conquest of "The Tin Land Country, which lies beyond the Mediterranean." This may have been a part of Britain. Cornwall and Somerset had valuable tin mines.

The Glastonbury Zodiac: It has been suggested that the natural form of the hills, rivers, etc., around Glastonbury suggested figures, from which the Zodiac was originated. Some human labour such as cutting and building up, made the figures clearer. The Zodiac is described as being developed at an early date, and originated in a *British latitude;* where else in such a latitude could it have arisen?

About 2000 B.C. people of the Early Bronze Age began coming to Britain. They had bronze weapons and implements, made of a mixture of copper and tin. Britain's possession of tin mines would have attracted traders from all bronze-using countries of that part of the civilised world. The "round barrows" were made by the Bronze Age peoples.

Construction of Stonehenge, a fertility temple, commenced about 1800 B.C. Avebury was probably commenced rather earlier. The "Chalice Well" at Glastonbury also probably belongs to this period. The Early Bronze Age was the period of the construction of most of the megalithic (i.e. "big stone") monuments, such as stone circles, etc. These continued throughout succeeding years, right up to the present day, to be the traditional meeting-places of the witch cult. (For example, the Rollright Stones.)

It should, of course, be distinctly understood that these very early dates are merely approximations, based upon the present state of archaeological knowledge; and that the various "Ages" are not sharply defined, but merge into each other.

In 1103 B.C. (according to Geoffrey of Monmouth) Brutus and his followers, refugees from Troy, sailed up the Thames and founded London. This date is, of course, approximate; but when Troy was destroyed some refugees may have come to the countries they had traded with, and they had trading relations with Britain. Such refugees, wishing to found a new colony, might claim to be of royal stock. Geoffrey of Monmouth's dates come from his list of kings, and in the length of their reigns; he got remarkably near to the date of Troy.

In the 5th century B.C. Celtic people of the Hallstadt Iron Age culture invaded Britain and occupied the south-eastern parts. They brought iron weapons and implements to Britain, and are generally thought to have been the people who brought the Druids as their priests; but it is possible that the Druids were partly descended from the earlier tribal priesthoods. The people who built Stonehenge and Avebury may have had a religion that remained until the later Druids merged with it. Only in this way, I think, can we account for the Celts in France and Ireland, who had numbers of Druids of their own, all agreeing that in Britain was the faith founded, and the true knowledge to be learned. The British Druids must have had an earlier tradition.

55 B.C. Julius Caesar's abortive attempt to conquer Britain.

About A.D. 37 Joseph of Arimathea, with some companions, refugees from Palestine after the Crucifixion, is said to have come to Britain and taken refuge in Glastonbury, then a Druid centre, where he built the first Christian church in Britain.

A.D. 43. A Roman army, despatched by the Emperor Claudius, landed on the coast of Kent, and during the next forty years the Legions gradually occupied the country up to the Scottish Highlands.

A.D. 61. The Revolt of Boudicca (Boadicea). Massacre of the Druids by the Roman army.

A.D. 120. Britain incorporated by treaty into the Roman Empire.

A.D. 324. By decree of the Emperor Constantine, Christianity became the official religion of the Roman Empire.

A.D. 410. The fall of Rome, and end of Roman rule in Britain. (It was in this fifth century that King Arthur must have lived, if he had an historical existence.)

A.D. 553. Council of Constantinople declares doctrine of reincarnation to be heresy.

A.D. 597. St. Augustine brings Papal Christianity to Britain, now extensively settled by Angles, Saxons, Jutes, and Danes.

A.D. 607. Refusal of the Celtic Christians to acknowledge the supremacy of Rome. Massacre of the Celtic Bishops and burning of Bangor Library.

7th century A.D. "Liber Poenitentialis" of Theodore forbids the practice of dancing in animal masks, especially those of horned beasts (so the people were used to dancing in masks, as witches did).

A.D. 900. King Edgar regretted that the Old Gods were much more worshipped in his dominions than the Christian Gods.

Circa A.D. 906. Regino, in *his De Ecclesiastica Disciplinis,* gives the famous "Canon Episcopi," denouncing "wicked women" who ride at night "with Diana, the goddess of pagans," obeying her as a goddess and being "summoned to her service on certain nights." This is described as a delusion of the devil. Regino ascribes this Canon to the Council of Ancyra, circa A.D. 314, but modern authorities think it possible that Regino wrote it himself. It was the official teaching of the Church about the Sabbat meetings until the publication of the *Malleus Maleficarum* in 1486, which denied its authority (backed by the Bull of Pope Innocent VIII in 1484, who called the authors of the "Malleus Maleficarum," Institoris and Sprenger, his "beloved sons"). It is a possibility that Regino forged the *Canon Episcopi;* and it is a certainty that Institoris and Sprenger forged the Approbation of the Theological Faculty of the University of Cologne which was affixed to the *Malleus Maleficarum.* So the "infallible Mother Church's" teaching on witchcraft began with a forgery, and continued with another forgery when the first one no longer served its purpose. It has been further suggested that the translation of the Authorised Version of the Bible of Exodus, Chap. XXII. v. 18, as "Thou shalt not suffer a witch to live" is yet a third forgery, perpetrated to please the witch-hunting King James I, in whose reign it was made. The word translated "witch" actually means "poisoner"; yet this text was the death-warrant of thousands. However, the Lutherans in Germany also used the text in the same sense, though I think learned men there must also have known that it was a false translation.

1066. The Norman Conquest.

1090–1270. The era of the Crusades, which ended in final failure.

1100. Death of William Rufus (who was almost certainly a pagan).

"In the 10th year of the reign of King John" took place the first recorded trial for witchcraft in Britain. King John is said to have been friendly with the witch cult. The verdict in the above case was "Not Guilty."

1207. Pope Innocent III commenced to preach the Albigensian Crusade, directed against the Cathari in the South of France.

1234. Extermination of the Stedingers.

1290. Edward I expelled the Jews from England.

1303. The Bishop of Coventry accused by the Pope of being a witch.

1307–1314. Persecution of the Knights Templars.

Pope John XXII was Pope from 1316 to 1334. He was the author of some of the earliest formal decrees against witchcraft.

1324. Trial of Dame Alice Kyteler of Kilkenny, by the Bishop of Ossory. She took refuge in England where she had "highly-placed friends." Later, King Edward III, in whose reign this happened, was in a state of feud with the Bishop of Ossory for some years. Was *he* one of the "highly-placed friends"?

1349. Foundation by Edward III of the Order of the Garter (which may have had connections with the witch cult).

1406. King Henry IV gives directions to the Bishop of Norwich to search for and arrest witches and sorcerers in his diocese.

1430. Trial of Joan of Arc.

1484. Papal Bull of Pope Innocent VIII, *Summis desiderantes affectibus.* (Particularly fierce attack on heretics and witches.)

1486. Publication of the *Malleus Maleficarum.* This was the signal for severe and widespread persecution.

1541. Witchcraft Act passed in the reign of Henry VIII. Before this time, according to Hale, "Witchcraft, Sortilegium, was by the ancient laws of England of ecclesiastical cognizance, and upon conviction thereof, without abjuration, was punishable with death by *writ de haeretico comburendo.*" (Quoted by H. E. Lea, *Materials Towards a History of Witchcraft.*) This looks as if witches were formerly recognised as being an heretical sect, and confirms the old story of the "burning time."

1547. The Act of Henry VIII was repealed under Edward VI.

1562. Another Witchcraft Act passed, in the reign of Elizabeth I. The punishment was the pillory for the first offence, and death after three separate convictions.

1563. The Parliament of Mary Queen of Scots passed a law decreeing death for witches. "Upon a very moderate calculation, it is presumed that from the passing of the Act of Queen Mary till the accession of James to the throne of England, a period of 39 years, the average number of executions for witchcraft in Scotland was 200 annually, or upwards of 17,000 altogether. For the first nine years the number was not one quarter so great; but towards the years 1590 to 1593, the number must have been more than 400." (Mackay, *History of Extraordinary Popular Delusions.*)

1584. First edition of *The Discoverie of Witchcraft,* by Reginald Scot. This was one of the first books to deny superstitious notions of witchcraft, and to treat the subject in a rationalistic manner. James I ordered it to be burnt by the public hangman. (He obviously thought that in the wrong hands it was dangerous!) It is a witch tradition that they influenced the writing of books to make people see reason and stop the persecution-mania; such books ridiculed popular superstition, even to the extent of suggesting that there were no such beings as witches. This book of Scot's may have been one of such. Scot may even have been a witch himself; he displays a suspicious knowledge of magical processes, showing that he had evidently studied the subject.

1597. James VI of Scotland (James I of England) published at Edinburgh his treatise on Demonology and Witchcraft. Witch-hunting was given Royal patronage.

1604. The Witchcraft Act of James I, the most severe yet introduced in English civil law. "Dr. Zachary Gray, the editor of an edition of *Hudibras,* informs us in a note to that work, that he himself perused a list of 3,000 witches who were executed in the time of the Long Parliament alone. During the first 80 years of the seventeenth century, the number executed has been estimated at 500 annually, making the frightful total of 40,000." (Mackay, Op. cit.) It must be remembered that this total applies to Britain alone, and takes no account of the terror that was raging on the Continent, and had been continuing for years.

1644. Matthew Hopkins started up in business as "Witch-finder General." He made a profitable career of it, claiming twenty shillings a head for every witch found, and lavish "Expenses" from the authorities who employed him. He has a number of imitators, especially in Scotland.

1681. Joseph Glanvil, in his *Sadducismus Triumphatus,* says, "Thousands in our own nation have suffered for their vile compacts with apostate spirits," i.e. as witches. It is notable, however, that *Sadducismus Triumphatus* was written as a pious protest against the growing disbelief in witchcraft. The more intelligent and educated people were growing sickened at the slaughter, and were beginning to doubt the whole phantasmagoria of the Church's teaching about witchcraft.

1711. Jane Wenham of Walkerne was tried as a witch and, being found guilty by the jury, was condemned to death; but the judge disbelieved the evidence and disagreed with the jury's verdict. He exerted himself to procure her pardon, and she was released. This is generally stated to have been the last trial for witchcraft in England.

1722. An old woman was burned as a witch at Dornoch, in Scotland. This was the last judicial execution in Scotland.

1735. In the reign of George II, the Witchcraft Act of 1735, which said in effect that there was no such thing as witchcraft, and no one in future should be prosecuted for it; but that anyone who *pretended* to supernormal powers should be prosecuted as an impostor.

1749. Girolamo Tartarotti published at Rovereto, Italy, his book, *Del Congresso Nottorno delle Lammie,* in which he stated that witchcraft was derived from the old cult of Diana, and drew a distinction between it and ceremonial magic that sought to conjure demons. He had to write very guardedly, because of the danger of too pointedly offending the clergy of Catholic Italy though he was upon the right track, and is, I believe, the earliest writer to take this line.

1809. Brown's Dictionary, published at Edinburgh, defines a witch as "A woman who has dealings with the Devil." (Old ideas evidently died hard in Scotland.)

1848. Modern Spiritualism was founded as a result of investigations into the phenomena produced by the Fox Sisters in America. (Such phenomena had appeared before, but people had been afraid to investigate them rationally.) The Church denounced Spiritualism as "diabolical," which it was not, and as "a revival of the old witchcraft," which in many respects it was.

1857. A French Spiritualist, Allan Kardec, upon instructions from his "Guides," reintroduced the ancient doctrine of reincarnation publicly into Europe.

1892–1897. One of the greatest impostures of modern times was perpetrated in France by two Freethinkers, Dr. Charles Hacks and Gabriel Jogand. They published a series of "revelations of Satanism," of the most sensational type, which were firmly believed in by large numbers of high-ranking clergy. Jogand was actually received in audience by Pope Leo XIII and patronised by Bishops and Cardinals. Then on April 19th, 1897, in the lecture room of the Geographical Society in the Boulevard St. Germain, he admitted it was all a fabrication, intended as an elaborate practical joke upon the credulity of the clergy. In spite of this, a number of them continued to believe in it, and most modern descriptions of "Satanism" are in fact based upon these fake "revelations." It had proved too good a stick to beat Spiritualism with! (Jogand had declared Spiritualism to be a branch of Satanism.) Daniel Douglas Home, the famous medium, was in his day declared by the Church to have a pact with the Devil, and to celebrate Black Masses.

1921. Dr. Margaret Alice Murray published her book, *The Witch Cult in Western Europe;* it was followed by *The God of the Witches.* In these books, Dr. Murray stated that witchcraft was the remains of the ancient pagan religions of Europe, and she identified the Horned God of the witches as being the oldest representation of a deity known to man, and identical with the deity depicted in the Palaeolithic cave paintings. Her books were attacked by the Rev. Father Montague Summers as being a revival of the heresy of Girolamo Tartarotti (see above).

1949. G. B. Gardner, under the pen-name of "Scire," wrote an historical novel called *High Magic's Aid,* which was published in this year. It was, so far as he knows, the first book written by an initiated witch, describing, under the guise of fiction, something of what a witch believes.

1951. The Witchcraft Act of 1735 was repealed, and replaced by the Fraudulent Mediums Act, which legally recognises the existence of genuine mediumship and psychic powers, and provides penalties only for those who fraudulently pretend to possess such powers in order to make money.

1954. *Witchcraft Today,* by G. B. Gardner, was published; the first book ever written describing what witches are and what they do, by someone who had actually taken part in their ceremonies, worshipped their Gods with them, and made magic with them.

1956. The August number of *Fate Magazine* (American edition) carried a story of how, on July 3rd, 1955, in Ojinaga, Mexico, eighty-five miles from Alpine, Texas, a woman named Josephina Arista was publicly burned at the stake as a witch, without trial, upon the orders of the local priest, carried out by the alcalde and the city police.

Appendix IV

The Forgeries of the Canon Episcopi *and the* Malleus Maleficarum

I HAVE PREVIOUSLY referred the reader to H. C. Lea's *Materials Towards a History of Witchcraft* for the full details of this matter; however, as that book is not one which is within easy reach of the general reader, and as the matter is of some importance in the story of the persecution of the witch cult, I will give a brief abstract of it here. Lea quotes a large number of relevant documents to show that the earliest teaching of the Church about the witches' Sabbat differed radically from the parade of horrors for which credence was, and is, demanded by orthodox writers. The foundation for this early teaching is a document called the Canon Episcopi, which was accepted as authoritative until the time of the publication of the *Malleus Maleficarum* in 1486, which finally threw it overboard, after it had been "interpreted " and "re-interpreted" until the final sense in which it was taken was almost the opposite of its original sense. Regino (circa A.D. 906) seems to have been the first publisher of it, in his *De Ecclesiastica Disciplinis*; and he ascribes it to the Council of Ancyra, which met in A.D. 314. However, Professor George Lincoln Burr, in a note to Mr. Lea's book, says, "Already the 16th century 'Correctores' of the Canon Law pointed out that this canon is not to be found in the genuine acts of the Council of Ancyra; but they find its substance in the (apocryphal) *De Spiritu et Anima* of Augustin and in an old life of Pope Damasus which seems to ascribe it to a Roman synod of his time. (A.D. 366–384: my note). But Friedberg (though in his ed. of the *Canon Law*, Leipzig, 1879, he retains without comment this note of the 'Correctores') has in his *Aus deutchen Bussbuchern* (1869), pp. 67–73, shown that the ascription to the Council of Ancyra is only a misunderstanding by Gratian, while the life of Damasus deserves no credit. He thinks it is an excerpt from some Frankish capitulary. According to so high an authority as Paul Fourier (Bibliotheque de l'Ecole des Chartes, lxxxi, 1920, p. 17ff.) Regino must not be implicitly trusted as an editor of canons. Il est incontestable qu'on trouve dans son oeuvre, en assez grand nombre, des textes retouchés et parfois plus ou moms remainiés. Nay more: not only are canons apocryphally ascribed to councils to which they do not belong, among them 'pseudo-canons d'Ancyre', but il est, d'ailleurs, dans le recueil de Reginon des textes qui sont incontestablement des apocryphes forgé de touter pièces. And, since we know that Regino retouched his texts, gave them fallacious labels, and admitted fragments wholly apocryphal, we cannot, thinks Fournier, help suspecting that among the capita incerta some may be of his creation. The Cap Episcopi Fournier does not mention; but the reforming purpose of Regino's book and his known interest in morals suggest the possibility of its coming from his pen."

In other words, this alleged *Canon of the Council of Ancyra* was possibly a forgery, and was ascribed to the Council of Ancyra to give it pretended authority. Its purpose was propaganda against the "night-riding witches," and its comparatively mild tone reflects the fact that the Church was not yet sufficiently firm in the saddle to be able to do more than disparage and mock at the nocturnal assemblies to celebrate the old Mysteries and worship the old Gods. The text, translated from the Latin, is as follows:

> Bishops and their officials must labour with all their strength to uproot thoroughly from their parishes the pernicious art of sorcery and malefice invented by the devil, and if they find a man or woman follower of this wickedness to eject them foully disgraced from their parishes. For the Apostle says, "A man that is a heretic after the first and second admonition avoid." Those are held captive by the devil who, leaving their creator, seek the aid of the devil. And so holy Church must be cleansed of this pest. It is also not to be omitted that some wicked women perverted by the devil, seduced by illusions and phantasms of demons, believe and profess themselves, in the hours of night, to ride upon certain beasts with Diana, the goddess of pagans, and an innumerable multitude of women, and in the silence of the dead of night to traverse great spaces of earth, and to obey her commands as of their mistress, and to be summoned to her service on certain nights. But I wish it were they alone who perished in their faithlessness and did not draw many with them into the

> destruction of infidelity. For an innumerable multitude, deceived by this false opinion, believe this to be true and, so believing, wander from the right faith and are involved in the error of the pagans when they think that there is anything of divinity or power except the one God. Wherefore the priests throughout their churches should preach with all insistence to the people that they may know this to be in every way false and that such phantasms are imposed on the minds of infidels and not by the divine but by the malignant spirit. Thus Satan himself, who transfigures himself into an angel of light, when he has captured the mind of a miserable woman and has subjugated her to himself by infidelity and incredulity, immediately transforms himself into the species and similitudes of different personages and deluding the mind which he holds captive and exhibiting things, joyful or mournful, and persons, known or unknown, leads it through devious ways, and while the spirit alone endures this the faithless mind thinks these things happen not in the spirit but in the body. Who is there that is not led out of himself in dreams and nocturnal visions, and sees much when sleeping which he had never seen waking? Who is so stupid and foolish as to think that all these things which are only done in spirit happen in the body, when the Prophet Ezekiel saw visitations of the Lord in spirit and not in the body, and the Apostle John saw and heard the mysteries of the Apocalypse in the spirit and not in the body, as he himself says, "I was in the spirit." And Paul does not dare to say that he was rapt in the body. It is therefore to be proclaimed publicly to all that whoever believes such things or similar to these loses the faith, and he who has not the right faith in God is not of God but of him in whom he believes, that is, of the devil. For of our Lord it is written, "All things were made by Him." Whoever therefore believes that anything can be made, or that any creature can be changed to better or to worse or be transformed into another species of similitude, except by the Creator Himself who made everything and through Whom all things were made, is beyond doubt an infidel.

It will be noted that the deity of the witches is not said to be Satan *in propria persona,* but "Diana, the goddess of the pagans." It is said, however, that this goddess is really Satan in disguise, and that the people who are "summoned to her service on certain nights," i.e. to the Sabbats, do not really and corporeally go there at all, but that the whole thing is simply a delusion of the imagination, the "illusions and phantasms of demons."

Hence, according to this, there is in reality no flying upon broomsticks, or goats, no kissing of the buttocks of goats or even of Grand

Masters, no performing toads, no cannibalism of unbaptised babes, no defiled Hosts, no copulation with demons, no transformation into animals, not even any black candles or crosses upside down—the whole thing is sheer imagination! Further, it is very plainly stated that those who believe the witches' Sabbat to be a physical reality are "infidels."

Now, *in the days in which it was written,* this fake addition to Canon Law was a clever and subtle piece of propaganda. Its purpose was to frighten people out of attending the Sabbats by sowing doubts in their minds about "delusions of demons." It ties in very well with the teaching of the Early Church that all pagan divinities were devils in disguise. This talk about phantasms and illusions was the sort of thing to confuse the minds of simple people and fill them with vague terrors of the unknown. Precisely the same technique is used by the Roman Catholic Church to this day in its attacks upon Spiritualism; all the "Guides," they say, are devils in disguise, and the whole thing is a diabolical illusion.

But as time went on, precisely the same thing happened with regard to the witch cult as is beginning to happen with regard to Spiritualism. So many people adhered to it that the charge of "illusion" would not serve. Darker allegations had to be brought; tales of "devil-worship" and "foul orgies" to which the external appearance of the cult was merely the outer court (vide Mr. Dennis Wheatley in *The Sunday Graphic;* it is wonderful how history repeats itself).

However, the two types of anti-witch propaganda were mutually contradictory; it was no use spreading "atrocity stories" if at the same time your Canon Law taught that the meetings at which these atrocities took place were imaginary. And as time went on the *Canon Episcopi* became more and more of an encumbrance to the witch-hunters, and needed to be "interpreted" with longer and longer arguments. The early Churchmen who had believed that a quick and decisive victory over paganism was a certainty were disappointed. It was proving a long-drawn-out struggle. The Judgment Day which they had expected in the year 1000 did not come off. The Crusades had ended in ignominious failure. And still the accursed pagans survived! Worse still, such men as Wycliffe had begun to preach against "the corruption of the Church," and to translate the Bible into English so that men could read it and think for themselves. The printing-presses were beginning to be set up all over Europe, and thereon were being printed, not only such books as were to the glory of Mother Church, but books of

Plato and the heathen Greeks. There was far too much free-thinking going on in the world, especially upon the subject of "pagan error," and strong measures were needed to cope with it.

Rome was quick to realise the formidable power of the new invention, the printing-press, as a means of controlling the minds of men and shaping public opinion. In 1484 Pope Innocent VIII published a Papal Bull which was a particularly strong attack upon heretics and witches. It said that witches copulated with demons in the forms of incubi and succubae, destroyed the offspring of women and cattle and the fruits of the earth, afflicted men and women with diseases, prevented intercourse between man and wife, making men impotent and women sterile, "with many other unspeakable crimes." It was the signal for a stepping-up of the campaign to exterminate the witch cult. Before this, there had been plenty of Papal Bulls directed against the witch cult, but they had been directed to special localities, and were but little known to the general public; this Bull, however, was *printed,* and spread broadcast over Europe as part of a book written under Vatican patronage by the Pope's "beloved sons," Heinrich Institoris and Jacob Sprenger.

This book, the famous *Malleus Maleficarum,* had a tremendous effect upon the persecution of witches. It was the forerunner of many similar works, all devoted to the promotion of witch-burning, and to removing the last arguments in favour of showing any clemency, including especially those drawn from the *Canon Episcopi.* It was not the first book to deny the authority of the *Canon Episcopi,* but it had a greater effect than any other on account of its widespread circulation, the official patronage of the Vatican, and the alleged patronage of the University of Cologne.

It commences with elaborate arguments that disbelief in the evils of witchcraft is heresy; arguments against unbelievers are set out at length, showing that such unbelievers existed and were a thorn in the side of the witch-hunters. It cites Pope Innocent's Bull as *proof* of the evil deeds of witches! There is a great deal of the usual monkish abuse of women; a number of weird and wonderful stories of people being carried off by demons, etc.; and innumerable alleged instances of "sorcery," most of which would insult the intelligence of any schoolchild. Witches are accused of using consecrated Hosts to work evil charms, murdering babies, afflicting people with all kinds of diseases, transforming people into beasts, raising storms, riding bodily through the air, killing people by mere touch, or even a look, "bewitching" cattle to madness or death, stealing milk by a kind of "remote control"—in short the book is a farrago of every superstitious horror conceivable.

The third part of the book urges secular as well as ecclesiastical courts to prosecute witches, and gives them minute instructions as to how to do so. Mere "ill-fame," and that upon the word of persons of bad character or simple mind, is sufficient to be accepted as evidence!

An explanation is indirectly furnished by this book as to why so many witches or alleged witches persisted to the last in "confessing" the most preposterous things. If they confessed, they were judged "penitent," and were accorded the "mercy" of being strangled before being burned; but if they refused to confess what was required of them, or asserted their innocence after they had been condemned, they were judged "impenitent" and burned alive. According to the tradition in the witch cult, if anyone was caught and the inquisitors tried to make them tell anything real about the cult, they were forewarned by the laws of the cult that they must not do so; but in order to obtain relief from torture, if they could see that there was no hope of escape they were told to confess to any horrors and impossibilities suggested to them because this would bring them a quick death.

At the time when the *Malleus Maleficarum* was issued, the University of Cologne was the appointed Censor of books, though this office was removed from it by a Papal Bull of 1487, and transferred to the Bishops; probably because of its refusal to cooperate in the matter of the *Malleus Maleficarum,* for when Sprenger and Institoris submitted their book to the Theological Faculty of the University, they could get only four of the professors to issue a cautious and guarded approbation of it; the rest would have nothing to do with it. Nothing daunted, this precious pair of scoundrels proceeded to forge a document which purported to show the approbation of the whole Faculty.

The forgery has been exposed in modern times by the learned archivist of Cologne, Joseph Hansen, in 1898. It appears that the copies of the *Malleus Maleficarum* which were intended for circulation in Cologne were specially printed without the "Approbation"; but the ones intended for circulation elsewhere had the "Approbation" inserted in them. In spite of this precaution, it became known to the University that the forgery had been committed; but it is probable that it was unsafe for them to have too much to say about it. Also, their office of censoring books had by now been removed from them, by Papal order, and placed in the hands of the Bishops, who could be relied upon to do as they were told.

However, the beadle, upon whose alleged word the "Approbation" rested, and the Dean of the Faculty, Thomas de Scotia, entered their formal denial in the records of the University; and, as a mark of their feelings upon the matter, when Sprenger, who was a member of the Theological Faculty, died, no Requiem Mass was performed for him by the University, contrary to the usual custom. There was little that they dared do or say; they were merely a handful of scholars against a formidable and pitiless totalitarian machine; but they made their mark in the archives, and that mark has come down to us. Their denial was noted in 1758, by Joseph Hartzheim, who was then Dean of the Theological Faculty, and as such had charge of the records. The records themselves subsequently disappeared; but the note of the Faculty's denial, in Hartzheim's handwriting, was preserved, and found by Joseph Hansen. An entry by Arnold Von Tongern, who was Dean of the Faculty in the early sixteenth century, has also been preserved: "*Liber qui Malleus Maleficarum dicitur falso facultati inscriptus. Examinandus traditur uni magistrorum cum relatione ad facultatem.*" It is apparent that some action was attempted, but the disappearance of the records prevents us knowing what came of it.

Great play has been made by such writers as Montague Summers upon the unimpeachable character and integrity of the authors of the *Malleus Maleficarum;* so I think it time that the reading public was presented with this sample of it.

The main purpose of the *Malleus Maleficarum* was to break down the opposition of reasonable and educated laymen to the cruelties and injustices of the witch-hunt as carried on by the Church. For this purpose, the backing of such institutions as the University of Cologne was vital; and so successful was the forgery that not only Catholic but Protestant circles came to accept the *Malleus* as authoritative. Its other purpose was to get rid of that awkward *Canon Episcopi;* it does this by blandly denying that this Canon applies to witches at all, and calls the idea that it does so "this pestiferous opinion." Yet Lea (Op. cit.) quotes document after document to show that for centuries the *Canon Episcopi* was the official teaching of the Church about witches.

So those who seek "the Church's teaching about witchcraft" in preference to that of secular anthropology have an intriguing choice before them; will they have the *Canon Episcopi,* or will they have the *Malleus Maleficarum*? These are the Church's official teachings. The authors of both were forgers. Which forgery do they prefer?

If they accept the teaching of the *Malleus Maleficarum,* how do they feel about the little matter of proven forgery as affecting the credit of its authors? And what becomes of the wisdom of the Church, which had been teaching false doctrine about witchcraft for centuries?

If, on the other hand, they accept the *Canon Episcopi* (overlooking once again the forgery committed by its author), what becomes of all the wonderful stories of "the horrors of the Sabbat"?

Being no theologian, I will leave them to work it out.

Appendix V

THERE APPEARED IN the *People of October 27th, 1957,* an article upon the existence in Britain of a modern cult of witchcraft. The writer of the article relates how he visited a large house in Finchley, in which he witnessed a witch ceremony which goes back to pagan times. Men and women took part in it, we are informed, who are regarded as reputable and respectable individuals by their unsuspecting colleagues and friends. "First one of the men lit some incense in a bowl. Soon the room was filled with pungent exciting fumes. Then one of the girls produced a length of white tape. She laid it round the floor in a circle nine feet across. She lit four candles and placed them on the floor round a wooden box—the altar. There were four knives, two jars of oil, some braided silk cord, a goblet, a silver plate and a candlestick. Then the electric lights were switched off and the four 'witches' undressed. Helping themselves from the jars, they rubbed oil into their hands, then stepped naked into the candle-lit circle. With heads bowed and hands raised before them they stood before the altar. Then one of the girls took a great sword inscribed with symbols and drew its point around the white circle." At this juncture, the writer informs us, he was asked to leave the room while certain highly secret rites were performed. When he returned he found that the witches were sitting on the floor around the altar. They were drinking rum. "Suddenly they rose, brandishing the ritual knives, and began a frenzied dance to the accompaniment of throbbing music from a tape recorder. They whirled, hopped and capered until the music died away. Then they stumbled exhausted to the floor. That was all. But one of the girls explained that at the end of the ceremony the men and women participants are quite free to pair off for what she insisted on describing as 'necking.'"

When the writer of the article left he immediately began his own independent investigation into the men and woman who had taken part in the ceremony. "Through them," he reports, "I came upon other members of the witchcraft sect. One is a thirty-five-year-old doctor who practises in a northern town. He, too, is a highly respected member of the community. He was therefore most anxious not to be identified. It is easy to see why. For he told me that, as a witch, he believes in magic. 'Orthodox doctors,' he said, 'would be horrified if they knew. But members of *any* religion hope, by prayer, to influence events over which they have no control. We merely employ different methods. Witchcraft has its imperfections, of course. They have crept in during the several hundred years in which we have been persecuted. Given opportunity, witchcraft could again become a practicable religion applicable to 20th century life.'

"Condemned by the Church as a monstrous evil, how could any responsible human being believe in it as religion?"

There was another article upon the same subject in the *People* for November 9th following. Amanda, a High Priestess of the cult, related to the writer of the article how the witches dealt with a man who was blackmailing one of their members. "We made a puppet," she said, "a wax image of the man—and bound it with string. Then we invoked a very special power. Suddenly, the blackmail stopped. His hands were tied. He could do no more harm." The eyes of the Priestess, we are told, blazed with conviction as she said this and as she made another astonishing statement: "If we witches did not invoke the assistance of our god and goddess, I believe that the sun would not return each morning." This strikes one as a rather wild assertion, and one wonders how far the writer embroidered it. It will be noticed that this absurd statement is recorded in both articles.

Bibliography

"A.E." (George Russell). *The Candle of Vision.* (Macmillan, 1920).

Alford, Violet, and Rodney Gallop. *Traces of a Dianic Cult from Catalonia to Portugal.* Article, *Folklore,* Vol. XLVI, 1935.

Anderson, M. C. *Looking for History in British Churches.* (John Murray, 1951).

Armitage, H. *Early Man in Hallamshire.*

St. Augustine. (A.D. 354–430).

Baring-Gould, Rev. S. *On Gables.* Article, *Murray's Magazine, 1887.*

Bede, The Venerable. *Historia Ecclesiastica.*

Bloom, J. Harvey. *Folklore, Old Customs and Superstitions in Shakespeare-Land.*

Boissier. *Receuil de Lettres au Sujet des Malefices et du Sortilege . . . par le Sieur Boissier.* (Paris, 1731).

Borrow, R. *Asiatic Researches.*

Bouquet, Dr. A. C., D.D. *Comparative Religion.* (Penguin Books, 1950).

Brewer, Rev. Dr. Cobham. *Dictionary of Phrase and Fable.*

Brown, Julian. *The Beauty of Mediaeval Illuminated Manuscripts.* Article, *The Sphere Christmas Number,* 1954.

Carpenter, Edward. *The Art of Creation.* (Allen and Unwin, 1912).

Cave, C. J. P. *Roof Bosses in Mediaeval Churches.*

———. *Chalice Well,* Glastonbury. Descriptive leaflet.

Cicero. *De Divinatione.*

Clinch, George, F.G.S. *Old English Churches.* (Upcott Gill, 1902).

Colson, Thomas. *Living Tissue Rays.* Article, *The Pendulum,* March, 1956 (from *The Electronic Medical Digest*).

Croker, T. Crofton. *Fairy Legends and Traditions of the South of Ireland.* (William Tegg. N.D., but first appeared in 2 vols., 1825 and 1828, by John Murray).

Crowley, Aleister, *Magick in Theory and Practice.*

———. *The Equinox of the Gods.* (The O.T.O. 1936).

Dacombe, Marianne R. (Ed). *Dorset Up-Along and Down-Along.* (Friary Press, Dorchester. 1951).

Davies, R. Trevor. *Four Centuries of Witch Beliefs.*

De Beauvoir, Simone. *The Second Sex.* (English Translation, 1953).

De Lancre, Pierre. *Tableau de L'Inconstance des Mauvais Anges.* (Paris, 1612).

Deren, Maya. *Divine Horsemen; the Living Gods of Haiti.*

Dio. *Roman History.*

Du Chaillu, Paul. *The Viking Age.*

Evans, Dr. Article on the Rollright Stones. *The Folklore Journal,* March, 1895.

Fabian, Robert. *Fabian of the Yard.* (Naldrett Press, 1950).

Fortune, Dion. *The Mystical Qabalah.* (Williams and Norgate, 1935).

Funck-Brentano, F. *Le Drame des Poisons.* (Paris, 1936).

Fyvel, T. R. *Unearthing the Holy Land's Past.* Article, *The Observer,* 10th July, 1955.

Gardner, G. B. (Pen Name "Scire") *High Magic's Aid.* (Michael Houghton, 1949).

———. *Witchcraft Today.* (Rider, 1954).

Geoffrey of Monmouth. *Historia Regum Britanniae.*

Gibbon. *Decline and Fall of the Roman Empire.*

Goetia, The. (Or Lesser Key of Solomon; also known as the Lemegeton).

Gomme, L. *Folklore as a Historical Science.*

Graves, Robert. *King Jesus.*

———. *The White Goddess.*

———. *Wife to Mr. Milton.*

Grimoire of Pope Honorius, The.

Guest, Lady Charlotte (Trans). *The Mabinogion.*

Hawkes, Jacquetta and Christopher. *Prehistoric Britain.* (Penguin Books, 1943).

Hayter, Col. F. J. *Deadly Magic: Including the Australian Pointing Stick.* (Rider, N.D.)

Hole, Christina. *English Folklore.*

Holmes, Edmond. *The Holy Heretics: the Story of the Albigensian Crusade.* (Watts and Co., 1948).

Hughes, Pennethorne. *Witchcraft.*

Insole, Alan. *Immortal Britain.* (Aquarian Press, 1952).

Jacobi, Dr. Jolan. *The Psychology of C. G. Jung.*

Jedwine, J. W. Tort, *Crime and Police.*

Kalevala, The.

Keating, G. *History of Ireland.*

Key of Solomon, The. Also known as the *Clavicule of Solomon.*

Kinsey, Dr. *Sexual Behaviour in the Human Female.*

Knight, Sir Richard Payne, and Thomas Wright. *Two Essays upon the Worship of Priapus.*

Leland, Charles Godfrey. *Gypsy Sorcery.*

Lea, H. C. *Materials Towards a History of Witchcraft.* (University of Pennsylvania Press. Philadelphia, 1939).

Lethbridge, T. C. *Gogmagog.* (Routledge).

Longworth, T. Clifton. *The Devil a Monk Would Be.* (Herbert Joseph, N.D.).

Mackay, Charles, LL.D. *Memoirs of Extraordinary Popular Delusions.* (Nat. Illustrated Library, 1852).

"Fiona Macleod" (William Sharp). *The Dominion of Dreams.* (Heinemann, 1910).

Malory, Sir Thomas. *Le Morte D'Arthur.*

Maltwood, K. E., F.R.S.A. *A Guide to Glastonbury's Temple of the Stars.* (John M. Watkins).

———. *The Enchantments of Britain.*

Mathers, S. L. Macgregor. *The Kabbalah Unveiled.* (Kegan Paul, Trench, Trubner and Co. 1887).

———. (Edited, with Introduction). *The Sacred Magic of Abramelin the Mage.*

Moseley, James W. *Mystery Ruins of Peru.* Article, *Fate Magazine,* December, 1955.

Murray, Prof. Gilbert. *Five Stages of Greek Religion.* (Watts and Co., 1946).

Murray, Dr. Margaret A. *The Witch Cult in Western Europe.*

———. *The God of the Witches.*

Nichols, Ross. *The Great Zodiac of Glastonbury.* Article, *The Occult Observer.*

O'Donnell, Eliott. *Haunted Britain.*

O'Donovan, Dr. (Ed.) *The Annals of the Four Masters.*

Paley, Archdeacon. *Evidences of Christianity.*

Plato.

Proclus. *The Theology of Plato.*

Raglan, Lady. *The Green Man in Church Architecture.* Article, *Folklore,* 1939.

Regnault, Dr. Jules. *La Sorcellerie ses Rapports avec les Sciences Biologiques.* (Paris, 1936).

Reid, Vera C., and T. Mawby Cole. *Gods in the Making.* (Aquarian Press, 1951).

Rhodes, H. T. F. *The Satanic Mass.* (Rider, 1954).

Rhys, Sir John.

Rolleston, T. W. *Myths and Legends of the Celtic Race.* (Harrup, 1912).

Romance of the Rose, The. (13th century).

Seltman. Charles. *Women in Antiquity.*

Shakespeare, William. *Henry V.*

———. *Twelfth Night.*

Spencer, Lewis. *Encyclopedia of Occultism.*

Squire, Charles. *Celtic Myth and Legend, Poetry and Romance.* (Gresham Publishing Co. N.D.).

St. Simon, Comte De. *Memoirs.*

Stubbes. *Anatomie of Abuses.*

Summers, Montague. *Witchcraft and Black Magic.*

Taylor, G. Rattray. *Sex in History.*

Tertullian. (2nd century A.D.).

Theodore. *Liber Poenitentialis.* (7th century A.D.).

Tres Ancient Coutumier De Normandie, Les.

Trial of Joan Of Arc, The.

Waddell, L. A. *The Phoenician Origin of the Scots and Britons.* (Williams and Norgate, 1924).

Wagner, Dr. W. *Asgard and the Gods.* (Adapted and Edited by M.W. MacDowall and W.S.W. Anson. Swan Sonnenschein, Lowrey and Co. 1889).

Waite, A.E. *The Book of Ceremonial Magic.*

———. *Elfin Music: An Anthology of English Fairy Poetry. (Walter Scott, 1888).*

———. *The Holy Grail.*

Witkowski, Dr. G. J. *Les Licences de L'Art Chrétien.* (Paris, 1920).

Wright, Thomas, M.A., F.S.A. (Editor). *A Contemporary Narrative of the Proceedings against Dame Alice Kyteler.* (The Camden Society, 1843).

Yorke, Gerald. *Tantric Hedonism.* Article, *The Occult Observer.*

———. *Dictionary of Folklore. Mythology and Legend.* (Funk and Wagnalls Company, New York, 1958).

———. *The Age of Chaucer: Vol. 1 of a Guide to English Literature.* Edited by Boris Ford. (Penguin Books, 1955). (Complete text of *Sir Gawain and the Green Knight*).

Also in Weiser Classics

The Alchemist's Handbook: A Practical Manual, by Frater Albertus, with a new foreword by Robert Allen Bartlett

Predictive Astrology: Tools to Forecast Your Life and Create Your Brightest Future, by Bernadette Brady, with a new foreword by Theresa Reed

The Druidry Handbook: Spiritual Practice Rooted in the Living Earth, by John Michael Greer, with a new foreword by Dana O'Driscoll

Futhark: A Handbook of Rune Magic, by Edred Thorsson, newly revised and updated by the author

The Herbal Alchemist's Handbook: A Complete Guide to Magickal Herbs and How to Use Them, by Karen Harrison, with a new foreword by Arin Murphy-Hiscock

Liber Null and Psychonaut: The Practice of Chaos Magic, by Peter J. Carroll, newly revised and updated by the author, with a new foreword by Ronald Hutton

The Magick of Aleister Crowley: A Handbook of the Rituals of Thelema, by Lon Milo Duquette, with a new foreword by Jason Louv and a new introduction by the author

The Mystical Qabalah, by Dion Fortune, with a new foreword by Judika Illes and a new afterword by Stuart R. Harrop

Predictive Astrology: Tools to Forecast Your Life and Create Your Brightest Future, by Bernadette Brady, with a new foreword by Theresa Reed

Psychic Self-Defense: The Definitive Manual for Protecting Yourself Against Paranormal Attack, by Dion Fortune, with a new foreword by Mary K. Greer and a new afterword by Christian Gilson

Pure Magic: A Complete Course in Spellcasting, by Judika Illes, with a new introduction by the author and a new foreword by Mat Auryn

Saturn: A New Look at an Old Devil, by Liz Greene, with a new foreword by Juliana McCarthy

Spiritual Cleansing: A Handbook of Psychic Protection, by Draja Mickaharic, with a new foreword by Lilith Dorsey

Taking Up the Runes: A Complete Guide to Using Runes in Spells, Rituals, Divination, and Magic, by Diana L. Paxson, with new material by the author

The Handbook of Yoruba Religious Concepts, by Baba Ifa Karade, newly revised and updated by the author

Yoga Sutras of Patanjali, by Mukunda Stiles, with a new foreword by Mark Whitwell